THOMAS WOLFE

THOMAS WOLFE

—————— ✥✥✥ BY ✥✥✥ ——————

Andrew Turnbull

✣ *New York* ✣

CHARLES SCRIBNER'S SONS

For Bayard and Margaret Turnbull

"Whatsoever thy hand findeth to do, do it with thy might; for there is no work, nor device, nor knowledge, nor wisdom, in the grave, whither thou goest."

—ECCLESIASTES, 9:10, quoted in *You Can't Go Home Again,* p. 733

❖ *Contents* ❖

❖ List of Illustrations ❖

LIST OF ILLUSTRATIONS

THOMAS WOLFE

1 · ASHEVILLE

On October 18, 1929, six days before "Black Thursday" when the bottom fell out of the market, a portentous first novel was published by Charles Scribner's Sons. In its odd originality it reminded Maxwell Perkins, the editor who had been instrumental in bringing it to light, of *This Side of Paradise,* which had crossed his desk a decade earlier.[1] For all its imperfections *Look Homeward, Angel* was almost physical in its impact, like some huge boulder being pried out of the earth. "A destiny that leads the English to the Dutch is strange enough;" it began, "but one that leads from Epsom into Pennsylvania, and thence into the hills that shut in Altamont over the proud coral cry of the cock, and the soft stone smile of an angel, is touched by that dark miracle of chance which makes new magic in a dusty world." Though inclined to hyperbole, the author wasn't exaggerating. The strains that had met in Thomas Wolfe and given him the groundwork of his autobiographical novel were fabulous indeed.

1

On his mother's side, he sprang from the Scotch-Irish Pattons and Penlands who had settled in western North Carolina before the Revolution. Peter Penland had been a captain under Washington during the French and Indian War, and Robert and Aaron Patton had fought with the Continental Army in the campaigns culminating in the victory at Kings Mountain. A great great great-aunt, Elizabeth Patton, was the second wife of the legendary Davy Crockett, killed at the Alamo. Thomas Casey Westall, the grandfather for whom Wolfe was named,[2] came of good English stock which had moved to Asheville from Winchester, Virginia, just after the Revolution. A builder-contractor and a major in the Civil War, Westall was also a versifier, the editor of a temperance sheet, a zealot who broke with the Presbyterian Church over predestination, and a mystic who in his last illness is said to have predicted the exact hour of his death, as his father had before him.

Of Westall's nineteen children, Julia Elizabeth, the author's mother, born in 1860, was the fourth of eleven by a second marriage. In later years she would describe her early environment as "the thorns & thistles of war, nothing but poverty, gloom, & sadness to remember. . . . We all struggled on just to live, older people spent lots of time talking of what they had suffered, in loss of life & of property—negroes set free & all seemed to fear the negro or what he might be persuaded to do. I remember lots of men, women would whisper, 'There are carpet baggers going among the negroes & they may burn us up any night.' . . . Every family had lost two to four young men in the Civil War."[3]

When Julia was six, her father bought a hundred acres in the mountains north of Asheville where he built a log house and his older boys did the work of farmers—plowing, splitting rails, and carrying corn to the mill in sacks when they weren't shooting possum, guinea, and wild turkey, or, for the fun of it, knocking a speck of a squirrel out of a tree. The younger children hoed the vegetable patches, and the cows and pigs were turned loose to fend for themselves. Julia was raised on such mountaineer staples as ashcakes and hoecakes and "roasten years" (corn covered in the ashes with the shucks on), and for sweetening they had sorghum and wild honey. One afternoon when she and a brother were up the mountain picking berries, they saw three wolves nosing along, and luckily the wolves didn't see them as they raced home. When their father went up with his rifle the animals had passed on, although that night Julia heard their mournful howling.

Largely self-educated, she went to school, if at all, for only a few months in the fall and spring, it being too cold to attend in winter, and Sundays she walked the miles to church carrying her shoes so as to look neat when she got there. She had inherited her father's strain of occultism and spiritualism. When she was seventeen, her older sister, Sallie, who had recently died of galloping consumption, came to her in a dream and took her to heaven. There was a searchlight slanting up toward the sky along which they sped, quick as a thought, to a land of beautiful birds and flowers. Sallie said the man riding toward them on a white horse was the first king of the earth, and Julia said, "Oh, we will meet a king—will he notice us?" and as they passed him, he patted Julia on the head and rode on with a radiant smile. Julia asked Sallie if she was happy, and Sallie replied that she was as happy as she knew how to be until she reached the higher sphere for which she was preparing. Julia wanted to stay, but Sallie said she must go back and await her turn, so they flashed down over the same white way, and then Julia was awake in her bed at four in the morning, knowing that what she had just experienced was reality and not a dream.[4]

After a year and a half of college she became a country school teacher, supplementing her income by selling books, in which capacity she met her fantastic husband. Of Dutch-German descent, William Oliver Wolf had been born near Gettysburg twelve years before the battle. On that fateful July 1st, 1863, the lean and tattered Rebels had marched past his house all day, and two of them had ordered him to take them to a spring—one of the two, he later found out, being the cavalry leader, Fitzhugh Lee. After the war Wolf had made his start in Baltimore as a stonecutter's apprentice and had worked for a while in York, Pennsylvania, and Columbia, South Carolina, before moving to Raleigh, North Carolina, where he married, divorced, remarried, and—ever restless—migrated to Asheville with his second wife, who died in February, 1884, while he was getting established in the tombstone business.

W. O. Wolfe, as he now called himself, having brightened his name with a final "e," was larger than life: an angular six feet four, with arms down to his knees and an oratorical, booming, yet strangely tender voice. In his descriptions of his father, Thomas Wolfe would emphasize the lonely, stricken quality of his cold, grey eye, the "blade of a nose" suggestive of a beak, and the "faint, uneasy grin" that played at the corners of his "thin, wailing mouth." Into his marble shop one day in October, 1884, stepped Julia Westall—no beauty, but trim of figure and white of skin, with black, shoe-button eyes and black hair drawn tightly back and a habit of pursing her mouth reflectively before she spoke. W.O., who was carving a tombstone when she entered, dove into his office as usual, where he threw off his apron, drew on a well-pressed coat of black broadcloth, gave his trousers a whisk and his shoes a brush, and came out looking immaculate. Having glanced at the book she was selling, he put his name down for it. Then he asked if she ever read novels.

"Oh, I read most everything," she answered. "Not the Bible as much as I should though."

W.O. said he owned some fine love stories, and that afternoon, by one of his colored helpers, he sent her Augusta Jane Evans' *St. Elmo.* A few days later when Julia was starting out to sell another book in which W.O. had expressed interest, she went to his shop at noon and found it closed. Knowing that he lived with his mother-in-law, she stopped by on her way home, and W.O. pressed her to stay for lunch, after which he took her into the parlor and showed her his stereopticon slides of the Civil War. Julia thought she ought to be leaving so he could go back to work, but he assured her his business didn't amount to anything. He said his mother-in-law wanted to return to her people in Raleigh and was staying in Asheville simply to look after him, and soon he must marry or sell his house. When Julia remarked that she thought marriage might be preferable to breaking up a home, he took her hand, said he had been watching her for quite a while as she passed his shop, and proposed.

Julia, who had been in love a few years before and was sure she could never love that way again, protested that they barely knew each other. W.O. was so adamant, however, that she finally said she would open the book she was selling at random and abide by the middle paragraph of the right-hand page. "Just a bit of foolishness on my part," she remembered long afterwards, and W.O. didn't want to risk it, but she did it anyway and hit on a description of a wedding with the words "till death do us part." "Oh, that's it!" cried W.O. "That's the very thing! We're going to let it stand!" and from then on he considered their marriage a foregone conclusion, though it took a little while to persuade her. For Christmas he sent her a white marble doorstop with a deep-carved inscription, "J.E.W. from W.O.W. 1884," together with some handkerchiefs and a note saying he had heard she was to be married and the handkerchiefs might come in handy should she regret her step. The wedding took place in January, a scant three months after his headlong proposal.[5]

It was an epic misalliance. Two people more temperamentally unsuited could scarcely be imagined. Like the fat, rich Pennsylvania Dutch country whence he came, W.O. was lavish, sensual, expansive, while Julia, whose family had scratched a living from the mountains, was flinty, parsimonious, repressed. She was basically kind and not as pinch-penny as Eliza Gant in *Look Homeward, Angel*, but she lacked the open-handed generosity of her husband, who one bitter night watched and did nothing while an old woman and a little boy looted coal from his cellar. Julia's acquisitiveness and unrelenting practicality irked W.O., whose temperament was artistic. As a young man in Baltimore he had delighted in the performances of Joe Jefferson and Edwin Booth, and with his histrionic flair there may have been lost in him a great actor or orator or prosecuting attorney. Carving tombstones was all right, but graveyards depressed him, and he was frustrated by the tedium and remoteness of the mountain town where he had cast his lot. To take up the slack of his unrealized potential, he drank; not habitually—he was never a social drinker—but every few months he went on a binge which might last days or weeks, often landing him in the hospital or under a doctor's care. Julia, a former temperance worker unaware of her husband's weakness when she married him, was humiliated. This naïve country girl, who had wanted affection, found herself putting up with periodic taunts and abuse. And yet the lips-that-touch-liquor-will-never-touch-mine attitude of her and her family only served to infuriate W.O. and drive him to further excesses. The Westalls, though industrious, upstanding, ambitious, and successful, were not overly endowed with that pity and concern for struggling humanity which would ennoble the writings of Thomas Wolfe.

He was born October 3, 1900, the youngest of seven living children. In uncertain health during her pregnancy, Julia spent the afternoons reading in bed, to which she attributed Tom's literary proclivities, for she believed in prenatal as well as post-mortal influences. And certainly books were his meat. The older children would pile them on the floor around him, and turning the pages he would say, "Read about that picture," memorizing the captions so faithfully that it became a parlor trick to have two-year-old Tom "read aloud" for guests. When his mother wouldn't send him to school the month before his fifth birthday, he went secretly with an older boy and was allowed to stay in view of his excellent progress.

The Wolfes lived at 92 Woodfin Street (several blocks from the square where W.O. had his marble shop) in the house he had built for his second wife, whose praises he often sang though he had been less appreciative when she was alive. The deep yard behind the house was lush with fruit trees, flowers, and vegetables. Grape-vines coiled around the high front porch, and standing on the railing the children would pick the overhanging clusters. Thomas Wolfe always associated the Woodfin Street house with his father's bounty, with the roaring fires he kindled each morning before whooping them down to breakfast, and with the whole hogs he bought from the butcher and cured himself, wearing a long work-apron with his sleeves rolled halfway up his lean, hairy arms. W.O. was never happier than at the dinner table, clanging the carving knife on the steel with his family grouped around him. Each plate would be heaped with half a dozen vegetables, and sometimes they began coming back for seconds before W.O. had had a bite himself. "Merciful God!" he would groan, with a smile just below the surface. "Look how they can eat! Will they never get enough?" He was always telling Tom who sat next to him that he wouldn't be a big man unless he "ate hearty," and prodding the little stomach, W.O. would say, "There's a soft place there" and cover the child's plate with another slab of beef.

Less cheerful were the memories of W.O.'s rampages, of his distant lion's roar as he reeled home from the square, with his head held so high to keep from falling on his face that it seemed he might topple over backward. Seating himself in a porch rocker, he would rock with ominous rapidity and suddenly rush into the house where his imprecations could be heard above the clattering of pans. His ire was aimed almost exclusively at his wife, and though he did her no physical harm, she often seemed in danger of it and took refuge in her locked room or at a neighbor's. Later came his remorse. "Oh my God, Julia, what have I done? I've ruined you all! It won't happen again!" But it would.

"From the first," wrote Thomas Wolfe in *Look Homeward, Angel*, "deeper than love, deeper than hate, as deep as the unfleshed bones of life, an obscure and final warfare was being waged between them. Eliza wept or was silent to his curse, nagged briefly in retort to his rhetoric, gave like a punched pillow to his lunging drive—and slowly, implacably had her way."[6]

The summer of 1906, during one of W.O.'s bad spells, Julia purchased a rambling house a block and a half away at 48 Spruce Street, and made up her mind to support herself by taking in boarders. It was partly a means of keeping her distance from a man whose drinking antagonized her and had, she felt, blighted her social life. A ceaseless talker, Julia liked people around, and if she couldn't have a proper home, at least the boarders would give her an outlet. Then too, no doubt as a result of her early privations, she had a lust for property which she would indulge more and more as her children grew up and off her hands. Even before her marriage she had begun investing in real estate with marked success, and it now became an obsession. "Over the wife, over the mother," wrote Thomas Wolfe, "the woman of property, who was like a man, walked slowly forth"; she of the knowing wink and "the curiously masculine gesture of the hand—the forefinger extended, fist loosely clenched." Thus, without there being an official break, two Wolfe ménages were established.

Tom lived with his mother at the boarding house known as "The Old Kentucky Home"—"[moving] inward," he said later, "on that house of death and tumult from room to little room, as the boarders came with their dollar a day, and their constant rocking on the porch." Julia thought of him as her baby and tried to keep him so. She had nursed him till he was three and a half, and now she insisted that he wear his hair in shoulder-length, Lord Fauntleroy ringlets, which she wound around her finger each morning. Imagine the anguish they must have caused a child of his deeply sensitive nature, especially when he was sent out on the street with his brother Fred to hawk *The Saturday Evening Post!* Once when he had been plaguing two older boys to buy, they began teasing him about his hair and calling him a little girl over his excited protests, until finally he opened his trousers and produced proof of his masculinity. With his thin, pixyish face and dark eyes he seemed a sad little fellow as he stood on the edge of a field where others were playing ball—already an introvert, already apart. When he was nine, he caught lice from a neighbor and his mother reluctantly cut off his curls.

Though he spent the nights in "the great, chill tomb" of the Old Kentucky Home, his heart was at Woodfin Street with his father and the other children, two of whom had already flown the coop. Effie, thirteen years older than Tom, had married in 1908 and moved to Anderson, South Carolina. She was a sweet, pliable, ladylike person whose life would be circumscribed by an unsuccessful husband and a large brood. Frank, a year younger than Effie, though intelligent and not without charm, was weak, spoiled, and dissolute; he had dropped out of school to roam the country on pick-up jobs and periodically he came back to Asheville to live off the family. In 1913, he would marry a woman some years older and settle in New Albany, Indiana, where he squandered his inheritance and went to sanitariums now and then to combat a craving for drink and drugs. Of Frank it might charitably be said that he had been seared and warped by his early experiences; as the oldest boy, he was the one sent to collect his father from bar or brothel during his sprees. But Frank had inherited his father's vices without the compensating strength, and his surrender to his appetites was a warning to Tom, who, despite the unflinching portrait of Frank as the corrupt and swaggering Steve in *Look Homeward, Angel,* sympathized at times with this least fortunate of his siblings. "Frank," Tom would write their mother in 1924, "whether by inheritance, environment or self-development, is, has been, and probably will be, diseased— as diseased as any child who comes into the world with a tubercular spine. . . . I pity him from my heart. . . . The light of his life has been blurred by an unseen hand; the hand of the Potter shook when he turned his clay."[7]

Mabel, next in line, was a thin boisterous Amazon ten years older than Tom with a face, as he remembered it, "full of heartiness and devotion, sensitive, whole-souled, hurt, bitter, hysterical, but at times transparently radiant and handsome." "When one suffers a hurt," he also wrote of her, "her voice is low and gentle: she has large, wonderful hands, and all the pain goes out under their touch." It was the law of her nature to give herself unstintingly, to complain of those who clung to her and turned her into a drudge, and then to give herself some more. From the time she was a little girl, she had been able to control W.O. in his cups, slapping sense into him and forcing him to eat, and now, as his housekeeper, she filled the maternal role which Julia had in large measure abdicated. Mabel's three younger brothers were like her own children, and she further unified the family by being its entertainer, for she sang and played the piano with compelling warmth. A few years later she and another Asheville girl would tour the South as a vaudeville team in small-town movie theaters.

Fundamentally extroverted, Mabel immersed herself in the lives of others, but this was becoming difficult with Tom because of his growing inwardness and withdrawal. Seeing him sprawled in a chair with his long legs dangling to the floor and his face hidden behind a book, she would turn on him with what he remembered long afterwards as hatred. "*Hatred* is the word—I am not afraid to use it. . . . She would scream 'bastard' at me, sneer at what she called my 'queer, dopey, freaky little face,' pout out her lips at me in mockery of my own, and let her head goggle and droop stupidly as my own did on its scrawny neck." She called him a Westall—"There's none of Papa in you"—when in their family "Westall" had become "a synonym for selfishness, coldness, and unpleasant eccentricity." A creature of impulse, by turns biting and caressing, Mabel could not know that her raillery was helping to foment in Tom a profound if fecund bitterness.[8]

Through it all, his protector was his brother Ben, eight years older. As Julia once remarked, "There was something between [them] from the time Tom was a baby that I could never explain." (Ben's promising twin, Grover, had died of typhoid in 1904 when Julia took her children to St. Louis, where she ran a boarding house for six months during the World's Fair.) Quiet, moody, and intense, Ben had "a pointed, bumpy, always scowling face" and "crisp, maple-brown hair" and "his extraordinarily sensitive mouth smiled briefly,

9

flickeringly, inwardly—like a flash of light along a blade." He had left school to eke out his independence by working in the circulation department of *The Asheville Citizen*, and though he lived at Wood-fin Street, he stalked through the house like a phantom, aloof from the family chaos.

The remaining brother, Fred, born in 1895, was more extroverted even than Mabel, with whom he aligned himself in family differences, as Ben and Tom were aligned. A personality boy and a go-getter despite a chronic stammer, Fred was generous, good-natured, and likeable—"his broad mouth," as Tom described it, "always cocked for laughter."

But in power of influence the stonecutter father transcended them all. His shop on the northeast corner of Pack Square fascinated young Tom. There, amid the granite from Vermont and the marble from Georgia, with his many-sized and -shaped mallets and chisels ranged on wooden shelves coated with emery dust, W.O., in wing collar and starched shirt protected by a striped apron, bent to his strong yet delicate task of carving inscriptions and designs—his entrance gates to heaven, his garland of roses, his crossed hands.[9] Tom felt sorry for the grocers and plumbers and haberdashers whose labors were so ephemeral by comparison. "He mourned for all the men who had gone because they had not scored their name upon a rock, blasted their mark upon a cliff, sought out the most imperishable objects of the world and graven there some token, some emblem that utterly they might not be forgotten." His father's love of beauty and craftsmanship carried over into literature. He would often read aloud the more sonorous passages of Shakespeare, varying them with the humbler pyrotechnics of "The boy stood on the burning deck . . ." or "Half a league, half a league, half a league on-ward. . . ." From his father, for whom the weather was never sim-ply bad but "hellish, fearful, awful, damnable, blood-thirsty," Tom inherited his taste for rhetoric. His mother gave him his appetite for detail, but the moment he went dramatic with a rhythmical flow of language, that was his father speaking.

By 1912, Asheville had grown from a mountain town to a small city of some 25,000, with a relatively plastic, democratic society. As yet there wasn't sufficient wealth to crystallize an upper crust, despite the presence of such economic royalty as E. W. Grove, whose patent medicines had underwritten the lavish Grove Park Inn, and George W. Vanderbilt, who had modelled the chateau in the midst of his hundred thousand acres on Blois and Chambord. With assets of nearly $100,000 and an annual income of $8,000 to $10,000 (a quarter of it real-estate rentals), the Wolfes were in the top two percent economically.[10] As it happened, next door to them in their middle-class neighborhood on Woodfin Street lived the Hazzards, an old South Carolina family with a liveried coachman and a splendid residence which afforded Tom an early glimpse of plutocracy. The Hazzards kept their distance from the Wolfes, who weren't close to anyone, even among their peers, and not just because of W.O.'s carryings-on. He caused less stir in Asheville, a tourist resort with many transients and outsiders, than he would have in a more settled community. No—the Wolfes by any standard were a race apart. With their wild energy and their rapid-fire, churning conversation they had, as Tom said later, "a mad, original, disturbing quality which they did not suspect." Or to quote his teacher, Mrs. Roberts, "The Wolfes are not common people—but eccentricity plus. Perhaps the bit of unusualness in each flowered in Tom."[11]

Margaret Roberts, the fairy godmother of Tom's youth, was a sensitive, intelligent, harassed woman in her mid-thirties with dark eyes, wavy hair, and a gentle, cameo face that lit up when she smiled. Somewhat wispy and scrawny, she kept going when it seemed as if her next breath might blow her away, for hers was a steely frailness, a nunlike steadfastness. Orphaned at fourteen, she had gone to a Nashville boarding school run by the family of her future husband, whom she had known ten years before they became engaged, and since they had to help support his younger brothers and sisters until they finished their education, it was another four years before they could marry. As she once confided to Wolfe, Mrs. Roberts loved "with an abiding love the brightness of spirit in a boy or girl—that quality whatever you call it that makes them the glory of the world." "Boys were her heroes, her little gods," Wolfe wrote of her. "She believed that the world was to be saved, life redeemed, by one of them. She saw the flame that burns in each of them, and she guarded it. . . . She spoke a calm low word to the trembling racehorse, and he was still."

Her husband—good, conscientious, a man of character—was by comparison rather blunt and pedestrian. He seemed earthbound to Wolfe, but Mrs. Roberts loved him with unquestioning fidelity. He was the principal of the Orange Street School the fall of 1911 when, as a means of comparing the progress in the different grades, the whole student body was asked to write a theme on the same subject. His wife, helping him correct them, was electrified by a ratty-looking paper signed "Tom Wolfe." Though she had never heard of the boy before, she was eager to enroll him in the private school she and her husband planned to launch the following year. When approached, Tom was so enthusiastic that his father agreed to foot the bill. A few days before the opening of the North State Fitting School, Mr. Roberts took Tom to meet his wife, who remembered the huge hands on the cornstalk body and the bright, fierce eyes that roved instinctively towards the bookcase. Suddenly forgetting his awkwardness, he began spouting about his favorite books, about this character and that, with a fervor that amazed Mrs. Roberts, who sent him home with one he hadn't read, *The Cloister and the Hearth*.

From the outset, books and learning had filled him with an almost sensuous delight. As a small child unable to read he had lain on the floor before a roasting fire and pored over the big, calfskin volumes of Ridpath's *History of the World*, exulting not only in the illustrations of battles but in "the musty odor of the leaves, and in the pungent smell of their hot hides." From his father's small, well-chosen library, he had progressed to the public one, which he greedily ransacked—the Alger and the Henty books sliding down with the *Iliad* and the *Odyssey*, the novels of Jeffrey Farnol and David Graham Phillips getting equal attention with those of Thackeray and Twain. But Mrs. Roberts found that his writing left much to be desired. His compositions sprawled across the page in an abominable hand, and she wrote on one of them that unless he observed the rules of paragraphing she would stop correcting them altogether. "Pegasus has to be controlled even though it must be by one who has no wings"—"Pegasus" because in every paper he submitted she could count on seeing a sentence, a phrase, or maybe just one word that lifted it far above the usual ruck of schoolboy efforts.

As Mrs. Roberts became his emotional center, he spent less time at Woodfin Street, where Mabel and Fred, a bit envious of his private schooling, were saying that their parents did more for Tom than for the others, and this was true. Reading his books, one gets the impression of a Titan battling against odds, but that was the stance from which it pleased him to write. Actually he was more fortunate than many an artist in the people who helped him and the opportunities afforded him. Fate, however, had saddled him with an odd physique which caused him increasing dismay. He was now a beanpole sprite of a fence-rail thinness, with absurdly long legs which gave him a curious, bounding, scissorslike stride. In a desire to appear shorter than he was, he had a tendency to stoop, and his mother was always telling him to throw his shoulders back like his father, who carried himself with a weird stateliness. Atop his spindly frame, Tom's delicate, brooding face seemed remote and misplaced, as though it belonged on another body. At times his glance was that of a trapped animal begging for release, who will tear your hand if you free him, but he had much natural sweetness in him too.

Knowing himself to be different and in some vague way superior, he was easily humiliated: for example, by the hauteur of his Westall kin, who felt that Julia had married beneath her and referred to her offspring as "those wolves." His boarding-house existence was another sore point. Like his father, who railed at Julia's "murderous and bloody barn," Tom hated the idea of paid hospitality, and he squirmed when his mother sent him down to the depot to drum up trade by circulating her cards. Nevertheless, the artist in him was bound to profit from the assortment of types that came to the Old Kentucky Home, just as his being born into a large, tempestuous family was a great human and psychological advantage, much as he suffered from their outbursts. Even his parents' mismatch was perhaps not wholly detrimental from the standpoint of his work, for as Freud has observed, bad relations between parents heightens a child's emotions by causing it to feel intense love and hate at a tender age.

The whole town was his theater of observation. Unnoticed, he would sit for hours in a corner of the firehouse listening to the banter of the firemen and policemen relaxing together. At fourteen he took on a paper route—not because his parents needed the money but because they wanted him to know the value of a dollar, and because, like everyone in the family, he was jealous of his independence. Getting up at four in the morning, he wandered through the rickety colored section known as "Niggertown" with a paper-filled sack tugging at his thin shoulder. His lengthening body craved the lost sleep, but the Negro ghetto intrigued him with its mystery, and he loved the poetry of the dawn. "He saw the pale stars drown, and ragged light break open on the hills. Alone, the only man alive, he began the day for men, as he walked by the shuttered windows and heard the long denned snore of the tropics." Later, sipping coffee in a diner with the other route boys, he learned to smoke.

His greatest joy was travel. Since the visit to St. Louis, his mother had taken him to Florida several times and once to New Orleans during Mardi Gras. When he was twelve, they went to Wilson's inauguration over the protests of his father (a Republican, who accused Julia of "wearing the boy out to see that miserable scoundrel sworn in") and of Mrs. Roberts, concerned about the algebra in which he was lagging. Telling her of the prospective benefits of the trip, he finally came up with, "But don't you understand—I'll hear the President and I'll see *the home of the United States!*" Conquered by that phrase, Mrs. Roberts gave in. Of course, the journeys he made were nothing compared to those he dreamed of making. Hemmed in by the cool, blue mountains, his desire whetted by isolation, he "nailed to the wind his heart"[12] when down some valley a train wailed to the East and he heard its retreating pulse—*thalatta, thalatta.*

His nature was centrifugal, expansive, yet he didn't neglect the possibilities at hand. Divinely discontented and observing, he was always on duty with his gift, losing all sense of time if, for example, a new building was going up and he stopped to watch it. Forever enlarging his scope and honing his awareness, he gravitated to older people, and his contemporaries were a little in awe of him which gave rise, on his side, to a certain reserve. Under Mrs. Roberts' guidance his reading had grown more selective, with an emphasis on poetry which was now almost a religion. Though W.O., who was more devout than Julia and said his prayers on his knees each night, had seen to it that his children went to Sunday School,[13] Tom stopped believing in the God of his fathers at fourteen or thereabouts. His attention shifting from God the Creator to man the creator, he dreamed of becoming a god himself.[14]

During his last year at the North State Fitting School, *The Independent Magazine* sponsored a city-wide, school essay contest to celebrate the Tercentenary of Shakespeare's death. Tom tacked the Chandos portrait of the Bard on his bedroom wall, writing beneath it Jonson's invocation, "My Shakespeare, rise!" Ben and Mabel took it up, calling him to the phone or sending him on an errand with, "My Shakespeare, rise!" and at table it was, "My Shakespeare, do you want another piece of pie?" But his essay on "Shakespeare, the Man" won the prize because of what the judges termed its symmetry, its evidence of wide and sympathetic reading, and above all its appreciation of Shakespeare's genius. Mrs. Roberts never forgot the glancing light in Tom's eye and the quizzical smile that played around his mouth when she suggested that he recast the essay in oratorical form for the school's declamation contest, which he also won. At graduation he swept the literary honors, but he wasn't *summa* or *magna cum laude*. He only excelled in the things he liked.

Sixteen his next birthday, he was markedly young for college, and the Robertses wanted him to stay another year and improve his weak subjects, but he had to press on. His father had destined him for a career in law and politics. "Don't laugh," W.O. would say, solemn-eyed and wetting his thumb for emphasis, "that boy will be governor someday." Though Tom would have preferred the University of Virginia ("a great name opulent with romantic suggestion"),[15] his father insisted he go to the University of North Carolina, where his contacts would help him to rise in the state. Another point in favor of Chapel Hill was Mabel's proximity. That summer she had married Ralph Wheaton, a salesman for the National Cash Register Company, and the couple were living in Raleigh.

"I arrived at my decision to attend our state university last Wednesday night," Tom wrote his new brother-in-law September 10th. "Perhaps I should say *forced* instead of arrived. For that was what it amounted to."

2 · CHAPEL HILL

WHEN TOM, accompanied by his brother-in-law who was helping him settle, showed up at Chapel Hill in September, 1916, this oldest of our state universities was not the mecca for 14,000 it is today. The students totalled 1,137, including the graduate school, and the town, named for a colonial chapel of the Church of England, was an isolated country village bounding the university to the north. Today's four-lane thoroughfare separating the two was then a sand-clay road—until lately in such disrepair that undergraduate wits would post "no fishing" signs by the potholes after a heavy rain. Crowding the campus from the south, where now there is a series of housing developments, lay five hundred acres of university-owned forest pierced by a few trails. On the campus itself the weathered buildings were clumped around a rough-kept, oblong common traversed by gravel paths and shaded by ancient trrees, with the inevitable Civil War monument at one end and a portico-covered well (the favorite student gathering place) at the other. In between, the focus and symbol of it all, was the gnarled and canted Davie Poplar, to which General William R. Davie had supposedly tied his horse when he headed the group of trustees who chose the site back in 1792.

Despite its depth of tradition, the outlook at Chapel Hill was somewhat narrow and provincial. James K. Polk, eleventh President of the United States, had been a Carolina man, as was Josephus Daniels, currently Secretary of the Navy, but the university ideal of public service meant service to the state. Its president—slim, ascetic, inspirational Edward Kidder Graham—was leading a crusade to lift North Carolina out of the primitive backwardness which had lingered on since the Civil War. Only a handful of students came from other states, the majority being from small North Carolina towns to which they planned to return after graduation. The norm of small-town success was thus the expectation for Thomas Wolfe, who wrote his father soon after his arrival, "I don't know if I will ever be President but I will promise you shall never be ashamed of me." Quoting the remark in a letter to Fred, W.O. commented that it sounded good to him and that he had high hopes for Tom "because he talks right and is a hard student, and if he keeps his health and lives he must necessarily succeed in the end, for Tom has good morals. It is the height of my life end ambition to see him through college . . . and unless I am greatly deceived you will be proud one day to call him your brother."

In *Look Homeward, Angel* Wolfe twisted and romanticized his college experience; both consciously and unconsciously he superimposed on the years at Chapel Hill some of the turmoil and frustration he was to know at Harvard and in New York while gestating the book. As early as 1919, discussing the possibilities for a college novel with one of his professors, he said that the profound truth could only be represented through an unappreciated student, because all students, no matter how prominent or successful, *felt* unappreciated.[1] But when he matriculated in 1916, the sorrows of Eugene Gant had yet to be distilled from the life of Thomas Wolfe who, considering the usual relentlessness of upperclassmen towards freshmen with any oddity of temperament or physique, got along rather well and quickly took root in the university. That fall he boarded in a private house, where his room cost twice as much as in a dormitory and where the food was excellent. Throughout his college career his father gave him the money he needed, though he had to be careful and his shabbiness and disorder led others to think of him as poorer than he was. Actually, he belonged to the privileged half of the student body, those who weren't obliged to work part time to meet their expenses.

Open, eager, and imaginative, he was one of the greener, more gullible freshmen. The sophomores took him snipe-hunting several times before he discovered what it was all about. After dark, a freshman would be posted with an open sack in a remote spot while the sophomores whistled up the snipe, which were supposed to run into the sack—the object being to keep the freshman sitting there all night. More embarrassing was his gaffe during his initiation with fifty classmates into the Dialectical Literary Society. Those who aspired to campus leadership joined either the "Di," recruited from the western half of the state, or the "Phi" (the Philanthropic), recruited from the eastern half. In the grandiose meeting hall—red carpet, green draperies, and chandeliers—the officers sat on a rostrum against a backdrop of the society's insignia, the president with a gold-headed cane for a gavel, while the members lounged on upholstered chairs ranged in semi-circular rows. At the start of the initiation a sophomore pretending to be a freshman made a boastful speech which supposedly set the tone. When Wolfe was called on next, he advertised himself for twenty-two minutes, pointing with a final flourish to the portrait of Zeb Vance, North Carolina's Civil War governor, and predicting that his own would one day hang beside it. Catcalls and exaggerated applause greeted this scarecrow of a freshman with his coat-sleeves too high on his arms and his pant-legs several inches above his shoe-tops, but he held his audience. Obviously he could talk in his nervous, stumbling way, in recognition of which he would presently be elected vice-president of the Freshman Debating Club.

From the first, Wolfe was articulate, noticed, and even a bit formidable, despite his self-doubt and his oscillations between joy and despair. The peak of his fall was the Thanksgiving Day football classic with the University of Virginia, which Virginia had won for the past eleven years. His enthusiasm had been kindled by Carolina's star, Bill Folger, who dominated the campus much as Hobey Baker had dominated Princeton's a few years before. A stiff-arming halfback of the Red Grange variety, Folger had graduated from The Citadel and played a season of football at the University of South Carolina before being persuaded by alumni to continue his triumphs at the Hill, while studying law on the side. This tramp athlete of casual ruggedness and manly grace could also recite Kipling and pick a mandolin. He was admired by men, adored by women, and —years later—immortalized by Wolfe as Jim Randolph, the football hero in *The Web and the Rock.*

The Virginia game was played in Richmond. After a bonfire rally, Wolfe and eight hundred other Tar Heels boarded the overnight special for the Confederate capital, where they marched to a midtown hotel and then were on their own until the kick-off. Wandering around the business district with a friend, Wolfe soliloquized on the beautiful women who were out in full force that day and on the evil and injustice of great cities with their extremes of poverty and wealth. He surprised his friend with his sympathy for the downtrodden; already this stripling seemed Atlaslike in his assumption of the world's burdens. Too keenly anticipated, the game was an anti-climax, although Folger, true to form, broke loose on a thrilling run that proved the margin of victory. Wolfe sent Mrs. Roberts a postcard: "We beat Virginia 6–0. It was a Thanksgiving Dinner that had been cooking eleven years."

Academically, his performance was respectable, but finding small nutriment in his courses, he got his real education from independent reading, which that year included Poe's *Tales, Frankenstein, Sir Gawain and the Green Knight,* and the plays of Lord Dunsany. Weekends he brought armfuls of books to his room, while those around him played poker. Nor was his reading, as Mrs. Roberts once observed, "mere gulping down. He literally crushed the bones of a book and extracted the marrow. I know whereof I speak because I was present at many a crushing." In class he seemed an awkward adolescent trying to grow up. Stumbling in after the attendance had been taken, he would hunch down in a rear seat and make himself as inconspicuous as possible, tittering defensively at the professor's barb, and enjoying it too, for he acquiesced in the role of clown. Whether he resisted using a Latin trot like the virtuous Eugene in *Look Homeward, Angel* is open to question, but he was sufficiently versed to make a trot and sell it to his classmates when none was available. Another time the teacher told them to skip a passage lest it offend the single coed present. Wolfe happened to be translating when the passage occurred and he plowed right through it—a discourse on the way the stomach grumbles when empty. He was never one to flinch at realities. Thus, when assigned an autobiographical essay entitled "Who I Am," he wrote and read aloud a description of his family, emphasizing his father's drunkenness and profanity which appalled the others, unaccustomed as they were to a side of life that Wolfe already viewed with a certain detachment.

He went home for Christmas, but the spring recess was too brief to make the cross-state journey worthwhile. Once his mother came to visit him and humiliated him by talking up the Old Kentucky Home among his acquaintance. "M-Mabel, M-Mabel," he said afterwards, with the stammer that took possession of him when upset or excited, "Mama's r-ruining me over at Chapel Hill! I'll sw-swear she's just r-ruining me with my friends!" When he went back to Asheville for summer vacation, it seemed dinky after Raleigh and Greensboro, and the boarding-house atmosphere depressed him more than ever.

His spirit found release in an unexpected quarter. A girl of twenty-one named Clara Paul, from the tidewater town of Washington, North Carolina, was staying at the Old Kentucky Home with her ten-year-old convalescent brother. The Pauls' parents had died, leaving them well-to-do, and Clara had just completed a business course at the Greensboro College for Women. She was slender, dainty, well made, musical, and a good dancer. She had hazel eyes, a pale, freckled skin, and curly hair, which Wolfe remembered as "corn-colored." In her photographs the tilted nose is perhaps a little large for the face, the chin a shade too long and prominent, the mouth a trifle wide and thin. But to Wolfe she was an oasis of loveliness.

Outgoing and considerate, she helped Julia with her chores, and Mabel, who had recently moved back to Asheville with her husband, smiled on her friendship with Tom. Clara encouraged him to go on excursions with her and her brother by paying his way, and though she had no taint of the siren or seductress and her engagement was common knowledge, Tom fell hopelessly in love with her. Responsive to his adoration, she may have permitted his advances, but all the evidence points to the fact that he never slept with her; in this respect the Laura James idyl in *Look Homeward, Angel* was a figment of his longing. The previous fall he had been cajoled by some upperclassmen into losing his virginity in a Durham whorehouse with the attendant disgust and disillusion one might expect in a youth of his poetic sensitivity. Now he wanted the physical with the spiritual, but it was not to be.[2] At the end of a few weeks Laura went back to Washington and got married, and two years later she died of influenza, closing the circuit of love and death in Wolfe's imagination and exalting the episode to a kind of religious ecstasy.

"He kissed her on her splendid eyes," Wolfe was to say of Eugene and Laura James in *Look Homeward, Angel*; "he grew into her young Maenad's body, his heart numbed deliciously against the pressure of her narrow breasts. She was as lithe and yielding to his sustaining hand as a willow rod—she was bird-swift, more elusive in repose than the dancing watermotes upon her face. He held her tightly lest she grow into the tree again, or be gone amid the wood like smoke.

"Come up into the hills, O my young love. Return! O lost, and by the wind grieved, ghost, come back again, as first I knew you in the timeless valley, where we shall feel ourselves anew, bedded on magic in the month of June. There was a place where all the sun went glistering in your hair, and from the hill we could have put a finger on a star."

In 1924 Wolfe would write Mrs. Roberts, "Did you know I fell in love when I was sixteen with a girl who was twenty-one? Yes, honestly—desperately in love. And I've never quite got over it. . . . A woman five years older can make putty of a boy. . . ."

At the time, his family was unaware of Clara's impact. In July, W.O. wrote Ben that Tom had "become suddenly *girl struck*, with two or three affairs lately" and that he had better restrain himself till he finished his education. Tom still had hopes of transferring to a more cosmopolitan university—that summer he corresponded with the Registrar at Princeton—but his father wouldn't hear of it, so he resigned himself once and for all to becoming a big fish in the relatively restricted pond of the Hill.

He returned to a campus muted by the war. In April the United States had joined the Allies. A fifth of the student body had left for the service, and in this smaller arena with its reduced competition he began to stand out for more than his resemblance to Ichabod Crane. The bookish, reclusive freshman was coming out of his shell. In those days it was customary to greet the other students as you passed them with a "Hi-ho, gentlemen" or a "Howdy-do, sir," and Wolfe, approaching you, would start his abashed smile at some twenty paces—a smile which seemed to say, "Yes, I know I'm a bit of an oddball, but I'm a friendly fellow really, and you look like one too."

Because of the national emergency, the football schedule had been cancelled, with military training taking the place of athletics. Twelve hours a week were devoted to close-order drill, digging trenches, and bayonetting straw dummies. An improbable soldier, Wolfe was known for the abruptness with which he changed from monkeyshines to hyperseriousness at the command of "Attention!" and when his squad fell out for a rest, he talked while the others listened. He had begun to find an audience, and in November he published a war poem in the university monthly, *The Carolina Magazine*. In succeeding issues more paeans to the soldiers of freedom and democracy appeared over his name, and one of them, "The Challenge" —its meter and emotion cribbed from James Russell Lowell's "The Present Crisis"—got reprinted in *The Asheville Citizen*, bringing a crow of delight from his ailing father, who was undergoing radium treatments for cancer of the prostate. W.O. wrote Tom that "The Challenge" has been "most favorably received by the people of this community, *your home*. And many have been the warm congratulations your mother and myself have received for you, by such men as Dr. R. F. Campbell, Col. Hodges, Dr. Purefoy, N. A. Reynolds, and men and women of such type who are among our best citizens and capable of judging." Mr. Roberts assembled his school to read the poem aloud, and newspapers elsewhere in the state picked it up. In May, when it was reprinted as far afield as Florida, W.O. wrote Tom, "I find it has been copied with your name as author more or less all over the country but then don't let it turn your head or make you vain. I suppose *I* am the *one* it has made *fool.* Robert M. Wells, a university man, declared Saturday eve it was the greatest patriotic poem published since the war commenced and would go down as such in history."

With surging ambition Tom now struck out in all directions. He had discovered the law that, up to a point, the more one undertakes the better he does each thing with his dilated energies. His work for *The Carolina Magazine* and for the college newspaper, *The Tar Heel,* had gotten him elected to Sigma Upsilon, a national literary fraternity, and he also made a social fraternity, Pi Kappa Phi—"the greatest thing I ever did and will mean much," he wrote his father after the initiation. Meanwhile, his grades improved, especially his Greek—thanks to a remarkable teacher, Professor W. S. "Bully" Bernard.

Son of a Confederate surgeon and the product of hard raising in a small North Carolina town, Bernard had scrabbled for his education and had ended up a groomed cricket of a bachelor with silvery hair and voice and a stern charm. He smoked cigarettes in a long holder, came to class in plus fours and daring hose, and careened around the campus in a tiny foreign roadster with wire-spoked wheels that seated one in front and one behind. Wolfe, on easy terms with him after two years in his classes, was a comical sight squeezed into the back with his doubled-up knees projecting above the sides.

Bully's passionate involvement with the Greeks was evident in the way he spoke the word—his voice clicking and trilling on the "G" and the "r," undulating and singing through the "e's," clicking again on the "k," and lingering with a sigh for the infinite on the "s." He made his students learn the language and bristled at their ineptitude, but his real concern was Greek culture. He sought to rekindle the glow of their superb civilizing effort, and in Wolfe he found an apostle who was instinctively drawn to the Greek perception of beauty in the commonplace, to their generalizing power through a brilliant use of details, to their bitter-sweet sense of life's transience, and to their broad humanity and final detachment. "How right the Greeks were in seeing the world as 'object,'" Wolfe would note in his Autobiographical Outline for *Look Homeward, Angel,* adding in paraphrase of Matthew Arnold, "To see life clearly and to see it whole." And in 1927 he would comment in a letter, "There's not much cant and twaddle to the Greeks; they are really the *living*, aren't they? The dead are all about us."[3]

His second year at Chapel Hill, though happier than his first, was marred by tragedy at the end. He had been rooming with Edmund Burdick, a brilliant Asheville boy who suffered from a congenital heart lesion. Pale and often out of breath, he had to withdraw from college in April and a month later he died. In their English course they had been assigned an essay on a theme from the Romantic Poets, and Burdick had chosen "Immortality." He was dead when the papers were returned, but the professor read his aloud to the class with dramatic effect and moving commentary. Wolfe was completely unhinged by the loss of his friend. He wandered around in a daze, asking, "Why has he died? Where has he gone? Is there a life after death?" Unable to sleep in the room they had shared, he spent his nights in an armchair in the suite of some other Ashevilleans, who finally installed a cot where he slept for the remainder of the term.

Summers, Tom was expected to earn money. The year before, he had gotten fifteen a week as Ralph Wheaton's office boy, but the war had made him restless and he was anxious to leave home. He had heard of the high wages being paid to unskilled labor in Norfolk, which also beckoned because Clara Paul was living there with her husband. His parents tried to dissuade him from going, but in the end they gave him his carfare, thinking he would soon grow weary and return.

He stayed away all summer without writing home for funds. Once, it is true, he looked up Fred—now a sailor stationed at Hampton Roads—who took him to the galley at the naval base and got him his first square meal in weeks. Revelling in the color and vitality of the war-swollen port, he sweltered, scrimped, stank, starved, and worked when necessary—first as a labor-gang timekeeper at Langley Field, then as a supply checker on the docks. Meanwhile he was fixing in his mind a variety of types from all over the country: Swedes from the Midwest, Jews from the sweatshops, Irishmen, Italians, Negroes, hunkies, Bowery bums. Having found out where

Clara lived, he reconnoitered her house from afar without seeing her, for he was too proud to make his presence known. He consoled himself at a brothel in the tenement district of Newport News, a hastily built shack of raw pine where he stood in line with the sailors, awaiting his turn in one of the cubicles. In September he went back to Asheville, matured and strengthened by his show of independence.

Ben was at the Old Kentucky Home, on leave from his newspaper job in Winston-Salem. Underweight and probably tubercular, he had been turned down by the armed services and his customary bitterness had increased to a quiet rage. "Good God, I wonder what I'm living for!" he said to Tom during one of their late talks on the sleeping porch which they shared. Puzzled by life's meaning, wanting to make the most of his own yet feeling his limitations, Ben kept urging Tom to press for advantages the others hadn't had.

Tom had been at Chapel Hill barely a month when word came that Ben was desperately ill. Staying on at the Old Kentucky Home he had caught flu, which turned into double pneumonia, and when Tom reached his bedside one look at the twisted and as if decapitated body gasping for breath told him that his brother was dying. The agony that followed, while the hysterical family sought to stave off the inevitable, raked Tom's spirit but quickened the artist in him. It reinforced his dark, unearthly side and filled him with the exultancy in life which follows the full realization of death. At the last there was a moment of supreme communion when the members of the family, for once lifted out of their private concerns, drew together in the face of Ben's expiring life and bowed to the majesty of his passing—"scornful and unafraid, as he had lived, into the shades of death. . . . O Artemidorus, farewell!"

"I think the Asheville I knew died for me when Ben died," Tom would write Mabel years later. "I have never forgotten him and I never shall. I think that his death affected me more than any other event in my life."

It was a grim season. Soon after his return to Chapel Hill, the flu epidemic, now at its height, struck down President Edward Kidder Graham. Desolation hung over the university like a cloud at the loss of its leader, whose inspired liberalism had helped to make Carolina one of the most democratic and self-governing campuses in

America. Because Graham had overtaxed himself with the regional directorship of the Student Army Training Corps, he was deemed a war casualty, and Wolfe was one of the few who, then or later, found fault with this exemplary man. "A bit of the prig to Graham," Wolfe was to say in his Autobiographical Outline. "Large spiritual eyes, the slightly beatified face. . . . How unsatisfying those speeches were [Graham's celebrated talks in chapel]—the core lacking—the terms of an abstract philosophy applied to hunger and thirst." It was the cloistered quality of Graham's idealism that put Wolfe off; he liked an idealism with its feet on the ground—one that took into account the passions, crudities, smells, and dissonances of ordinary life.[4]

Since September the university had been an armed camp. The newly established S.A.T.C. dominated the curriculum, and save for the physically disqualified, everyone eighteen and over was an enlisted man on his way to becoming an officer. Not Wolfe, however. Two weeks short of his eighteenth birthday when the term began, he had been excluded and impatiently awaited the next draft. When the Armistice was signed in November, he felt cheated again, for like most of his generation he longed to go overseas.

As life on the Hill fell back into peace-time routine, the students returning from the service found Wolfe an established personality— an off-beat but respected individual who represented the arts in a healthy way. His looks alone were enough to set him apart—and above. He was six feet three and still growing in that pre-vitamin age when the race was several inches shorter than it is now. Long-limbed, sinewy, thin-chested, and raw-boned, he had high, square shoulders and huge, stringy hands which he twisted together in moments of tension, or flailed dramatically as he talked. Head forward, stooping slightly as if prepared to duck through a door, he swung across the campus with a loping, loose-jointed stride. His wavy, uncombed hair was always in need of a cutting (he was letting it grow extra long to cover the patch of eczema that had lately appeared on his neck), and in his rumpled, ill-fitting clothes with his tie off center and a bit of shirttail extruding, he looked—though not actually dirty—as if a bath would do him no harm. The dark intensity of his glance, however, made it clear that such externals were the least concern of this busily preoccupied young man.

His living habits continued migratory. He had a room by himself which he seldom used. Sometimes he spent the night in the dormitory suite of Forrest Miles, editor of *The Tar Heel,* Wolfe being the managing editor or second in command. In after years, Miles would picture Wolfe at the close of an evening: still talking as he undressed, still gesticulating with a shoe in his hand, he would suddenly grow abstracted and sit perfectly still, staring at the wall for minutes on end. Wolfe was an energetic sleeper who ground his teeth and snored until just before his first class, to which he dashed without breakfast and with his assignment hastily scrawled on scratch paper, or even a paper bag. When called on to recite, he was voluble in a diffident, slightly apologetic manner, as if afraid of seeming too knowledgeable or assertive, and after the bell he would go on arguing with the professor, not polishing the apple but from a sincere interest in the subject.

A frequent companion that year was "Big" Terry, or John Double-Terry, as he was known, to distinguish him from the Terry of ordinary dimensions. Both Wolfe and Terry were oddities—the one outlandishly tall and gangling, the other outlandishly round and fat —and both were indoor-literary. Though Wolfe occasionally kicked a football or pitched a game of horseshoes, he was too awkward and lunging for team sports, and as for Terry, his favorite exercise was eating. Moonfaced, multi-chinned, and bespectacled, he kept his coat buttoned to conceal his girth and had a hard time catching his breath when he lapsed into his habitual, good-natured laugh. Six years older than Wolfe, he had graduated from college and was now attending the medical school, and sometimes Wolfe accompanied him to the dissecting room where he forced himself to look at the cadavers. Terry's real enthusiasm, however, was conversation and the arts, and he would end up an English professor at N.Y.U. and Wolfe's first official biographer.[5]

Wolfe's wide popularity at this point was founded on his wit. His muttered asides in chapel convulsed his neighbors, and his flow of homespun jokes made him much in demand as a speaker at smokers and banquets. At a meeting of the Di Society, when fines were being imposed on absentees unless they had a plausible excuse, Wolfe parodied the various types of alibi so uproariously that a motion was passed cancelling all the fines. During the fraternity rushes it was he who provided the entertainment at Pi Kappa Phi with his travesty of King Arthur's Round Table. ("My Lord, my lady waits without." "Without what?" "Without food and clothing." "Feed her and bring her in.") But his best-remembered burlesque took place in the advanced composition course of Professor Edwin Greenlaw, a plump, grim-jawed scholar with a concealed sense of fun.

One morning the class assembled as usual on the second floor of Old East, and Greenlaw, having noted the absences, was saying, "Well, gentlemen, let's get on," when feet clattered on the stairs, the door flew open, and Wolfe peered in. After he had taken his seat, Greenlaw broke the silence with, "Brother Wolfe, we welcome you. Will you read us the burning words you have written?" Standing up in his overcoat, for the building was poorly heated, Wolfe cleared his throat and began reading a manila sheet covered with his headlong scrawl. Running off it in mid-sentence, he fumbled in his pocket, drew out a typed page, read it, searched his pockets again, and came up with a ragged envelope covered with more writing. Odd scraps of paper followed, testifying to the white heat of his inspiration. At one point a match cover yielded a sentence. Everyone was chuckling as Wolfe with furrowed brow dug into his pocket one last time and produced a roll of toilet paper, from which he read scroll-like as he unwound it onto the floor. When he had finished, poker-faced Greenlaw commented that the essay was well suited to the paper on which it was written, and Wolfe's shout of merriment swelled the general uproar.

He could afford such capers because his literary reputation was secure; it was indeed his only vanity. He seemed to consider a few things he had written the best around, though he gave you to understand that they were child's play compared to what he would do later on. Crossing the campus with a friend, he would reel off purple passages plucked from the air, crowing with delight when he hit on a phrase that particularly pleased him. In Greenlaw's class they had collaborated on a novel about a strike, and Greenlaw told Wolfe that in his part of it he had achieved what most men didn't get till they were forty—namely, style. Wolfe, however, dreamed of something more. Since the arrival that fall of Professor Frederick Koch, his heart was set on becoming a playwright.

"Proff" Koch (two "f's" if you please), as this boyish and least professorial of zealots liked to be called, had taught theater at the University of North Dakota for thirteen years before coming to Chapel Hill. His passion, indeed his monomania, was the folk drama. Scorning the decadence and false sophistication of the contemporary stage, he asked for plays rooted in the American soil; plays about the customs, legends, and superstitions of a pioneer people; plays full of tall tales, square dances, corn shucking, quilting, cane stripping, and log raising; plays about the long, hard winter in the little sod shanty and about the prairie springtime gay with wild roses and brimming with the song of the lark. Koch believed that every locale had its drama, just as every person had a creativity which would blossom into art if wisely directed. "You're potential poets and you're hiding it!" this irrepressible enthusiast with the Norfolk jacket, Windsor tie, and ubiquitous pipe would tell his pupils.

When Koch invaded the Hill with his "experiment in folk democracy" there were only twenty-five coeds in the university, but since most of the male population had been absorbed by the S.A.T.C., his first playwriting class consisted of seven girls and Thomas Wolfe. Early in the game Wolfe took Koch aside and said, "Proff, I don't want you to think that this Ladies Aid Society represents Carolina. We've got lots of he-men interested in writing, but they're all disguised in uniforms." Wolfe found Koch no stickler for technique. Long on encouragement and short on criticism, which according to him made young writers self-conscious and dried up their natural impulses, he would boast that "We don't need any rules—we write from our hearts." The essentials were spontaneity and relentless pursuit of the folk. He had his students combing country newspapers for human-interest stories about fishermen and sharecroppers, and if one of them had heard of a settlement called "Hanging Dog," Koch would say, "Magnificent! There's your title!" and the student, like it or not, would be stuck with writing a play about Hanging Dog.

To decide which ones should be enacted, a reading was held, open to faculty, students, and townspeople alike, for Koch thought of the folk drama as a community project, and when it came to the staging, everyone was on tap. The lighting, for instance, would be dumped in the lap of a professor of engineering, and costumes and furniture were requisitioned from houses in the village. Members of the scene-painting committee went out in the country and made sketches of real log cabins, because Koch demanded authenticity. If the script called for breaking a plate, you broke it, and if it was meal-time, you ate an actual meal. One of the pleasanter incidentals in a Koch production was the odor of frying bacon.

In March, 1919, the Carolina Playmakers presented their first program—three one-acters including *The Return of Buck Gavin* by Thomas Wolfe. Tossed off in several hours on a rainy afternoon, Wolfe's play had been inspired by an old newspaper clipping about the capture of a Texas outlaw in a Chicago tenement. He transposed the incident to the familiar setting of the mountains around Asheville and gave it a sentimental twist: Gavin is captured when he goes home to put flowers on the grave of a fallen comrade. Koch persuaded Wolfe to play the title role on the grounds that no one knew the life as he did. Wolfe, after all, was a mountaineer (albeit a city one), and something about him brought to mind the drovers and the rough, gaunt men in covered wagons who came down with their apples and whisky and cider and camped in vacant lots. But if any of this spirit got into Wolfe's acting, it was mingled with another element peculiarly his own which astounded the audience of six hundred. In the angular, mat-haired, wild-eyed outlaw they were suddenly conscious of a primitive force, an enraged rebellion that far exceeded the requirements of the trifling play. Koch was lyrical. "You can smell the mountain air," he said afterwards, "*Buck Gavin* has its furies as the Greek dramas have theirs." A few weeks later at Class Night, Wolfe was hoisted onto a table and made to repeat his triumph, but this time he turned it into a farce that had faculty and students screaming with laughter.

In the uncut version of *Look Homeward, Angel*, Wolfe would satirize Koch as Professor Hutch, "the little man with the urge." "Gene, Gene, have I shown you this?" gasps Hutch, taking out a pocketful of letters and clippings. "Have you seen this yet? By God, boy, you'll be famous. They're reading about us all over the country." Koch may have been egotistical in his naïve way, but he gave his students a sense of their immediate worth, and his enthusiasm launched Wolfe on the course which—though it turned out to be the wrong one—he pursued for the next eight years, not without profit.[6]

That June he went home loaded with honors. Editor-elect of *The Tar Heel* and a member of next year's senior council, he was one of seven juniors tapped for the Golden Fleece, the Carolina equivalent of Skull and Bones. He found his father in the hospital, and when he called on him, he would slip off to the operating room and watch the nurse tidy up after the surgeon had left. Sitting on the operating table, he would ask her the name and function of each instrument as she cleaned it and put it away. Another pastime was wrestling with J. B. ("Big Mac") McIntosh, a policeman who had won the championship of the Allied Armies in elimination bouts after the Armistice. McIntosh had a mat in his barn, and it amused him to roll around with Wolfe—this tangle of limbs with the biggest hands he had ever seen. Once Wolfe brought several friends to watch, and McIntosh, suddenly in earnest, squeezed Wolfe's stomach so hard that he vomited. When he could speak again, he said, "Mac, I wish this whole barn would go up in flames"—mental violence being his usual response to humiliation.

In September he went back to the Hill, pleasantly aware that he was a big man on campus. He had gotten there by brains and personality, for he had no athletic or social qualifications. Society, it is true, counted for less at Carolina than at Princeton or Virginia where Wolfe mightn't have fared so well, yet even at Carolina it was a consideration, and Wolfe had mixed feelings about it. Although in his secret heart he would have liked to shine as he swept a beautiful girl around the dance floor, a complex of ungainliness kept him on the sidelines at proms. Nor did he belong to the Asheville clique which qualified automatically for the old-line fraternities, and he resented the snobs who stared superciliously from the porches of fraternity row. Almost in protest against their meretricious values, he had joined his bob-tailed fraternity, Pi Kappa Phi. Recently established in a house in the village and devoid of social pretensions, it nevertheless had more than its share of leaders—of able, purposeful men like Wolfe himself.

And Wolfe was not only a leader: he entertained. Push your way through a crowd at the Old Well and the chances were he would be at the center of it, grinning roguishly as he got off one of his big lies. In any bull session he took the lead in a perfectly natural way, preferring to talk, yet willing to listen, especially to contrary views that burnished his own. Though usually in a hurry, he was never in too much of one to pause for an animated discussion, and he had a warm way of putting his arm around you and showing that he liked you. He did not cultivate or reject anyone, but was interested in all types and met them on their own ground.

The seat of his authority was the weekly newspaper, *The Tar Heel*, which he presided over with loose-reined élan. As managing editor the year before, he had given out the assignments but was so lax about collecting them and so hard to locate that he ended up doing much of the writing himself. Now, as editor-in-chief, he waited till the day the paper went to press before checking the copy, and having corrected it, he dashed off the needed fillers on the bus going over to Durham. Once when he learned a day in advance that the copy was almost non-existent, he sat up all night and wrote the entire issue himself. One way or another the job got done, and every Thursday, just before the deadline, he breezed into the Seeman Printery, reeling off explanations as to why he was just a wee bit late with stuff. If the editor of the Trinity (now Duke) *Chronicle* was on hand, Wolfe would joke that he didn't see why the "Chronic-Ill" couldn't wait another week—it wasn't worth printing anyway—and then, having emptied his pockets of what appeared to be the contents of several scrapbaskets, he would assemble *The Tar Heel* in fifteen minutes of intense effort. He stayed on afterwards to see it through the press, which sometimes occupied him till late at night when the jitney had stopped running, but such was his energy that he thought nothing of walking the twelve miles of rough, winding road to Chapel Hill.

He was fond of Mr. Seeman, the printer, who always remembered a meal with Wolfe and several of his companions. Tom was moody that day, and the others kept trying to draw him out for Mr. Seeman's benefit. "Say, Tom," one of them finally asked, "when you get to be a famous author, are you going to use your middle initial, or just sign yourself 'Thomas Wolfe?'" The sensitive face brightened. With a shrewd, slightly contemptuous smile Wolfe said, "Use my middle initial? Hell no! How would it look if Shakespeare had signed himself 'William J. Shakespeare?'" What struck Seeman was an underlying seriousness. The boy isn't joking, he thought; he really means to win a glorious name.

In his work for *The Tar Heel* Wolfe varied his style, slipping easily from the sprightly to the hortatory, or from the caustic to the grave. In his column "With Apologies to Pepys" he satirized such grievances as the meals in the university commons. "Thence to dinner," he would write, "where we had a stew smelling of goat but dessert was good" or "Infinite busy in the afternoon and with eagerness to supper, finding a rubber heel with gravy in side dish at my plate." When gubernatorial candidate Max Gardner gave a hackneyed speech at the university, Wolfe sounded his note of reform: "Tell us something we don't already know. We will agree quite freely that the Old North State is the peer of them all and that the labor situation is serious. But if you will come boldly forward and exhibit two or three planks in your platform that show you have been doing some real thinking on your own part, we will have more respect for you, no matter if we don't all agree with you." (To Wolfe's delight, his editorial would be quoted in the ensuing campaign.)

Meanwhile he continued to write and act for the Playmakers, and he helped to edit a humor sheet, *The Tar Baby*, for which he wrote an entire issue parodying *The Raleigh News and Observer*. By way of preparation he spent a day in Raleigh covering the capital beat with a reporter, after which he went through *The News and Observer* files till 3 A.M. With so many commitments it was surprising that he had any time left over for his studies, but he repeated his performance of junior year, getting mostly 2's, or B's, with a sprinkling of 1's, or A's.

In class he didn't hesitate to raise questions which embarrassed the instructor. Thus in Koch's Shakespeare course,[7] which covered most of the plays, he and another student challenged the validity of such a survey. Wanting to concentrate on *Hamlet* from a literary, philosophical, and psychological point of view, they subjected Koch to a barrage of arguments and objections that degenerated into bullying, and Koch seemed on the verge of tears when another student reminded Wolfe that he was getting what had been described in the catalogue: Shakespeare from the standpoint of staging and acting alone. Wolfe craved challenge and resistance of the sort he came up against in the courses of Edwin Greenlaw, that brusque, businesslike, but magnificent English teacher who fielded the most intricate questions without a moment's delay. Articulate, wide-ranging, and erudite without pedantry, Greenlaw stood for something he called "The Great Tradition." Beginning at the headwaters with the Hebrews, Greeks, and Romans, he carried his students down the stream of literature to modern times, not overlooking a single tributary. He read with fine eyes that aroused both one's sympathies and one's critical faculties, his specialty being the Elizabethans, whose gusto, grandeur and physicality had always appealed to Wolfe.

In his Autobiographical Outline, Wolfe would call Greenlaw "one of the great creative forces of my life"—but there was a hitch. Sooner or later there always was, with everyone. Greenlaw seemed muffled by a rigid scholarly discipline; his fires were banked as he constantly checked the luxuriance of Shakespeare and Spenser with the cold intellect of Francis Bacon. "A thorough-going, Teutonized scholar [who swore] by the Ph.D.," as Wolfe described him, he belonged to a new, aggressive, essentially scientific wave of educators whose watchwords were "method" and "research." And since Wolfe's love affair with literature had little to do with these, a side of him remained untouched by Greenlaw's enlightened pedagogy. This was the Wolfe who roamed the campus in the small hours, hobnobbing with cops and cab drivers in all-night diners; who registered in the cheap hotels of neighboring towns as Thomas Chatterton or Samuel T. Coleridge; and who gravitated to courses like News Writing and Dramatic Composition which gave him a chance to vent some of the emotions that seethed within him.

Oddly enough, the professor who meant the most to him was a philosopher with small appreciation of literature as such. "Horace Williams and the Liberating Breath," he would write in his Autobiographical Outline after touching on Greenlaw's limitation.[8] Wolfe thought Williams not only the greatest teacher he ever had but one of the great lives of the period, quietly unfolding itself in a remote college town.

A North Carolina farm boy born on the eve of the Civil War, Williams had worked his way through Chapel Hill and gotten fellowships at the Yale and the Harvard Divinity Schools, where he stitched together a philosophy from Plato, the Bible, the Upanishad, and German metaphysics. ("The crazy patchwork of three thousand years," Wolfe called it in *Look Homeward, Angel*, "The forced marriage of irreconcilables.") Yet if Williams' philosophy was gnarled and abstruse to the point of incoherence, the man himself was vivid and convincing in his determination to challenge and, if need be, to madden people into using their minds. North Carolina was Democratic, so Williams—an independent at heart—took pleasure in voting Republican. Since the majority of the students at Chapel Hill came from fundamentalist backgrounds, Williams, albeit a Christian, went out of his way to upset Baptist and Methodist credulities. His never-ending war with dogma and complacency made him an uncomfortable person to have around. Walking to class with the head of the math department, he would ask, "What is a one?"—and then boast to his students that the head of the math department had been unable to give him a satisfactory answer. At faculty meetings he would interrupt a serious debate with a motion that they consider the question, "What is the educating act?"

He lived in a rambling house without screens, furnace, telephone, or plumbing, and until suit was brought against him he ignored the town ordinance forbidding farm animals on the premises because of the flies they attracted. His disdain for scientific materialism, which he considered the canker of the age, extended to simple hygiene. "In the Middle Ages, vulgar superstition vented its passion and its credulity upon the devil," Wolfe quoted him as saying. "Men called it religion. More recently vulgar superstition vents the same passion and the same credulity against the fly. We call it science—sanitation." Wolfe thought this "unfair but magnificent" and went on to speculate that "all great creatures perhaps have in them a touch of magnificent unreason." Out in the country, Williams had a farm where he spent part of every day, and a student who came to see him might be asked to go to the pasture with him while he salted his bull. Enjoying the company of the simple and unlettered, he frequented the village drugstore and the livery stable, where he gathered homely illustrations for his classes. He was penurious as a result of early hardship and rejoiced in a shrewd bargain and had a spice of the devil in him—what Wolfe called "a genius for occasional and conscious malignancy." It was aimed, however, at the foolish and the pretentious. Wolfe had never known him to despise the worthy.

Spare and erect, with heavy laborer's hands, Williams had a bulging forehead, a cropped mustache, and a thin, seamed face surmounted by rimless spectacles. With his soft, persuasive voice he could have been a country parson save for the gleam in his eye when he chuckled satirically at the world. He lived in and for his classes, where he parried and probed like a psychiatrist, answering a question with a question. A master of suspense, he would bring a discussion to a head just as the hour was ending, and then say, "Well, I see we've gotten ourselves into quite a turmoil—perhaps we can straighten it out next time." Wary of too much reading lest it become a substitute for thinking, he assigned few books and did not check to see if they were read. His themes were honor, truth, wisdom, spirit, God, immortality, and the like—the great intangibles with which a man must come to grips if he is to be educated in the deepest sense.

Though his critics dismissed him as a crank, they had a hard time explaining away his attraction for the ablest students—"my boys," as he called them—to whom he was a sage lacking only a loincloth to give the illusion of having been lifted bodily out of the Lyceum. Concerned with all phases of college life—from athletics to debating, from fraternities to the honor system—he imparted to his disciples a sense of the campus in the making, while holding up the example of former students of his who had gone on to triumphant careers. "Be yourself," was his doctrine. "Be a man. If you follow the crowd, the crowd will never follow you." It was the old appeal of Socrates and of Luther, whose *Ich kann nicht anders*, first heard in Williams' classroom, would come back to Wolfe at the turning points of his life.

During his last two years at Chapel Hill, Wolfe belonged to Horace's elite, Williams rating him among the half-dozen remarkable students he had ever taught. As a junior, Wolfe had won the coveted Worth Philosophy Prize for an essay entitled "The Crisis in Industry," championing labor against capital. Williams had called it "a great utterance," and Wolfe felt big with prophecy. In class, Williams joked about "the flood of feeling on Mr. Wolfe's face," and about "Mr. Wolfe who lies awake o' nights thinking of things," but there was respect and understanding between them. Williams had that final innocence which often goes with eccentricity, and summing him up, Wolfe wrote that "Horace, if not as profound and singular a mind, [was] probably as profound and virginal a person as America has produced."

As the air grew thick and sweet with the Southern spring—his last in this glade of learning—an indolence crept over Wolfe that made it hard to go to class. Nights he roamed the campus unable to sleep; it seemed to him that the huge moon over the treetops had never spread such enchantment. Already he felt nostalgic for the scented lawns and wisteria-draped arbors he would soon be leaving forever.

His parents came to graduation and listened proudly as Tom, the class poet, read his ode of farewell under the Davie Poplar. The president of the university whispered in W.O.'s ear that Tom was destined for great things. In the senior poll he was voted Best Writer, Wittiest, and Most Original, and the paragraph under his name in the yearbook called him "young Shakespeare" and "a genius," but this euphoria, endemic to graduating classes, needed to be taken with a grain of salt. As yet his writing, for all its energy and fluency, gave little promise of the splendors to come. At Chapel Hill the real phenomenon was Wolfe himself, this tumult of contradictions—haphazard yet intense, friendly yet withdrawn, humble yet assured, moody yet farcical, interested in all around him yet self-absorbed.

His future was a puzzle. Lately he had been dreaming of graduate work at Harvard, whose name conjured up visions of "elegance, joy, proud loneliness, rich books, and golden browsing." Horace Williams thought it the place for him to go on developing, and Koch was a former student of George Pierce Baker, Harvard's famous professor of playwriting. But Wolfe hadn't broached it to his family, who were now expecting him to earn a living.

3 · HARVARD

He lingered at Chapel Hill a few days beyond graduation, ostensibly to gather his things but really to savor the atmosphere in solitude, and after a final session with Horace Williams, he left with a feeling of "the vast champagne of earth [stretching] out for him its limitless seduction." Somewhere along the way he had been bitten by strangeness and possibility and number; a Renaissance lust for uncharted coasts lived on in this twentieth-century American.

The situation in Asheville made him eager to escape. The inexorable spread of his father's cancer had turned him into a piteous old man, sunk in "a semi-life of petulant memory." His mother was sixty and hale, but because of a supposed heart ailment she had given up boarders for roomers at the Old Kentucky Home, and the reduced work allowed more time for her real-estate mania. Mabel, childless and frustrate, found release in talking jags, pointless outbursts, and concealed drinking. Frank drifted in from the West, Effie and her children came up from South Carolina for a visit, and Fred—now a travelling salesman of electrical equipment—was often on hand, but the meeting of the clan made for squabbles and resentment. Since Ben's death they seemed to Tom a rudderless crew.

That summer he had an affair with a married woman at the Old Kentucky Home—until his mother found out and broke it up—and once he went camping with three college friends who called for him in a Model T, expecting him to bring some of the necessities. His sole contribution was a carton of the little Haldeman-Julius paperbound books which he read far into the night, holding them against a candle on the tent floor. His future remained uncertain. His father, still wanting him to be a lawyer and a power in the state, was too sick and despairing to press for an ambition which Tom dismissed as forlornly limited, and yet to his family his literary ambitions seemed equally forlorn. Practical people, they thought of authors as a race apart and couldn't imagine their flesh and blood turning into one. Then too, in the South of that day as in the West, the arts were less esteemed than in New England, where the intellectual tradition had never been broken; Wolfe was reared in a society where "writer" had rather the connotation of "sissy" or "ineffectual."

He had been offered a teaching post at a nearby military school, and he told the doctor he would take it if his father was expected to die that year. Unable to predict, the doctor encouraged him to go to Harvard if that was what he wanted, as the Robertses had been urging him to do all along. Tom had made up his mind to borrow the money if necessary when his mother, seeing how much it meant to him and also perhaps from a subconscious desire to keep her baby dependent, agreed to finance him for a year. When the other children grumbled, she told them that had they shown the same determination, a way would have been found to give them a higher education too. On August 10th Tom mailed his application to the Harvard Graduate School of Arts and Sciences, and was accepted September 13th as a candidate for the M.A. in English.

A week later he set out, after sending Fred a letter drawing the line between them. Fred had rebuked him for not writing their parents more often from college, and though he granted he wasn't much of a correspondent, Tom went on to say that he had done nothing during his four years at Chapel Hill to make his father regret having sent him, and that those four years represented more sweat and midnight oil than Fred would ever know about. Such was to be Tom's method of fulfilling his obligations. If Fred valued the friendship of the only decent brother he had—and Tom thought he could say this without too much conceit—he must mind his own business. Characteristically, Tom added that one could never accuse another without a sense of regret which he now felt, especially as Fred had so much that was fine and generous in his make-up.

And now the journey to "the proud, fierce North"—his father's land—and the sense of delirious expansion as he boarded the train. He would come to view all life as from a speeding train—fleetingly, hauntingly, panoramically, with a never-to-return poignance. Trains, his symbol of escape to brighter worlds, plucked his heartstrings: "At the same moment, I heard the whistle of the great train pounding on the rails across the river. It swept past us leaving the lost and lonely thunder of its echoes in the autumnal hills, the flame-flare of its terrific furnace for a moment, and then just hearing wheels and rumbling, loaded cars—and finally nothing but frost, the silence it had left behind it, and October."[1]

Of course Wolfe's judgment at times like these was none too reliable. The first morning of the trip the train was standing still when he awoke at daybreak, and he and several companions went out to see where they were. They had stopped in the midst of a large apple orchard, and since the section of Virginia above Greensboro, North Carolina, where they had turned north during the night was famous for its apples, Wolfe began describing the change in atmosphere, the subtle yet unmistakable feeling of being in old Virginia, mother of Presidents and bulwark of the Confederacy. When a passing trainman told them they were still in North Carolina, Wolfe laughed it off. "The serpent tempted Eve with an apple," he said, "and now these apples have taken advantage of me."

After several days in New York ("the ecstatic Northern city," he would call it in his Autobiographical Outline, "no other city has ever given me anything to compare with it"), he went on to Cambridge, whence he wrote his mother on a note of isolated grandeur: "Now, foolish or headstrong, as you will, I must make or ruin myself from this time on, by my own pattern. . . . I have chosen—or God has chosen—a lonely road for my travel." Not that he was totally bereft. The first-year graduates from Trinity and Carolina ate at the same table in Memorial Hall, and Wolfe roomed with three who were going to the law school, on the top floor of a house where the landlord was a Carolina professor on sabbatical. Nevertheless, he missed the relaxed friendliness of the Hill. He had come to Harvard to study playwriting under George Pierce Baker, and when he tried to register for the course, he found it restricted to a hand-picked dozen who had submitted samples of their work the previous spring. In desperation he went to see Baker, and the professor thawed out immediately on learning of Wolfe's connection with Koch, whom Baker described as one of his "pets." Thus Wolfe was admitted without the usual preliminaries to the charmed circle of English 47, better known as "The 47 Workshop," and Baker became his greatest influence—"the unfailing wise and strong and gentle spirit who knew all, had seen all, could solve all problems by a word, release us of all the anguish, grief and error of our lives by a wave of his benevolent hand."[2]

Generally speaking, the literary sense, which functions most happily as a powerful exception, is wary of too close contact with the academic, but Baker had reconciled the two: his students were free to follow their creative demons wherever they led, while buttressed by the standards and prestige of a great university. Baker was something of a sport in an English department dominated by that impeccable Shakespearean, George Lyman Kittredge. Not that Baker shunned scholarship—his lectures in the history of the drama were solid enough—but his passion lay elsewhere. He had launched his playwriting course in 1905, subsequently organizing the Workshop to produce the plays that were written—the whole thing in the face of considerable opposition, for though Harvard approved the study of drama as literature, acrobats, jugglers, clowns, and trained pigs were deemed more appropriate for peasant fairs. Besides which, a stigma of frivolity and immorality clung to the theater. Should Harvard, whose watchword had been "Veritas" for going on three centuries, ally itself with the shoddy of the commercial stage?

For Baker's enterprise *was* commercial, albeit in the best sense. With his belief in the theater as a civilizing force, he took pride in those of his students who went on to New York successes, and their success had been sufficient to win him an international repute. English 47 had been famous from the start; one of its charter members, Ned Sheldon, had written his hit *Salvation Nell* while still an undergraduate, and now another Baker alumnus, Eugene O'Neill, was spearheading what looked like a theatrical renaissance. By 1920, when Wolfe appeared, Baker had sent a score of playwrights to Broadway—also some prominent directors, stage designers, and critics—and the talented and ambitious from all over the land were funnelling into his course.

Baker, or "G. P." as his students called him behind his back, was a curious blend of a reserved New Englander and an actor, a showman striding in from the wings. As a young man he had been thought to resemble Edwin Booth, and something in his present mien suggested that other virtuoso, Sir Henry Irving. He wore pince-nez attached by a black, flowing ribbon, and despite the irony of his glance an understanding smile constantly got the better of his thin, determined lips. Wolfe detected an occasional mannerism in his sonorous speech—for example, the exclamation "Puffeckly extrawdn'ry!"—yet the fictional portrait of Baker as Professor Hatcher in *Of Time and the River* damns him with a more unctuous urbanity than he in fact possessed. Baker was too engrossed in his work to waste much time on affectations of worldliness; indeed like all dedicated men he seemed a bit removed from the world. Nor did he drop names with the blatancy of a Hatcher. Having met the leading playwrights here and abroad, he might quote his friend Arthur Wing Pinero or read a letter from Eugene O'Neill to clinch his point, but he did so less in a spirit of self-glorification than to give his classes the zest, the authenticity, and above all the professional touch his students longed for.

The Workshop had its headquarters in the oldest building in the Yard, trim, red-brick Massachusetts Hall, which had been a barracks during the Revolution. Its 30'x50', double-story ground floor was Baker's kingdom where he met his budding playwrights, who sat on paint-specked chairs at a long table. As he hurried in—pleasantly serious, not looking at anyone in particular—he brought with him the excitement of important doings. It might be that he had seen the Moscow Art Theatre in New York the previous day, returning on the midnight train so as to meet the present class, whose members he treated less as students than as adults practicing their métier, and they tended to be a mature lot since Baker preferred working with those who had had some experience of the world. Thus Wolfe, still nineteen when the term began, was the next to youngest in his group of ten, four of whom were in their twenties, three in their thirties, and one in his forties.

As a warm-up for writing an original one-act play, each student was asked to select and dramatize a current short story, Baker meanwhile using the class periods to discuss the theater informally, delightfully, at times eruditely. Though most of his illustrations were drawn from contemporary Broadway, he didn't hesitate to bring in Terence or Molière when they applied. The one-acters having been submitted, he read them aloud in class. For the sake of objectivity, he never told who had written the play under consideration though it was usually no feat to glance around the table and spot its nervous, red-faced perpetrator. An accomplished reader, Baker made the most of each script, and then, removing his pince-nez with a distinguished jerk, he asked, "Well—what about it?" In the free-for-all that ensued he stayed in the background, usually reserving his criticisms for a private conference from which the author came away feeling that Baker, no matter how censorious, was on his side. Never bored or indifferent, he drew the utmost from his students because he himself was so unflagging. They slaved to meet his standards, writing and rewriting for a word of encouragement, a wry, commending smile, anything on which to base their hopes.

According to Baker, the best means of judging a play was to enact it, and he threw himself into the nightly rehearsals with professional zeal. There was a no-nonsense attitude among the young men and women (he also taught at Radcliffe) going over their lines and smoking a last cigarette outside Massachusetts Hall when he appeared at 7:30 sharp, stepping briskly for a man of his heft. Indoors, amid the chaos of flats and props stacked ceiling high—for here the Workshop made and stored its sets—a 12'x20' area had been marked off, these being the dimensions of the stage in Agassiz Hall, which could only be spared for dress rehearsals and final performances. Baker's seat was a gilt, high-backed royal bench drawn up to a small table—gifts of the celebrated Hamlet, Forbes-Robertson, who had used them during his farewell tour of America. On Baker's right sat the author to whose judgment he deferred. He never imposed his ideas, though when the action foundered he might stop the play to inquire of the author, "Is that right? Is that the way you want it?" If the fault lay in the acting and he could stand it no longer, he would rush out on the stage and with short, mincing steps and rapid gestures show how the part should be done. While avoiding the sarcasm so many affect when directing amateurs, he was chary of praise, but the ease, the quiet elation with which he went about his utterly congenial task inspired the whole company.

During Wolfe's first year in the Workshop, since Baker was much occupied with the writing and directing of the Plymouth Tercentenary Pageant to be held the following summer, his assistant—Kenneth Raisbeck—often stood in for him at classes and rehearsals. Raisbeck and Wolfe quickly became intimates, though one could hardly imagine a more unlikely pair. Not yet twenty-two and thus considerably younger than most of his charges, Raisbeck was a strange, blighted, talented mixture of fineness and meanness, of honesty and pose, with an enigmatic coolness and subtlety that belied his appearance of a young Santa Claus. His dark, chestnut hair was parted neatly to one side, and his merry, mocking, understanding brown eyes registered permanent amusement at the state of the world. When he spoke, the upper lip of his thin, split-watermelon mouth moved hardly at all, and the high flush on his apple cheeks gave him the healthy look which Wolfe likened to a Raeburn portrait, although around his cleft chin the ruddiness shaded towards the blue of a strong, close-shaven beard. His laugh, while not high-pitched, was girlish and irresistibly mirth-provoking—a sort of musical gurgle or "burble," as Wolfe called it. He affected an English accent—saying something like "ace" for "yes" and "a-d'ye-do" for "how do you do"—and in meditative moments he paid out his words one at a time as though each meant worlds. Of medium height and build, with small feet and capable, short-fingered hands, he walked with a springy, coltish grace and was so agile he could run backwards almost as fast as forwards. He dressed in becoming tweeds, sometimes wearing an ascot inside his open-necked shirt *à la* Noel Coward, and one imagined him drinking tea from Chinese porcelain while discussing the ballet. No dilettante, however, he was fiercely ambitious, and hoped to become the American Chekhov.

His background, to Wolfe's surprise, was small-town Midwestern. He came from Moline, Illinois, where his father, an immigrant of Manx descent, worked for a farm-machinery company. The youngest of nine, Kenneth had been an asthmatic child who stayed indoors reading and drawing. He had first thought of becoming a painter, but after a summer at the Chicago Art Institute he had veered towards writing and had gone to Harvard on a scholarship, attaching himself to the Workshop by preparing posters for them. He quickly impressed Baker, who had made him his assistant while still an undergraduate and who had taken him abroad to help with the research for the Plymouth Pageant. The year before Wolfe's arrival, a Workshop production of Raisbeck's *Torches*, a tragedy of the Italian Renaissance, had scored brilliantly.

One of his duties was to befriend the newcomers in English 47, and early that fall he invited Wolfe to dinner, suggesting they meet in Raisbeck's tiny, fifth-floor suite on Massachusetts Avenue, fronting the Yard. His sitting room was neat and attractive with its Japanese prints and Goya drawings on loan from the Fogg Museum, and its few pieces of nice old furniture lent him by two spinster aunts who lived nearby and spoiled him within their limited means. Raisbeck's mannered aloofness put Wolfe off at first, but it soon came out that the pattern of their lives was identical. The precocious youngest sons of large families who didn't share their interests, they had gone to Harvard in the hope of writing immortal plays. Sainte-Beuve has noted the life-long importance of the milieu or group in which an author begins to find his bearings, of that "natural and as if spontaneous association of young minds and talents, not precisely similar or of the same family but of the same *flight* and of the same spring, born under the same star and who feel themselves made for a common task." These words explain as well as anything can the basis of this most improbable friendship.

Though Wolfe tolerated Raisbeck's preciousness because of a redeeming excellence, others in the Workshop chilled him with their "not of this world accent which might be English but isn't. 'My dear fellow' and so on." He had never before encountered male apartments with chintz curtains, flowered coverlets, brass bedwarmers, and Tobies on the mantel. At first he tried to ape the prevailing aestheticism, but his heart wasn't in it. Whereas at Carolina he had championed art and ideas against the yokels and philistines, at Harvard he found himself defending the earthy and spontaneous against the self-styled artists—or "ottists"—of English 47. After quoting some of their high-flown criticisms in a letter to Koch, he asked sympathy for "a raw Tar Heel who, with native simplicity, has been accustomed to wade into a play (at Chapel Hill) with 'that's great stuff' or 'rotten'—simple and concise." The Workshop sophistication turned him in on himself. "Utter rebellion from the group," he wrote of this period in his Autobiographical Outline. "Sullen resentment for the group."

He was now six feet four and still growing. At Chapel Hill his elongated frame had been taken for granted, but at Harvard he was once again an oddity as he crossed the Yard at his swift, bowling gait. His dark, disordered clothes looked as though they had been slept in, and he punctuated his talk with explosive gestures intermingled with a feeling of his ear or a scratching of his thigh, a pained wrench of the mouth or a fierce nod of emphasis. The length of hand below his cuffs together with his soft uncouthness and inherent dignity were vaguely Lincolnesque, though he was too much of an individual to be ticketed. He wasn't a hillbilly exactly, for when he opened his mouth you found he had read all those books, and yet in another way you were surprised he wore shoes.

His attic room at 48 Buckingham Street in a nice part of Cambridge was a perpetual rat's nest. As he was always writing and rarely collected his effusions, papers were scattered everywhere, and books too—some of them opened face down, others stuffed with markers. Dirty linen accumulated on the furniture and in the closet until he vowed to send it out next day, but postponing it to the next and the next after that, he finally became reconciled. When the black rims on his collars and cuffs got too noticeable, his tendency was to buy a new shirt rather than send the soiled ones to the laundry. Likewise, when his shoes wore through he lined the soles with cardboard as long as possible—then bought a new pair. He was keeping even later hours than at Chapel Hill, often roaming about till two or three in the morning, and since the landlord locked the door at eleven and Wolfe had a habit of forgetting his key, it was sometimes necessary to wake his roommates by throwing pebbles at the window. When they came down to let him in, he would want to converse with them or read them something he had written.

His chief companions, aside from Raisbeck, were a group of North Carolina law students (three of them his roommates) who thought of him as a card, as "a long old boy from Asheville who can really write." They would take him to dinner just to get him started on affairs back home, after which they might go to the theater where they sat in the cheap top balcony, or to the burlesque at the raucous, smoke-filled Old Howard. At the end of one such evening, during which large quantities of alcohol had been consumed, Wolfe's comrades—these were North Carolineans who roomed elsewhere—walked him home from the subway for fear he would topple in the gutter. While they were puzzling over how to get him into his darkened house without waking the neighborhood, they became aware that the object of their solicitude had draped himself over the picket fence that enclosed the yard and was being ill to his heart's content. A few moments later, as they lifted and pulled in an effort to dislodge this human clothespin, a policeman came by and began questioning them—at which point Wolfe separated himself from the fence and rising to his full majesty asked what all the excitement was about. Head high, he went sedately up the walk, let himself in with his latchkey, and disappeared with a parting bow, leaving his friends to placate the law.

He often spent his Sundays in Medford at the home of his mother's brother, Henry Westall, a Unitarian minister turned real-estate conveyancer. In *A Portrait of Bascom Hawke,* a burlesque of his Uncle Henry highlighting the Westall peculiarities, Wolfe would liken him to "the great Ralph Waldo Emerson—with the brakes off," and indeed he bore a faint, if horse-faced, resemblance to the Concord sage. In Uncle Henry, the Westall materialism had been tempered by a learned idealism. As a young man he had found the ambition to leave Asheville and work his way through Tufts and Harvard Divinity School. The novelist in Wolfe was fascinated by this odd transplant, this booming egotist full of family lore, who wrote poetry in imitation of Matthew Arnold's and who gave his nephew a much needed *point d'appui* in the North.

For Wolfe, though more befriended and appreciated than many a graduate student, felt lonely and abandoned. In his Autobiographical Outline he would tell of "the ineradicable stain of solitude upon my spirit," and looking back, he realized that even at the height of his Chapel Hill gregariousness, he had in fact stood apart. He recalled "periods of content with different boys. A brief adventure or two together—but never a complete unfolding. With older men— partly with Horace Williams—but cautiously, mentally." A brooding isolation was his normal state.

That fall, in addition to English 47, he was taking American Literature, Baker's survey of the drama from the Greeks to modern times, and John Livingston Lowes on the English Romantics. He also audited Kittredge's Shakespeare, but his favorites of the moment were Shelley and Coleridge. Although his taste as he grew older inclined towards what he called the "earth poets"—Chaucer, Whitman, Keats, and other celebrants of the senses—his early addiction was Shelley, the sky poet and winged fancifier whose defiant spirituality remained a part of his make-up. Lowes' course also brought home the genius of Coleridge, that "chief prince of the moon and magic" as Wolfe called him, who ended by influencing him more than any other Romantic. "The Rime of the Ancient Mariner" seemed to him the pinnacle of Romantic verse. "You can no more," he was to say a few years later, "stop the necessity of that poem midway than you can stop the wind by opposing to it your little finger."[3] Professor Lowes, a tiny, scowling man with a deep voice and vast erudition, was then preparing his magnum opus, *The Road to Xanadu*, in which he traced many of the words and images in "Kubla Khan" and "The Ancient Mariner" to Coleridge's reading. This demonstration of the way a poet's subconscious had transmuted learning into art of the highest order encouraged Wolfe and seemed to justify his being, like Coleridge, "a library cormorant." Already pitting himself against the great, he was not afraid to see in Coleridge's experience a portent of his own.

His reading had slacked off somewhat during his last two years at Chapel Hill because of his other activities, but now he hurled himself at books as never before. Widener Library, dominating the Yard with its raw, un-ivied newness, reminded him of all there was to know. Daily he visited the Farnsworth browsing room where the light was mellow, the decor soothing, and the furniture "spacious and rump-receiving." He gutted its shelves of the classics he hadn't read, but his mind kept reverting to the stacks, and as he roamed those ten, dried-paper-smelling floors, he despaired of making a dent in their million and a half volumes. "Yes, but, damn you," he would tell himself, "look at those given over to Shakespeare! In different editions of Shakespeare alone, English and foreign, there are almost 5,000 volumes. And you can get him all in the one-volume Cambridge edition. Very well—1,500,000 divided by 5,000 gives 300. Ah, but you fool, they're not all Shakespeares! You have chosen the one author most numerously represented. Yes, but, curse you, 300 books is nothing. One can do a hundred times that. Consider the repetitions with Milton, Pope, Wordsworth, Tennyson, Dickens!"[4]

Whereupon he would go to one of these shelves, count the duplicate editions, and gloat if they were numerous.

Though his intake was large, how can one believe that he, like Eugene Gant, read twenty thousand books in ten years ("deliberately the number is set low," wrote Wolfe) when Van Wyck Brooks estimated that during a twenty-year period of intensive study he had read less than six thousand? Wolfe's technique, of course, had little to do with scholarship. It was more akin to rape, or at times to an athletic contest as he scanned a page, watch in hand, to see how long it took. His thirst for omniscience was that of a Balzac or a Faust in its fruitful absurdity—fruitful because to aim at the impossible is to enlarge one's powers.

His Widener researches were sometimes interrupted by unbookish reveries. He might, for instance, imagine that the librarian with the provocative smile was waiting for him in the stacks, and then goodbye to books as he embraced her "in the grand, approving and most silent audience" of Shakespeare, Donne, and Herrick.[5] Or again, when a distant automobile horn broke the stillness, he would remember the wisdom of the streets, and rushing to the subway he would end up on the Boston Common or down by the wharves with an ear cocked for the conversation of passers-by. He began to visualize his life as "a vast tapering funnel" into which everything must be poured. "I shall make one globe," he wrote in his notes, "not of my learning but of all learning, I shall make one globe not of my life but of all life. . . ."[6] And yet the principle of selection was in him.

Tortured by the philosopher's riddle of the One and the Many, he saw himself condemned to waste and confusion as he sought to encompass the whole. He dreamed of chemicals which would quicken his faculties and enable him to absorb more information in less time. He dreamed of his intake becoming a perfectly governed stream, with the requisite knowledge arriving at the precise moment when it was most needed. He dreamed outrageously, but as Renan remarked, "Man is by nature mediocre—he is good for something only when he dreams."

In November, 1920, having submitted his short-story adaptation, Wolfe set to work on *The Mountains,* a one-act folk play begun at Chapel Hill. Baker liked its rustic material; he told Wolfe that he was getting entirely too many high-society dramas by authors who knew nothing of high society. Wolfe wrote Koch of his going ahead in "pure exaltation. . . . This thing has seized me with a death-like clutch." Having read it, Baker told Wolfe he was proud of him for writing it, and after a trial rehearsal it was included in the Workshop program for the following year—an auspicious beginning, since only a handful of the plays submitted could be given full-dress performances. His morale soaring, Wolfe began a three-acter depicting the ruin of a post-bellum Southern family, with the harsh New England winter spurring him on. There was a feeling in the air just before a snowstorm that affected him powerfully, and it seemed to him that he never wrote better than on a snowy night when the street noises were muffled. With the first spring he went for walks along the Charles River in the lengthening twilights, sometimes stopping by a stone near Gerry's Landing which bore the inscription, "On this spot in the year 1000 Leif Erikson built his house in Vineland." Sitting beside it one evening, Wolfe said to his companion, "You know, I've always wanted to be like this guy, discovering new lands and frontiers, but geographically discovery is almost over. What I'd like to explore is man's innermost mind and spirit. I'd like to lift the veil, if I can, from some of the mystery surrounding life and death."

He was certainly in no hurry to get his degree, or he wouldn't have cut back from the standard four courses to a mere two his second term. He may have wanted the extra time for his writing, or to concentrate on French and German for his language exams, but whatever the reason he ended up two half-courses short of the eight required for his M.A. Afraid to go home lest his family contest the second year at Harvard on which his heart was set, he lingered at Buckingham Street neurotically undecided. For six weeks, an almost total suspension of the will kept him in a mental sweatbox—doubly afflicting because of the summer heat. He thought of working his way to Europe on a steamer, and at one point he almost took a job as a Cambridge ice-man. The second week of July he pulled himself together, moved to 42 Kirkland Street nearer the Yard, and enrolled in the Harvard Summer School for a course in English History which, as he wrote his mother, would place him "within a half course of my master's degree & leaves the way open to undivided work on playwriting next year if I can arrange to return." Ideas for plays revolved in his mind, and in the back of his English History notebook he sketched a situation which began: "The Groodys were a strange family. They never saw each other's good points till one of their number died. Then they were lavish in their affection. In their cooperative maudlinism. . . ."

He continued in this vein for several hundred words, a first fumbling with the materials of *Look Homeward, Angel.*

Separated from his family for so long a time, he saw each member with increasing clarity. His father, now a feeble old man awaiting death, was past being interested in Tom's affairs, and hadn't approved his going to Harvard in the first place, so his mainstay, moral as well as financial, was his mother whom he began to reassess in a more favorable light. "I think it is only within the past year," he wrote Mrs. Roberts, "and through the medium of her letters that I have realized what a remarkable person my mother is." Having seconded his literary ambitions by sending him to Harvard, having joined her indomitable will to his, she never lost faith from this time on. It is true that she conceived of writing largely in terms of worldly rewards—of "fame and fortune," to use her repeated phrase. When she learned of the success of *The Mountains* in trial rehearsal, she wrote Tom, "I am very much lifted up on what you say about your play & wish it will be a beginning for a *great big name*, also a promise of financial substance to make smooth your future pathway. The first step towards success is to be self-supporting. Don't think I am only thinking of *money* but it takes a certain amount to be able to meet the best people, this you already know. Let us hope not only honor & fame but the luxuries of life will be yours." Though disapproving of his mother's materialism, Tom began to count on her interest in his work. He wrote her fully of his plans and accomplishments, and sending her a copy of *The Mountains*, he explained, "All the critics in the world may *say* it's good, but a man's mother will *know*."

She had embarrassed him by neglecting to pay his second-term bill until the Bursar's Office threatened to suspend him, yet sooner or later he got the money he needed, and the $2,156 he spent during his first six months was a sizeable sum in the currency of that day. His mother kept urging him to remember his health and to "eat plenty of good nourishing food." She would pay for it, she said. Let him economize in other ways. "Stop spending money for cigars or cigarettes, they only do harm and decrease your ability as well as your purse." A smoker from the age of fourteen, Wolfe had affected a pipe during his last year at Chapel Hill, but now he confined himself to cigarettes, which he smoked incessantly. His reference to colds accompanied by fever suggest that he may have been suffering from low-grade T.B. The tuberculars, who flocked to Asheville for rest cures and sat on the porches sunning themselves, had given him a dread of this disease, which was scary then, like cancer, or the unmentionable syphilis. Soon after his arrival in Cambridge, a wracking cough had led to his spitting a little blood, but despite his fright he hadn't gone to the doctor, and it hadn't recurred.

When summer school ended the middle of August, he didn't know what to do. Though Baker had invited him to return for the advanced playwriting course, English 47a, he lacked his mother's permission. "I want to go home," he wrote Mrs. Roberts, "I've *got* to go somewhere, but I'm afraid they won't want me to come back next year, and I've got to do that also." He knew his family was critical of his going to school so long and spending so much money. Fred, usually a good correspondent, hadn't answered his letter written the end of May, and during the summer he had heard from his mother only twice. "You may talk all you please of the misfortune of being 'old and alone,'" he wrote her, "but I tell you that approaches not one degree the misfortune of being young and alone." As September wore on, he grew desperate. On the 19th, he wrote his mother that his twenty-first birthday was two weeks off and that if the time had come to go out on his own, he would do so, but that she would hear from him no more unless she answered. Then, just as the fall term was beginning, he got a letter saying that she was accompanying his father to Johns Hopkins for radium treatments and suggesting he join them in Baltimore.

It was the first time he had seen any of his immediate family since coming North the year before. On his way to Harvard he had stopped in Baltimore for a glimpse of his father, then at the Hopkins for treatment, but their hospital meeting in *Of Time and the River* was based on this second visit, when he remained two weeks. In the interim the old man had failed markedly; there was now a transparency about him that accentuated the bladelike nose and the bony, almost reptilian slant of his forehead. His chin hung loose and petulant as he took the air on the fifth-floor porch and stared dully across the city of his youth where he had gone to work as a stonecutter's apprentice, but his huge, shapely hands reminded Tom of the man he had been. W.O., once so ambitious for Tom, told him during the visit, "You are the disappointment of my life," and there was a constraint between them. However, Tom had his way with his mother, who finally agreed to give him one more year at Harvard, and he went back late for classes but triumphant.

Everything now turned on the production of his play. The Workshop performances in Agassiz Auditorium were attended by four hundred select invitees, who in place of admission were expected to send in written criticisms which the author used as the basis for further revision. The press was excluded, but sometimes an established playwright or a Broadway mogul graced the audience, and production by the Workshop had proved the opening wedge for more than one illustrious career.

The Mountains, performed on the evenings of October 21st and 22nd, was about a young doctor just returning from medical school to minister to his people in western North Carolina. Sworn to combat their misery and ignorance, he finds himself involved in a family feud his first day home, and as the curtain descends he goes out to fight the opposing clan. Wolfe was trying to show the warping tyranny of environment, but his treatment contained too much exposition of the "He could shave ye with one shot an' come back an' give ye a haircut with t'other" variety, and too little action. After reading the criticisms, he decided that the audience hadn't been up to his bitter ending. They had wanted the young idealist to triumph over circumstances, but Wolfe said he would rather jump into the Charles than cater to such sentimentality. "I thank God that the far-reaching wisdom of the founders saw fit to remove the names from the criticisms," he remarked to Baker of one particularly infuriating stricture, "for if I knew who wrote that, I would no longer be responsible for my actions."

He was angriest at those who had formerly admired his play and now saw no merit in it. "How they turn on you when it fails!" he would write in his Autobiographical Outline. "The coldness! The neglect!" In despair he went to see a fellow student—a clergyman in his forties named Ketcham—who had warmly praised *The Mountains* when Baker read it in class. Ketcham still maintained there were fine things in it, but added that a play might read well and act badly. He was sure, however, that Wolfe was mistaken in fancying that Baker had passed him the night of the performance without speaking and had been cool ever since. Wolfe was young and had much to learn, said Ketcham, and he ought to be prepared for worse setbacks than this.

The imagined rift with Baker was short-lived. Presently G.P. was suggesting that *The Mountains* be expanded to three acts, so he must have felt it had possibilities. Wolfe took everything so hard—nothing was light or inconsequential—the substratum of his nature being a delicate, agonized, highly emotional sensitivity which demanded constant expression. And how he could talk! Haltingly at first, especially with those he didn't know well, stammering jerkily with a faint lisp as though his tongue were a bit too large, blurting out questions that expected no answer, swallowing and beginning again—"I know I'm saying this badly but what I mean is"—until finally he got rolling, and then the language streamed forth as from a fire hose. His eyes bright and piercing as he warmed to his subject, he seemed unaware of the saliva gathering at the corners of his mouth and occasionally seeping down. If elated, he would seize your arm and shake you as he poured his excitement into you. If angry, he would thrust his head forward and nod emphatically, the words

coming into his mouth in great groups as he ripped and pounded
and demolished till even his shirt seemed to grow excited, the droop-
ing points of his collar turning up and out. Listening to him was
exhausting, but it was seldom dull.

He might be letting you in on a family squabble, growing wild-
eyed because his mother, sister, or brother wouldn't do this or that.
Or he might be describing a prize fight he had seen the night before
in Mechanics Hall. Or again, he might be analyzing his courses outside the Workshop—the English Drama from 1590 to 1642 and
Lowes on the English Renaissance—in which case he would adopt
a somewhat sardonic tone, for he was losing patience with minds
which did no more than annotate the utterances of the great, and
congratulated themselves on superior wisdom in so doing. In his
notes of this period he cited Coleridge's remark that everyone is
either a Platonist or an Aristotelian, calling it "a striking manifestation of the power to generalize in a man of profound and varied
genius. But," he continued, "along comes your learned professor,
who quotes Coleridge's statement, and, after coughing drily behind
his hand, adds: 'Strictly speaking that is not quite correct. What
Coleridge means—(this symptom is almost infallible!)—is that every
man possesses to a greater or lesser degree either the power of synthesis or the power of analysis. But of course Aristotle at times shows
the power of synthesis, Plato can be closely analytical. In general,
however, Coleridge's statement is true.'" Of such hemstitching
Wolfe observed, "Very well. *That* goes down in our notebook but
we *quote* Coleridge."[7]

Unlike the Ph.D. candidates he saw all around him—"intellectual
peasantry," he called them later, "dull, cold, suspicious of any idea
they had not been told to approve"[8]—Wolfe conceived of learning
as an extension and enrichment of his daily living. Except where his
courses required it, he didn't read to compare one text with another;
books referred him to life and vice versa. Thus he might be eating in
a restaurant, observing the solemn animality at a nearby table, the
fowllike thrust and retreat of a long horse face at a soup spoon, when
suddenly, by what magic of association he knew not, he would be
with Shakespeare in a tavern, partaking of a cold pork pie and wash-
ing it down with a jug of porter or sack. They would have met that
morning at the Globe Theatre where Shakespeare was rehearsing

his new play, *King Lear*. Sensing a strangeness in the encounter (for Wolfe imagined himself a visitor incognito from the twentieth century), Shakespeare had pursued it with the solitary intensity which the creative man bestows on the unknown. Now, as they ate together and Wolfe explained his miraculous projection back into Elizabethan times, Shakespeare responded electrically, accepting the fact and understanding the means almost before they were revealed. Wolfe produced documentary proof: photographs of the Tower and the Strand in their modern surroundings, a postcard of the *Aquitania* leaving Southampton docks. He was struck by the ease and simplicity of Shakespeare's conversation, his words being in no way remarkable except that they seemed to come from a bottomless well. A self-contained universe, Shakespeare left the plumes and flourishes to the little fellows. His talent no longer surprised him, but he thrilled to the pageant of the succeeding ages as Wolfe sketched it in: the rise of science, the power of the press, the march of democracy, the religion of progress. "And the pox?" Shakespeare asked. "We can cure it almost infallibly with an infusion in the blood," Wolfe replied. Then Shakespeare listened intently as Wolfe described the subsequent developments in literature, including the decline and revival of Shakespeare's own reputation.[9]

Wolfe often imagined himself conversing with the literary immortals. Insatiably curious about their careers, he read their biographies to find out when they had begun to write, and at what age they had done a good thing. Though obliged to consider form and technique for his playwriting, he was really more interested in what might be called the personality of authorship; also in grappling with ideas and establishing his point of view. Horace Williams' philosophical idealism, which had seemed so attractive at Chapel Hill, was losing its authority. The Truth, Goodness, and Beauty which Williams upheld as absolutes excluded too much that vitally interested Wolfe. He had to believe in Ugliness, Evil, and Falsehood as well, for without this duality and conflict the world seemed pale. Why was the idea or plan of a wheelbarrow which Plato called reality any more real than the concrete wheelbarrow which hauled dirt and stubbed one's toe? "What is real?" Wolfe asked himself in his notes, and answered, "Anything is real of which we find ourselves obliged to take account in any way. . . . That man is a fool who in his climb for knowledge seeks to build beyond and apart from the facts of this world." And yet the questions Williams had posed—How can there be unity in the midst of everlasting change? In a world of decay what is fixed, real, eternal?—continued to haunt him. Perhaps he could square the circle. Might it not be possible to march through the thick of life, immersing oneself in all its horrible and lovely detail, and yet achieve some degree of permanence and universality?

In his notes he had already hit on his fundamental assumption that "life, at its pinnacle—or of pain and ugliness: or of tragedy and beauty—escapes us. We never escape life save on an inferior landing stage—romantic escape is mean, base, and transitory: it cannot rise to meet the great facts. . . . Death itself the most magnificent fact, the most inexorable fact—has always overtopped the poor dignity of human emotion." A few years later he would restate this idea in his Autobiographical Outline: "Ultimately I came back to the same blind faith. That life in itself was very full, that what failed in it was our own apprehension. Is not this the true romantic feeling—not to desire to escape life, but to prevent life from escaping you." And a few years after that he crystallized it once and for all in *Look Homeward, Angel*: "Since Ben's death the conviction had grown on him that men do not escape life because life is dull, but that life escapes from men because men are little. He felt that the passions of the play were greater than the actors. It seemed to him that he had never had a great moment of living in which he had measured up to its fullness."

Though Wolfe has been criticized for an unbridled egotism amounting to solipsism, his subordination of the individual to the larger pattern of existence is classic, is Greek. His central concern was not himself but the stream of life flowing past him.

On his return from Baltimore in October he had taken a dormitory suite with several others, and a month later he moved to a single room at 67 Hammond Street back of the Divinity School. With his peculiar hours and his absorption in his work, he was better off by himself though it aggravated his loneliness, and he wished he could solve the girl problem. Weekends he visited the students at Wellesley, meanwhile devoting his carnal energies to another type of female whom he sought out in the environs of Scollay Square. But this expedient left him parched and dissatisfied, and in his Autobiographical Outline he would write of "the brooding romance in my heart" and of yearning for every pretty face that lost itself in the crowd.

As the year wore on, with the prospect of theatrical success as remote as ever, he had to think seriously of supporting himself. The matter came to a head in the red, wintry bleakness of a waning March afternoon when he asked an unspecified older man on whose judgment he relied—perhaps the aforementioned Ketcham—whether he would ever succeed as a playwright, and the answer was that, frankly, his abilities seemed critical rather than creative, and that he ought to get his Ph.D. and teach. The year before, Professor Lowes, struck by his essay on "The Supernatural in the Poetry and Philosophy of Coleridge," had likewise urged him towards an academic career. And so the last week of March, 1922, he filed his application for a teaching job with the Harvard Appointment Bureau, notifying Baker of the fact in a letter which, like so many written to unburden his mind, he kept unmailed among his papers. Thanking Baker effusively for all he had done, Wolfe said the conviction had grown on him that he could never express himself dramatically.

Two months later he was talking quite differently, after Baker had pronounced his prologue to the three-act version of *The Mountains* the best ever submitted in the course. "At times the work over which I expend the most labor and care," Wolfe wrote his mother, "will fail to impress while other work, which I have written swiftly, almost without revision, will score. Such was the case with my prolog: a thing of the utmost simplicity." In this description of two men and a boy building a rail fence on a spring afternoon, Wolfe's characteristic sweep and vividness begin to appear, as when he speaks of the "wind [snaking] in vast curves through the long grass in the field." Also prophetic were the evocations of trains in the play's stage directions. "Below, far in the distance, the train rushes out of the mountains. The pounding of its wheels can be faintly heard and its ghostly whistle floats back from some moonlit plain." With hope reborn, Wolfe told his mother that such taunts as he might receive in the future would "strike against as tough a hide as a sensitive fellow can call to his defense. I tell you if success depends on desperate determination I will not fail." Baker had asked him back for a third year, but the end of May he was offered an instructorship in English at Northwestern, and simultaneously he passed his language requirements, thus completing his work for the M.A. He had hoped for a job in a large city where he could keep in touch with the theater, and certainly Chicago qualified. Reluctant to teach, however, he was still weighing the offer on June 19th when a telegram late at night told him his father was dying. He started home at once. When his train stopped at Morganton fifty miles from Asheville, he read in the paper that his father was dead.

Since Chapel Hill, W.O. had written him hardly at all, though one of his last scrawls summarized his attitude: "Am glad you think you are getting along so well and hope you will soon find a place to stop and go to work and make a noise in the world." After eight years of illness the end had come swiftly; a severe hemorrhage and two days later W.O. was dead at the age of seventy-one. As he lay in his coffin, Tom touched his hands and found them "cold and firm, almost like marble, and I ran my fingers along the big veins which stood out in sharp, bold relief." In a letter to Mabel he pictured those unforgettable hands as "sinewy lengths of bone and muscle, browned with toil and bearing ridges of thick veins on their backs which stood out like cord-rope. His fingers were likewise long, huge-boned, and muscular with big, shiny, and well-formed nails. They were, in a word, the hands of a man who had done heavy labor, but not the hands of a laborer which suggest stubby nails, stubby fingers, and, all in all, blunt solidity. I rather believe the sculptor Michelangelo had hands which were like my father's."

In answer to Baker's letter of sympathy, Wolfe described his father as "really one of the most vigorous and distinguished personalities I have ever known. . . . It's hard to see a big, strong man break down and lose his strength. They drink life in with great gulps and their experience of pleasure and pain is crowded and poignant." Then passing on to his father's taste in literature: "He had an inexhaustible memory for poetry, one of his favorites being Gray's 'Elegy' which I suppose the master minds who write our imperishable verse today would characterize as 'artificial and declamatory.' Nevertheless it's a great pity, for there's a fire burning there. And that's what counts. Somehow not many of them seem to have it today. They are passionately concerned with form; their delicately attuned senses recoil at the faint suggestion of sentimentality or mawkishness. Byron is artificial to them, Kipling 'declamatory'—the unpardonable sin. Of course any intelligent person will recognize these faults, but, nonetheless, must we recognize the colossal and unquenchable energy which generates their work. This is what I understand by 'genius' and though a man's work may be as full of flaws as a Swiss cheese it will somehow continue to endure if only it has fire, when all the faultless little concoctions of the faultless little anemics have been buried. To me the standard of judgment exhibited by a natural, forceful personality like my father is far more valuable than that of the super-sophisticated, for I know that if artificiality and declamation had been all, it would never have appealed to him."[10]

After the two-year hiatus, Asheville had a strange, dreamlike quality. People looked at him indifferently, some had forgotten him while others had moved away, children had grown up, and there were new faces and voices everywhere. W.O.'s death intensified his feelings of emptiness and dislocation. Perhaps the sight of his father walking down the street was what was needed to bring to life this town so steeped in his personality. Tom amused himself by paying mild court to a cousin, Emily Westall, reading her Tennyson's "Come into the garden, Maud" with just enough of a lisp to be charming—"Queen rothe of the rothebud garden of girlth." One day he and a friend borrowed a car to take two girls to the top of Sunset Mountain, and driving through the Grove Estate a tire went flat. They had begun their unaccustomed struggle with the spare when an elderly man in tan dungarees emerged from the forest and offered his services. With his aid the job was quickly done, and Tom handed him a quarter which he accepted with a bow, though had they looked back as they drove away they would have seen him smiling. Some years later, Tom's brother Frank heard the story from the man himself; he was E. W. Grove, owner of the Grove Park Inn and the six thousand acres of Sunset Mountain. Frank asked if he had thought of returning the quarter. "No, I still have it," said Grove. "First I kept it because it was the only tip I ever received, and then its preciousness grew in proportion to Tom's fame."

His happiest moments that summer were spent with the Robertses. As he later wrote of Eugene Gant, "He was more even than most young men, fiercely amorous of praise and almost fanatically grateful to the giver when he got it," and Mrs. Roberts had remained his radiant center of approval. Stopping by to see her, he would stay for dinner with the family and on past midnight, reading them fragments of his plays and talking, forever talking. Mrs. Roberts hadn't the slightest doubt of his ultimate success. "Boy, nothing can stop you!" she would exclaim. "It's in you, writing is—it's the marrow of your bones!" Her one concern was his health; she feared he would burn himself out living under such constant pressure. She encouraged him to continue in the Workshop, and his bargaining power had increased since his father's death. According to the will, Tom was to inherit $5,000, which he agreed to waive in view of his educational expenses. (Fred, who had recently returned to Georgia Tech to complete his degree begun before the war, did likewise.) In the end, Tom's single-mindedness prevailed, his mother agreed to support him for one more year, and he turned down the job at Northwestern.

Back in Cambridge he installed himself at 21 Trowbridge Street, two blocks from the Yard. Once, when his landlady announced that Professor Baker was there to see him, Wolfe called jocosely from his room, "Throw that man out of here!" Baker's inscrutable reserve had modulated to distinct cordiality where Wolfe was concerned; in November he took Tom to the opera three times besides having him to his Brattle Street home for Thanksgiving dinner.

As for Kenneth Raisbeck, Wolfe thought of him as his best friend, and Raisbeck had a knack of making friendship with him seem a rare privilege. They were an odd twosome strolling the streets of Cambridge: the intense giant with the tip-tilted nose on his hollow-cheeked, still adolescent face would be balancing from foot to foot as he slowed to keep pace with his smiling, compact associate whose flaming cheeks and russet tweeds heightened the contrast. Raisbeck was more or less in technicolor, while Wolfe with his pallor and his dark hair and eyes was very much black and white. Together they explored Boston, seeking little-known restaurants and speakeasies to replace the too-familiar Jake Wirth's and Durgin-Park. Sometimes they were accompanied by other members of English 47 who pounced on every witticism—"Can I use that?"—relinquishing it good-naturedly if its originator objected. In such a group Raisbeck stayed in the background—listening, prodding, dissenting—a cherubic Mephistopheles full of quiet raillery. Nothing escaped his provocative, feminine glance, while Wolfe was only half there, now intruding a fiery monologue that had little to do with the subject, now withdrawing to outer space. He took pleasure in the simplest experiences, which kept him on a constant voyage of discovery. Thus he might report that the setting up and dismantling of the circus on Huntington Avenue was more exciting than the actual performance under the big top. In minute detail he would then describe the night-to-dawn tableau lit by flares: the elephants pushing the loaded vans into place, the strength and skill of the roustabouts pounding in the pegs, the whole organized chaos which, to add to its attraction, had been free of charge.

Because of his openness and susceptibility, Wolfe was extremely vulnerable. His look of touching, eager enthusiasm would change abruptly to hungry disappointment, and yet withal he had a magnitude, a sincerity, and a driving force the others lacked. Raisbeck, whose plays were tatting, who couldn't write three words without self-criticism, admired Wolfe's ability to pour it out—the strange, powerful way he had of approaching a subject in its relation to his appetites. Raisbeck could imagine Wolfe evolving into another Whitman, and Wolfe battened on Raisbeck's praises, finding him a delightful companion as well. Many a night they reeled home from Boston full of cheap wine, laughing and singing with the exaltation of youth that knows it will be famous and can never die. At the same time Raisbeck had begun to get on Wolfe's nerves with his growing furtiveness, secretiveness, and affectation. He carried a Malacca cane and went around with a terrier named Bran (after the dog of the Irish folk hero, Cuchulainn), and before he entered a building he hung his cane on a tree, and much to everyone's annoyance Bran sat obediently beneath it until his master came out. To visit a museum with Raisbeck was particularly trying, Wolfe thought. Shunning the big canvasses that drew most of the attention, Kenneth would gravitate to a tiny still life tucked away in a corner, and when asked his opinion of it he would say sorrowfully, "It's *very* beautiful and *very* moving and altogether quite perfect. It's like a fugue, you

know." At such moments Wolfe felt utterly alien from this corn-belt
aesthete with the dry, impeccable mind and feline perceptions.

There were other members of English 47 who considered Raisbeck
excessively arty, but Wolfe criticized them too. Indeed he faulted
all his peers, especially those who had had a measure of success by
Workshop standards. This one—an earnest, well-meaning New Englander—complained of the hardships of the creative life while enjoying a large private income. That one—a simple Midwesterner—was
devoid of standards or ideals and enviously mocking of those who
had them. Still another—an ex-vaudeville writer who had the advantage of knowing life in the raw—seemed capable of nothing but
dramatic clichés. What they all lacked from Wolfe's point of view,
though he didn't realize it at the time, was his central heat, his need
of utterance, the poetic intensity on which his conception of art, and
therefore of the theater, was based. He was soaking himself in dram-
aturgy, which he called "the greatest art in the world—above painting, sculpture and novel writing," and yet it seemed to him that
when a play succeeded it was because the author had the genius of
a poet—a passion and a truth that somehow broke through the shop-
worn conventions. Eugene O'Neill's *Beyond the Horizon* was a case
in point; like O'Neill, Wolfe wanted to strip his characters bare
against their environment instead of manipulating them artificially
in the approved Broadway manner.

"What we need, Proff," he had recently told Koch who heartily
agreed, "is a robust drama! There are too many dilettanti in the
theater." And in his notes he promised, "I shall write a play that will
be so brutal it will be artistic."[11] Casting about for a subject, he kept
bringing new scripts to class until one day Baker removed his pince-
nez with a let-us-discuss-this attitude. "Mr. Wolfe," he said, "you
have written us six one-acters, and I don't want you coming in here
again without the second act to one of them." Wolfe had been contemplating the "spirit of world-old evil" he had felt in Asheville the
previous summer, and he now decided to expose the greed and
hypocrisy of his home town. With his instinct for fullness, for what
he called "the broadside view of things," the idea grew under his
hand till it burst the bounds of the usual three acts and crystallized
as ten lengthy scenes, requiring seven changes of set and more than
four hours to perform. In January, when he submitted his leviathan

to Baker, he explained in a covering letter that there were thirty odd characters plus a mob because the subject demanded it, not because he didn't know how to save paint. "Some day I'm going to write a play with fifty, eighty, a hundred people—a whole town, a whole race, a whole epoch—for my soul's ease and comfort."

Baker, who preferred abundance of powers to freedom from faults, thought *Niggertown* might be trimmed to workable proportions, and to allow plenty of time for revision he scheduled it for a May production. During the winter and spring, Wolfe rewrote it with growing assurance that it would win the Belmont Prize, a $500 award sponsored by producer Richard Herndon which carried with it the guarantee of a New York production. Covering page after page with his soft-pencilled, hard-driving script, Wolfe stored the grubby manila sheets in cartons under his bed. He seemed unable to work unless books were scattered about, giving him a sense of being up against all print. Sometimes he would pause and read along in the first volume that caught his eye, examining its particles with icy matter-of-factness. "A masterpiece," he would think, "and yet there isn't a line or a word in it that's beyond your powers." The problem was how to sustain such excellence. A masterpiece, after all, was a triumph of structure and organization. No matter; it all began with the seedling word, and if he could equal it now in one of its parts, wasn't there a hope that someday—?

Although in his plays he sought to write objectively about large, impersonal issues, memory and imagination kept perversely dragging him back to his own, most private past. "I think often of my childhood lately," he wrote his mother in January; "of those warm hours in bed of winter mornings; of the first ringing of the Orange St. bell; of papa's big voice shouting from the foot of the stair, 'Get up boy,' then of the rush downstairs like a cold rabbit with all my clothes and underwear in my arms. As I go through the cold dining room I can hear the cheerful roar of the big fire he always had kindled in the sitting room. . . . Then breakfast—oatmeal and sausages, eggs, hot coffee, and you putting a couple of thick meat sandwiches in a paper bag. Then the final rush for school with Ben or Fred, and the long run up the Central Avenue hill with one of them pulling or pushing me along." The memories of Ben and his father were particularly insistent. "Each tone of their voice, each peculiarity of their expression is engraved upon my mind—yet it seems strange that it all could have happened to me, that I was part of it. Someday I expect to wake and find my whole life has been a dream."

Three months later he was writing: "Mama, in the name of God, guard papa's letters to me with your life. . . . There has never been anybody like papa. . . . He is headed straight not for one of my plays, but for a series. . . . He dramatized his emotions to a greater extent than anyone I have ever known—consider his expressions of 'merciful God'—his habit of talking to himself *at* or *against* an imaginary opponent."

And three months after that: "I never forget; I have never forgotten. I have tried to make myself conscious of the whole of my life since first the baby in the basket became conscious of the warm sunlight on the porch, and saw his sister go up the hill to the girls school on the corner (the first thing I remember). . . . This is why I think I'm going to be an artist. The things that really mattered sunk in and left their mark—sometimes only a word—sometimes a peculiar smile—sometimes death—sometimes the smell of dandelions in Spring—once Love."

Niggertown went into rehearsal April 23rd under the chastened, ironic title, deemed more appropriate for its Cambridge audience, of *Welcome to Our City*. The play concerned the struggle between Rutledge, an old-line Southern aristocrat, and Johnson, an up-and-coming mulatto doctor who had gained possession of the Rutledges' former residence. When Johnson finds his daughter being seduced by Rutledge's son, he breaks off negotiations with Rutledge, who is attempting to buy back the house. The rebuff is avenged by young Rutledge, who kills Johnson when the National Guard is called out to quell a Negro riot. Broadening his canvas to include the whole city and by implication the whole South, Wolfe satirized politics and education, boosterism and babbittry, though his central theme was the race issue, which he called "the sore spot in our life here in the South—the forbidden fruit of conversation and exposure." Against a sinister, prophetic background of shifting race relations, he had written a forward-looking, almost an integrationist play in its sympathetic yet unsentimental portrayal of the Negro doctor, and its probing of white hypocrisy and injustice.

Baker, though a Victorian moralist at heart, gave his students wide latitude in their choice of subject, drawing the line only at downright cheapness. Race riots and miscegenation did not daunt him, especially when handled with Wolfe's passionate sincerity. Hurting with ideas, Wolfe had plenty to say but didn't know how to say it, for he refused to see that condensation is the cornerstone of the dramatic art. Bent on emptying his mind in one titanic burst, he churned out great gobs of powerful stuff, much of which didn't belong together. Baker had accepted *Niggertown* for production with the understanding that it would be cut, and yet the rehearsal version was as long as the original.

Wolfe felt sure that the enthusiasm of the actors and the force of the writing would reconcile Baker to his gawk of a play, while Baker was equally sure that once it was "on its feet" Wolfe would appreciate the need of shortening it. During the nightly rehearsals in Massachusetts Hall, these two and the stage manager sat side by side at the edge of the brilliance cast by a single drop light, the scene docks looming in the shadows and the smell of paint, glue, and lumber permeating the air. Leaning intently forward, Baker glanced from the script to the actors' faces with a driving will sometimes relieved by his sardonic twist of a smile. Wolfe lounged nearby on a paint-specked chair, now stretching out almost horizontally as if to put himself on a level with the rest of the world, now lunging upright, turning sidewise, and winding a long arm around the chair back, now throwing himself restlessly forward, chin on fists, elbows on knees, his piercing eyes never leaving the stage.

One night, after a week of rehearsing, Baker proposed some cuts. Wolfe made a gesture of agreement, promptly followed by reasons why the lines in question should remain. Baker listened politely, then turned to the actors and read them the cuts, while Wolfe, sitting erect, began weaving back and forth in his chair like a polar bear suffering from the heat. Finally he sprang to his feet with an anguished cry and rushed out into the night, returning quietly a few minutes later as if he had left for a smoke. He made no reference to the amputation, though each time Baker—contrary to practice—made another one a similar outburst occurred.

Despite his artistic torments Wolfe that spring was living in a dream, in what he later remembered as "a radiance drunken with joy and with power." His masterpiece was about to be staged as the last climactic play of the year, and then the gates of heaven would open. Baker saw it from a slightly different angle. "I've got a student," he told a friend, "who's a crazy, wild, six foot five Southern boy. He's written one of the most brilliant plays ever submitted in English 47, and we're trying to put it on in spite of him. He's shy, he stammers, and he upsets the cast. When anything goes wrong, he bellows at them." Baker might have added that Wolfe waylaid him outside every class, to walk beside him and argue about his play. One day Baker humorously suggested that someone tie a rock around Wolfe's neck and drop him off a Charles River bridge ("Tell me if he gurgles much"). The crowning annoyance was when Wolfe refused to pay the stenographer who, he felt, had overcharged him for typing his play, and Baker was called in as a referee. In this harbinger of future law suits, Wolfe congratulated himself on beating the stenographer "from bonnet to bootstrap," adding that he would be ashamed of his vindictiveness had he not been forced to suffer from her "false and perjurous tongue."

Far away in Asheville his mother prayed for his success. "My whole soul is in it for you," she wrote him, "& I am sure you will yet win. You were born in [the] month of writers so astrology teaches, & you had a father who was a natural born actor. . . . I feel certain that you will be [a] success as a writer—if not [a] playwrite." *If not a playwright*—Wolfe echoed these words in a cold-eyed notation the day of the opening: "Friday, May 11, at 5:55 in the afternoon, with the first Workshop performance of my play less than two and one quarter hours distant, I want to record here, for my personal satisfaction, my belief that the play which I have written has no better show than that of a snowball in the infernal regions. I can only hope that the cast and producing organization will give a performance superlatively better than any they have previously given. And even then? And even then??"

Actually the play was far from a flop. It impressed the audience as vivid and real, if somewhat episodic and inconclusive. During the intermission Wolfe was seen plunging about, incoherent but obviously quite happy. At one point Baker got word that he was creating havoc backstage, and the person sent to coax him away found him muttering that if the actors wouldn't do such and such "his career was at an end." Despite Baker's cuts, the mammoth performance with its unwieldy cast and multiple changes of scene on the tiny Radcliffe stage was far too long, and the audience grew restive as it dragged on towards midnight. Afterwards an Asheville girl who chanced to be present, and who claimed to recognize the real-life counterpart of every character, took Wolfe to task for lambasting the South—to which he replied, "Now it's the truth, isn't it?" Disappointingly, the Belmont Prize went to another play, and Wolfe began to boil as the written criticisms came in, some of them attacking his ruthless candor. He told an acquaintance that he was going to New York with *Welcome* to make his fortune and that on the train he would shred the criticisms and flush them down the toilet, strewing their debris the whole length of the track. Baker made such revenge unnecessary by recommending *Welcome* to the Theatre Guild so enthusiastically that they asked to read it.

As he set about compressing it to two and a half hours to insure its acceptance by the Guild, Wolfe felt his moment had come. According to Baker, *Welcome* had a better chance of success than the Guild's last production, Elmer Rice's *The Adding Machine*. "I know this now," Wolfe wrote his mother: "I am inevitable, I sincerely believe the only thing that can stop me now is insanity, disease, or death." Emboldened by a friend's home-made wine, he went even further in his next letter: "This thing inside me is growing beyond control. I don't know yet what I am capable of doing but, by God, I have genius—I know it too well to blush behind it—and I shall force the inescapable fact down the throats of the rats and vermin who wait the proof." His mother answered temperately that she hoped his play would sell. "I know you deserve it & should not have to wait long. . . . Be careful & don't rush on & lose your health. I must confess I worry quite a bit about you. For my sake go slow—you have plenty of time to make a name and money too."

4 · FRUSTRATION

AFTER a visit with friends in Westchester County, Wolfe holed up in Cambridge the second week of June to abbreviate *Welcome* and finish his other long play, *The House* (his saga of a decaying Southern family). "Raisbeck," he said in a letter, "is here with his dog—or vice versa—but I rarely see him." Once again Widener was "crumpling" under his attack—"ten, twelve, fifteen books a day are nothing." In July, when "Summer School arrived in a swirl of petticoats and lilac-colored drawers," he made a play for one of the newcomers who had "all the seductive tenderness of a tigress." At the end of the session they planned to meet in New York and go to Norfolk by boat if they could get a double stateroom—she being the third woman he had promised to meet in New York—"but where in the name of God do you take them?" he wrote a friend. "There is a mighty conspiracy everywhere abroad—the more terrible because

silent and veiled in holy words—which crushes us slowly and relent-
lessly into the [souls] of the domestics and the Pure Young Men.
Any suggestion that a male may hold physical communion with a
female without first propitiating the priest and the Holy Ghost is
met with invective, hatred, and relentless opposition."

By mid-August, having revised *Welcome* without cutting it appre-
ciably, he took it to New York where he fussed with it some more,
had it retyped, and submitted it to the Guild. If they accepted it, he
thought that a run of six or eight weeks would be sufficient to launch
him. In his penniless state, meanwhile, he seethed at the prosperity
he saw all around him. "Women—" he wrote his mother, "cheap,
vulgar women—the parvenu wives of soap manufacturers, usurers,
grafters, politicians, hog-butchers, and God knows what else, put
thousands on their backs, while the artist, the poet, the man with a
mind, sensitive to beauty and nobility, longs in vain for a few of the
wonderful books displayed in the windows." In mid-September he
went back to Asheville to live off his mother while waiting to hear
from his play.

At this critical juncture, his family—meaning Fred, Mabel, and
Julia, since Frank and Effie no longer impinged—treated him more
sympathetically and considerately than he had reason to expect, for
to these down-to-earth, unsophisticated folk, each scratching for a
living, his aspirations in a world they knew nothing of began to
seem like madness.[1] They feared for him and suffered with him
when day after day no word came from the Guild, yet they were
agreed that the time had come when he must support himself, and
in terms of his artistic development it was just as well, since his
dependence on his mother was keeping him a child. Despite his
family's forbearance, he quarreled with them at times. Julia had a
notion which she never really abandoned, that writing was light,
easy work compared to business enterprise. Equally exasperating
was Mabel's cynicism about his chances, because of her own unrealized ambition to be an opera singer. As for Fred, back selling
electrical equipment after graduating from Georgia Tech, his sur-
viving letters to Tom during the Harvard period are loyal, big-
brotherly exhortations "to give 'em hell, boy—I'm pulling for you."
But face to face they got on each other's nerves.

Late in October, with still no word from his play (the letter of refusal in *Of Time and the River* is a fiction), Tom set off by bus to visit Effie in South Carolina and was picked up en route by three joy-riding acquaintances. As they drove through Greenville roaring drunk, they were arrested and jailed. Tom thought, or perhaps imagined—he was never clear about it in his own mind—that the cell where he was confined contained a young Negro. Furious at being taken advantage of in his drunken state, he went berserk and got beaten up by the police, and when he came to, the Negro—if he ever existed—was gone. Fred was summoned to bail them out, but made such a row when he heard about the Negro that the police locked him in with Tom until a friend negotiated their release. After this escapade Tom felt disgraced in the eyes of his mother who had suffered so much from W.O.'s and Frank's drinking and who now imagined Tom following in their footsteps. His sense of guilt and general worthlessness made home unbearable, and early in November he went back to New York, temporarily employed as a fund-raiser for the University of North Carolina.

His soliciting had a way of getting mixed up with matters closer to his heart. When the head of American Tobacco asked him what he did, Tom answered with a fascinating half-hour lecture on the writing and marketing of plays. Meanwhile he lived in an uptown flat with a bachelor contingent that included his football idol, Bill Folger—still adventurous and magnetic and adored by women, though touchy about his forgotten fame. He was Wolfe's contact with that American type, the college athlete who never grows up, who reaches "such an acute, limited excellence at twenty-one"—as Fitzgerald was to put it in *The Great Gatsby*—"that everything afterwards savors of anticlimax." In December, having kept him on the rack for three months, the Guild declined his play, though Lawrence Langner, one of the Guild directors, was sure he could get it produced if Wolfe would tighten it and reduce the running time by thirty minutes. Wolfe agreed to try, but his aim, he said, had been to dramatize a whole civilization, not just a few people, and when he got down to it, he was unable to meet Langner's specifications. Just before Christmas, his work for the university completed, he went to Cambridge to talk to the Appointment Bureau about teaching jobs and to Baker about his future as an artist.

The ambivalence of his friendship with Baker was plain to see in unmailed scraps of letters written that year; though the drafts exist in Wolfe's papers, no corresponding copies are to be found in Baker's. The previous winter when Baker had accepted *Welcome* for production, Wolfe wrote him, "You have something more than a play to deal with, sir. You have the fate and destiny of 190 pounds of blood, bone, marrow, passion, feeling—that is, your humble servant in your keeping. I hope that's not an undue responsibility—but it's true and you must know it." His abject dependence gave way to rebellion, however, when the criticisms of *Welcome* began to come in and Baker told him that the ability to take such criticisms might make the difference between a second-rate artist and a great one. "I do not believe this," Wolfe replied. "Being a great artist depends no more on such callousness than does his ability to swallow castor-oil, or blue-point oysters, or fried pork chops. . . . You, or no man else, can make me a great artist, or a second-rate artist, or any kind of artist. That is a matter which was settled in my mother's womb—she, whose blood fed me, whose heart and whose brain lighted me and gave me being. That part of our destiny, believe me, is fixed, and nothing save death or madness can check or change it. And worldly wisdom on life, from an experienced traveller, is of no avail. If there is genius, the thing is a marvellous intuition, little dependent on observation. If there is no genius, I'd as soon draw wages from one form of hackery as another."

Before the last visit to Asheville Wolfe had asked Baker to write his mother, and the professor had outdone himself, telling Julia that Tom saw life as a dramatist should, that talent such as his couldn't be repressed without grave danger, and that were he free to devote himself to the work he loved, he would certainly make a name within the next decade. ("Ten years!" Julia had thought to herself. "That's a mighty long time!") While thus relying on Baker's support, Wolfe felt free to reject his advice. "Do not deceive yourself," he had written Baker that fall. "You can teach me no balance, equipoise, or moderation. Nothing will be gained by putting a fence around me: I will burst forth the more intemperately at the end."

The showdown occurred on January 3, 1924, when Baker returned to Cambridge after a talk with the Guild. Wolfe had assumed that following its Workshop production, *Welcome* would be snapped up by a New York producer, and when it wasn't, money became his obsession—not as an end in itself but as a means to the normal comforts of existence which the artist needed like everyone else. The artist-in-a-garret myth seemed to Wolfe the equivalent of saying that because three-fingered Mordecai Brown was a great pitcher, all the other pitchers should immediately have two fingers cut off. Uppermost in his mind was the practical problem of how to earn a living, about which Baker was maddeningly indefinite, except for his insistence that Wolfe mustn't teach lest it stifle his creativity. Instead he should go abroad and write, write—do nothing but write.[2] When Baker showed Wolfe a book on the American theater which praised the Workshop production of *Welcome* for being "as radical in form and treatment as any play the contemporary stage has yet acquired," Wolfe was pleased, but as he commented drily to someone else, you couldn't eat praises. After the long preliminaries, he wanted concrete, paying results and felt cheated because they weren't forthcoming.

In fairness to Baker it ought to be emphasized that his claims were modest. Unlike the extravagant Koch, he merely said that if a student had the necessary talent—a large "if" to begin with—the Workshop might speed his apprenticeship, and he had been unusually patient with the stubborn, idiosyncratic Wolfe. For despite a readiness to experiment, Baker was primarily interested in the viable, the saleable, the going thing. Not innovation but getting his young men and women on to New York was his heart's desire, his pride of the moment being Wolfe's former classmate in English 47, Philip Barry. This twinkling, fastidious Ivy Leaguer, whose notable career would be climaxed by *The Philadelphia Story,* specialized in "high comedy" not devoid of intellectual content. Gracefully attuned to current modes, he was more Baker's dish than the inconoclastic O'Neill, who as a Workshop student had resented being told that *Bound East for Cardiff* wasn't a play. But if O'Neill had lacked definition and restraint in Baker's eyes, what was he to make of Wolfe with his spilling profusion and his urge to say everything at once?

In *Of Time and the River,* Wolfe satirized the Workshop (or "Playshop" as he sometimes called it) with a harshness it scarcely deserved. True, this worthy experiment had its frauds and dilettantes, but most of its members had tried according to their lights, and some had succeeded brilliantly. When Wolfe scorned their dreams of accomplishment, he failed to point out that he, the most impassioned dreamer of them all, had also been the greatest dupe of the myth which Baker sought to discourage—namely, that by a wave of his wand he could transform anyone into a playwright. A few years after the publication of *Of Time and the River,* when Wolfe was asked why he had written so acidly of the Workshop, he replied, "I'll have to admit it was a case of sour grapes—I wasn't much good in that class."[3] He might have added that during his Harvard years he was more interested in life's possibilities than in Baker's precepts of dramatic form. Instinctively he knew that his cornucopia must be full to overflowing before he could shape its contents. Still green and growing, he wasn't ready to cross the line which every artist crosses alone and in his own good time with his tidings for mankind.

Therefore he turned to teaching as the likeliest means of supporting himself. His letter of application for an opening at N.Y.U. pleased his prospective employer with its candor. Admitting his lack of teaching experience, his playwriting ambitions, and the startling effect which his six feet five sometimes had on strangers, Wolfe promised to give the most faithful and efficient service of which he was capable if a satisfactory offer were made him. On January 21st, after a visit to the Washington Square campus, he accepted an instructorship in English paying $1,800 for seven months of teaching beginning February 1st.

Till then, he stayed on in a rented room at 10 Trowbridge Street in Cambridge. A friend who stopped by to see him in the afternoons would find him reclining before a wood fire in a Morris chair, with a half-filled glass on the arm and a bottle on the floor beside him. After an experimental binge freshman year, Wolfe had drunk comparatively little at Chapel Hill, but at Harvard his drinking had increased, especially during the crises of the past year. Alcohol gave him a respite from the endless drumming of impressions on his tightly strung nerves, and under its sway the past rose before him clothed in splendid words and images. "Proud, magic liquor" was his name for this life-enhancing genie.

In bowing to necessity Wolfe had postponed, though in no sense abandoned, his long-range ambitions. Indeed he had chosen to teach at the newly established Washington Square Branch of N.Y.U. for non-academic reasons: because of its proximity to Broadway and

Greenwich Village, and because he thought the rough-and-tumble student body, largely Jewish and second-generation immigrant, would give him material for his plays. "I teach! I teach! Jews! Jews!" he wrote a friend of college days, admitting elsewhere that he had come to N.Y.U. "without racial sentimentality—indeed with strong prejudice concerning the Jew which I still retain." With only eight hours of teaching per week, and with Mondays, Wednesdays, and Fridays entirely free, he had planned to do a lot of writing but soon found that correcting the themes for his three sections of Elementary Composition, totalling one hundred and four students, left him little time for other pursuits. On a treadmill that offered no escape, he nevertheless dreamed of a distant day when he would be composing great, verbal symphonies—books, plays, poems, he knew not what. He was no longer thinking quite so narrowly in terms of the theater. Writing his mother in March, he said his idea of success would be to produce "a fine and noble play or book" and in the next letter he likened his life to water that has passed the mill and turns no wheel: "The great play is yet unwritten; the great novel beats with futile hands against the portals of my brain." It was the first indication that he felt he had a novel in him.

Despite flashes of enjoyment, teaching was a torment—at the outset because of fears of inadequacy, and then, as he gained confidence, because of a drudgery which his conscience would not permit him to shirk. Huge, raw, gangling, shabby, and shy, he lectured pell-mell to his noisy classes with occasional musical interludes when he read aloud. He poured out his most intimate feelings about Donne, Milton, and Wordsworth—"You *do* see, don't you? You *do* see?"—snatching eagerly at any tidbits his students offered in return. On a theme describing a rundown cemetery where rats prowled by night he wrote, "If this cemetery really exists, please let me know where it is." (To his disappointment, the cemetery was real but the rats were imaginary.) Forever seeking the alive and beautiful in a welter of inconsequence, he corrected the unending themes doggedly, meticulously—sometimes writing criticisms as long as the themes themselves, which he was apt to return coffee-stained or grease-marked. Once he brought in a batch stuck together with condensed milk.

He found release in roaming the city and absorbing its color, although for the most part his life ran on a narrow track between the factorylike building where he worked and his cell of a room at the nearby Hotel Albert.[4] He gave the job his all and felt appreciated by students and faculty alike, yet he knew from the start that he wasn't a teacher and said so to everyone. "I don't regret the experience," he wrote a friend, "but this year ends my pedagogic career. I may, conceivably, tap on the sidewalk with a cane next season, having bought a pair of smoked glasses: I may shout 'Times! Woild! Joinall' in a raucous bellow. But—I shall not teach." As his salary was being paid in twelve monthly installments, $750 would be due him when he finished his stint in September, at which time he was going to England, bury himself in a village, and write for as long as his money held out.

Spring came, with its promise of adventure. One afternoon a pretty coed called on him in the English office. She had asked for an appointment, though her work was satisfactory. Suddenly she burst out crying and covered her face with her hands, and before he knew it her head was against his shoulder. Having ascertained that the chairman of the department was nowhere in sight, Wolfe went on with the interview. Nothing was wrong with the girl, except April stirring in the blood. Though Wolfe knew better than to get involved with students, he was enjoying himself with two women employed at the hotel who phoned him and left notes in his mailbox and didn't tell each other they were seeing him. Love affairs, yes, but marriage hadn't the slightest appeal. That year the Robertses were distressed because their son, aged eighteen, threatened to leave college in order to marry, and Wolfe threw himself on the parents' side. "My God," he wrote young Roberts, "take your youth, your glorious, irreclaimable youth and go where the wind listeth. . . . This is the Satanic period of our lives—Satan was young and the first great rebel—and only so, I think, do we reach ourselves and God at the end. . . . Love in our youth is not to seize and hold but to pursue—it should be the will-o'-the-wisp forever eluding us, yet forever taking us to higher, better ground."[5]

Teaching on through the summer, he fretted over *Welcome to Our City*, which was now in the hands of the Provincetown Players. When the Players kept it four months without even reading it, he fumed in a letter that "so help me God, the day will come when, unaided, I shall hammer them down upon their creaking knees"—

confessing a moment later that there was something schoolboyish in his ravings. He then offered his play to the Neighborhood Playhouse, and one of their directors wrote him in August that it was unusually fine and promised well for young America, but did he have another with fewer characters? As he hadn't heard from Baker since coming to New York, he inferred that his former mentor was disgusted with him for going into teaching. Koch, however, had bounded into town and asked permission to include *The Return of Buck Gavin* in a forthcoming edition of *Carolina Folk Plays*. Embarrassed by what he looked back on as his juvenilia, Wolfe consented with reluctance, feeling that all would be well when he went abroad and finished his sure-fire masterpiece, *The House*.

N.Y.U. had at least given him the satisfaction of paying his way, or almost paying it, for several times his $150 a month hadn't been enough to tide him over, and he had fallen back on his mother for additional funds. He enjoyed her forthright, informative letters—unparagraphed streams of consciousness in a loose masculine hand which made no distinction between the trivial and the important, human problems being interlarded with the weather, what she had eaten for lunch, and endless real-estate dickerings. Undaunted by the Guild's rejection of *Welcome*, she thought it might in the end prove advantageous since early success had ruined many a career. She advised him not to be too conscientious about his teaching. "You don't get paid enough, so take a hint. You [are] not in that line for [your] life time." When her letters lagged, he accused her—as she sometimes accused him—of not caring, but she remonstrated that "you & your work keep me living—sometimes I think I am still young & will be here long in the future to see you famous. I believe in you & I am sure in a few short years the whole community will know you." As she wanted to see him before he went abroad, he visited Asheville the end of September, staying on into October—his month of homecoming, recollection, and return.

Mrs. Roberts was as excited about his European trip as if she were going herself and wanted him to stay so long that "trip" would no longer be the applicable word. Many a book had wafted her across the Atlantic in her imagination, though she had never actually been for lack of funds, and because her conscience drove her to do the duty that lay nearest. "Tom, don't ever do your duty," she had written him when she heard of his travel plans. "It is a tyrant, tyrannical beyond words." She wanted him to plunge headlong into the new adventure, "[draining] the cup *to* the dregs—but no more." Many geniuses, she granted, had drunk "the cup of experience not only *to* the dregs" but had then "inserted their tongues in the not always silver goblet." Had it made them greater artists, or shortened their lives and tainted their genius? An avowed Victorian, she inclined towards the latter view, knowing that Tom disagreed. But some of her unquenchable idealism had gotten into him. "Above all don't lose faith," she had written him. "A man must suffer before he can write. I believe that. But I don't believe any man who has lost faith in God and man (whether his be an orthodox conception or not lies with him) ever wrote a line that was a farthing's worth to the world. . . . If I were you and had the gift of the pen, I'd rather be able to interpret the beauty of the world, the beauty and tragedy and mystery of men's lives, than to have all the gold that has ever been mined."

Words, in all their bloom of suggestiveness, were his kingdom. "Make them shine, Tom. You are a star and you must make your words shine like stars."

Pausing here to chart Wolfe's progress, we notice that he has moved outward through a series of pressure chambers—from Asheville to Chapel Hill to Harvard to New York—each widening his horizon and freeing him a little more. Now he was going to Europe, for generations of American artists the widest, freest, and most self-revealing chamber of them all. In his luggage was the manuscript of his play which he hoped to perfect under foreign skies, but when he boarded the 17,000-ton Cunarder *Lancastria* on October 25th, he unconsciously put aside the corset of the theater and began to function as the novelist and prose-poet he really was. In his voluminous journal of the voyage, the author of *Look Homeward, Angel* is suddenly manifest.

The first day on board he watched New York receding in the distance—"bound half way up her thin, far spires by a flanking girdle of cloud and mist." The city seemed "to swim insubstantially in smoke, its slender soaring lines contributing to the illusion, its steel and granite weight forgotten in a moment"—to be replaced by a new reality, the sea, which Wolfe evoked with Conradian echoes. When he went on deck at sunset the third day, the waves, under the fading light, "had turned to the cold, evil color of steel; a wind came up and a swell, the heaviest of the voyage, lifted and swung the ship with a combination of rotary and horizontal motion. She reeled like a horse under us and far ahead we could see her nose plunge steeply in a mounting coil of water and emerge after a perceptible time, in a smother of foam and spray." The sun had gone down, leaving a line of brilliant red along the horizon against which the hull of a tramp lay silhouetted, and as Wolfe watched the jaunty little captain pace the bridge with a short black pipe clenched in his teeth, he went ultra-literary and "thought—call it sentimentality if you like—of Frobisher and Drake and Nelson and of the mighty men of his race who have made the sea their mistress and their slave." But then a touch of pure Wolfe in its pictorial exactitude as the captain "looked to where the black hull of the tramp cut the last red of day."

At Harvard Wolfe had been a compulsive eavesdropper, memorizing every conversation, studying every gesture and intonation to see what they meant dramatically. Now he was sinking himself into people with the same alertness but with a more leisured relish, savoring the human manifestation for its own sake. The quartet at his table included an Englishman in plus fours and tasseled stockings "with a thin, sharp, rather furtive face which sloped forward to a long narrow beaklike nose." At lunch the first day, while the *Lancastria* was slowly revolving in the North River, a big two-funneled ship steamed past their porthole, and Wolfe asked the Englishman if he recognized it. "Oh yes," he replied, "she's the *Eyedrietic* [the *Adriatic*]." For the first time in his life Wolfe was talking to a cockney, who a moment later told him of the efforts of English scholars to reintroduce in America the accent used in England—which labor of enlightenment he called "restorin' the purity of the nitive tongue."

The other Englishman at the table—a blond, small-boned aristocrat —was returning from five years in the Washington embassy. His cordiality annoyed Wolfe, who found something "a little revolting in the inheritance of a gentleman which demands a schooled and polished courtesy towards everyone." The diplomat's tireless circulation from group to group smelled of hands across the sea and the destiny of races, and led Wolfe, with his interest in how things got to be as they are, to speculate on the evolution of the English gentleman. Thinking back to the etiquette books of the Renaissance, he recalled the gentleman's need of doing everything with apparent ease. He might engage in contests with his inferiors so long as he was sure of being returned victorious ("which always seemed to me, by the way, like very bad sportsmanship," Wolfe commented). Rightly conceived, Wolfe thought it took tremendous courage for a gentleman *not* to be brave. What else, in God's name, could he be? The gentleman was protected in his valiance, assured of a graceful dispatch. "A small hole under the wave of thick, bright hair, or a clean, small place drilled through the heart—'face to face and leading the charge'"—such was his predestined end. "Only the peasants," wrote Wolfe, exposing his plebeian bias and foreshadowing his own struggling death, "get it through the bowels, the noisy men, who cry loudly in their throats before they die, as if they love life well and would proclaim their sorrow as it goes."

One installment of his journal, anticipating his autobiographical essay "Gulliver," described an excessively tall young man on shipboard who had about him "a kind of brooding and subdued excitement; his eyes gleamed madly and from time to time darted sidelong glances; and though he spoke little at first, he was liberal in passionate and half-arrested gestures, as if he were already making preparations for an eloquence yet to come." As he strode the decks, elderly gentlemen occasionally stopped him to ask in the kindest tones imaginable, "My boy, how tall are you?"—causing him to mumble some unintelligible reply and rush angrily away. When he awoke in the morning, the young man stared across his angled shanks to where his distant toes sprawled on the footboard; they seemed hardly to belong to him until he moved, and then he realized that he was progenitor of the whole abominable distance. Not only beds but all human contrivances were a tantalizing fraction too small or scanty for his needs. "I have not felt the world's imprisonment," Wolfe had previously written in his notes; "I have wanted a key to enter, not a key to set me loose." His pathos was that of an outsider, subtly excluded from the world of ordinary men and seeking a back-door admittance through his work, which helps to explain the fanatical drive that went into it.

Because of engine trouble, the voyage lasted eleven days. The night they sighted the beacons of the Scilly Isles, Wolfe lay in his bunk a long time before he slept as through his porthole he watched "the great stars ride up the sky." (This identical phrasing would appear in *Look Homeward, Angel*.) At dawn they entered Plymouth harbor, quietly enclosed by green hills, and soon afterwards they were pitching in a heavy channel cross-chop towards Cherbourg to unload more passengers. Next morning they were going up the Thames estuary where "busy little tenders puffing nervously through their gay red stacks steamed round us and ragged tramps, their funnels far astern, slid past us in the fog, bound seawards." In Wolfe's observation, the strange was invariably tinged with the familiar; thus the huddle of warehouses and docks and chimneys along the shore seemed to him all that one might reasonably expect of Hoboken. As the passengers got into the tender which would take them ashore at Tilbury, he had his first glimpse of those in third class—"poor, harassed, badgered-looking men and women who for the lack of a few dollars *extra passage* were detained on the slightest irregularity." It troubled him to think that they, too, had lived in that hull, looming so monstrously above them, without his suspecting their existence.

The tender's deck was just beneath the *Lancastria's* lowest portholes, at which the strange, wild faces of the engine-room crew now appeared. Wolfe stared at them—"straight into their small, evil eyes —and I knew that in their hearts they hated us." Then there welled up in him that sense of the interdependence of all human life which would undergird so much of his writing. He realized how little of the ship he had actually seen: two strips of deck, three tiers of cabins, a music room, a writing room, a lounge, a dining salon. It had seemed spacious, but in the greater spaces hidden from view these drudges had toiled while he sipped his broth at eleven and his tea at four. In the huge imprisoned well, small, white, grease-smeared men had turned a brass wheel half around, watched a gauge, paced a catwalk with wadding in their hands. Wolfe took it all in at a glance and sympathized, and for a moment he *was* those men.

Looking back at the *Lancastria* as the tender made for shore, he thought of the legend of the ghost ship which drives before the moon or setting sun, exposing its spectral ribs and vanishing—the legend so perfectly told in "The Rime of the Ancient Mariner." The *Lancastria* and its crew now had the insubstantiality of New York when he last saw it, obscured by mist halfway up its gleaming towers. Wolfe's perceptions—so vivid and concrete—were dream-encased; how often he leaves us, as he himself was left, with a feeling that "we are such stuff as dreams are made on, and our little life is rounded with a sleep!" The charm of travel was founded on illusion, and perceiving it now, Wolfe noted in his journal that he would never again visit England with his present élan, for the Actual was always a poor thing beside the Expected. "The green-golden little kingdom on the isle, nested so long ago in the mind and heart of a boy with a book" was already slipping through his fingers as he approached it that morning in the yellow fog and heard the dim creakings and rattlings of the invisible shore.

During his first days in London he mainly walked "the queer, blind, narrow, incredible, crooked streets," looking at the people, hearing them, "getting them," and late at night and early in the morning when the streets were empty, he stopped at pubs, taxi stands, and refreshment wagons and listened some more, making notes all the while on London versus New York and England versus America. Having worn out his shoes with walking, he bought a pair of broad, shiny English boots which made him feel very John Bullish as he clumped along. Once he joined a crowd outside a shop from which G. K. Chesterton's famous bulk presently emerged, his great red face turning purple with embarrassment. The crowd parted to let him through, and at a distance of twenty yards, he whirled and glared back at them in horror before hastening on. When Wolfe visited the Tower of London, he was specially moved by a dim-lit chamber whose stone walls bore the inscriptions of doomed men. One that he could read—"My heart is yours to dethe"—had over it the name of the author, a London goldsmith, and beneath it the year 1564, and to one side a heart with leaves and blossoms sprouting from it. At the end of several weeks, tired of city fog and greyness, he went west to Bath, the old Roman settlement he recalled from his reading in Chaucer and Sheridan and Arthurian legend. Abruptly hemmed by smooth, green hills, Bath would linger in Wolfe's memory as the loveliest of English towns. Street by street, it climbed one of those intimate hills with others leaning down on it, so that the onlooker (said Wolfe in his journal) got "something of the sudden, sharp nearness-in-farness, steepness-in-lowness" of the early Italian paintings—"Christ in the foreground with a mob on the way to Calvary with the hill standing like a tower in the middle distance." From Bath he went to Bristol where the nightly chimes, high above the tiled roofs and gabled eaves, rang back the centuries and peopled the winding streets with the phantoms of the burghers and adventurers who had built the city with their distant trade. By early December he had gotten his temporary fill of England and crossed the channel to France.

His third evening in Paris, when he was still befuddled by the language, he rented a fifth-floor room in a cheap Latin Quarter hotel. The *concierge*, a limping *mutilé de guerre*, groaned at the sight of Wolfe's three suitcases, so he took two of them up himself, leaving the third behind till morning. During the night it was stolen, and when Wolfe found out he came close to losing his mind, for the bag contained the manuscript of his unfinished play, *The House*. Moving to another hotel, he filed suit at the local court with the aid of a Harvard acquaintance who spoke fluent French, and was awarded five hundred francs, or $25. When he went to collect it, the *patron* accused him of being in cahoots with the stranger who had stolen the bag. Muttering that he had always been an honest man but would never be again, the *patron* finally made out a release for the five hundred francs, and when Wolfe had it safely pocketed he called the *patron* a dirty scoundrel and his wife a liar, rather enjoying it as they followed him to the door, their faces contorted with rage and hatred.

During December he rewrote his play, changing its title to *Mannerhouse*, and was glad in the end he had lost the original, since the new version seemed to him the best thing he had done. Save for an excursion to the Château-Thierry battlefield with several friends he had known at Chapel Hill, he saw no one and was homesick and forlorn. His difficulty with the language cut him off from his surroundings, and his sense of isolation had grown acute when quite by accident he ran into Kenneth Raisbeck on New Year's Eve.

In *Of Time and the River* Eugene meets Starwick (Raisbeck) on the steps of the Louvre, but what actually happened was this: passing the museum at closing time, Raisbeck was attracted by a hubbub at the front door, which turned out to be Wolfe tussling with several guards. He had been drinking and was determined to see more pictures, closing time or no closing time. Catching sight of Raisbeck, he yielded the point, and after a joyous reunion the two old friends spent the evening touring the working-class bistros around Les Halles, returning in the dawn to Raisbeck's flat at 18 Boulevard Edgar-Quinet. Like Wolfe, Raisbeck had gone abroad to write his way to glory. First he had stayed in Cannes with Philip Barry who owned a house there, but a falling-out had terminated the visit. The end of November he had come to Paris were he joined the two young women whose studio apartment he was now occupying. They had lent it to him in their absence, and they returned unexpectedly New Year's Day while Wolfe and Raisbeck were sleeping off their excesses.

During January Raisbeck stayed on at the studio with "Elizabeth Johnson" and "Faith Cummings" as we shall call them—the Elinor and Ann of *Of Time and the River*—while Wolfe lived some distance off at the little hotel in the Rue des Beaux-Arts where Oscar Wilde had died. But the four of them were constantly together, "doing" Paris with all the fervor of Americans kicking over the traces. Elizabeth, a twenty-nine-year-old Boston matron, had left her husband and child to follow Raisbeck abroad, which performance seemed to delight him as "utterly *mad*—Boston." Faith was accompanying Elizabeth partly for the sake of appearances; she was thirty and unmarried and had gone into nursing against her parents' wishes. Under the guidance of these seasoned travellers (Elizabeth had done refugee work in France during the war), Wolfe began to feel at home, though Raisbeck's deterioration since their last encounter exasperated and appalled him.

At Harvard, Raisbeck's ascendancy had stemmed not merely from his having something thoughtful or beautiful to say on almost any subject, nor from his Celtic flair for making life glamorous and surprising; one had respected his integrity, the severity and accuracy of his criticisms, the way he stood up to Baker when defending a play he believed in, and the few times Wolfe had joined others in ridiculing his mannerisms he had felt bad afterwards. But now something was awry: Raisbeck seemed content to vegetate without purpose or ambition, growing pettish when Wolfe criticized his self-indulgence.

Not until this point in *Of Time and the River* does Eugene discover Starwick's homosexuality through his infatuation with a parasitic Frenchman, though actually Wolfe must have known it at Harvard, withholding it in the novel for the sake of the story. In the Twenties, to be sure, homosexuality was more under wraps than now, and because Raisbeck had been preoccupied with earning a living and building prestige at Harvard, his affairs had been discreet. The trip abroad had represented, among other things, a chance to indulge his appetites, and in Cannes he had been so blatant about picking up sailors on the wharves that Philip Barry had sent him away in disgust.[6] Wolfe reacted similarly to "the little cootie of a Frenchman" (Elizabeth Johnson's phrase) who attached himself to Raisbeck in Paris, although this entanglement merely dramatized and brought home to Wolfe's senses what his intuition must have told him all along.

From the start, Wolfe had been troubled by Raisbeck's exoticism, his lack of anything resembling the common touch. Passionately concerned with his own origins, Wolfe wondered why Raisbeck never spoke of his home in the Midwest or showed the slightest inclination to return; he seemed devoid of either love or hate for the soil which had nourished him. Correspondingly, in literature, though Raisbeck was an authority on Wilde, Huysmans, and the corruptly elegant Restoration Drama, he knew little of the robust music of Chaucer, Wordsworth, and Milton and claimed he couldn't read Dickens and Thackeray at all. In painting, Wolfe admired the brawling, bursting plenty of the Dutch and Flemish masters—their canvasses packed with everyday life—but Raisbeck, though too intelligent to deny their merit, was more deeply stirred by the drawings of Aubrey Beardsley. Shrinking from all that was coarse and full-blooded in art as well as life, he had taken refuge in the "amusing," by which he meant the rare and the perverse.

The long-smoldering antagonism between them caught fire when Wolfe fell in love with Faith Cummings, only to discover that she was already enamored of Raisbeck. Faith was a large, graceful Juno with thick black hair boyishly cropped, a peaches-and-cream complexion, and a generous smile that radiantly transformed her usually sullen expression. Having had scant attention from men, she was jarred by Wolfe's thunderous assault, and in any case Raisbeck was blocking the path, subtly manipulating both Elizabeth and Faith who pampered him and spent their money on him. Had Raisbeck taken a normal interest in either, Wolfe would have been less incensed, but obviously Raisbeck was leading them on to no purpose, out of vanity, caprice, and feline spite.

More offensive to Wolfe than Raisbeck's homosexuality was his arrogance in captivating, using, and discarding other people as if they were merely a backdrop for his romantic personality. Essentially frivolous for all his cultivation, he had spent his life weaving little webs of charm. Like a young girl before she forms a serious attachment, he had flirted indiscriminately with men, women, children, and probably with dogs, to fill the bottomless void in a nature which lacked the strength to love and be loyal. Sensing this hollowness at last, Wolfe quarreled bitterly with Raisbeck and withdrew from the auto trip to southern France which the four were planning to take at the end of January. He hoped that Faith, who was fonder of him than one might surmise from *Of Time and the River*, would also stay behind, but she didn't, and after four weeks of hectic conviviality he was by himself again, picking up the pieces of his debauch.

He had left N.Y.U. knowing he could return in February at an increased salary, but the middle of January he had written the head of the department that what was happening to him was "too important to be checked violently" and that his mother, he thought, would help him stay abroad some months longer. Nearing the end of his resources when he met Raisbeck, he had cabled home for money and gotten $125, which he quickly spent in the company of his high-living friends. In response to a second cable, his mother had sent him a check made out to her which he was unable to cash, and to add to the confusion he lost it. Then came a letter from Fred suggesting that three months abroad ought to be enough and that if he had finished his play, New York was the place to sell it. Tom answered defensively that he didn't mean to burden the family and was quite prepared to earn his living as a teacher, but that he was working hard in a last effort to save himself from "the deep damnation of Freshman composition." Simultaneously, he wrote his mother that if she could spare another $500, it would allow him to remain six months longer, visit southern France and Italy, and "do his work" —whatever that meant. He talked grandly of settling down to write short stories ("cheap ones if necessary") in order to make money, but his real desire was to cram in as much Europe as possible before the gates slammed shut.

Penniless, he fell back on the bounty of an American widow who occupied the room next to his at the hotel. He had previously scorned her when she invited him to lunch and now he was ashamed, realizing that the lonely and broken are often the readiest to help in time of need. She gave him the key to her little apartment on the Montmartre where she no longer lived; it was crowded with souvenirs of her past life, and he went there daily to read and write and meditate. His literary output during February consisted of interminable letters to Faith filled with young moralizing and faked insouciance. He told her of receiving news from home which had put "their pretentious and rather sordid little comic opera" into perspective. His sister Mabel had had a serious operation, and the very day "her flesh was riven by the surgeon's knife" he had participated in a "paltry little stew of concocted emotion" with Raisbeck, Elizabeth, and Faith, during which there had been much talk of honesty by people who had to think about being honest, and of unconventionality by people who had to think about it—"and who can never do anything but flutter around the safe edges, with a rather kittenish feeling that they are getting very *near* at times."

Meanwhile the bountiful widow had grown possessive. When she suggested that he accompany her on a visit to her married sister in Tunis, Wolfe temporized, for as soon as more money came from home he was planning an escape to the Midi. He received another check from his mother late in February, and drunk with the ecstasy of liberation, he wrote Faith of dropping from his monastery window into the moonlight and hearing laughter by the distant fountains. Or, in more prosaic terms, he paid his arrears at the hotel and headed south.

In his travels Wolfe was always attaching and being mothered by elderly women who poured their tragic histories into his wondering and sympathetic ear. At Orleans, where he stopped for the night, he was taken in tow by a half-demented countess with a scrapbook of clippings about her tour of America in behalf of the Allied war effort. She drank horse's blood for her anemia, and after listening to her prevarications for a week, Wolfe lost patience and went on to Tours where his money ran out and forced his return to Paris. There he found another check from his mother as well as a letter from N.Y.U. offering him a job in September which he accepted, hoping that by then some means of escape would present itself. Having expanded his journal, which he called "A Passage to England," to almost fifty thousand words, he sent it to Mrs. Roberts for editing and possible publication in *The Asheville Citizen*. She praised it enthusiastically but doubted whether *The Citizen* would take it because of the interspersed satire of Asheville. Wolfe said he had written those parts in sadness of heart. "It is done nevertheless," Mrs. Roberts replied, "and your big foot, however much sadness may be controlling your leg muscle, comes down with squishing force upon the godlets of our daily lives and Sabbath meditations." In the end, only a brief excerpt about his visit to the Tower of London was printed.

Heading south once more, he settled at St.-Raphaël, so as to be near the family of a Chapel Hill professor on sabbatical. They would remember Wolfe as starved for companionship and eager to tell anyone who would listen about the theft of his manuscript and the countess who drank horse's blood, as if relating his adventures was a means of fixing them in his mind. The end of May he visited northern Italy and was lyrical about Venice, with "its dark, innumerable little side canals slapping gently under your window" and its gondolas "which come curving out of the water like carved smoke." A month later he was in England, winding up his *Wanderjahr* with a feeling that at last he had something to say, that his life till now had been a mere gathering and sorting of materials. He wrote Mrs. Roberts' sister that she was right in supposing he would return a sadder person. "My eyes are a little darker, I think, a bit madder than before, but you will not notice this when you see me, for I shall smile a great deal with my mouth, and no one has ever known me well enough to make the very simple discovery that laughter died in my eyes six years ago when Ben died."[7]

The end of August he sailed for home on the *Olympic*, an ocean-going colossus which fed his future visions of "the huge nocturnal slant and blaze of liners racing through immensity." He was travelling third class, and the next to last night on board he went to a gala in second where he met a Mrs. Bernstein, a stage designer who had come down from first for the festivities. Though her brisk competence and ruddy good humor did not portend romance, Wolfe felt in her a combination of qualities he had long been seeking, and despite the difference in their ages he gave amorous pursuit. Back in New York Mrs. Bernstein would laugh with friends about the enormous, vociferous young man she hadn't been able to get away from on the boat; wherever she went, there he was! But Wolfe had made an impression with his violence, his vague hunger, and his furious questioning which insisted on knowing everything about her, down to how many pairs of shoes she owned. At one point he had upbraided her for her connection with what he called "the dung-heap of the theater," and remembering the incident long afterwards she wrote that his "iron grip on her arms was wonderful, she discovered it was what she had wanted all her life." She told him he was crazy, for she knew of his yearning to sell a play. In her suitcase at the time was the copy of *Welcome to Our City* which he had submitted to the Neighborhood Playhouse.

The evening after they met, they exchanged their first endearments as the *Olympic* lay anchored in quarantine off Staten Island with the towers of Manhattan glimmering in the distance.

5 · ALINE

"THE true artist," wrote Shaw in *Man and Superman*, "gets into intimate relations with [women] to study them, to strip the mask of convention from them, to surprise their inmost secrets, knowing that they have the power to rouse his deepest creative energies, to rescue him from his cold reason, to make him see visions and dream dreams, to inspire him, as he calls it. He persuades women that they may do this for their own purpose whilst he really means them to do it for his. . . . Perish the race and wither a thousand women if only the sacrifice of them enable him to act Hamlet better, to paint a finer picture, to write a deeper poem, a greater play, a profounder philosophy! . . . In the rage of that creation he is as ruthless as the woman, as dangerous to her as she to him, and as horribly fascinating. Of all human struggles there is none so treacherous and remorseless as the struggle between the artist man and the mother woman."

And what if the "mother woman" is herself an artist?

An actor's daughter eighteen years older than Wolfe, Aline Bernstein had been born on a bright starlight night in December, 1882, when the cold made the horses' hoofs ring on the cobbles of New York like metal on metal. Her father, Joseph Frankau, was in his dressing room at the Madison Square Theatre, fastening his wig to his forehead with spirit gum, when a messenger came in to announce the birth of his first child. Aline always attributed her father's quixotic temper to his oddly assorted parentage. *His* father, a German-Jewish immigrant, had married a girl of old Connecticut stock, who by way of preparation had spent a year in the household of a rabbi. During Aline's girlhood there were family reunions at her grandmother's ancestral home in Farmington, which breathed the style and decorum of the eighteenth century. One must remember that Aline's bohemianism was grounded in a fundamental propriety and sense of order.

She was reared in uncertainty. Her mother, a sweet homebody of Dutch-French-Jewish descent, had suffered her father's road tours, drinking sprees, and infidelities, and there was never enough money. Aline loved her mother and sympathized with her lot, but her idol growing up was her mother's sister, Aunt Nana, who had married a doctor for the characteristic reason that she loved someone else and wanted to teach that someone a lesson. As Aline pictured her in later years, Nana had the tall, curvaceous splendor of a full-rigged ship. She wore too many rings, her bodice was cut too low, her train was too long, and the excess of ruffles beneath her skirt made a silken whisper as she walked. Men were her *raison d'être*, and as Aline described it, "Discipline was unknown to her. . . . She was never selfish in the narrow sense, she would give the dress off her back, and she had a beautiful and embracing pity for anyone in poverty or pain; but she was morally blind to what was near, and all thought of living was in a dreamy present which she expected to be indefinitely extended."

Once, by mistake, Aline drank a dose of some drug which Nana had begun to indulge in and might well have died but for the timely ministrations of the physician husband.

Aline's other aunt ran a boarding house where the Frankaus lived because of their straitened circumstances. Sitting beside her Aunt

Mamie as she carved the roast for the boarders, Aline was permitted to fish out the succulent bits that fell in the gravy on the platter. She loved to eat and she loved to go marketing, rejoicing in the spiced dinginess of the old-fashioned grocery stores where one took the tops off barrels to sniff the pickles or run one's hands through satiny coffee beans. Later the Frankaus occupied a house with Aunt Nana and her husband, until he became so exasperated with her amours that he left her; then Aline's mother opened a boarding house where Nana continued her life of a demimondaine. Aline liked to watch her aunt decking herself before the cheval glass, in preparation for the gentlemen who swept her off in hansom cabs or stayed for private dinners in her apartment. Meanwhile the house teemed with actors, for Aline's father was popular with his fellows. Accompanying him on road tours in England and America, she learned what it meant to be a professional—the steely strength required to keep one's weaknesses from interfering with one's work. From an admirer of Nana's, a wealthy art collector, she learned the equally valuable secret of living in the moment. "Only remember," the collector had said, revolving a piece of jade in his hand, "not to love it so that it costs too much to relinquish it"—a caution she threw to the winds when she met Thomas Wolfe.

By the time she had completed her education at public school and Hunter College, both parents were dead, and save for their aunts, she and her younger sister were alone in the world. A month before her twentieth birthday she married Theodore Bernstein, a rising young broker who adored her and offered her a security she had never known. As a girl she had dreamed of becoming an actress, but her father had discouraged it while encouraging her talent for drawing. After the birth of her children, a girl and a boy, she studied painting for several years with that incomparable teacher, Robert Henri, who stressed the importance of trusting one's instincts, seeing freshly, and preserving a sense of wonder.

"Blunder ahead with your own personal view," he told his students. "The thing that makes the artist is a gigantic individual development." He knew the price of going it alone, of denying the normal urge for friendship and approval, but alone one got acquainted with himself—grew up and on, not stopping with the crowd. "Do not let the fact that things are not made for you, that conditions are not as they should be, stop you. Go on anyway. Everything depends on those who go on anyway." Such notions, filtered through Aline, would stiffen Wolfe on his solitary road.

Later she had studied at the New York School of Applied Design, and when friends launched the Neighborhood Playhouse in 1915, she had made sets and costumes for them, becoming in due course the first woman member of the United Scenic Artists, which qualified her for the big Broadway productions. By the time Wolfe met her she was a leader in her field. She loved the sticks and stones of her profession and used to say that the best moment in the world, bar none, was when she faced her drawing board with a blank sheet of paper on it. She had taken courses in cutting when draughting was thought sufficient, she had unwrapped mummies to see how Egyptian costumes should be made, she never missed a rehearsal or fell behind in an assignment, and she fraternized with her co-workers and sought to improve their lot.

While holding up her end in a man's world, she had lost none of her delicious femininity. Soft-eyed, soft-haired, soft-skinned, she ingratiated with a trusting eagerness, a gentle, yielding vivacity. Attractive as a bun is attractive, or an apple turnover, she had the sweetness of someone's good little wife, and her slight deafness became an asset when she tipped her ear to give you her full attention. She dressed with quiet distinction, wearing East Indian fabrics when they were still a novelty, and the finest English tweeds, and turn-of-the-century veils that went over her hat, tied under her chin, and framed her face, which was open and rosy as a peony. People of all ages and conditions were drawn to her, for she was devoid of snobbery and treated stage hands no differently from a Theatre Guild director. She was the kind of person who kept up with her friends, and when she ran into you, she would be bubbling with anecdotes. It might be that she had visited her wig-maker in the Village, only to find that his place had been converted into a speakeasy, and though it was 10 A.M., she had said, "All right then, give me an Old Fashioned." (Here she would lapse into hysterical shrieks at her own audacity.) Or she would tell you of her masseur's remark when he met her unexpectedly on the street: "Mrs. Bernstein, it's so nice to see you with your clothes on!"

Her great quality was her vibrant, sentient appreciation, her capacity to enjoy and to share her enjoyment. Generous to a fault, except where it conflicted with her vital interests, she had the best of two worlds—bohemian and bourgeois—and she couldn't have stood one without the other. The envious who criticized her for "having her cake and eating it" forgot that a nature as rich as hers has the right to make demands, and that she gave as much as she got. It was Aline who brought the excitement into the Bernstein ménage, and without intending to she rather took the color out of those near at hand. Her amiable, prosy husband who spent his evenings playing bridge at the club (he was an impassioned gambler) had been the lover in what for her was more a *mariage de convenance*, and at some point they had reached an understanding which permitted her to go her way. Not that she was promiscuous. On the contrary, her affairs prior to Wolfe had been real relationships with men whose character and ability she admired. But like her father and her Aunt Nana before her, she was a romantic who came at life expecting miracles such as her shipboard meeting with Thomas Wolfe.

They did not see each other for several weeks after they landed. Almost immediately Wolfe went to Asheville where a real-estate boom was in progress, symbolized by the levelling of the old Battery Park Hotel. This antiquated structure with its wide porches and comfortable rockers, its eaves and gables and labyrinthine corridors, had crowned a green hill in the center of town, and from its windows one had looked out on a vast panorama of mountains in the smoky distance. Now the hill had been razed to make way for garages, stores and office buildings, and a charmless, up-to-date hotel sixteen stories high was being erected to replace the old one. Everywhere there was talk of enormous profits, and amid the general inflation it somehow got in the paper that Wolfe was a "professor" who held "the chair of English" at N.Y.U. He realized more clearly than ever that Asheville wasn't for him, that he couldn't return and become a crusading editor as some of his friends had been urging him to do. "There are kinds and kinds of provincialism," he had written in his notes; "New England is provincial and doesn't know it, the Middle West is provincial, and knows it, and is ashamed of it, but, God help us, the South is provincial, knows it, and doesn't care."[1] He recalled a conversation a few years earlier with a local banker who had asked him what he wanted to do. When he spoke of becoming a playwright, the banker looked crestfallen until Wolfe added, "You know, if you hit it right, it's very profitable. Eugene O'Neill has made a million dollars already." "Oh!" said the banker, seeing the light. "Is that so? Why that's just fine!"[2] From discussions of this sort Wolfe had gotten the impression that art *per se* was considered queer and almost immoral in Asheville; it suggested, he wrote his mother, "an unending succession of pictures of naked women."

During the weeks at home he had thought a great deal about Mrs. Bernstein, and on his return to New York he was disappointed not to find a message from her at his hotel. He now took a cynical view of their encounter, classifying it as married-woman-toying-with-young-admirer-during-the-isolation-of-a-voyage. To drive her out of his mind, he immersed himself in academic routine, but she wouldn't be driven: her jolly look, her spunky walk, her excited voice, her hearty laugh, her large, liquid brown eyes, and above all the magic of their last evening together kept returning. At the end of several days he wrote her a pompous letter, informing her that he had "never truckled to the mob" but that if she remembered him (he knew perfectly well she did) and felt like seeing him again, he could be reached at the Hotel Albert. No sooner was it mailed than he cringed to think of her reading it.

His suspense was brief. She phoned next morning to invite him to a performance that evening at the Neighborhood Playhouse. This fashionable little art theater which had come into being as an adjunct of the Henry Street Settlement was a handsome, red-brick façade sprouting among the tenements of the Lower East Side. When Wolfe got there, Aline was waiting for him on the sidewalk, and comparing her with his idealized remembrance, he was conscious of certain defects. Her sturdy neck was slightly worn and pleated, her legs were too thin (or rather the calf muscles began too high up), her dark hair was streaked with gray. But once again he admired her shapely hands with their look of strength like the arch of a bird's wing, her beautiful mouth and teeth, her luscious smile, and from his point of view her embonpoint was all to the good; the slim-hipped, boyish flappers who had set the styles these past few years repelled him with their barrenness.

Aline had wisely arranged to meet him in the context of her work. He couldn't help but be impressed by the theatrical big-wigs who came up to her between the acts to congratulate her on her sets. Afterwards, she took him backstage to meet the actors—then up to her workroom to see her costume drawings, so sure and swift. There was a diffidence between them as they reconnoitered each other before taking the plunge, obscurely sensing its profound import for them both. Though they saw each other several times before then, it wasn't till Wolfe's twenty-fifth birthday on October 3rd that Aline became his mistress. That day they had agreed to meet for lunch on the steps of the New York Public Library, and Wolfe was twenty minutes late (not Aline, as one would infer from *The Web and the Rock*),[3] and their immense relief on finding each other told them they were in love. During their meal at a speakeasy Wolfe drank too much, while Aline poured out her belief in his talent and his future, and later she remembered that day as typical of all that ensued: Wolfe angered, then delighted her, made her laugh, then brought her to the edge of tears. It was a series of violent contrasts with never a moment's ennui.

"The met halves of the broken talisman," in Wolfe's lovely phrase, these two exceptional beings now united their lives, and for a comparison one looks back a century to Balzac and Madame de Berny, where the discrepancy in age and experience was greater still. Balzac had been a lout of twenty-two, completely ignorant of women, when he fell in love with the accomplished, forty-five-year-old goddaughter of Louis XVI and Marie Antoinette who enveloped him in a mothering tenderness that broke the shackles of his family and liberated the artist. Aline's love for Wolfe also partook of this maternal element, but with a difference. Though others might regard her as matronly, in her own eyes she was ever young and desirable. Balzac's liaison with Madame de Berny had cooled to an abiding friendship which she gladly accepted, but would a quiet resolution of this sort be acceptable to the eternal feminine in Aline?

A woman's love for a man depends in large measure on what she can do for him, and Aline Bernstein could do everything for Thomas Wolfe. It wasn't simply a matter of his physical helplessness and disorientation, of his needing someone to look after his clothes and remind him of his engagements. The essential lack lay deeper. For years he had gnashed his teeth at the thought that others were be-littling—or at least insufficiently appreciating—his talent, and enjoy-ing his failures. The devotion of this sought-after, successful woman redeemed his self-respect, while affording him a window on the world he longed to penetrate, for she knew everyone connected with the arts. At the start, their affair gave him a feeling of lightness and elation; he was pleased with himself for bagging such an elegant mistress. Then all of a sudden he was desperately in love and wanting to control her every move.

She phoned him each morning at the Albert to wake him and start him writing, for he had wangled an afternoon teaching schedule which left his mornings free for his own work. Her cheery voice describing the busy day ahead roused him to emulation, and when they met for lunch or dinner she would be full of her doings with carpenters, electricians, costumers, actors, directors. Often he called for her after her evening show, and they would conclude their day with a midnight supper at Childs. As they toured the city, he rediscovered it through her eyes and through her memories, which went back to the Eighties and Nineties. During his first year in New York, the throngs and the nervous flux had wearied him, but now he felt attuned to its poetry.

He went to Asheville for Christmas and wished he had stayed in New York. "My family," he wrote Aline, "is showing its customary and magnificent Russian genius for futility and tragedy." His arrival having coincided with the death of a bibulous cousin, Fred met him at the station "with the news that another member of my damned and stricken family has been lost: that he was troubled by his ap-pendicitis, my mother by a severe bronchial cold which might de-velop into pneumonia, and that my sister, just returned from an in-terrupted rest cure at the hospital, had hysteria and had broken down under the nervous strain of Christmas preparation. He then wished me a merry Christmas."

On his return to New York, Wolfe and Aline were no longer satis-fied to live apart, and during the winter of 1926 he moved into the "loft" at 13 East Eighth Street which she had rented as a studio, though on his insistence he let him share the rent. In the center of this fourth-floor room running the length of the building was a sky-light from which the ceiling sloped towards the front and rear windows, so that Wolfe had to stoop at either end. The whitewashed walls bulged in places, and in others the plaster had been knocked away. The floorboards sagged and creaked under his tread, but the space and privacy were a luxury after the Albert, and during the next few months this dilapidated roost with its meager furnishings afforded him some of the happiest hours he would ever know.

Each night Aline went home to her brownstone at 333 West Seventy-seventh, and her mornings were taken up with the theater, but around noon Wolfe would hear her step on the stair, a key would turn in the lock, and the door would open on her beaming face. Often she was full of some humorous detail observed in the street —for example, a vendor giving his fruit the once-over with a feather duster. As they hugged each other, his love words stripped away the years; she was his "lass," his "pet," his "plum-skinned wench." Sometimes he would break away from her to pace the attic crooning with delight, and there were moments when he danced with glee, clumsily leaping and cavorting and throwing his head back, while Aline, catching his mood, circled nearby in demure waltz step. After the first elation of being together, she turned her thoughts to food.

A superb cook whose dishes were full of butter and wealth, she read recipe books in bed at night, sometimes thinking to herself, "My, that sounds good!" and straightway jumping up to prepare it. "I tell you what I consider a good meal—" she once wrote Wolfe, "a dish of fine, salty oysters, a clear soup (strong chicken broth with hair-thin noodles), maybe some lobster newburg (optional), a grilled fillet of beef, young peas cooked with lettuce and tiny onions (my own specialty), a cool green salad simply dressed, a raspberry ice, coffee, any good wine, and plenty of love from or with your loved one. There is something to make you believe in God. What?"

When she did their marketing, he stalked in her wake tweaking the legs of chickens, plunking melons, reading the labels on cans with lustful eye, and having brought home the packages, he poured himself a drink and settled back to admire her concentration as she gave herself to the cooking. On afternoons when he wasn't teaching, food would be followed by love and by interminable conversations during which they swapped their past lives. Aline agreed with her Aunt Nana that nothing was quite as satisfactory as talking to someone you loved in a prone position; it made you think of things that never would have occurred to you standing up. Nestling against him, she could feel his shivers of laughter at her deft characterizations, for she saw into others at a glance and ticked them off in a sentence or two. They were physically attuned, although from the outside theirs seemed less a passionate than a comfortable, working relationship. Visitors to the loft would find Aline, besmocked and bespectacled, at her drawing board, while Wolfe, sprawled on the sofa, would be reading or correcting themes.

They were discreet but not furtive. They loved and didn't much care who knew. In a dark-blue suit less spotted than of old, his mane of hair slicked down, his normally scuffed shoes suggesting a hasty shine, Wolfe attended the evening receptions at the Bernsteins, where he rubbed shoulders with the magnates of her world—everyone from Alexander Woollcott to Eva Le Gallienne to Theresa Helburn to F.P.A.—conscious that in their eyes he was a nobody, or at best just another of Aline's young protégés. Specially painful had been his introduction to Helen Arthur and Agnes Morgan, the business manager and stage director of the Neighborhood Playhouse. Shortly before his trip abroad he had been visiting friends in Pleasantville where Miss Arthur and Miss Morgan had a cottage, and one evening they had returned from New York to find a manuscript wedged inside their door. It was the version of *Mannerhouse* subsequently stolen in Paris, and the accompanying note asked them for an opinion on its suitability for production. They quickly saw its hopelessness as a play, but because the writing showed promise, they typed out their comments and left them at the house where Wolfe was staying. Next evening, on their return from the city, they were greeted by a note which said, "Mesdames: Thank you for nothing. I didn't ask for criticism—I asked for a production. I am going abroad to write more plays, and when I return, my foot, like Caesar's, will be on your neck."

Meeting Wolfe at last, Helen Arthur—a sparrow of a woman—gazed up at him and said, "Mr. Wolfe, you didn't scare me with your note, but now that I see you I realize it would be quite something if you put your foot on my neck"—which left him blushing and gawking until she set him at ease by drawing him out about his European trip.[4]

Through Aline he had every entrée an aspiring playwright could hope for, but his plays weren't selling. *Welcome to Our City,* resubmitted to the Provincetown Theatre, bounced back, while *Mannerhouse,* which he considered his chef-d'oeuvre, had been rejected first by the Theatre Guild and then by the Neighborhood Playhouse. Aline tried to suggest that his talents might not be suited to the theater. Of course he could write, but she pointed out that only a fraction of a play exists on paper; it couldn't be judged until the actors got up and walked around and spoke their lines. The stage was a corporate enterprise in which one had to adjust to others and heed their criticisms, but Wolfe, a creative autocrat, wanted everything his way. As his hopes waned, he stopped revising his plays and applied his energies to sketches, satires, and reminiscences which no one saw. Discussing his childhood with Aline had brought it vividly to life, and during the spring he made a few notes for a novel which struck her as such a good idea that she offered to stake him to a year abroad while he wrote it.

As he shifted his weight to her, his arrogance towards his family increased. "There are few heroic lives," he had written his mother in January: "about the only one I know a great deal about is my own. This is boastful, perhaps, but as it is also true, I see no cause to deny it. Year after year, in the face of hostility, criticism, misunderstanding, and stupidity, I have been steadfast in my devotion to the high, passionate, and beautiful things of this world." Simultaneously he was telling Koch, "For two years now I have worked and travelled alone, ordering the events of my life as courageously and honestly as I could, compromising for my existence by teaching in order to escape the more odious restraints incurred by demands on my family." He wrote Mrs. Roberts of having been "forced into work for which I had no affection, at the penalty of what talent I had. It may be said that I was not 'forced,' but I insist that money has been held over me like a bludgeon. Recently what little help I have secured from home to eke out my salary (and, I confess, my own lack of economy) has been withdrawn."

The self-pity seems unjustified. To be sure, his mother talked poverty while speculating in real estate both in Asheville and in Florida where she had recently spent her winters, and Tom had waived his patrimony because of his educational expenses, in effect donating his share to the other children. But the fact remained that Julia had financed his graduate work without reimbursement to herself, had sent him money when he couldn't make ends meet on his N.Y.U. salary, and had paid for a large part of his year abroad. Why, in any case, should he have expected his family to go on helping him? Hemingway and Fitzgerald, driven by similar ambitions, had been self-supporting from the time they were twenty-one. By comparison Wolfe seemed pampered, and yet there was something admirable in his self-conceit and the obeisance he demanded to his extraordinary though still unproven powers. The artist, after all, must believe in himself before anyone else can.

In letters to his mother he had mentioned Aline, and Julia wrote back that he was fortunate indeed to have found "a financial friend —I trust she has the beautiful character you speak of & there is no mistake." She counselled him to be wary of women "except a young loving girl—or a truly generous Christian woman, that has a young man's interest at heart." Mrs. Roberts, in whom he had confided the affair, was afraid of the consequences and urged him to break it off, but he replied that he had no intention of striking love in the face and driving away the only comfort and security he had ever known. The soft, enfolding type of female he would have liked for a mother, Aline Bernstein differed from Julia Wolfe somewhat as a pillow differs from a table edge.

After completing his year at N.Y.U., he drove South with a hard-drinking acquaintance who later committed suicide, and when he wrote Aline that they had parted ways in Baltimore, she answered that "it was a relief to know you are no longer with your wild companion. You are my wild companion and I hope you will always be so. The way I care for you is like a cube root. It just multiplies in every direction." From Norfolk he wrote her, "I am sleeping, you observe, 'Where life is safe' [the slogan on the hotel stationery] and have spent part of the day in a series of parleys, debates, and refusals with one of the negro bellboys, who wants to sell me a pint of corn whisky, a quart of gin, and a girl 'who's jest beginnin' at it'— all reasonably priced. . . . Here, in this dying town, the drear abomination of desolation, I spent a summer of my youth eight years ago, gaunt from hunger and wasted for love, and I saw the ships and the men go out, the buttons, the tinsel and the braid. But my heart has ticked out madder time; the dogs have howled too long for the men who will come no more; and a great deal of blood has gone under the bridge. (Are you moved, girl?)"

Proceeding on to Asheville, Wolfe found his family preoccupied with the real-estate slump, and after he left he wrote his mother of "the spiritual sea which separates our lives. . . . I believe we are worshipping different gods, but if we can't understand, let us try to be loyal."

He sailed for Europe June 23rd on the *Berengaria*. Aline had preceded him and they met in Paris. As a warm-up for his novel he filled a notebook with early memories which rose before his eyes with the sudden splendor of a volcanic isle. The middle of July he and Aline went to England where she had theatrical business to attend to, he meanwhile completing a second notebook of reminiscences (the two together made up the Autobiographical Outline from which *Look Homeward, Angel* would evolve). Late that month they visited the lake country, where he began his novel in earnest. Sitting on a hillside near Ilkley, he wrote the opening lines in one of the legal-sized ledgers which Aline had bought him for the purpose. She was sketching the landscape, and suddenly he turned to her and said he was going to be a great writer and that long after her death people would know about her because she would be "entombed in his work."

At Ambleside Aline ran into Theresa Helburn and her husband, who invited her and Wolfe on a day's excursion in their rented Rolls-Royce. Aline wasn't sure how Wolfe would react; he was jealous of her friendships in the theater, and she feared he might sulk and withdraw into that vast interior region of his. But no—the golden weather and the luxurious car in which he could stretch his limbs appealed to him, and he obligingly sat in front with the chauffeur while Aline occupied the back with her friends. After lunching at Windermere, they slid through valleys dark as twilight and up hills that overlooked silver lakes, reaching Grasmere in time for tea which they had in sight of Dove Cottage, once the home of William and Dorothy Wordsworth and later of Thomas De Quincey. Naturally their conversation centered on the poets, and as Wolfe warmed to his favorite subject, his face took on the exaltation of a young god.

Years later, describing him as he appeared that afternoon, Aline
stressed the fateful opposition of eyes and mouth. "The eyes were
not beautiful," she said, disagreeing with most observers, "they were
brown, and flat and cold in expression, in the eyes was the coldness that balanced his passions, and checked his excesses, and saved
him." But the mouth "was magnificent, the most expressive feature
[Aline] had ever seen; . . . the upper lip was thin and firm and
echoed faintly the coldness of the eyes, the lower lip was enormously full, with an outward thrust, and held the look and the
promise of all his passions, all his violence, all the voracious appetites that fed his mighty nature, and all the beauty and sweetness
as well." And the mouth was in command that day. When Theresa
Helburn and her husband had gone, tears started from Wolfe's eyes
because Aline, he said, cared for her successful friends more than
she cared for him and was impatient to return to her life in New
York. He begged her never to stop loving him, and in what she
remembered as the happiest moment of her life, she promised she
never would.

From Ambleside they went to Glasgow, then back to London
whence Aline sailed for America August 19th, leaving Wolfe to
wrestle with his book. In one of his texts at Chapel Hill he had
marked a passage in Horace's ninth ode: "Many brave men lived
before Agamemnon: but all of them, unlamented and unknown,
are overwhelmed with endless obscurity because they were destitute
of a sacred bard. Valour, uncelebrated, differs but little from coward-
ice when in the grave." Wolfe saw himself in this bardlike role,
vanquishing death and oblivion with timeless words. Aiming at
universality, he had written his Workshop plays on large, objective
themes—the race question, the decay of the Old South, the boosterism of the Twenties—but his kind of objectivity presupposed an intense subjectivity. "Are you not an artist?" he had written in his
notes. "Then begin with your own life."[5] And again: "It is not for
us to write 'why' across the firmament and to try and answer it. It is
rather for us to write 'why' across the scroll of our being, and there
to answer the question we have raised."[6]

The creative life is often a groping, a terrible stumbling until the
artist finds himself doing what his subconscious has demanded all
along. For Wolfe the turning point occurred that summer of 1926

when he dropped through the trap door of his past and came to grips with the dark thing in him, with the tragic vision brewed in childhood and consciously cultivated at Harvard, though not expressible in the theater. Yet who is to say that his theatrical apprenticeship had been wasted? The years of frustration and yearning had widened and deepened him and given his pent-up emotions an explosive force.

After Aline's departure he found lodgings in Chelsea: a bedroom and a sitting room with a cupboard for tea things, and a large table to write on, and shelves that were soon populated with the second-hand books he was always acquiring. Each morning he worked for four or five hours, and during his afternoon rambles the novel went on flowering in his mind. Lying awake at night with hands folded behind his head, he would hear the footbeat of the bobby pass his window and remember that he had been born in North Carolina and wonder why he was all alone in a London flat. With a hollow feeling he would switch on the light and read what he had written that day, asking himself once more, "Why am I here? Why have I come?" But there were moments of exaltation as his book gathered momentum and took on a life of its own. Doing 3,000 words a day, he wrote a friend that his novel would be "Dickensian or Meredithian in length" and that the cutting—"which means, of course, adding an additional 50,000 words"—would come later.

In mid-September he went to Belgium for two weeks, taking his ledgers with him and continuing his daily stint. Always reborn when travelling, he wrote Aline that his life was assuming "the remote and lovely quality it had when I was wandering before—I seem to be the phantom in a world of people; or the only person in a world of phantoms—it's all the same." On a bus from Brussels to Waterloo he recognized James Joyce, with whom he had shaken hands that summer in a darkened hallway when Aline had gone to see him on business. But now Wolfe shied away from the awesome, fastidious Irishman with the black patch over one eye under his rimless spectacles. During a guided tour of the battlefield he fell into conversation with Joyce's son who did not, however, invite Wolfe to join him and his sister and his parents when the party stopped at a café.

Seated at a nearby table, Wolfe listened to the Joyces conversing in French and felt they were observing him—"the great man himself," he afterwards wrote Aline, "taking an occasional crafty shot at me with his good eye." Wolfe liked Joyce's "highly colored, slightly concave" face with its thin mouth, "not delicate but extraordinarily humorous" and its "large powerful straight nose—redder than his face [and] somewhat pitted with scars and boils." Joyce had an air of niceness and simplicity, although driving back to Brussels he got a bit stagey, Wolfe thought; "draping his overcoat poetically around his shoulders," he sat on the front seat cross-examining the driver. Wolfe could not know that Joyce had made the trip to Waterloo to gather material for *Finnegans Wake*.

Lounging in the rear of the almost empty bus, Wolfe crooned to himself and made idiot noises of delight to think that he should be travelling with the author of *Ulysses*, a smuggled copy of which had fallen into his hands at Harvard. He had been thrilled by its iconoclasm, its technical innovations, and its delicate, discriminating word-magic, and he felt a kinship with this proud and lonely writer exhuming his past in self-imposed exile, bringing all Dublin to life as Wolfe hoped to bring Asheville, elevating the common experience to the dignity of myth, and weaving human destinies into a tapestry so wide that it took the sting out of death and decay.[7]

Back in London, Wolfe grew tired of his isolation and moved to Oxford because he knew one of the Rhodes scholars. He lived in a country house up an avenue of trees flanked by rugby fields, where in the afternoons tousled, red-cheeked players with scurfed knees swayed and scrambled and filled the damp air with their cries. His book was going well; for the first time in his life he felt that he was hurling his strength at a definite object. By November 8th he had done 100,000 words, already a fair-sized novel, and the end was not in sight. "I have somehow recovered innocency—" he wrote Aline, "I have written it almost with a child's heart: the thing has come from me with a child's wonder, and my pages are engraved not only with what is simple and plain but with monstrous evil, as if the devil were speaking with a child's tongue. The great fish, those sealed with evil, horribly incandescent, hoary with elvish light, have swum upwards."

Aline's letters bemoaned their separation. Though she prided herself on her ability to turn away from things that hurt her, her present sorrow she could only take close and press to her inmost self. As she thought back over the summer, a few moments stood out like lightning flashes: a night at York when she had watched Wolfe in his sleep and had felt such a premonition of doom that she dared not put out her hand to touch him; Wolfe in a pub at Ambleside, radiating affection for the shepherds and their dogs; their parting at the station in London—she had never seen him so pale, nor known him to be so tender and considerate. Sometimes she spoke his name aloud and stretched her arms out to him, and only the knowledge that he would hate it prevented her, when she wrote him, from staining the paper with her blood or enclosing a lock of hair. When the phone rang, her heart leapt at the thought that it might be he come home on one of his wild impulses—except that if it were he, the phone wouldn't just ring, it would peal ecstatic chimes.

The only time she forgot him was when she had to concentrate on her work, and the moment she finished he was back again. She lived for the evenings when she no longer had to talk or make arrangements and could shut herself up with her thoughts. Until he returned she would have preferred not to raise a finger, except to get a pass to meet him at the boat, but she went on with her stage designing out of habit. With an ocean between them, she lived in perpetual anxiety lest he drink too much, or drift around the continent and never return, or take up with another woman despite his vows. He had always wanted to be loved, and now that he was she suspected it didn't wholly please him. "The thing that constantly torments me is that how on earth we can have any life together, with all these years between. If it were not for that, I know you would not allow us to be separated even now."

Wolfe's letters brought more heartache than joy, ending too often in what she called "a hellish dance on paper about my unfaithfulness." He pointed out that despite their absorption in each other she had terminated her summer on schedule, going back to New York not a day or a steamer late—to which she replied that her other commitments had required it, and besides she had sensed that he wanted to be alone. He said their affair was costing her nothing, that she kept her two lives separate, enjoying the best of each, but as for him, "Why, God's wounds, His liver and His guts,

I have torn my accursed heart away from its moorings, I have ladled it up to you with smoking blood; I have unspun my entrails, counted my slow pulses, distilled my brain for you. . . . I gave you the ticking minutes of my life," he rumbled on in his father's rhetoric, "and all of it never weighed as much as a pair of ruffled drawers, a wig, a flowered waistcoat for your man Carrol [the star of the play Aline was working on]." It was all very well for Aline to speak of spending his birthday in seclusion, but what of the other days when she "jigged wantonly with [her] retinue?" "Does it please you to be a romantic figure—to look mysterious grief? Think what a light you will throw with that when my successor comes. Or when he came." Aline assured him that with her he would have no successor, but going to bed at night he imagined the simultaneous occurrences across the ocean—"darkness drops, the revelry begins, the flashing lights blaze on the sky, and women, fatal, false, silken, soft-breasted, cushion-bellied women, awake to lust."

Sometimes he apologized for his "abominable ravings" but he sent them nevertheless, determined that Aline should know him for the "half-monster" he was. Part of his resentment sprang from his ob-scurity—his life, as he put it, having grown "sick and thwarted for lack of a hearing." It also rankled him to be living off Aline, who said they would get the book done without further assistance from his family. When she mildly suggested that after his novel he might consider going back to his plays, he lashed out at her, "Good God, can you not have kindliness and decency enough to refrain from writing me about them again, with slobbering generalities about 'going on,' 'eventually,' 'wonderful writing.' Must I be depressed and nauseated helplessly when I'm trying to forget them in something else?" He was so insecure that he didn't hesitate to remind her of her race, addressing her as "Jew," "my dear Jew," and even "my grey-haired Jew." Her only comeback was to regret there wasn't a Jewish nunnery she could enter. "We would wear dark-brown velvet habits, with gold and ivory rosaries, and sleep on the best mattresses. But nuns, nevertheless." She felt as chaste as a young girl, and was saying her prayers at night for the first time since she was seventeen.

By November she was begging him to return. From her stand-point, correspondence was a poor substitute for being together, though it gave him the satisfaction and release of a sub-literary exercise. He wrote that he was putting on weight—"I swing heavily along now with a man's stride—the racing, thin boy who leaped into the air is gone; but through all this gathering flesh, this growing heaviness, I exult to see the faun's face shining yet—the ancient eternal morning madness that grows wilder, younger as my body ages." Youth in others bored him, however; he dreamed no longer of maenads but of "Helen and Demeter moving their rich bodies in the ripening fields." That was the way he thought of Aline, his "autumn home." "At the time of life's heat my rich fidelity to you, my grey-haired, wide-hipped, timeless mother."

He was keeping the faith, as he constantly reminded her in letters and cables. GOING BELGIUM SPOTLESS DEAREST and MONASTIC ORDERS LONELY WORKING she understood, but WORKING CONTINENT DECEMBER DEAREST gave her pause. Did it mean he was faithful and returning in December, or did it mean he was visiting the European continent that month? It meant the latter; feeling stale, he had decided to refresh himself with a trip to Germany. The end of November found him in Paris among "the hating and hated French" with their smiles "thin and furtive as snakes" and their "horrible nervous pettiness" all too evident in the way they drove—"swarming, honking, tooting along the narrow streets and two-foot sidewalks, while the heavy busses beetle past."[8]

His father's origins had given him a warm spot for Germany, and he felt instantly at home when he reached the frontier at Strasbourg, where he remained several days, gorging himself on dark beer and goose-liver pie. On the train crossing the Rhine, he rushed from one side of his compartment to the other, looking down at the river and exclaiming, "I have fooled you, you swine!"—for he sometimes imagined that he was being hunted, thwarted, checked. The Germans were friendly, and he refused to believe that their heartiness and bonhommie was part of a malevolent plot to dominate the world. As the Bavarian hills and woods and gabled toyland villages rushed past the train window, he had a mystical sense of their sounding in him and of his giving them a life they never had before.

At the Hofbrauhaus in Munich he came up against a phenomenon he would be pondering for the rest of his days. "In this vast smoky room," he wrote Aline, "there were seated around tables 1200 or

1500 people of the lower middle classes. The place was a mighty dynamo of sound. The floors and tables were wet with beer slop; the waitresses were peasant women with smooth hard kindly old faces —the beer slopped from their foaming mugs as they rushed through this maelstrom. A choir of drunken voices sang beyond the doors —women and men—ugly and hearty, swaying towards each other in a thousand natural powerful mug-lifted postures, as they do in Teniers. The place was one enormous sea-slop of beer, power, Teutonic masculine energy and vitality. It was like watching some tremendous yeast unfolding from its own bowels—it was the core, heart, entrails of their strength—the thing unfolding and unpremeditated that cannot be stopped or stoppered."

"Head-and-heart tired" but "loaded to the lips," he felt the time had come to go home and wind up his book. He returned by way of Switzerland and sailed from Cherbourg December 22nd. He and Aline exchanged Christmas messages by radio, but in one of the pocket notebooks he had begun keeping that summer he registered his ambivalence: "What rut of life with the Jew now? Is this a beginning or a final ending? Get the book done." When the *Majestic* docked at 8 A.M. on December 29th and Aline saw him on the deck, she began jumping up and down at the end of the pier. After their long separation the first hours together were like a dream, but next day Wolfe found himself coming back to reality in the wine-cold air of New York.

"Reality," of course, being only a manner of speaking in the America of the moment. With the Boom nearing its peak, 1927 was a year of marvels and sensations, of the first trans-Atlantic telephone call and the first nationwide hookup. Lindbergh flashed across the heavens, and Calvin Coolidge startled the nation with, "I do not choose to run." Sacco and Vanzetti went to the electric chair, Peaches and Daddy Browning filled the papers with prurient exposé, and Tunney out-pointed Dempsey in their rematch before a record crowd of a hundred and fifty thousand. *Rio Rita* was the Broadway hit, and Clara Bow, the "It" girl, dominated the movies, which that year began to talk. None of it, however—save the final agonies of Sacco and Vanzetti—made much impression on Wolfe, who was living in his novel and in the Asheville of a bygone day.

Turning down a $2,200 instructorship at N.Y.U. (that door, he knew, would always be open), he moved back to the Eighth Street loft and buried himself in his work. He was trying to rediscover language "in its primitive sinews—like the young man, Conrad—Joyce gets it at times in *Ulysses*,"[9] and build his book with a new kind of brick. Huddled in a blanket after the heat went off, whipping himself on with noxious coffee of his own brewing, he sometimes wrote till his garret trembled with the first milk wagons rattling past in the dawn. He seemed to function best in the small hours when the real world went ghostly and his imagined one peopled the dark. "In my experience," he later observed, "the period of darkness brought with it first, during the early hours of the night, a sense of weariness, confusion, sterility and horror, then a sense of growing triumph, assurance, and elation, and finally a state of exultant wakefulness in which my energy purred softly like a mighty dynamo and my spirit brooded with a sense of demonic ecstasy over all the earth."[10] The moist smell of the glycerine, Vicks, pneumonia cure, and mentholatum which permeated the Old Kentucky Home assailed his nostrils as though he were living there. Out of the stillness came his father's voice at the foot of the stairs before breakfast, commanding the damned rascals to crawl out of bed before the roof fell in. When spring came and he opened his window to its soft airs, the back yards of Woodfin Street rose before his eyes in tangible seas of bloom.

He was seeing hardly anyone save Aline. Touchy about her financial aid (it was her own money, she insisted, her theatrical earnings), he lived frugally and apart. Once she got him into a tuxedo and took him to a party for Carl Van Vechten, Elinor Wylie, and William Rose Benét, but he instantly disliked these celebrities and managed to insult all three before the evening was over. His closest companion, next to Aline, was a young painter named Olin Dows (Joel Pierce in *Of Time and the River*), whom he had come to know at Harvard as a result of Olin's enthusiasm for the Workshop production of *Welcome to Our City*. This gaunt, engaging ascetic four years younger than Wolfe was in mild yet obstinate rebellion against his plutocratic origins. He displayed a veneration for Wolfe's talent and a belief in his star which was the sine qua non of a friendship with him before he arrived.

ALINE

Wanting to seem like everyone else, Olin had affected poverty at Harvard, so that when Wolfe first visited the Dows in Rhinebeck the spring of 1924, he had been flabbergasted by their two-thousand-acre estate. He had gaped at the green-uniformed footman who opened the door, as if to say, "What manner of man is this, and where does he fit in?" and when Olin's mother descended the stairs in a tea gown, he had looked at her as if she came out of a pumpkin. He had returned several times since, and in June, 1927, when the loft grew uncomfortably hot, Olin persuaded him to spend three weeks in their gatekeeper's lodge, where Wolfe lived alone and worked as much as he pleased, stepping out the door at night to watch "the moon-blaze and wink, the herring glamor, the dancing scallop fires" of the nearby Hudson. Word having gotten around that one of Olin's bohemian friends was visiting him, the neighboring gentry included him in their parties. Thus he spent the evening of July 4th at the Vincent Astors, watching them shoot off a small fortune in fireworks.

Too big for a petty envy of riches, Wolfe couldn't help wishing he had the freedom and security of these people to speed him into the one aristocracy that mattered—that of artistic achievement. In human terms he wasn't overly impressed; indeed as he surveyed the guests on the Astors' lawn that Fourth of July, he felt a surge of pride for his own family. These Rhinebeck swells were interchangeable with thousands of their kind, while the Wolfes with their meanness and vulgarity and dignity and mad authority were like no one else on earth. Thus he accepted the Dows' hospitality without obsequiousness, as if it were his due, although at their dinner table his mussed hair and the spots on his clothes and his general awkwardness made him seem a little like a harvest hand at a polite gathering. Once he was talking so hard that he hadn't begun to eat when the dishes were passed again, and without interrupting himself he heaped seconds on top of his firsts.

During the visit to Rhinebeck Aline wrote him about an afternoon she had spent cleaning out the loft. Under the debris on the floor she had found two of her love letters which she tore up—hurt that he should treat them so lightly. She was put out not to have heard from him during his absence, but in a postscript so faint he could

111

barely read it, she asked, "Would you like to go to Europe with me?" and fainter still: "Vienna, Prague, Budapest."

Indeed he would! With his novel nearly completed, or so he thought, he was ready for a lark. Shortly before their departure July 11th, he looked up a college friend interning in a New York maternity hospital, and was persuaded to watch a husky Irishwoman give birth to an eight-pound boy. Every time she screamed Wolfe screwed up his face and clenched his teeth, but he found it a thrilling spectacle. "Come on, momma!" said the intern in charge. "Do your stuff now! Give us some help, momma! Push! Push! Do you want to have this baby or not? It's your kid, momma, not mine!" At last the little skull began to emerge and then the body, and when the intern held the infant up by his heels and spanked him to make him yell, Wolfe could restrain himself no longer. He gave a yell of his own and said, "Come on, baby! Come on!"—much to everyone's amusement. He wrote Mabel that the experience had made a great music in him and that something gathered in his throat when he thought of all the pain and wonder that little life must come to know. "I hope to God those feet will never walk as lonely a road as mine have walked and I hope its heart will never beat as mine has at times under a smothering weight of weariness, grief, and horror; nor its brain be damned and haunted by the thousand furies and nightmare shapes that walk through mine. This is no sentiment —but the stark truth, from a very deep place in me."

Abroad with Aline, he added Vienna, Prague, and Nuremberg to his collection of cities, and staying on in Paris after she went home, he visited a brothel—the first evidence of his being unfaithful to her. Back in America he resumed his teaching at N.Y.U. on a schedule that gave him four consecutive days free of classes. A favorite of Homer Watt, the head of the department who had originally hired him, he enjoyed preferential treatment, taking leave of absence whenever he felt like it and coming back to a schedule adapted to his needs. "Papa" Watt, a burly, bustling Scot with great admiration for the creative temperament, believed in hiring would-be writers to teach composition, and Wolfe wasn't the only prima donna on the staff, though Watt's vicarious pleasure in Wolfe's escapades caused him to be spoken of as the departmental wild oat. Playing up to Watt's Villonesque conception of him, Wolfe seasoned his letters from abroad with glimpses of flophouses, workingmen's dance halls, and disreputable pubs. Once he had written Watt on the notepaper of a Paris *brasserie,* "used, generally, I believe, by young men and women naming a time and place" which was "no reason why it should not Serve a Worthier Purpose."

Struggling to finish his book, he resented more than ever the drain of teaching, but he threw himself into it wholeheartedly, for it wasn't in his nature to do things by halves. That year he had mostly night classes, and his students, fatigued by their day's work in sweatshop, bank, or market, would snap out of their lethargy at the blast of his entrance. Coming in with a rush, Wolfe would unpack his briefcase and immediately start pacing to and fro at the front of the room, passionately absorbed in whatever he was expounding. His approach was serious and workmanlike, with no monkeyshines or playing to the gallery. Inadvertently getting a laugh, he would join in if he saw occasion for mirth, and if not, he would shrug it off. His moods were paradoxical and rapidly changing. At times he seemed so fey that one wouldn't have been surprised to notice faun's ears sprouting from the disproportionately small and delicate head above the high, broad shoulders, and the next moment he would be ranting like an Elizabethan tosspot, spraying the front-row students as he literally frothed at the mouth. His spluttering, stammering earnestness—the hesitation of someone with more on his mind than he can articulate—was reassuring proof that though he might have three brains, like other mortals he only had one tongue. Reading his favorite passages aloud, he forgot where he was and went on after the bell, above the shuffling of feet and gathering of papers, until checked by the incoming class. His constant aim was to get at the emotion behind a piece of literature and evoke an honest response. Once when he referred to Tennyson's "As Through the Land at Eve We Went" as a rather slight poem, a student somewhat older than the rest raised his hand and said, "Mr. Wolfe, may I suggest that those who have lost a child would not consider it a slight poem?" The comment was clearly inspired by personal experience, and after a moment's reflection Wolfe said with deep sincerity, "You're absolutely right."

In October he and Aline, feeling more flush now that he was on salary, rented a commodious, second-floor apartment with a bath at

263 West Eleventh Street. (Heretofore, he had taken his showers at friends' apartments or at the Harvard Club where he often stopped to read and write letters and collect his mail.) Aline used the front room as her studio, while Wolfe occupied the rear one overlooking a small garden. Here, pushing himself to exhaustion, he finished the novel late in March. For twenty months he had written it with mounting confidence and joy, and the result seemed to him a strange, deep, unique picture of American life. His first act on reaching the goal was to send Watt his resignation. He thanked his chief for his many kindnesses, adding that on his side he had tried to give faithful service and was proud of having missed only one class in three years. Nor had he ever put a grade on a paper without venturing a few lines of honest criticism. But now the time had come to devote his whole energy to his chosen work, and if his novel failed to get published, he planned to support himself by some form of writing. (Lately, he had been investigating the possibilities in radio, movies, and advertising.) He knew he was taking a chance, but he thought one could afford to gamble once or twice in his life to gain his heart's desire. "The most reckless people, I believe, are those who never gamble at all."

His next problem was the marketing of his 350,000-word behemoth, whose title, *O Lost*, had been drawn from its tag line, "O lost, and by the wind grieved, ghost, come back again." Aline, having read it and found it good, took it to Boni & Liveright where she knew the managing editor. After keeping it five weeks, they declined it, for despite its quality and originality they were loath to publish yet another young man's autobiography, especially such a long one. The legal adviser of Harcourt, Brace, the next friend of Aline's to read it, had a similar reaction: though he recognized in *O Lost* the pulse and energy of the real thing, he doubted that any publisher would have the patience to remedy its excesses.

Meanwhile Aline had given the manuscript to the Irish savant and critic, Ernest Boyd, who passed it on to his wife, Madeleine, then starting out as a literary agent. Dismayed by its bulk, this lusty, strident Frenchwoman put off looking at it for several weeks, but once she got into it she was unable to tear herself away. At the end of twelve hours' consecutive reading, she rushed out in the hall of her apartment house, shouting, "A genius! I have discovered a genius!" Her first meeting with Wolfe a few days later confirmed this view. Instead of the small aristocratic hands of the Irish literati she had met through her husband, Wolfe had the monumental hands of a sculptor, together with the flowing hair of a musician and the dark, dreaming eyes of a poet. He seemed to her no ordinary mortal but someone living on another plane entirely.

Warmed by her enthusiasm, he was only too glad to have her undertake the placing of his manuscript. She sent it first to Longmans, Green, & Co. and then to the enterprising young firm of Covici-Friede, both of whom declined it, although Covici-Friede asked for an option on Wolfe's next book, saying they would publish it if he held it to a reasonable length. He had started a second novel which he called *The River People*, based on his experiences in Rhinebeck with an interweaving of European motifs. He felt whipped, and yet when he went abroad towards the end of June after a brief visit to Asheville, he wasn't devoid of hope. If his second book was accepted, perhaps someone would publish the first, which at least was in professional hands.

Paradoxically, though Aline had been doing everything she could to help him, their relations had deteriorated to the breaking point. The tension of completing his novel and the anguish of having it rejected had brought Wolfe to the edge of nervous collapse, and he had had to prime himself with liquor to be able to face his classes, meanwhile taking out his bitterness and frustration on Aline. They had always known how to make the fur fly, but where their previous battles had been spiced with histrionic enjoyment (Aline, after all, was a professional actor's daughter and Wolfe the son of a rollicking amateur), now they were fighting for keeps. On the one hand, Wolfe was insanely jealous. He was haunted by the words of a troublemaking acquaintance of Aline's who had told him at the start of the affair, "She *likes* young men—I'm sorry but that's the way it is." He couldn't bear to have another man show interest in her, and in recent months had so far forgotten himself as to phone her late at night to see if she was home or out on some "bawdy mission," as he called it. And yet, on the other hand, he resented being tied to a woman old enough to be his mother. He hadn't planned to marry till he was thirty-five or so, after possessing hundreds of women all over the globe. Aline knew he was bringing girls to their apartment in her absence, and once when he invited two of them for dinner along with another N.Y.U. instructor, she showed up as if to make a scene, but he quieted her and sent her away.

In June he told her point-blank that he wanted his freedom, and when she preceded him to Europe with Theresa Helburn, it was understood that they weren't to meet there. Knowing the sadness of coming away from a foreign mail window empty-handed, Wolfe asked half a dozen friends to write him—an unnecessary precaution, for once he and Aline had separated they were in constant touch. Oddly enough, his letters were the most devoted he had ever written her. Confessing his shabby treatment of her, he called her his "great Star," his "other loneliness," and "the only clasp of hand and heart" he had found "in the enormous dark." When he visited Beethoven's house in Bonn and saw his earhorns, he was reminded of Aline's deafness and her "lovely *listening* quality," as though she were hearing music somewhere within. At a prehistoric museum in Mainz he was touched by a female skeleton in a stone coffin, the wife of some Bronze Age chieftain—by "her small head, her little gleaming teeth, her straight and delicate bones. . . . And around the small straight bones of her forearm, there was a round heavy bracelet of bronze, and around her neck a heavy bronze ring that made me think at once of the ornaments you wear. As I stood there I felt the eternity of love—the Romans had gone, the Vandals had gone; but these two people had defeated time and death. . . . I thought of you, and I knew then that my love for you was the most enduring thing in my life, and would hover above our bones when the great towers of America are forgotten, and the great chain rusts about your neckbone."

He had never sounded so loving, and yet his words seemed rhetorical and strained at times, as if the idea of her meant more to him than the reality. "You are the most precious thing in my life, but you are imprisoned in a jungle of thorns, and I cannot come near you without bleeding." When he spoke of seeing her again, it was in terms of loving *friendship* (the platonic implications chilled her), and he sidestepped her suggestion that they meet in Berlin before she went home in August. From the boat she wrote him bitterly that he thought only of himself and finding his way. "It is sad to think that in all your letters you dismiss my condition by saying I will be all right because I have work to do. I would dearly love to see once that you wished to comfort me and hold me near to you." From his accounts of his frantic sight-seeing and careless misadventures, she gathered that he had done little about his new book, and it angered her that he should let his talent go to seed. "I wonder if you know what you do," she concluded her letter. "Take care of yourself, and be faithful to your own goodness, and don't for God's sake waste everything as you have me."

For two months he wandered through France, Belgium, and the Rhineland, drinking it all in: art, architecture, plays, scenery, people, parades, markets, bars, bookshops. On a guided tour of Frankfort he once more encountered James Joyce, who motioned him to take the adjoining seat in a crowded bus, but again nothing was said. After visiting Goethe's house and the Town Hall where Wolfe and Joyce bowed each other through the doors, the tour disbanded, and Wolfe told Joyce he was going back to the Old Town. When Joyce said he thought he would also "get lost there for a while," Wolfe was too shy to ask his company, so they walked in the same direction down opposite sides of the street, Wolfe peering into shop windows and observing Joyce from the corner of his eye.

In September he went to Munich for the annual fair, or *Oktoberfest*, which began the end of the month. At this Teutonic Coney Island in the Theresien Fields on the city's edge, there were merry-go-rounds, entertainment booths, innumerable sausage shops, sheds where whole oxen were roasted on the spit, and—the feature attraction—vast beerhalls which dispensed liter mugs of double-strength October beer. When the revellers stood on chairs around their tables with arms linked and swayed to the blare of a Bavarian band in that "great smoky hell of beer," they seemed to Wolfe to embody "the essence of the race—the nature of the beast that makes him so different from the other beasts a few miles over the borders." It was uncanny and a little sinister. Prejudiced though he was in their favor, Wolfe had felt a disquieting brutality in the Germans from almost his first contact with them.

Like many big, shambling men conscious of their power and bulk, he was naturally gentle, though he loved prize fights. He had seen Dempsey axe down the bull-like Firpo, describing it later as less an athletic contest than "a burning point in time, a kind of concentration of our total energies, of the blind velocity of the period, cruel, ruthless, savage, swift, bewildering as America." A favorite pastime of his Harvard days had been the fights at Mechanics Hall, where he would go wild with excitement, pummelling those around him when someone was batted to the floor. Imagining that he was the beaten man, he would see himself rising time and again, though blind and mutilated, till the look of him horrified his opponent. Now at the Munich fair, quite unexpectedly, his dreams of valiance were put to the test.

As he was leaving a beerhall one night with seven or eight liters under his belt, a man standing in the aisle addressed him in a friendly manner and held him by the arm as he started to move on. More in a spirit of exuberance than of irritation, Wolfe knocked him over a table and ran exultantly from the hall, feeling like a child who has thrown a stone through a window. He was too drunk to run very fast, and by mistake he took a side entrance which led to an enclosure at the rear of the building. It was raining outside, and behind him he heard shouts. Looking back, he saw several men pursuing him, one of them brandishing a folded chair. Too wild for fear, he closed with them and went down in a sea of mud. The heavy bodies on top of him snarled and grunted and smashed at his face and back until wearily he rose up under them as out of quicksand, only to slip and go down in an ocean of mud that seemed to be choking him—though what was really blinding and choking him was the blood streaming from his head wounds. Breaking free at last, he flailed at the dark forms, wanting only to end it, to kill or be killed. At one point he was conscious of a woman clawing his face and screaming, *"Lassen sie mein Mann stehen!"*—"Leave my man alone!" Then the police intervened and hustled him off to the station, where he was found to have a broken nose.

He spent the next six days in the hospital. All his hair was shaved off, and when he emerged he covered his baldness with a black skull cap such as the students wore after duels. It made people stare at him and whisper, and a waiter who asked him very respectfully whether he had been in a sword fight was visibly disappointed when Wolfe told him the truth. The middle of the month he went to Vienna where he got a cable from Aline saying that Scribners was interested in his book, but it failed to excite him. Hurt by the general indifference to *O Lost,* he was trying not to think about it and had begun to wonder if he weren't just another self-deluded aesthete with nothing to contribute. A week later he heard from Madeleine Boyd about Scribners; she hoped he would take no action except through her. He answered that she could depend on his sticking closer than glue, yet he doubted that anything would come of it when he pushed on to Budapest early in November. In the village of Mezö-Kövesd on a sodden, steaming plain a hundred miles beyond Budapest (the furthest east he would ever travel), the children giggled at him but saw nothing comic in the men with "their embroidered aprons and their ridiculous derby hats stuck straight off their heads" or in the bewildering costumes of the women, though "any one of these people," he wrote Aline, "would have stopped the traffic in New York." Back in Vienna the middle of the month, he found a letter from Scribners' editor Maxwell Perkins—the name meant so little to him that he called him "Mr. Peters" in a letter to Aline—expressing admiration for his book and asking to see him as soon as possible. Wolfe answered that the praise was worth its weight in diamonds, but instead of rushing home as one might have expected, he spent the next month loafing through Italy and sailed from Naples December 22nd.

"Never has the many-ness and the much-ness of things caused me such trouble as in the past six months," he wrote in his pocket note-book during the voyage. "But never have I had so firm a conviction that our lives can live upon only a few things, that we must find them, and begin to build our fences." As he lay in the hospital after the *Oktoberfest* brawl, his thoughts had reverted to Aline, whose love then seemed his only support. Lately he had written her of resuming their old relationship and of his contrite desire to make it work. "I am yours forever," she answered joyously. ". . . No one exists for me in my heart but you. . . . I don't know what you want but I am here for you. You write now that you are coming back to make something of your life, you said you were going away to make something of your life. The thing to do is to do it, and no one can do it but yourself. There are plenty of places in the world to get your head cracked and your nose broken if that is what you are after, but why? Isn't once enough, or did you like the way it tasted? As soon as you come back, we will sum up what you want and what you can do, and for once in your life make a plan and see where you stand. You are too good to waste. We will hold together."

Wolfe landed New Year's Eve with twenty-seven cents in his pocket, and the morning after New Year's he phoned Perkins, who told him to come right over. He was entering the orbit of one of the most remarkable men this nation has produced.

6 · ARRIVAL

MAXWELL EVARTS PERKINS was an aristocrat not only born and bred but of mind, heart, and instinct. Proud of his Yankee forebears who had served their country with distinction, he was showing a like devotion to honor, duty, and standards of excellence in his chosen field, the republic of letters.

His life-long friend Van Wyck Brooks once said of him that he knew few Americans in whom so much of the nation's history was palpably and visibly embodied. Perkins' great great grandfather, Roger Sherman, had signed the Declaration of Independence for Connecticut, while William Maxwell Evarts—the grandfather for whom he was named—was a United States Senator who had been Attorney General under Andrew Johnson and Secretary of State under Hayes.[1] Max's other grandfather, Charles Callaghan Perkins, had infused an aesthetic strain. A descendant of prosperous and philanthropic Boston merchants, this friend of Browning, Motley, Landor, Lowell, and Longfellow was an authority on Italian sculpture and painting,[2] and his cultivation had rubbed off on his son Edward, Max's father, who had lived abroad until he was twelve. To keep up his French, Edward Perkins read to his children—translating as he went along—such works as General Marbot's *Memoirs* and Erckmann-Chatrian's *A Conscript of 1813*, thus launching Max on his worship of Napoleon. For Max was addicted to heroes: Shelley and Napoleon in his youth and later Mark Twain and Jefferson and General Grant.

Born September 20, 1884, the second in a family of four boys and two girls, Max was brought up in Plainfield, New Jersey, a short commute from New York where his father practiced law. His earliest memory was of Grandmother Evarts leaning over the foot of his bed and chuckling when he had the measles; having produced twelve children of her own, she was used to seeing small boys lying swollen and spotty. He also retained an indelible impression of the cook calling him into the kitchen one morning where he saw a little man about a foot high dancing in a shaft of sunlight in an awkward, crippled way. When he was four and his brother Edward five, the family decided that these two mustn't miss the opportunity of seeing Washington while Grandfather Evarts was still in office. After an exciting journey on the *Royal Blue*, the boys were disappointed by their grandfather's speech in the Senate, for he looked and talked just as he always did, and they fidgeted so much and kicked the balcony so loudly that they had to be taken out. But next day they had an unforgettable experience. They were playing in their grandfather's drawing room off the front hall when the doorbell rang, and rather than face the visitor they hid under a table. The door opened on a spare, erect man whose tightly buttoned frock coat emphasized his angularity. Greeting him warmly, Max's Aunt Mary told him the Senator was out and added, "General Sherman, if you have a minute I'd like you to meet my sister Betty's two boys." She peered into the drawing room. "Edward! Maxwell! Now where can they have gone?"

The brothers began to giggle, and spying them under the table, William Tecumseh Sherman stooped down and said, "If you two young rascals don't come out of there, I'll send for one of my big guns and blow you out." So they emerged and shook hands with that terrible annihilator, and looking up at Sherman's close-cut white beard, Max was reminded of the pin feathers on a chicken. Then he listened, entranced, while Sherman went on to tell Aunt Mary about some magnificent new ordnance the Army had just acquired. Back in Plainfield, Max named a lead soldier "General Sherman." A few years later, as he was going to bed one evening, the phone rang and there were excited voices and his mother came in to say that General Sherman was dead, and Max felt very sorry about it during the five minutes before he went to sleep.[3]

As a rule Max spent his summers at the family seat in Windsor, Vermont,[4] where Grandfather Evarts had bought several houses and a large tract of land. From his earliest days Max loved this trim New England village almost in the shadow of Mt. Ascutney, which he thought the most beautiful mountain in the world, with the most beautiful name. (Later, he wanted to name one of his daughters Ascutney but was overruled.) In Windsor he found an outlet for his adventurous streak, jumping on and off the freights as they rounded the bend and rolling logs with the lumberjacks in the Connecticut River. When Theodore Roosevelt's sons came to visit, Max looked down on them for being afraid to dive off the boathouse roof.

At St. Paul's School in New Hampshire, he was known for his impishness. On one occasion he and another boy ran the elevator up and down with everyone chasing it, and Max didn't mind his punishment of a long walk around the pond, since hiking was his favorite pastime. Senior year he was taken out of St. Paul's and sent to day school in Plainfield, and that fall when his father died of pneumonia, leaving the family in financial straits, Max's fundamental seriousness and responsibility began to assert itself. Of all the children it was he who seemed most concerned with their mother's plight. She continued their father's practice of reading morning prayers, and once when she broke down and couldn't go on, there was enormous comfort in the way Max went over to her and put his arm around her without saying a word.

But he still had plenty of hell in him. As Van Wyck Brooks has analyzed it, Perkins was part romantic, insouciant Cavalier and part grim Roundhead who believed in living against the grain and doing things the hard way, and during his freshman year at Harvard the Cavalier predominated. He joined a raffish club, neglected his studies, and spent a night in jail when he tried to prevent a cop from arresting a tipsy companion. (Their cellmate was a sad Negro who kept repeating, "I'm in great trouble" as he worked his way through Max's supply of Richmond Straight Cut cigarettes.) After nearly flunking out at mid-years, the conscientious, disciplined Max took hold and his marks rose to respectability. Though he much preferred literature courses, he majored in economics because his New England conscience told him that medicine ought to taste bad to do him any good. However, in pieces for *The Advocate*, the Harvard literary magazine he helped to edit, the Cavalier struck back. "On Taking Things Easy" stressed the advantage of taking things easy, just as "On Getting Up in the Morning" sympathized with the desire to stay in bed and "On Bluffing" praised the ingenuity of the bluffer. Writing was already a passion with him, though his essentially critical and reflective nature inclined him towards essays rather than fiction.[5]

On the social side, Max, without being a snob, had an element of exclusiveness in his make-up. He went around with the right men, dressed carefully and inconspicuously, and despite his limited budget was able to join a final club, the Fox, as well as the Signet, which he found more congenial because of its intellectual bias. There the lunch-table discussions centered on books, the theater, and ideas in general, without much attention to politics and economics; Socialism did not strike the campus until a few years later with the generation of John Reed and Walter Lippmann. Also in the Signet were John Hall Wheelock, the poet who later became Perkins' colleague at Scribners, and Van Wyck Brooks, genially shy and already writing about American literature. These two had found their direction while Perkins was still groping, yet his kindly, unobtrusive intelligence commanded respect. Firm without being hard and serious without being heavy, he had a rapt Shelleyan quality; his pointed observations were often accompanied by a quizzical smile and a momentary brightening of his vivid, blue eyes. Fair-haired, straight-nosed, smooth-limbed, and slender, he brought to mind the statues of Antinoüs, immortalized by Hadrian, though he seemed a bit uneasy with his classic perfection of form and face, as if he didn't want to be noticed for mere looks. Girls, on the whole, found him courteous, reticent, and charmingly indifferent.

As a Harvard senior, his future remained uncertain, but the Evarts ambition was already stirring. He used to talk to John Hall Wheelock about his dream of becoming President by literary means: starting as a reporter he would gain control of a newspaper or a publishing house and use it as his political springboard. It would have been natural for him to enter the law, which had attracted the men of his family for several generations, yet something in his nature resisted the mold. After his graduation in June, 1907, he worked for several months in a Boston settlement house and then became a reporter for *The New York Times*.

He loved the job with its Richard Harding Davis glamor and unending surprises. Now he was on the trail of a murder in Chinatown—now listening to William Jennings Bryan weave his spell in Madison Square Garden.[6] During his third year on *The Times* he fell in love with a Plainfield girl—pretty, artistic Louise Saunders who wanted to be an actress. Four years younger than Max, she had been aware of him from the time she was a little girl, when the Perkinses had sat several pews ahead of the Saunderses in church. Studying the brothers from behind, she had decided in favor of Max because his black stockings were always neatly pulled up and because once she had seen him lift his head and gaze at the blue ceiling with the silver stars as though even then he were wondering what could possibly be understood. It wasn't till much later that *he* became aware of *her*. Then one of the first things to delight him was her reply when he asked her to return his pajamas which he had left behind while visiting her family at the shore. Unable to find them, she sent him a man's bathing suit that had turned up with the comment, "Here are your pajamas—I'm afraid they have suffered a sea-change into something rich and strange." Max and Louise were married December 31, 1910.

Ambitious as ever, without knowing where he was headed, Max had told Louise that he would like to be a little dwarf on the shoulder of a great general, advising him what to do and what not to do without anyone's noticing. Before his marriage he had left *The Times* to become advertising manager at Scribners, for much as he enjoyed reporting he felt that the irregular hours would be hard on his family. Duty triumphed again during the First World War when he wanted to volunteer and stayed home with his dependents, but the Mexican border crisis the previous year had given him a taste of adventure which he cherished for the rest of his life. Called up with the New Jersey National Guard, he spent several months as a cavalryman in Douglas, Arizona, and though the hoped-for battle with Pancho Villa failed to materialize, Perkins delighted in the masculine solidarity of camp routine.[7]

Meanwhile his star had been rising at Scribners. When he transferred to the editorial department after four years in advertising, he knew at once that he had found his métier, and before long he was made a director and secretary of the corporation. His fine-bred, New England (by way of New Jersey) conservatism seemed perfectly adapted to this genteel, tradition-encrusted house which had been under the management of the same family since its founding in 1846. A citadel of good taste, Scribners published not only Henry James, Edith Wharton, and Thomas Nelson Page but Meredith, Stevenson, and Barrie in an age when Americans still looked to England for literary guidance. Theodore Roosevelt, one of the firm's most lucrative "properties," was thought by most of the staff to be too radical a politician, while Galsworthy, their spokesman for the younger generation, was deemed a bit subversive, although sound at heart. It is safe to say that prior to 1920, when the rockets began to go off in its sedate offices at 597 Fifth Avenue, Scribners had never published a line that would cause a schoolgirl to blush. By this time Perkins was for all intents and purposes executive editor, though he still deferred to venerable, stately William Crary Brownell, dean of American critics and the firm's "literary adviser." Yet Perkins had a comparatively free hand at this critical juncture in American letters, for the renaissance heralded by such "realists" as Dreiser, Anderson, and Sandburg had gained momentum with the war. A new energy, a new freedom, a new tempo had widened the range of artistic possibilities, and his latent daring now asserting itself, Perkins felt it his mission to seek out the young, indigenous talents and bring them together with their public.

This phase of his career began with Scott Fitzgerald's *This Side of Paradise,* an early version of which Perkins had ruefully declined in 1918. At Fitzgerald's request he had sent it to several other publishers, hoping they too would reject it, for he recognized its extraordinary merit and believed it could be rewritten into an important work, as indeed it was the year following. Even so, Perkins had trouble getting Scribners to accept it. Charles Scribner II, the head of the firm, was proud of his imprint and reluctant to bestow it on a book which he considered frivolous, while the Olympian Brownell couldn't stomach Fitzgerald's flappers at all. When Perkins met the boyish author, he thought to himself, "Hang it, he's too attractive!" Fitzgerald's blond, incisive good looks were coupled with an improvising charm and grace that made others seem like old ginger ale, and Perkins feared an inordinate personal acclaim that might distract him from his work. In any event *This Side of Paradise*, published the spring of 1920, gloriously vindicated Perkins' belief. Overnight it made Fitzgerald the spokesman of the younger generation and proved to be the first rolling stone in a literary landslide for Scribners.

Several years later, when Perkins brought forward a book of stories by Ring Lardner which Fitzgerald had helped to collect, he ran into similar opposition among his colleagues. To them Lardner was a mere sports reporter, another Perkins roughneck like the ex-marine Tom Boyd, whose combat novel *Through the Wheat* had nevertheless won comparison with *The Red Badge of Courage*. Lardner's *How to Write Short Stories* caused a similar stir, the critics hailing his hitherto scattered and neglected work as that of a master. In 1924 Fitzgerald began writing Perkins from Europe about a young American named Ernest Hemingway who had achieved an underground repute with his pieces in the little magazines. "I'd look him up right away," said Fitzgerald, "he's the real thing," and Perkins had only to inspect Hemingway's first book of stories, *In Our Time*, to know that Fitzgerald was right. Yet when Perkins received the manuscript of *The Sun Also Rises*, there ensued a stormy editorial conference. Charles Scribner thought it a vulgar novel, not only in its use of four-letter words but in the turpitude of its heroine; he had always felt that a woman should at least have some affection for the men she went to bed with. Perkins countered that a publisher's first allegiance was to talent and that *The Sun Also Rises* showed more talent than he had seen in a long time. If Scribners didn't print it, they might as well go out of business; they couldn't maintain themselves forever on Galsworthy, Theodore Roosevelt, and Thomas Nelson Page. Besides, Hemingway had agreed to eliminate some of the words which Mr. Scribner found objectionable.[8] Asked which ones, Perkins jotted them down on a slip and handed them to his chief who said with a twinkle, "Max, if Hemingway knew you didn't dare pronounce these words, he'd disown you." In the end Scribners published *The Sun*, which quickly became a classic of expatriate life. The youth in his mid-twenties who had minted its trenchant, economical prose was already a legend, and when they met Perkins was charmed by Hemingway—this big, bluff, barrel-chested bully-boy and *beau garçon* with the wide, irresistible grin and the passion for boxing, bullfighting, and above all war, of which he spoke with the authority of one who has been blooded.

Perkins, of course, had many irons in the fire. He had gathered around him a wide diversity of talents, having found what he was looking for in the ex-cowboy Will James no less than in James Boyd, author of *Drums*, who rode to the hounds. One of his coups had been the former art critic, Willard Huntington Wright, who as "S.S. Van Dine" was breaking sales records for detective fiction with his Philo Vance series. But Hemingway and Fitzgerald remained in a sense his favorites—these young, high-mettled, supremely gifted artists, either of whom, he felt, might one day write *the* novel about America. (Fitzgerald's virtuoso performance in *The Great Gatsby* augured well.) With his deep ancestral stake in this country, Perkins hoped to play a part in seeing it revealed as Tolstoy had revealed Russia in *War and Peace*—for Perkins, the masterpiece of all time.

The influence of a great editor, like that of a great teacher, is a subtle, atmospheric thing not easily defined, but with Perkins the root of it was his integrity. Meeting him, you knew right off that here was a man incapable of a cheap or shabby act and one you could trust forever. His respect for others followed naturally from his deep self-respect (not to be confused with self-regard or conceit), and he gave his authors a sense of caring as much about their work as they did. Besides which, he had an uncanny knack of putting himself in their places and visualizing their problems from the inside, for Perkins was essentially an artist whose medium was the writing of other men. Like an artist, he trusted his instincts and shied away from the prescribed or formularized, even to the point of discouraging advance summaries of novels lest they fetter the author's imagination.

His criticism, as a rule so keen and unerring, was offered tentatively, obliquely, half-reluctantly; as one writer described it, asking Perkins for advice was like dropping pebbles down a well and listening for the splash. "Don't *ever* defer to my judgment," he wrote Fitzgerald early in their relationship, his humility before the creative act rivalling that of Rilke who said that with nothing so little as with critical words can one touch works of art, mysterious existences whose life endures while ours passes away. And yet for all his identification with the artist, Perkins was no visionary but a hard-headed realist with a sound grasp of the business end of publishing and a shrewdness about what would click and what wouldn't. Having, moreover, the complete confidence of his chief, he was able to push through the books he believed in. No one would think of contradicting Mr. Scribner, a stern old gentleman who ruled his kingdom like a benevolent despot, but when they disagreed, Perkins would, as he put it, "lean a little," and next day he leaned a little more, and in the end he got his way.

Or rather what the welfare of Scribners required, for Perkins was that rarity, a truly disinterested man, who gave the impression of being in touch with ultimate justice. He wanted nothing for himself, hardly ever took a vacation, and brought home a loaded briefcase each weekend, his one interest outside of his profession being his family. Eager for sons, he had produced five daughters (after the fifth he had wired his mother, ANOTHER), yet he was an affectionate, even a doting, parent who treated his daughters more like younger sisters. Still boyish in middle age, he played cops and robbers and kick the can with them, and on visits to Windsor he took them on hikes to the top of Mt. Ascutney, making them walk for thirty minutes and rest for ten like soldiers on the march.[9] After dinner in the evening he often read aloud to them from the classics, growing annoyed when they asked him to skip the battle scenes in *War and Peace* since those were his favorite parts.

Patient and long-suffering though he was with his authors, at home he could flash a disquieting irritability, and around the office he would go white with anger at laziness or ineptitude, glowering at the offender and shaking his head in wordless disgust. His silences were epic because his work had trained him to listen and because small talk bored him; he never spoke unless he had something to say. In answer to your question he might look at you inscrutably or gaze off into space, and with the flibbertigibbet who tried to draw him out at a dinner party he went completely dead. A mild eccentric, he had taken to wearing his hat in the office, sometimes tipped back reporter-style but more often resting low and level on his long, rather narrow skull. No one knew for certain why he wore it. "I've often wondered," said a fellow editor, asked about it in later years. "I don't think it was a question of a draft on his head." According to one theory, the brim of the hat acted as a sounding board, for he had begun to go a little deaf. Another school maintained that it made him seem about to leave the office, thus enabling him to get rid of the stray callers, friends of friends, and literary cranks who ate up his time.

Whatever its rationale the omnipresent grey fedora symbolized his non-conformity: Perkins had his own unique way of doing things. Walking in the country, for example, he would toss a rock from hand to hand, insisting that this way you exercised your whole body instead of just your legs. With the same daft logic he would argue that honey should be sold in tubes, like toothpaste, and that typewriter paper should come in rolls, like paper towels. He had a somewhat embarrassed belief in phrenology and would tell you that no one with a small nose or a flat back to his head—he was cursed with neither—could possibly amount to anything. Acutely sensitive to personal appearance, he would pronounce someone a fine fellow for no better reason than that he liked the shape of his ears or the cut of his mustache.[10]

Forty-four when Wolfe began to occupy him, Perkins was still classically handsome, his face having gained in gravity and a quality of estrangement with the years. His hair had darkened to light brown with a hint of grey at the sides; and his skin tightly drawn over his high cheekbones, patrician nose, and cleft chin had a faintly weathered look, but his eyes were young—those level blue eyes which Wolfe described as "full of a strange misty light, a kind of far weather of the sea in them"—eyes that took you in dispassionately, as if looking for something, and perhaps hoping for something. A lean, upright five feet nine, he gave little thought to his clothes, though his worn grey suits were of good, conservative cut, and in his bearing there was a touch of elegance, a muted swagger. He often stood meditatively rocking with thumbs hooked in the armholes of his vest, gesturing when he spoke with feminine sensitivity but without effeminacy; and as he strolled about the Scribner offices making inspections and interviewing the heads of the departments, his hands would be clutching his lapels. For one so up on things, he was oddly distrait. An author meeting him for the first time might find Perkins standing helplessly at the entrance of the railed-in reception space, evidently not seeing anyone or anything, until the author made a guess and went up to him. Then Perkins would shake hands indifferently and lead the way back to his cubicle, turning en route as if it had just occurred to him that someone was with him, and what business did he have here anyway? The blue eyes would flash appraisingly, and if he liked what he saw Perkins would give a genial sniff and smile his slender, enigmatic, but enormously reassuring smile, and handing the visitor ahead to his office, he would clasp his lapels and follow behind.

Carlyle, for whom Perkins had an old-fashioned enthusiasm, once wrote: "It is the property of the hero, in every time, in every place, in every situation, that he comes back to reality; that he stands upon things, and not the shows of things." Perkins had never had any trouble recognizing a new reality when he came across it, whether in the guise of a Fitzgerald, a Hemingway, or a Wolfe—writers so different as to be virtually three points of a triangle—and having found his reality he backed it to the hilt. "Looking round on the noisy inanity of the world," Carlyle says again, "words with little meaning, actions with little worth, one loves to reflect on the great Empire of *Silence*. The noble, silent men, scattered here and there, each in his department; silently thinking, silently working; whom no Morning Newspaper makes mention of! They are the salt of the Earth. A country that has none or few of them is in a bad way."

Perkins first heard the name Thomas Wolfe in September, 1928, when Madeleine Boyd, who had come to see him on other business, kept bringing up "a wonderful novel about an American boy" which was seeking a publisher. His curiosity aroused, Perkins asked to see it, and she agreed to send it on condition that he read every word. Although delighted with the opening pages—a description of Eugene's father as a boy watching Lee's ragged horde march on Gettysburg—Perkins was disappointed by the ensuing section about Gant's life before he settled in Altamont. He went back to other matters, delegating the reading to a lieutenant who presently drew his attention to the scene where Ben Gant, the undertaker, and the doctors are conversing in the greasy spoon. Perkins now dropped everything and read straight through the manuscript, knowing when he finished that it had to be published whatever the difficulties, and he anticipated the worst—especially after Wolfe's first letter from abroad which told of having his head bashed and his nose broken at the *Oktoberfest*.

On January 2, 1929, when Perkins glanced up from his desk to see Wolfe's giant frame filling the doorway, he was reminded of Shelley, who also had a disproportionately small head and wild hair and a luminosity of expression. Visibly trembling, Wolfe took off his coat and sat down as this mild-mannered, New England-looking gentleman, with almost no preliminaries, began discussing the scene in *O Lost* where the madam buys a stone angel from Gant for the grave of one of her "girls."

"I know you can't print that," Wolfe broke in. "I'll take it out at once, Mr. Perkins."

"Take it out?" The blue eyes looked offended. "Why, it's one of the greatest short stories I've ever read!"

Perkins said he had been reading it aloud to Hemingway the week before, and he thought *Scribner's Magazine* might buy it, whereupon Wolfe jumped to the conclusion that this little bit was all they wanted, and his heart sank. But then Perkins went on to speak of the book as a whole and of problems arising from its length and lack of coherence, and when Wolfe saw that Perkins was seriously interested, he talked wildly of cutting this and that, only to have Perkins reply in a well-bred half-whisper with a faint rasp to it, "No, no— you must let that stay word for word—that scene is simply magnificent." Referring now to a sheaf of handwritten notes, Perkins went over the manuscript in detail, and for the first time Wolfe felt he was getting criticism he could really use. The parts Perkins suggested cutting or altering were invariably the least interesting and essential, while the parts Wolfe had thought too earthy or profane for publication, Perkins urged him to keep.

At the end of the conference Wolfe was told to go home and think it over, and five days later he came back with an outline of his contemplated revision. When he asked Perkins if he might say something definite about publication to a dear friend—meaning Aline—Perkins smiled and said he thought so, that their minds were practically made up. On his way out of the office Wolfe ran into John Hall Wheelock, the poet who was also a Scribner editor; Wheelock said he hoped Wolfe had a good place to work—"you've got a big job ahead"—and Wolfe reeled out of the building in a drunken glory, knowing that his book would indeed be published. Scribners is at Forty-eighth Street, and when Wolfe came to his senses, he was on One hundred and tenth with no memory of how he had gotten there. He spent the next week in a delirium that reminded him of the Stephen Leacock character "who sprang upon his horse and rode madly off in all directions." He would be sitting in the Harvard Club staring stupidly at the publisher's letter of acceptance, when suddenly he would get the urge to rush outside and walk up Fifth Avenue for miles, pausing now and then to inspect the unsigned contract and the uncashed $450 advance which lived in his breast pocket. On January 12th, having worked off some of his buoyancy in a forty-five-page screed to Mrs. Roberts, he finally got down to work. (Mrs. Roberts, on hearing the news from Fred, had written Tom, "Good Lord, Boy, my heart thrills so I can't think. . . . It had to come, but I never dared to hope that it could come to you *so young*. . . . I should think the stars would just be swarming about you so that they bump into each other, and knock off great swirls of star dust.")

Though Tom and Aline were back together and the prospect of being published had made him easier to live with, he had taken an apartment by himself at 27 West Fifteenth Street, not wanting to merge with her as completely as before. A few years later she would write a story picturing a typical day in this Indian Summer of their love.[11] It is spring, and going to Wolfe's apartment, she finds him sprawled across the bed in trousers, shirt, and shoes, his face spangled with sweat, his hair glistening, his shirt damp. Beside him is a coffee cup whose unmatching saucer overflows with cigarette butts. Scattered about the floor are more butts, sprinklings of ashes, odd socks, a collar or two, several neckties, and myriad books—some open face up, some open face down, some piled together. She kisses him awake, saying, "Your neck is all sweaty, you smell like a little baby out of its nap, you smell like musty books and I love them!" Holding her tight and trying to draw her back into sleep with him, he answers, "You smell like goose grease, all Jews smell like goose grease, but you smell like a flower too, a fresh dewy flower just out of the bathtub."

Wolfe has a lunch date with Perkins, and Aline has bought him a blue polka-dot tie which is "going to make that new blue suit hum, and all the lunch you don't spill on the suit you can sop up with the tie. You tell your friend up on Fifth Avenue that he had better bring an extra fifty cents along to feed the clothes."

Wolfe explains how he happens to be sleeping fully dressed. He had worked till five that morning when two friends from Asheville had turned up with a bottle of corn liquor, and after a few drinks it had seemed only fair to show them his new suit. He had put on the trousers—then one of the friends had phoned his girl, and they had another drink because she was angry. Wolfe had tried to pacify her. "Think of all the girls," he said, "who are never called up at 5:30 A.M., all the girls who are never called up at all! How the hell would you like to be one of those girls?" When his friends had left, he had fallen asleep reading a poem of Herrick's, and opening the volume now with Aline at his side, he says, "Listen to this, my dear, how beautiful, they can't do it any more. That ungainly minister in his country parsonage, writing about a little child, about the little child's faith."

Aline lies very still, transported by his reading, until she remembers his appointment. She tells him to shave and bathe, while she makes his coffee.

"Right you are," he says, springing to life. "You're not right often, but this is one of the occasions. Coffee is the correct word, coffee and no bath. The papers will carry tomorrow morning, 'Mr. Thomas

Wolfe introduced a novel custom for breakfast yesterday. He had coffee and no bath. Mr. Wolfe is the son of Mrs. Julia Wolfe of Asheville, well known in real estate circles.'"

"If you will kindly move your great hulking frame away from the sink," Aline interrupts, "I will fill the kettle and make the first item of the new-style breakfast."

In the midst of shaving at the dish-laden sink, Wolfe cranes around to see what Aline is doing and drips lather on his new pants. The hot water is running, and the stream catching the edge of a plate spurts fine beads down his leg. His mind is a battlefield. He wants to stay and lunch with Aline, he wants to go uptown and lunch with Perkins, he wants to walk uptown, he wants to ride up on the bus, he wants to take a taxi and dash up to the door, he wants to stay home and write, he wants to lie on the bed and hold Aline close to him, he wants to tease and torment her and make her cry, he wants her to go away and leave him alone, he wants to stand by the window and let his soul float out into the infinite, he wants to think about all the books he is going to write, he wants a long drink of gin that is in the closet where Aline won't be likely to see it, he wants to live in everyone's house and find out what they are like.

At the last minute Aline notices that a sleeve of his new jacket reposing on the floor has taken a little drink of coffee from a used saucer, and having cleaned it as best she can, she hustles him out the door only half an hour late for his appointment.

To keep him solvent until his book appeared, Wolfe was working part time at N.Y.U. He had one section of English Composition and was marking papers in a Bible course as well, "the hated teaching now become strangely pleasant," he wrote Mrs. Roberts. Musing on his possible access of fortune, he told the student who was typing the revision of *O Lost*, "I wouldn't know how to spend more than $6,000 a year. I'd like to have ten thousand books. I'd like to spend about a thousand dollars a year for books [and have] a two or three room apartment with a Negro chef about forty years of age—I love to eat, you know. I shall marry at seventy-three. Life is too short to be mixed up in nasty complications with other people. A shack on a sea cliff in summer. Then Europe perhaps once a year, a few months at a time, living liberally. Two thousand dollars is a sufficient sum for that. But it all depends on the success of the book, and if it should fail, it would hurt terribly."

By the end of March he had finished the revision to his satisfaction but not to Scribners', for the manuscript he brought back was only eight pages shorter than the original.[12] His cuts had been virtually nullified by additions, and Perkins realized he must step in or the job would never get done. So began their collaboration; during the next two months they met at Scribners in the evening to decide what should be left out. Though they haggled at times, Wolfe for the most part accepted Perkins' suggestions with good grace, grumbling to friends, however, that "those bastards at Scribners told me they'd publish my book and now they want to tear it to pieces." Once he pounded up the stairs to Madeleine Boyd's fourth-floor apartment bellowing, "Madeleine, they're cutting the balls out of my novel!" and the French hairdresser on the second floor went to Mrs. Boyd wringing his hands and saying, "My ladies, my ladies—they are shocked—can't you do something?"

Legend exaggerates the extent of the editing. In the end eleven hundred typewritten pages were cut to about eight hundred. To give the story the unity of unfolding through Eugene's memories, the father's pre-Altamont existence, which Perkins had found slow going, was omitted, as were Wolfe's digressions on politics, morals, and religion, and the histories of minor characters were thinned. Rambling sequences, such as Eugene's career at the state university, were condensed, and one important transposition was made: Gant's homecoming trolley ride through Altamont was shifted from Part II to Part I for greater impact. Here and there, gutter words were euphemized, and a few of the coarser passages were toned down.[13] But in his original "Note to the Publisher's Reader" accompanying the manuscript, Wolfe had said that it did not seem to him the book was overwritten and that what came out "must come out block by block and not sentence by sentence," and so it occurred. Perkins' editing was chiefly a matter of architecture, of eliminating chunks so as to give harmony and proportion to the whole. He didn't tamper with the actual writing, which in his estimation bore the signature of a great artist. He asked for a better title, however, and Wolfe drew an inspired one from the couplet in "Lycidas"—

ARRIVAL

Look homeward, Angel, now, and melt with ruth.
And, O ye Dolphins, waft the hapless youth.

A month later, when Wolfe visited the Scribner art department to see the first printed sample or "dummy" of his book, the two young women who worked there were non-plussed by the colossus who ducked his head and thrust his shoulders sideways to get through their door, talking all the while in an eager, resonant stammer to Perkins who was leading him along. After the introductions, Wolfe sat down and immediately rose again on hearing an ominous creak. "D-do you mind?" he said. "I th-think I'd better try another chair." When one of the girls pushed forward a substitute of solid oak, he thanked her as if he were being offered a golden throne. His suit was rumpled, there were spots on his tie, and he kept thrusting his fingers through his slicked-down hair, causing it to stand up in oily little anchovies, but his warmth and his delight in the occasion made one forget his peculiarities. When the dummy was brought out—a few printed pages with the blue binding and rainbow-hued wrap of the first edition—his huge hand clamped round it and held it at arm's length. After gazing at it in silence, he said to Perkins, "You know, it's like a m-miracle. Six months ago if anyone had s-said I'd be holding my own book—a *p-printed book* right here in my own hand—I'd have t-told them they were crazy."

Early in June the manuscript went to press, and the last part of July he and Aline took a cottage in Maine where he slept on a porch surrounded by spruce woods, with the ocean lapping twenty-five yards away. He fished off a rotten wharf and walked along the shore road of Boothbay Harbor by moonlight. His days were spent correcting proof, and in the process of making the final version deeper, fuller, and truer to himself, he interpolated so many things that the printer's surcharge came to $700, which by rights he should have paid, but Scribners absorbed it. Now that he was doing the work he loved, his whole life seemed miraculous. A boy from the mountains born in a strange, wild family, he had gone beyond the mountains and known the state, had gone beyond the state and known the nation, had attended its greatest university and worked in its greatest city and travelled beyond the seas. "Because I was penniless and took one ship instead of another," he wrote

137

Wheelock, "I met the great and beautiful friend who has stood by me through all the torture, struggle, and madness of my nature for over three years." And now, to top it all, a fine publisher was bringing out his book, a sample of which appeared in the August issue of *Scribner's Magazine*. "An Angel on the Porch," Gant's interview with the madam which Perkins had admired, was offered as "The first work of a new writer about whom much will be heard this fall." Wolfe expected the story's publication to be accompanied by convulsions of the earth, falling meteors, and a general strike, but a few friends mentioned it and that was all.

In September he went home—his first visit for over two years, his last for eight to come—and as the giant worm of the train twisted through the slashed, red gorges up into the mountain fastness whence he had begun his trek across the world, his feelings were a mixture of fatality and elation. He had made good; he was a credit to his community still blissfully unaware of its impending exposure at his hands. In Asheville everyone was cordial and rooting for his success. He wrote Perkins that in his family "we get one another crazy —I've been here a week and I'm about ready for a padded cell. But no one's to blame." His reluctance to discuss his book made Mabel fear, she later confessed, that it was "one of those boring philosophies or criticisms or a book on the Negro Mulatto subject." She doubted that ten Ashevilleans would read it, even after Tom took her aside to say he had written some things people weren't going to like and that next time he came home it would probably be incognito. But he hoped Mabel would understand and realize that he had tried to do his best.

As an insurance against the oblivion that awaits most first novels, he went on teaching at N.Y.U., for though his heart was "beating a roll-call against [his] ribs," he thought it "just as well, perhaps, to have an anchor that will keep me on earth, unless I go into the balloon service permanently."[14] In his classes he paced back and forth with the same brooding intensity, his eyes blazing when he was moved, which was most of the time. One day he came in exulting that "they've given me a whole window at Scribner's"—referring to the bookstore's display of *Look Homeward, Angel*—and thereafter part of every hour was devoted to behind-the-scenes anecdotes about its reception.

For a man, what can compare to living with a dream and realizing it after long struggle? In Wolfe's case, coming as he did from a comparatively simple, unlettered background, the romance of the printed word intensified the rapture of literary success. Though the first review of *Look Homeward, Angel* in *The New York World* made fun of its "musings over destiny, fate, love, ah me, ah me," the all-important ones in the Sunday *Times* and *Herald Tribune* were such unqualified raves that Perkins ordered a second printing. At which point Wolfe was brought up short by repercussions from home.

Asheville had been reading his book as confession or autobiography, which in a sense it was. In the original version of *O Lost,* the members of his immediate family had been called by their real first names, although before publication all were changed except Ben's, Grover's and W.O.'s—the three who had died. In many cases the names of subordinate characters pointed to their flesh-and-blood counterparts; thus Horace Williams was Vergil Weldon in the novel, French Toms was Tom French, Roy Dock was Guy Doak, and so on. When Perkins had voiced alarm about the family's naked portrayal, Wolfe had said, "But Mr. Perkins, you don't understand—I think these are *great* people who ought to be told about,"[15] and Perkins realized that, in the profound sense, *Look Homeward, Angel* was transcendingly a work of the imagination. He had never had an author who gave such a sense of creating a universe *ex nihilo,* as in the first book of Genesis. More seer than reporter, closer to reality than to actuality, Wolfe couldn't help transmuting everything he touched.[16] "There is scarcely a scene that has its base in literal fact," he had said in the "Note for the Publisher's Reader." "The book is . . . a fiction that grew out of a life completely digested in my spirit, a fiction which telescopes, condenses, and objectifies all the random or incompleted gestures of life—which tries to comprehend people, in short, not by telling what people did, but by what they should have done."[17]

Though his characters invariably took off from persons he had known whose mannerisms were recognizable in the finished portrait, he infused them with his own vitality, and by heightening this trait and suppressing that, he distorted his models in a way that made them truer to the human condition. In this respect he was the source and root of his characters, their lives flowed from him, and the country at large welcomed *Look Homeward, Angel* as a powerful and original work of art. Asheville, however, which had given the potter his clay, reviled it as malicious gossip.

On the street, at clubs, bridge parties, teas, and social gatherings of every kind, *Look Homeward, Angel* was Asheville's major topic in the weeks following its appearance.

"Have you read it?"

"Isn't it awful?"

"Such a terrible thing to write about his own people!"

"He's a mad genius."

"Did you recognize——?"

"Now that Tom mentions it, I remember quite clearly—"

And the person would go on to certify as historical fact some peccadillo which Wolfe had made up out of whole cloth. Soon he was getting anonymous letters which began, "Sir: You are a son of a bitch," and an old lady he had known all his life wrote him that though she had never believed in lynch law, she would do nothing to prevent a mob from dragging his "big, overgrown karkus" across Pack Square. His mother, she said, had taken to her bed white as a ghost and would never rise again.

Actually, Julia was behaving with her usual fortitude. "I don't object," she told Fred and Mabel. "He can paint me up like old Carolina Peavine [a local beggar woman] if he can make a success of his writings." If Julia was hurt, she concealed it and brushed aside those who sought to commiserate with her.

For example, the woman who phoned her and said, "I knew Tom when he was a little boy, and I always liked him."

"Yes," said Julia expectantly.

"And I know you always tried to bring up your family the best you could, but Mrs. Wolfe—"

"Well, thank you," Julia cut in. "It's very nice of you to say that. Tom's doing fine, and we're all well. Goodbye."

Recalling the incident in later years, she would shake her head and laugh. "I knew what she was trying to say, but I tell you, I just didn't give her a chance."

Mabel was less controlled. She felt that Tom had blackened their origins, and she suffered acutely when some of the women at her club cut her because of the book. Presently she rallied, writing Tom that he had put them on the map and that she would sell her ticket to heaven for a little of the recognition he was receiving. Fred, too, when he got over the initial shock, sided with Tom and was able to joke about it in a letter. He said that in the next book he hoped Tom wouldn't write "so damn deeply. *Look Homeward, Angel* gave me a few headaches trying to fathom out Greek Mythology and Egyptology. And don't lose everything. [In] your first Book everything was lost. In the next hope you cry out, Eureka! I have Found it."

Hardest hit of all was Margaret Roberts. Tom had tried to prepare her when, after reading "The Angel on the Porch" in the August *Scribner's,* she had written him that she feared the story would distress his family. Wincing at the rebuke, he had started to answer that her letter seemed false and sentimental to him, that she was being a little too consciously "the fine woman" and that she no longer thought of him as he was, but as the boy she had known. Then he reconsidered, and putting the letter aside, he had written her another saying she was "one of the high people of the earth, with as little of the earth in you as anyone I have ever known—your understanding is for the flame, the spirit, the glory—and in this faith you are profoundly right."[18] But he added that anyone who was offended by what seemed to him "a very simple and unoffending story" would have much stronger feelings when the book came out.

That fall she was suffering from a toxic goiter which almost killed her, and she chanced to be alone in the house when she heard the postman deposit what she knew was *Look Homeward, Angel* inside the screen door. As she went to collect it, her heart was beating so loud and fast that she thought it would leave her body. Joyfully, she took the book back to bed with her, and by chance it fell open at the chapter about the North State Fitting School which she read with mounting anguish. Then, as she laid it aside feeling hurt and helpless, she noticed the inscription: "To Margaret Roberts, who was the Mother of my Spirit, I present this copy of my first book with hope and with devotion. Thomas Wolfe, October 15, 1929."

What pained her most was the portrait of her husband, who had been satirized as a leaden oaf given to inane, whining laughter and to stroking himself and others with chalky fingers—a description which shocked her the more because it had never occurred to her that Wolfe's attitude towards her husband was substantially different from his attitude towards her. When Wolfe had been with them the month before, he had talked congenially with Mr. Roberts and had given her no warning, and now she felt betrayed. The rest of the novel, when she mustered the strength to read it, bore out her first impression of ruthlessness, and although in writing Wolfe she tried to do justice to his artistry, her conclusion was, "You have crucified your family and devastated mine."

He answered with what she later called "a short dear letter," saying he had shown hers to Perkins who pronounced it that of "a splendid person." In February, when some of the dust had settled, he wrote her again trying to meet her objections. He said that the bitterness in his book had been aimed not at individuals but at the structure of life, which seemed to him cruel and tragically wasteful. Angry Ashevilleans were claiming that *Look Homeward, Angel* had been written to pay off old scores, and indeed some of his characterizations may have begun that way. (A friend to whom he had read the early chapters of *O Lost* remembered him pausing to gloat, "His real name is——. Do you know what that son-of-a-bitch did to me once? Well now, just wait till he sees this!") And yet the end product had little to do with revenge or petty malice.[19] As he wrote Mrs. Roberts, "My book was called up from the lost wells and adyts of my childhood—for twenty months that experience blazed and was shaped and fused into a mold of my own creation—my own reality. . . . Do you think that if the reality in my book was only the same reality that walks the streets I would take the trouble of writing at all?"[20]

Mrs. Roberts wanted to send him a more understanding letter, which in her weakened state it took her months to compose. Then, feeling it was inadequate, she didn't mail it and for a long time there was silence between them.

In later years he liked to remember that October, 1929, the turning point of his career, had also been a turning point for the nation, *Look Homeward, Angel*'s publication having coincided with the Wall Street crash. That autumn stock prices stopped rising, indicating that the supply of speculators buying for an increase was exhausted, and since ownership "on margin" now became meaningless, large numbers rushed to sell in a snowballing action that wrecked the market and inaugurated a decade of depression. The economy might be toppling but Wolfe, whose gains during the Boom had been intellectual and spiritual rather than financial, was going on. He was, indeed, just hitting his stride.

Across the nation *Look Homeward, Angel* got superlative reviews, the best of any first novel in several years. The critics compared Wolfe to Whitman, Dostoyevsky, Rabelais, Melville, and Joyce, and Ben's death to that of Madame Bovary. John Chamberlain in *The Bookman* called *Look Homeward, Angel* "a rich, positive grappling with life," adding that "no more sensuous novel has been written in the United States," while *The New Yorker* thought that Wolfe's "exposé of the boy's soul, in all its idealism and obscenity, makes Dreiser's youths seem like Frank Merriwells." Of the personal tributes, none meant more to him than Edwin Greenlaw's. The Renaissance scholar who had taught him at Chapel Hill said the novel didn't contain a shoddy line, and that he would go back to it now and then—"Something I don't do very often with modern books." Fellow authors, that most exacting class of critic, were quick to recognize a new power in their midst. Hugh Walpole, visiting this country, said of Wolfe in an interview, "Let America awake to him, for he has the making of greatness." And James Boyd wrote Perkins, "I have an uneasy feeling that the little fellows had better move over for this bird. But whether I mean the little fellows on Parnassus or on Blackwell's Island I don't yet know. I only know somebody's got to move. And on personal grounds there's no writer I'd rather move over or down for myself. Although there will be no question of volunteering. It will be a case of the brewer's big horses."

Wolfe had never gotten enough mail to satisfy him, and now he was glutted with effusions from remote places. A clergyman in Portage, Wisconsin, thanked him for "breathing on the valley of dry bones" and making them "bloom and dance." A mother in Santa Fe wrote him that in the faraway gaze of her seven-year-old son she recognized the questing spirit that had been frustrated in her and prayed it might carry on. "Why, I do not know because the questing is pain. But that is *life*, the life you have made us feel—inevitable, beautiful, deep-rooted in the past." Wolfe heard from a trainman who had been inspired by *Look Homeward, Angel* to finish his novel called *Sidetrack*, which told of the human wrecks who cling to railroading. (Drawn by the subject, Wolfe met this man and tried unsuccessfully to interest Perkins in his work.) There were invitations from women to come to tea, cocktails, dinner, whatever suited him, sometimes with the polite addendum that he bring Mrs. Wolfe if such there be. An actress wanted to introduce him to a young playwright of her acquaintance. "I'm sure you would find much in common. He has the same *zest* for life that is in you and your *grand* book."

Around New York, Wolfe was a phenomenon. There had never been anything quite like this giant Ariel with the policeman's shoes and the unshorn locks that swirled low on the nape of his neck in a Byronic ringlet or two. His sprawling disarray was appealing in its ingenuousness; so much was happening to him that he simply didn't care whether his tie was straight or his coat and pants matched. When asked to dinner he would dominate the evening with intimate outpourings as wide as the horizon, though he was shy too, and easily hurt, blanching with anger at the supercilious smiles if, for example, he sopped up his gravy with a piece of bread. Like Robert Burns come to Edinburgh from rustic seclusion, he had an unimpeachable sense of his own dignity and worth.

It didn't take him long to weary of the speaking engagements, the autographing parties, the celebrity hounds, and the high-strung women who said they had wept over *Look Homeward, Angel* and wanted to be a part of all that beauty. He complained of the Park Avenue ladies who threw themselves in his arms, but if they hadn't, he would probably have complained of that too. He was clear on one thing, however: that his importance had nothing to do with money or social position or the current brouhaha. He remained immovably centered in his work. *Look Homeward, Angel,* he noted, had taken him "approximately 500 days (and nights) of writing, revising, correcting, with an average of five hours a day of actual composition. From ten to fifteen cups of tea and coffee a day and from 40 to 60 cigarettes, from 6 to eight miles a day walking about the room or up and down the streets of Europe and New York, during which I thought constantly about the book. Months and months of thinking about it from the time of waking until the time of sleeping. I hope to repeat this process about 20 times during my life."[21]

Having lost interest in *The River People* begun the previous year, he was casting about for a subject. Perkins had remarked that he thought a good story could be written about a boy who had never seen his father and who after a series of adventures came across him in some odd situation—Perkins throwing it out casually, for as he later said, "Such a story as I was thinking of could only be written by one of those fairy-tale writers we all publish."[22] It wasn't intended for a serious novelist like Wolfe, who surprised him by answering, "I believe I could do something with that." Wolfe was taking it in the metaphorical sense of that search for a spiritual father—for an all-wise counsellor and friend—which had been his life-long quest.

Perkins himself was the new candidate for this exacting role. In a Christmas letter of gratitude, Wolfe called Perkins "a heroic figure . . . one of the rocks to which my life is anchored." Perkins thought Wolfe's greatest need was to be able to devote full time to writing, and since he wouldn't draw his first royalties until June, 1930, Perkins got him a generous $4,500 advance, on the strength of which he quit teaching in February. In March he was awarded a $2,500 Guggenheim Fellowship and decided to go abroad for a year—a mortal blow to Aline. He had dedicated *Look Homeward, Angel* "To A.B.," and in the copy he inscribed for her on his twenty-ninth birthday, he had said, "At a time when my life seemed desolate, and when I had little faith in myself, I met her. She brought me friendship, material and spiritual relief, and love such as I have never had before." But now that he was launched, she felt him slipping from her grasp. There were accusations, recriminations, and scenes after one of which she wrote him:

"My dear—I hope you will find it in your heart to forgive me. But since you have turned me away from your love, I seem to have lost all control of myself. I know you will say you still love me, and want me to be your dear friend. Try to bear in mind that it is you who are turning from me and not I who go from you. My love swells up and crowds my body and my mind grows desperate with it. I know you are so tired—you will write the best book as soon as you are quiet. Try to bear with me till you go. Tom, you must know this much about people, that a relation such as ours can't be wiped away with words. You are a great person, and just walking out of this does nothing good. You have always talked to me of faithfulness and fidelity. You have always said that I would leave you and stop caring for you first. Well, it's the other way, isn't it? I know I have been pretty trying just now, but it's only since this has happened, I mean since you tell me you will leave me. Try to bring what goodness and greatness you have to bear upon keeping me just now. I hold you in such high and glorious love. Maybe some miracle will happen. Knowing you these years has been a miracle. I can't put you out from the inmost part of me. I will do the best I can to be good before you go, and put no more enemy into my mouth. Never lost myself that way before. But never before have I lost you. —Aline."

Wolfe has described this period in one of his unpublished manuscripts. "Each day when she came to see him now, the little head bent tragically into his arm, the small flower face wept bitterly, bitterly, they held each other tightly; he pressed her to him hard and close, but all he could say was, 'Oh stop, please stop, my dear!' because they knew there was no medicine for their woe, no check against the marching grief of time."[23] The day of his departure, May 10th, she helped him pack, and they stood together in the bow of the ferry going over to Hoboken. It was dusk when they reached the pier. They went straight to his cabin and drank a bottle of champagne he had received as a going-away present, and she gave him an old medal which the painter, Marsden Hartley, had given her. Back on deck they kissed each other tenderly amid the idiot shouting from ship to shore, until it was time to leave and Aline descended the gangway crying.

The *Volendam* blew her whistle and eased out of her slip. The tugs nosed her downriver, and Wolfe was at the railing as she slid past Manhattan under a blazing moon.

7 · TORMENT

"A MAN who strives after great things," wrote Nietzsche, who might have explained Wolfe to Aline better than Wolfe could explain himself, "looks upon everyone he encounters on his way either as a means of advance or as a delay and hinderance—or as a temporary resting place. His peculiar lofty *bounty* to his fellow men is only possible when he attains his elevation and dominates. Impatience and the consciousness of being always condemned to comedy up to that time—for even strife is comedy, and conceals the end, as every means does—spoil all intercourse for him; this kind of man is acquainted with solitude and what is most poisonous in it."

For the moment solitude, or rather the semi-isolation of shipboard, was what Wolfe craved after the turmoil of recent months. The Dutch beer was excellent, and he liked the Dutch themselves with their brittle blue eyes and clean, hearty innocence. He sat at a

147

table with a middle-aged French couple, an old Viennese and his wife, and a young German girl with straw hair, and they laughed a great deal as they drank their wine and compared notes on Europe and America. In the evening when the moon made great pools of light on the water, he strolled the deck and pondered his success, hoping the bad part was behind him—"the ballyhoo, the gush, the trickery, the intrigue, the envy, the hatred, the horrible weariness." He had decided that any writer who was impressed with the kind of notoriety that might come to him in New York, and who tried to serve and justify it, merited the disillusion which most certainly lay in store.

From Boulogne he went directly to Paris where his mail contained a bill for $525 from a New York dentist who had removed several teeth and replaced them with bridgework. He thought it a fantastic overcharge and fired off angry letters in all directions, brooding over it and dramatizing it till it seemed as if the whole world were conspiring to ruin him. A letter from Fred described the latest scandal connected with his book. An Asheville paper had printed a photograph of a stone angel said to be the one which Gant had sold the madam for a prostitute's grave, but Tom, who had invented the episode, knew nothing of this angel; actually it stood over the grave of a prominent Methodist lady, whose outraged family had written the paper demanding a retraction.

In Paris he was pursued by Emily Davies Vanderbilt, a friend of Aline's. This hectic divorcee, the model for Amy Carleton in *You Can't Go Home Again*, showered him with invitations, but he soon lost patience with her and her current escort, a young Frenchman in riding clothes whose "black sheiky hair," he wrote Aline, was "plastered down with 8 ounces of vaseline." This "bad edition of the late Rudolfo Valentino" could "stand on his hands, and cut flips, and pick your pocket without you knowing it. He also jumps from one airplane to another, so he says, and hangs down by one foot." Emily thought him a genius and hoped that he and Tom would come to feel like blood brothers. She tried to persuade Tom to smoke opium with her because "she has some silly idea in her head," he wrote Aline, "[that] she is a terrible 'destructer-ess' who wrecks men's lives etc. I don't think she's ever going to wreck anything, not even herself. There's nothing to wreck—she'll be hanging around this way

20 years from now, trying to fill up her own emptiness with other folks' richness." (A false prophecy: in 1935 Emily Vanderbilt, alone on the New Mexico estate of her estranged husband, would put a bullet through her heart.)

The first week of June, Wolfe shook her by going to Rouen and returning to a different hotel where he holed up to write. Paris had always seemed to him "the most homesick city in the world," and since his arrival he had been filled with unspeakable longing for America. As he later described it, he would be "watching the flash and play of life before me on the Avenue de l'Opéra and suddenly I would remember the iron railing that goes along the boardwalk at Atlantic City. I could see it instantly just the way it was, the heavy iron pipe; its raw, galvanized look; the way the joints fitted together. It was all so vivid and concrete that I could feel my hand upon it and know the exact dimensions, its size and weight and shape. . . . Or again, it would be a bridge, the look of an old iron bridge across an American river, the sound the train makes as it goes across it; the spoke-and-hollow rumble of the ties below; the look of the muddy banks; the slow, thick, yellow wash of an American river; an old flat-bottomed boat half-filled with water stogged in the muddy bank; or it would be, most lonely and haunting of all the sounds I know, the sound of a milk wagon as it entered an American street just at the first gray of the morning, the slow and lonely clapping of the hoof upon the street, the jink of bottles, the sudden rattle of a battered old milk can, the swift and hurried footsteps of the milkman, and again the jink of the bottles, a low word spoken to his horse, and then the great, slow, clopping hoof receding into silence, and then quietness and a bird song rising in the street again."

Out of such recall Wolfe began to weave the chants of his second novel. In the pocket notebooks of this period one finds the seeds of these prose poems in such lines as "Play us a tune on an unbroken spinnet" and "He wakes at morning in a foreign land" and "October had come again, had come again." Not infrequently Wolfe's writing urge began with the sort of ache which in other hands might have become a lyric or an ode. That summer he was soaking himself in the poetic books of the Bible—in Ecclesiastes, Job, and Song of Solomon—and he had finally gotten around to *War and Peace,* which consoled him with its length and its autobiographical underpinning.

"If we are going to worship anything," he wrote Perkins, "let it be something like this. . . . You get the stories of private individuals, particularly of members of Tolstoy's own family, and you get the whole tremendous panorama of nations, and of Russia. This is the way a great writer uses his material, this is the way in which every good work is 'autobiographical.' . . ."

Buried in his writing, he saw hardly anyone during June, his companions when he needed them being two young American couples who lived in a hotel back of the Bibliothèque Nationale. The five of them would sit at the sidewalk café watching the old men with great loads of books totter back and forth across the endless tiers of the Bibliothèque, while other men, young and old, went in and out of the doors of the nearby brothel known as "The House of Nations." Wolfe spent an evening with Michael Arlen, Richard Aldington, and the Irish poet, Thomas MacGreevy, who remembered him as "still a bit country boyishly wide-eyed and certainly trusting and ready to be friendly." At the suggestion of Max Perkins, who liked his chicks to stay together so to speak, Wolfe wrote Scott Fitzgerald, then shuttling back and forth between Paris and Switzerland where his wife was in a sanitarium. "In some occult way—" Perkins was simultaneously writing Fitzgerald, "for he [Wolfe] is so utterly different, and so is his writing, from yours—the appearance of his manuscript here, and of himself, recalled to me your apparition eight or nine years ago. It is because of the extraordinary wealth and variety of talent."

Perkins was hoping that Wolfe might bolster Fitzgerald, who had fallen on evil times. The Crash had been the knell of the irrepressible decade which, in Fitzgerald's words, had "[borne] him up, flattered him and [given] him more money than he had dreamed of, simply for telling people that he felt as they did, that something had to be done with all the nervous energy stored up and unexpended in the War." *The Saturday Evening Post* still paid him top prices for his stories, but he looked down on them as mere potboilers and was stuck in the novel which he had begun in 1925, after publishing *The Great Gatsby*. In recent months his wife's sanity had given way—the doctors called it "schizophrenia"—and since his drinking had long been out of control, he feared he might lose custody of his child. Thus his mood, when he answered Wolfe's note by inviting him to lunch, was something like the embattled wistfulness of Charlie Wales in "Babylon Revisited."

Wolfe and Fitzgerald spent a congenial afternoon and evening together, predisposed in each other's favor by the bond with Perkins, though at one point they hotly disagreed on what it meant to be an American: Wolfe said we were a homesick people who belonged to the earth and the land we came from as much as any race he knew of, while Fitzgerald said we weren't even a country, and that he himself had no feeling for the land. At ten o'clock that night they parted in the Ritz Bar where, according to Wolfe, Fitzgerald "was entirely surrounded by Princeton boys, all nineteen, all drunk, and all half-raw. He was carrying on a spirited conversation with them about why Joe Zinzendorff did not get taken into the Triple-Gazzazza Club: I heard one of the lads say, 'Joe's a good boy, Scotty, but you know he's a fellow that ain't got much background.'—I thought it was time for Wolfe to depart, and I did."

The second week of July he went to Montreux where the balcony of his hotel room looked across fifty yards of flower-embroidered lawn to the brilliant blue of Lake Geneva with the mountains rising steeply on all sides. Occasionally the stillness would be broken by "the fast thrash of the paddles as the lake steamers, white and clean as swans, came into the landing down below, disgorged and took on, and then, with startling speed, were on their way again." Here the chaos which had been gathering within him like a black cloud suddenly burst with hurricane violence, and he abandoned himself to the flood. The words poured out as never before, though he still had nothing which could be called a novel. He wrote of night and darkness in America, of the faces of sleepers in the little towns, of "the hissing glut of tides upon ten thousand miles of coast," of the moonlight beating down on the wilderness and "[filling] the cat's cold eye with blazing yellow." He wrote of "that enfabled rock of life we call the city" and of trains and men in harbors and the traffic of ships.

One evening at the Casino he ran into Fitzgerald who suggested they explore the night life, which proved disappointing until Wolfe began to improvise. Striding along and flailing his arms as he talked, he "found to his amazement," Fitzgerald recollected (it was one of his favorite anecdotes), "that not only could he reach the street wires over his head but that when he pulled them he caused a blackout of Montreux. To the inquiring mind this is something of a discovery, not a thing that happens every day. I had a hard time getting Tom away from there quickly. Windows opened, voices called, there were running footsteps, and still Tom played at his blackout with the casualness of a conductor ringing up fares."[1] Wolfe had asked Fitzgerald not to tell Emily Vanderbilt his whereabouts lest she notify Aline, with whom he had made up his mind to sever relations. And, rightly or wrongly, he held Fitzgerald responsible when soon after their encounter heartrending messages from Aline began to reach him in Montreux.

Living with her family in their newly built house in Armonk, Aline had gotten two letters from Wolfe on his arrival in Paris. He had spoken of visiting their old haunts and of being reminded of her everywhere he went, and he quoted a line of Horace's which she had tacked up in his apartment: "You can change your skies but not your soul." Later there had come a joint postcard from him and Emily Vanderbilt. Then silence.

Since he was planning to bring Aline into his next book, Wolfe had asked her to jot down her recollections of her girlhood. She found it a congenial task and wrote him that she was putting in all sorts of extranea, including descriptions of food which showed "the influence of Thomas Wolfe, early period. . . . First thing you know it will turn into a novel and then I'll have to use it myself." For the rest she gardened, made curtains, waxed floors, and spent a good deal of time just looking at the landscape and wishing she could become a part of it. She had thought of going back to her painting but was unable to concentrate—"All art seems like a terrible pain." Searching for echoes of Wolfe's voice in poems he had read her, she went through *The Home Book of Verse* which reminded her that suffering was no new thing, although Keats' "Ode to Melancholy" made her angry. "Such sentimental nonsense to think we can glut our sorrow on the morning rose. I used to think it was fine until I had this real sorrow. Now the rose I want to trample in the ground with my sorrow. I want them all to wither."

It seemed to her that every day she went through enough torture to last a lifetime. "If only some change would come upon me, something would open up and show me how to become this calm and loving friend you want." She wished it were possible to live back-wards, like a motor in reverse—then she would run it to the point where they had met and switch it off. "Tom," she begged, "if you'll only work and not drink all over Europe there will be at least some justification for your desertion of me. Will you write and tell me about it, tell me you have started? Not just little scraps when you come home late at night but real hours of steady work. Please make a schedule and stick to it. You are blessed with genius."

When the weeks lengthened without hearing from him, she wrote, "My dear, if you have ever valued my love and my friendship, let me know what is the matter. I have been true to you since we first came together, does truth and love deserve this? I know that you think I am considering only myself, I know your side too, I know I am older than you, but you always have said it made no difference." She re-minded him of his birthday less than a year before when he had given her the inscribed copy of *Look Homeward, Angel*. "Time is not a dream, time was when we were not as we are now—I want to know about your book. Since it has taken this to write it, it de-serves to be a great one. Your pen writes with my blood. I trust it is more expressive than ink or lead pencil. But still I love you and I think you love me. And I think that if I could look into your face, it would be well."

Her pleading only increased his determination to break away. "My life is divided between just two things—" he had written Perkins on his arrival in Montreux, "thought of my book, and thought of an event in my life which is now, *objectively,* finished. I do not write any more to anyone concerned in that event—I received several letters, but since none have come for some time I assume no more will come." Though Aline's psychological hold on him was deeper than he realized, she no longer held him physically, and now that he was writing about her he viewed her with clinical detachment. About this time he drafted a questionnaire which mercifully he never sent her, though it gives an idea of the kind of grilling she must have been subjected to. In it he asked for a minute description of her feelings when stage designing, giving birth to a child, making love. He asked about her previous affairs, especially the one with the painter, George Bellows. "Why did he stop being your lover? Why did you love him to begin with? Did you feel grief when he died?

What sort of man was he? Tell me why you thought he died because he could not be a great artist. Give me some idea of it. Why did you tell me the name of George Bellows but not the name of any other lovers? Was it because he was the most celebrated man who had been your lover?"

Shortly after the meeting with Fitzgerald came a cable from Aline: ARE YOU ALL RIGHT. LET ME KNOW AT ONCE. OTHERWISE SAILING TO FIND YOU. The threat threw him into a frenzy, and when a friend of Madeleine Boyd's came to see him, he suspected the young man of being an informer of Aline's. "This woman of course is behind it," he wrote in his notebook. "She wrecked me, maddened me, and *betrayed* my love constantly, but she will not leave me alone now." He went on a binge and stormed back to his hotel at 2 A.M., where he pounded on the doors and rushed up and down the corridors cursing, singing, and howling with laughter. Next day he moved to Geneva, and in a chastened mood he wired Aline, LET'S HELP EACH OTHER. BE FAIR. REMEMBER I AM ALONE. LETTER FOLLOWS. He wrote her that though he would never forget their years together which nothing in the future could equal, his only concern was his work and she too must give herself to her work and her family. When she answered that she wanted no future without him in it, at least as a friend, he let it drop. By now another matter was upsetting him.

In July *Look Homeward, Angel* had been published in England and well received, the influential *Times Literary Supplement* praising Wolfe's "great talent, so hard, so sensual, so unsentimental, so easily comprehending and describing every sordidness of the flesh and spirit, so proudly rising to the heights." Wolfe had asked his editor at Heinemann not to send him any reviews since he was hard at work and they would distract him, but the editor sent some anyway, assuring Wolfe that he had nothing to fear. He read them with jubilation, and then received a second batch which contained a panning by novelist-critic, Frank Swinnerton. "Amid the squalor of a disagreeable family life," wrote Swinnerton, "[Wolfe] suddenly begins crying 'O this' and 'O that,' as if he were parodying the Greek Anthology as a last resort. . . . It is emotional without feeling, crowded with violences and blasphemies, and to one reader it appears incoherent, not from strength or intensity, but from overexcited verbosity." On the heels of the Swinnerton came a still more acid attack in *The London Observer* which Wolfe chanced to see in Geneva. The reviewer claimed to be unable "to form the remotest conception of what *Look Homeward, Angel* is about, though I have been humbly gnawing at it for weeks. There is an untidy American family which, for the six hundred pages already mentioned, manages to continue in a state of almost unbroken excitement about everything and nothing. To scream, to leap, to whine, to roar is for these persons the work of an odd moment: and all their moments are extremely odd. Eugene is the hero, and is perhaps a shade more violently silly than the others."

Though he toughened a little towards the end of his life, Wolfe was pathologically sensitive to criticism—a defect of his qualities—for his childlike openness and vulnerability, his refusal to callous, was an asset to the artist. The two British attacks overwhelmed him. He wrote John Hall Wheelock that his book had "caused hate and rancor at home, venom and malice among literary tricksters in New York, and mockery and abuse over here. . . . Life is not worth the pounding I have taken from both public and private sources these last two years." In a letter to Perkins he said he would write no more books and asked for a statement on the money owed him by Scribners. In his distress he began wandering again. One morning he packed a suitcase, went to the Geneva airport, and caught the first plane, whose destination happened to be Lyon. High over the Rhone valley he looked down and "saw a little dot shovelling manure in a field and recognized a critic." He had never flown before and wondered why, since it afforded the panoramic sweep and Zeuslike perspective which he constantly sought in his work. After a week in Lyon, he flew to Marseilles, making the following notes in the air or soon after landing:

"We roared right off (I was the only passenger) without turning —the great machine bumped over the ground—bounded heavily— was in the air—we circled the field—almost immediately when you take off, the ground seems 100's of ft. below you—it has that minimized look as if a man would be 2 inches high— Then we roar far up over the hangars and see the little dots there. Then over the Great Rhone valley—The tens of thousands of farms below—the minute cultivation of everything—the bright rich clayey looking strips (perfectly neat) and the strips of green—the poplars, the hedges—the roads straight where they can be like white chalky arteries—and curving elsewhere—over all the enormous fruitful rolling countryside groups of villages—clots of farms—sometimes big towns—the fat rich green reaches right up, is cloven right to, is sewn right on the massed *clean edges* of the rich woods—sometimes below us—sometimes far away the winding snake—the hot, bright, silvern snake of the Rhone that is drinking France down— Then the Alps march in to the left, the East—then the other mountains to the West and valleys below— then the calcareous sub-alps—the chalky buttes and tables with their mass of runt pines, etc.—the rich clay land gets grey and chalky— we still have rich valleys but the color of the land has changed—a sickening lurch and tilt around the corner at Avignon—one pilot pumps furiously—the land rushes towards us at a slant—I think I'm done and see a race course, 1000's of little dots of people, and big stands below— Then we right ourselves and go on down a valley— Almost before I know it, the great hot wink of the sea—the chalk buttes—the blasted rent calcareous mountains—We fly over the sea a little and then land on the grey aridity of Mentigrave."

After several weeks in Marseilles and Provence, he flew back to Geneva to collect his things and found a steadying letter from Perkins, as well as one from Wheelock who claimed to have "some understanding of the excitements, sufferings, and nauseas to which the man who is trying to do the almost impossible is subject. . . . I am not saying that there are no faults in your first book; doubtless there are many which might be pointed out by careful analysis; but these are faults which are the reverse of great qualities, qualities very rare today, such as vigor, profusion, and vitality. . . . Why in God's name should you allow yourself to be cast down by a few unintelligent or prejudiced English reviews? The greatest writers of all periods have been subjected to just this sort of thing but have had the courage and the serenity to come through it and to weigh it for what it is worth, which isn't much."

In Geneva Wolfe once again ran into Fitzgerald who meanwhile had read *Look Homeward, Angel* and had wired Wolfe that he was ENORMOUSLY MOVED AND GRATEFUL. He asked Wolfe to accompany him on a visit to the Gerald Murphys then living in Switzerland, and when Wolfe declined, Fitzgerald accused him of avoiding people because he was afraid of them. Actually Wolfe had decided that

Fitzgerald, unable to work himself, was trying to demoralize others and prevent them also. "I am sorry I ever met him," he wrote a friend; "he has caused me trouble and cost me time; but he has good stuff in him yet." Some months later, when his irritation had cooled, Wolfe would characterize Fitzgerald to Perkins as "a very generous and at heart a very kind and sensitive person, and also a man of talent."[2]

Of course their whole conditioning had been different. Four years older, Fitzgerald belonged to an earlier decade, to the Twenties, which Wolfe from his seat on the sidelines had been accustomed to disparage for its shallow optimism and materialism, its headlong pursuit of pleasure. He had always known that work is freedom and self-indulgence is slavery, that great gifts impose great obligations, while Fitzgerald—this handsome, ruined boy with the undertow of sadness—was having to learn it through hard experience. Still, their viewpoints when they passed each other that summer of 1930—Wolfe on the upgrade, Fitzgerald on the down—were not as far apart as Wolfe imagined. From the start of his joy ride Fitzgerald had sensed that something was wrong. "All the stories that came into my head," he said, looking back, "had a touch of disaster in them—the lovely young creatures of my novels went to ruin, the diamond mountains of my short stories blew up, my millionaires were as beautiful and damned as Thomas Hardy's peasants."

But where the dark Wolfe had been weaned on tragedy and took it as the norm, for the lightsome Fitzgerald it was more of an acquired taste.

From Geneva, Wolfe went to Freiberg in the Black Forest where there was rioting in the streets. In the national election then taking place the Nazis emerged as a major party. The end of September he stopped at Colmar in Alsace Lorraine to see the *Isenheim Alterpiece* of Mathias Grünewald and was overwhelmed by the agony in the contorted body of Christ and "the *sinister gold light* . . . the almost unholy glee" in the faces of the angels. In the graphic arts it was the Teutonic spirit in its various guises that touched him most deeply. He loved what he called "the great, cruel, vulgar Dutch and Flemish paintings"—the Hondecoeter tables loaded with fruit and flesh and fowl, the sunny cows of Cuyp, the deep-bellied goddesses of Rubens, the bawdy taverns of Teniers. He delighted in pictures that "showed men drowning their heads in burst hogsheads, tearing wolfishly at a leg of ham, pouring the contents of a wide-lipped ale jug indiscriminately into a woman's throat and down her neck, while all about the swarming place men fumble in a woman's rich bosom, relieve themselves against a wall (children on the ground), while dogs crawl hungrily to the groaning tables, groups dance drunkenly in a ring, thick-set sweating men rush out of doors with foaming jugs, and in the distance, at a church, a procession winds slowly in to a service."[3] For Wolfe the master of them all was Brueghel, whose canvasses he called "cosmic spectacles. There are a thousand stories in each one, and as you begin to examine them, you see that each story is touched with this superhuman penetration—this unearthly quality." He thought Brueghel "one of the greatest story tellers and dramatists that ever lived," bringing over into paint "a talent that is incredibly like the one Rabelais used in writing."[4]

In October he went to London and rented the top two floors of a house on Ebury Street, complete with a charwoman who "cooks for me, brings her darling tea in his little beddy, coddles and coaxes him, and is in fact a perfect priceless damned Kohinoor." In this atmosphere of order and repose, he settled down to a midnight-to-dawn routine of work, at the end of which he would sit by his window and watch London awaken. He would notice how the light fell on the yellow walls and smoky brick as the milkman came through with his odd cry and the housemaids emerged to scrub the stoops. When November closed in—"lovely London November—soft, wet, woolly, steamy, screamy, shitty November"—he was content to stay in his apartments, brooding and writing. Thanks to his English publisher he got plenty of invitations, but wasn't too keen about drinking weak tea and eating cold lamb by the "cheerful fumes" of a gas burner in parlors "reeking with gravedamp chill."

A year earlier Sinclair Lewis had written him out of the blue to congratulate him on *Look Homeward, Angel.* "It and [A] *Farewell to Arms*," said Lewis, "seem to me to have more spacious power in them than any books for years, American OR foreign." In November Lewis became the first American to win the Nobel Prize for Literature, and in his acceptance speech he named Wolfe as one of a handful of young writers who seemed on the verge of giving America a literature worthy of its size. At a press conference Lewis announced that if Wolfe maintained the standard set by his first book, he had a chance of becoming "the greatest American writer. In fact, I don't see why he should not be one of the greatest of world writers."

Wolfe wrote Lewis his thanks, and Lewis replied that he would be in London that winter and hoped they could get together. When they met early in February, 1931, Wolfe flinched, as so many had before him, at Lewis' appearance. This gaunt, sandy jumping-jack with the puckered mouth, protuberant eyes, and corrugated skin had a death's head ugliness for which he compensated with endless mimicry and horseplay, but Wolfe instantly recognized and liked the honest, brave, tormented spirit behind the mask. Their week together was climaxed by a nightmarish ride in a rented limousine to the country place of a mutual friend, which Wolfe would describe in *You Can't Go Home Again* with fictional embellishments. There he pictures himself as the sober guardian of an exhausted Lewis, when actually both were so drunk on arrival that they had to be helped into the house. During the visit Lewis got sick and Wolfe cleaned up after him, but in the written account he spared the great man this indignity. Later he joked that they had given Lewis the Nobel Prize for the wrong accomplishment, that he had known some pretty fair drinkers in his day in and out of the mountains, and that none could equal "Red."

For once Wolfe was up against a vitality as overpowering as his own and more capricious. Late one night after leaving Lewis at his hotel, Wolfe had made the long journey to Ebury Street and was getting into bed when the phone rang. "Come right back over here," snapped Lewis and hung up. Somewhat in awe of his new friend, Wolfe wearily got dressed and returned to find Lewis entertaining a stranger. "See!" crowed Lewis as Wolfe entered. "Didn't I tell you? Isn't he a big son-of-a-bitch?"

After ten months abroad Wolfe decided to go home and finish off his novel, whose working title was *The October Fair*. He had begun to group his material in loose chapters, one of which he called "Time and the River"—his symbols for memory and change. The much-publicized encomiums of Sinclair Lewis had made him uneasy, and he wrote a friend that if he was going to blaze out in all this glory, he hoped the boys would give him a few more years in which to do it. Not that he was reneging. On the contrary, he was more resolute than ever, his recent reading of Trollope's *Autobiography* having confirmed his view that "tenacity is one of the chief elements of talent—without it there is damned little talent, no matter what they say." He thought the best writers weren't necessarily those with the greatest endowment. Joyce, for instance—"I don't believe he begins to have the natural ease, fluency, and interest of, say, H. G. Wells. But he had an integrity of spirit, a will and a power to work that far surpasses Wells. I don't mean mere manual and quantity work—Wells had plenty of that, he has written a hundred books—but I mean the thing that makes a man do more than his best, to exhaust his ultimate resource. That is the power to work and that cannot be learned—it is a talent and belongs to the spirit."

Unlearnable though it might be, one could court it by avoiding the limelight, and when Wolfe landed on the *Europa* early in March, he headed for the wilds of Brooklyn and took an apartment at 40 Verandah Place.

Forsaking Manhattan symbolized a break not only with the flummery of the "literary life" but with Aline, who now precipitated a crisis. The previous summer, after Wolfe stopped writing, she had gone on sending him pathetic cables, climaxed in the October by LIFE IMPOSSIBLE. NO WORD FROM YOU. ARE YOU WILLING TO ACCEPT CONSEQUENCES. Wolfe did not answer, but thereafter he collected his mail in trepidation, and kept an eye on the obituaries in the New York papers. At one point he was so distraught that he lay in bed for two days, unable to eat or get dressed, and he had begun to fear that Aline was dead and that her embittered friends were keeping him in the dark when he heard of a great success she had had with her sets, and someone who had seen her recently told him she was blooming. In December she resumed the despairing cables, but in January her sister, who had always disapproved of the relationship with Wolfe, looked him up in London and assured him that Aline had never been happier. The sister said Aline's messages should not be taken too seriously; emotional and impulsive, she might think she meant these things when she sent them but she soon regained her equilibrium. Wolfe felt hoodwinked and was doubly irritated when the sister repeated the one really boastful thing he had ever heard Aline say; namely, that she always got what she wanted in the end. "You can 'get your way' with people," he wrote Perkins, "but you cannot 'get your way' with life—she must grow old and die. Also she has failed this time with me."

Whatever her mental state, Aline had been physically unwell during Wolfe's absence. She had suffered from fainting spells and was just recovering from a painful attack of sinus when she read in the paper of his return. Dashed that he should come back without notifying her, she took an overdose of sleeping pills and was rushed to the hospital where she remained for several weeks with an aftermath of pleurisy and pneumonia. When Wolfe heard about it, he wrote her declaring his eternal love but adding that the time of "madness, darkness, [and] passion" was over, and asking instead for her friendship and belief. Aline replied that if she knew he wanted her for only a small part of his life, she would be content, and they went on seeing each other, though now the initiative lay almost entirely with her.

During his time abroad Wolfe had heard much talk of the Depression at home which, far from being checked as the government kept announcing, was about to enter its bleakest phase. After a brief rally early in 1930, the stock market had continued its descent into the abyss. Business was languishing, factories were shutting down, beggars and panhandlers were multiplying, and Hoovervilles (clusters of tarpaper shacks inhabited by the homeless) were springing up in vacant lots on the edge of town. In Asheville the outlandish Boom had ended in an equally spectacular bust. The two principal banks had failed, the mayor had shot himself, and a wave of scandals and investigations had ensued. With virtually all their savings invested in real estate, Wolfe's family was wiped out, and his oldest sister Effie, saddled with seven children and a ne'er-do-well husband, was in dire straits. In September Tom had offered Fred $1,000 to be distributed as he saw fit, and when Fred accepted $500, Tom told him not to worry about paying it back because "one of the greatest pleasures is helping out someone of your own . . . in time of trouble. I don't think it matters so much at other times, you can fight and squabble as much as you damned please when things are rosy, but when trouble comes you stick together."

Meanwhile Tom was settling into the Assyrian quarter of South

Brooklyn where his apartment, on a narrow side street that was almost an alley, consisted of a high-ceilinged bedroom and beneath it a study that opened on a little tree-shaded garden all to himself. In the neighborhood he was soon a familiar figure swinging along with his majestic tread. Sometimes he would pause to accost a truck driver, a hobo, or a policeman without the least trace of self-consciousness or embarrassment. Stopping at a diner for a cup of coffee, he would smile to himself when the counterman wiped his place with a greasy cloth that only made it dirtier, but his sharp, realistic appraisal of the little fellows was touched with poetry too. He could describe an incident down the block or the waitress at a corner stand in terms that exalted others inured to city drabness, and walking the streets with him, as he drank in their life with animal intentness, was an experience in itself. Nothing escaped his restless, flickering glance though part of him stood aloof, forever weaving a fabric of what he saw. He was involved and detached, at once the wide-eyed stranger and the knowing familiar—the artist, in short.

Unwilling as ever to be a sideshow, a mere entertainment piece, he avoided the rich and fashionable who angled to meet him, but was warm and welcoming to chance acquaintances with no axe to grind. There was a quality in his sociability—a lack of reserve, a headlong rapport—that suggested the solitude in which he lived. If he showed up on your doorstep shyly twisting his hat and you asked him in for a drink, he would stay all night if you let him. A friend of this period remembers standing in the hallway with Wolfe for what seemed like several hours; Wolfe had made the move to go, but on his way out something had occurred to him and talking about it he grew more and more excited and wouldn't leave, though intermittently he apologized for keeping his friend awake.

Starved for intimacy, for enduring human contact, he had written his mother, "For the first time in my life I have begun to think of getting married and to wonder if there is some nice girl somewhere who would have me." But a handsome, intelligent young woman he had an affair with that summer ran into difficulty when she tried to steer the relationship to firmer ground. Wolfe wasn't to be relied on; absorbed in his work, he would go for days without phoning, and his idea of marriage was primeval, impossible—a man, a woman, and a child in an updated Garden of Eden. The compromises and adjustments of ordinary life were not for him.

To escape the city heat he spent the first part of August on an island in Casco Bay, and on his return he received a note from Perkins saying he should make every effort to complete his manuscript by the end of September. Perkins knew the danger, in building a reputation, of there being too long a hiatus between books, and his jog brought Wolfe to an instant reckoning. He answered that he couldn't possibly finish the book in a month's time and began to wonder if he would ever finish it. He spoke of the self-doubt that came from living in the public eye and hearing it whispered that other writers were getting ahead of him, and that his next book better be good or he was done for. According to a recent squib in a Boston paper, he had taken half a million words to Maine with him, and Scribners had been telegraphing him their pleas to cut and condense it. It was the kind of exaggeration on which his legend battened, but it drove him to despair. "In spite of my size, appetite, appearance, staying up all night, 500,000 words etc.," he wrote Perkins, "I am not a cheap and sensational person: if there is going to be publicity, why can't it tell the truth—that I work hard and live decently and quietly."

Money was worrying him. He hated pinching pennies, especially where food and drink were concerned, and he felt an obligation towards his family, especially his mother whom he had pledged to support in case of need. *Look Homeward, Angel* had sold well for a first novel—some 15,000 copies—but that was hardly a bonanza. The $5,864.63 which he received from Scribners during the first three years of their association almost exhausted his royalties, and his proceeds from the English edition were less than he had hoped. He could always draw on his advance (Fitzgerald had told him that the way to become really important to your publisher was to owe him large sums of money), but Wolfe believed in delivering the goods before payment. And so to replenish his pocketbook and restore his confidence, it was decided that he should prepare a section of his work in progress for immediate publication in *Scribner's Magazine.*

Across the nation it was a gloomy fall, with seven million unemployed—the figure would presently rise to twelve. Hoover had called for a twenty-million-dollar relief fund "so that each of the unemployed will have $2.50 to squander away during the winter," Wolfe wryly observed. The end of September he was stunned and saddened by the death of Kenneth Raisbeck, whose body was found in a Westport, Connecticut, graveyard. The coroner's first report stated that Raisbeck had died of acute spinal meningitis, but the police were skeptical because of bruises on his throat, bloodstains on his shirt, and other signs of violence. After a second autopsy a new certificate was filed indicating "strangulation homicide" as the probable cause of death. On the fatal day, Raisbeck had been driving by himself from Boston to New York and was last seen near Westport sitting in a parked car with another man, which raised the suspicion of homosexual foul play, though the mystery was never solved.

Since their falling-out six years earlier, Wolfe had avoided Raisbeck who had nevertheless written him a beautiful appreciation of *Look Homeward, Angel,* and subsequently Wolfe had helped get a play of Raisbeck's produced on Broadway.[5] As always death touched a deep chord in Wolfe, whose bitterness was cancelled now by memories of Harvard when he and Raisbeck were young and idealistic and full of hope.

Aline had also had a bad year. In a moment of candor after Wolfe's death, she was to say that falling in love with him had been akin to a Japanese maiden's self-immolating leap into a volcano: she knew it would be fatal but she couldn't resist.[6] For a woman used to getting her way he had the fascination of an indomitable force. She had never wholly possessed him as he possessed her, though she had helped to mold his character and his tastes, had housebroken, tamed, and civilized him—all but the untamable kernel.

Since his return from Europe she had seen him every Thursday in his Brooklyn apartment, and between visits she fought off the temptation to phone by writing him letters full of a piteous and inexhaustible love. "Remember," she said in one of them, "you are perfectly free from me, but remember that I am bound body and soul to you," while in another she signed herself, "your faithful and always loving but dethroned and deposed concubine, Scheherazade Bernstein." Though she confessed the difficulty of holding "the lover Aline in check," all she now asked was the right to look after him. "The wind is blowing like mad here today," she had written him that summer from her hill in Armonk, "and I hope it is blowing over Brooklyn, blowing the heat and the flies and the cobwebs, blowing with puffed cheeks on your forehead and on your eyes, waking you up to work and fulfill your beautiful destiny." She promised to pickle a mackerel for his lunch—"a toothsome and palatable morsel [that] will shoot cool little silver wires to your brain, and stir up words to put on paper." She wished that every day she could cook him a meal "flavored with the richness and delicacy of my feeling. I would design better meals than scenery, and to better purpose."

She took him to see *Grand Hotel* for which she had done the sets, although the only success she cared about was his. Heartsick when he talked wildly of giving up writing and looking for a job, she refused to believe "the thing you keep saying, that something has died within you. A gift like yours does not die, for if it did you would die with it." She granted that as one grew older and lost the fire of youth, he had to dig deeper for his inspiration, but his work profited thereby. Her old teacher, Robert Henri, used to say that if an artist had but one other person to believe in him, he could go on to his conquest through struggle, and she would be that person for Wolfe. She would stand guard while the book flowered within him; she would guide him to the heights so that his soul might sing again, as it had when the *Angel* came from the press. "Today, now," she wrote him, "is the turning point of your life. You can take the hard road, the beautiful road, the road the great men of art have worn with their feet, or you can stroll down the easy path with all the little people. If you are my Tom, the great man who has lived in my mind, you will gather yourself together. It is inconceivable that you can waste yourself."

When Wolfe had broken with her the previous summer, she had torn up the girlhood memories she had written for him, and she didn't feel like rewriting them, but her past was their chief topic of conversation. At times they seemed to be back on the old footing, and then unpredictably he would turn and rend her, calling her maudlin and melodramatic and saying he was ashamed of their relationship. He would ask her why she wasn't home with her family where she belonged, and once he intimated that it might have been better had her suicide attempt been successful. He dismissed her love as nothing but glands, menopause, pathology, and while boasting of his own conquests, he accused her of hideous liaisons with "the corrupt and poisonous vermin of the theater." Thrown down and beaten by his tongue, she tried to understand where she had failed. She knew that at the start she should have given more thought to the difference in their ages, but her spirit was young and her body strong, and when he loved her it had seemed perfectly natural. She had worked for his success, and no one knew "the sum of his wonder" as she did. "Why I cling to you so," she wrote him, "God only knows, but you are made of stuff so glorious, so terrible, and if I let you go, you will be lost."

In her novel-memoir, *The Journey Down,* Aline would describe an afternoon in Wolfe's apartment that summer of 1931. For several hours she has been watching him as he sleeps on the couch. Change is spilling out of his pocket from which the tip of his latchkey protrudes—should she take it and go to market? Though weary of her person, he is still enthusiastic about her cooking. He starts to move in his sleep and gently she lays her hand on his head so as to keep him from turning away. The huge shoulders heave and sink back ineffectually. Things have come to a strange pass, she muses, that it should be her bliss to watch him sleep.

A thunderstorm is brewing, and at the first flash of the lightning his eyelids open, the eyes themselves still glazed and unseeing. Anxiously she wonders what his mood will be when he wakes. Another flash and the eyes come to life. "She held her hands to her sides so they would not go out and offend him by a caress. Her active body held so long in this prison of heat and quiet, longed so to move, but she must put her strength to hold it another moment. He moved his great mass away, leaving room beside him on the couch. He looked at her, smiling as only he in the world could smile, and patted the place he had made vacant. Quietly she placed herself beside him, alive again if only for a moment."

In January, 1932, Wolfe's mother came to visit him. By this time he had moved to an airy, third-floor apartment at 111 Columbia Heights adjacent to the harbor and only a step from Brooklyn Bridge which he loved to walk across, especially at sunset. On her way to New York, Julia had stopped in Washington to stay with Mabel; her husband had lost his job and Mabel was supporting them by renting furnished apartments. Aline, then in Washington for the opening of a play, had on her own initiative called on Tom's mother and sister, and from all reports the meeting had been a success.

But now disaster. The morning after Julia's arrival she and Tom were finishing a late breakfast when the doorbell rang, he pressed the catch, and Aline came up. He had just received a letter from a German publisher asking him to sign a contract they had sent him a year ago; evidently Madeleine Boyd had sold them the rights to *Look Homeward, Angel* without notifying Wolfe or sending him the advance, and describing the matter to Aline, he called Mrs. Boyd names and threatened to have her jailed.

"And you're to blame for it," he added unreasonably. "You gave her my manuscript in the first place. You're the cause of my getting mixed up with a woman like that. You're two of a kind."

Julia tried to calm him, while Aline kept saying she would take it up with Madeleine, she would do anything he asked because she loved him.

"You know how much I love you, Tom."

Julia let it pass, but when Aline persisted in her endearments, Julia said, "Well, it's all right if you love him as a friend, a dear friend—or do you love him as a mother? Is it possible you have a mother's love for him? That's all right."

"Oh no," said Aline with lowered eyes. "You don't understand."

Julia replied that she did understand, and if it was any other kind of love, she would call that illicit. "You have a family, don't you? A husband and grown children almost as old as Tom?"

"You don't understand," Aline repeated.

Tom sided with Julia.

"My mother's not an ignoramus," he said. "She knows what she's talking about. Go away and leave me alone. I want to be left alone."

"You go," said Julia, "and let Tom quiet down."

Aline refused to go unless he kissed her.

"Yes, you will go," said Julia. "Tom's in no mood to kiss anybody just now, and I didn't come up here to get all worried and excited this way."

After an angry debate, Julia pushed Aline out of the apartment and locked the door. When the bell rang later that morning, Julia went to the window, saw Aline on the front steps, and motioned her to leave.

"We live in a crazy world—" Aline wrote Wolfe in a letter he received next day, "here it is a sin in the eyes of ninety-nine people out of a hundred that I love you. But money grabbing is not such a sin. Speculating in real estate is noble and fitting, but love is wrong. It is not so wrong as hate. I had five one hundred dollar bills in my purse yesterday, which you asked me to bring you Monday morning. When I left you today, I took one out and threw it over the Brooklyn Bridge, I thought if they cannot understand how I love you, here is something to appease the Gods your people worship. . . . If ever you need a friend you need one now, and here you have thrown me out and allowed your mother to insult me, to call my love licentious. Her love for you was noble when she deprived you of your rest to make a few pennies [his boyhood newspaper route], when she made you wear tight shoes to save the pennies for new ones. You all have learned that pennies, even grown to dollar size, can melt away, disappear even under the eyes of avarice. But love, my love, is great, radiant, lasting. It is not a sin, it is a glory and those who say it is a sin are degrading themselves. . . .

"There is a measuring stick for you, and put a notch in it part way up, that is the place to throw out the friend, no use any more. That's the Asheville code, and look at the town, it's the greatest, cleanest, most beautiful, happiest in all this broad land, its citizens prosper, its artists are encouraged and supported, its wives stick by its husbands, except in one instance where a wife walked out on her family in order to make herself some money. But that one doesn't count, because of its noble motive. The next four days I am going to throw a hundred dollar bill over the bridge into the river, just to show God I don't come from Asheville. I assure you we need the money, too. . . .

"Do you know it was only Monday that you were sweet and friendly with me? I have tried for hours to see things as you would have me, but I cannot believe I have ruined your life and work. For while we were really together you wrote your beautiful book. . . . After you and your mother threw me into the street I still love you and I am faithful to the highest emotion a human being can know. I love you without hope, without hope even of any understanding from you, I love you knowing that my beautiful soul is twisted by your mouths, by the horrid cruel phrases of your mother and yourself. I was a fool to let you both torture me into losing my control. But I was bared to the quick, I have carried this pain of my rejected love since you went and it is wearing down all of my resistance. It is useless to ask you for love or your favorite word, friendship. Tom dear, if only I could live backward from now on, to see where my fault with you has lain. I wish I believed in God, I wish I believed in anything, to ease my tortured mind. I wish that someday there would enter your mind some sense of the value of what I give you, I wish for you everything to make you happier."

Wolfe read parts of it aloud to his mother, and in an interview long afterwards she recalled:

"I said [to Tom], 'Call her up right now.' He laughed about it. I said 'Call her up right now; tell her that she's a Jew and I've never known one yet that if you drop a nickel but what they'd jump over and scramble for it. And tell her to leave the one hundred dollar bill on the bridge.'

"Oh Tom enjoyed—you know—the thought because I spoke about her jumping off to get the nickel—scrambling in the river for a nickel. I said to leave the one hundred dollars on the bridge and jump for the nickel. I remarked to Tom, I says, 'She's the silliest woman I believe I've ever heard talk or seen,' and he laughed and jollied over it, laughing over the letter. And he told me that she'd threatened to jump off the high building, some of the highest buildings. And I says, 'Well, let her jump!'

"And he says, 'Well,' he says—

"I says, 'She's crazy! Something's wrong with her.'

"He says, 'Well, yes,' he said, 'lots of silly things—but there's a lot of good things about the woman, yes.'

"I says, 'Well, it'd be a bad make-up if there wasn't anything good about a person, but I says, 'I just think that she's silly.'"[7]

A few days later came another letter from Aline apologizing for her previous one but adding, "I maintain that neither you nor your mother have any understanding of myself, of the freedom I demand for my mind and my life. I will not be bound in thought nor behavior by anything I do not choose myself. I have lived a fine life, I have held to the performance of my duties at home, and if I have not lived sexually with the man I married, it is nobody's business but ours, certainly not your mother's. I have retained purity in the practice of my work. I have been an uncompromising artist in a world that is full of compromise and ugliness. When we met and loved each other, I gave you the whole strength and beauty of my free soul and free mind. . . .

"I have concluded that it is time we see each other no more. I have fought against this so long, and now I know I will have to withdraw into myself the outgoing love which you are unable to take. I wish I could find an open place in your mind where I could lay all this I have written. I love you forever, and now we drop in a great unknown pool, separate."

Nevertheless she kept writing him, asking his plans and telling him hers, hanging on hope against hope, until finally he scribbled this note to her son on the back page of one of her letters: "To Theodore Bernstein, Jr.: I have this to say to you: if you are a man with a shred of pride or decency left in you, you will see to it that your mother no longer disgraces herself and her family by wilfully running after and doing the utmost in her power to wreck the life of someone twenty-five [sic] years younger than she is. I here and now demand, having exhausted every other means long ago, that you see to it that your mother no longer tries to see me or communicate with me in any way."

Whether he sent it is not clear, but something happened at this point which caused Aline to abandon the pursuit and face the necessity of rebuilding her life without him. In the clash of wills, the mother had triumphed over the mother-mistress. On her return to Asheville, Julia wrote Tom that he was "strong enough to pull out of this mudhole you have allowed yourself to slip into. . . . I expect a cheerful letter that you have broken loose, pulled away, and henceforth will not be under the spell and influence of that woman, a selfish villain, that has made it her purpose to divert your thoughts and actions all for her glory. I am sorry to have to speak so, but can't help feeling bitter."

In after years when the subject of Aline came up, Julia was apt to say succinctly and unfairly, "If there had been less of her, there would have been more of him."

The anti-Semitism evident in Wolfe's treatment of Aline cannot be blinked but must be qualified. He had inherited a small-town prejudice against, and suspicion of, the alien, the outsider. In the Asheville of his youth there were very few Jews and those few were ridiculed, though not with the hatred reserved for the poor whites. But if Wolfe was anti-Semitic, he was also at times anti-German, anti-French, anti-Irish, and even anti-American. And he was pro-Semitic too: he admired their lavishness, warmth, humor, and persistence, and he sympathized with the tortured intellectualism of his Jewish students at N.Y.U. His portrait of one of them, Abe Jones in *Of Time and the River,* while harshly satiric, betrays an underlying affection. In his relations with Jews and Gentiles alike, he was capable of cruelty, yet he was too conscious of belonging to what he called "the family of earth" to be malignantly anti-Jewish, and when confronted with those who were, he took a clear stand, as we shall see.[8]

January, 1932, was a new beginning for Wolfe, not only in the break with Aline but in his writing. That month he sold *A Portrait of Bascom Hawke,* a short novel culled from his manuscript, to *Scribner's Magazine* for $500, and at once set to work on a second one, though impeded by an accident sustained one evening when he accompanied Perkins to Grand Central Station and boarded the train with him. They had had a few drinks, and Perkins had suggested that Wolfe spend the night at his home in New Canaan, but as the train was pulling out, Wolfe changed his mind, rushed down the aisle, and jumped from the moving coach. Thrown violently on the concrete platform, he severed a vein in his left arm, and after receiving first aid at Grand Central, he went back to his apartment, where about 1 A.M. he phoned a girl he knew and asked her to make him some milk toast. She begged off, but when she stopped by to see him next morning his sheets were bloody and he was sure his arm would have to be amputated. "And they aren't going to take it off here," he gloomed, pointing to his wrist, "or here"—pointing to his elbow—"it'll be way up here, and I just won't have an arm." The girl got him to the hospital, and when the X rays showed there wasn't a fracture, he felt better right away.

In March he turned in his second novella, *The Web of Earth*— a carefully wrought tapestry of his mother's recollections inspired by her visit. Perkins later adjudged it the most perfect thing Wolfe ever wrote in the technical sense; on reading it, he said not one word should be changed. When *A Portrait of Bascom Hawke* appeared in the April *Scribner's*, Laurence Stallings commented in his book column in *The New York Sun*, "There's an eddy of energy for you . . . a lyrical paean to life" and predicted that Wolfe's second novel would be even finer than his first. But on the debit side, he was once more under attack for defamation of character.

Bascom Hawke, the stringy zealot turned real-estate conveyancer, had been patterned on his fantastic uncle, Henry Westall, whose home he had often visited in his Harvard days. When Uncle Henry and his two daughters denounced Wolfe's portrait as vicious satire, he could only repeat what he had said to the Asheville critics of *Look Homeward, Angel*: that he wasn't concerned with praising or denigrating living individuals and that if Uncle Henry had provided some of the clay for Bascom Hawke, the rest came from sources that the Westalls knew nothing of. The roots of all literary creation were, as he put it, "fastened in autobiography," but a writer didn't proceed by "calling Greenville Jonesville or by changing the name of Brown and Smith to Black and White: if it's that easy let's all start out for the nearest town with a trunk full of notebooks and pencils and start taking down the words and movements of the inhabitants from the most convenient corner."

Wolfe drew his authority not from his models but from his manner of viewing them and from a feeling for the whole of existence which he brought to bear on them. The previous summer Aline had sent him an article on Brooklyn Bridge by a well-known social critic, remarking that the man wrote well—"I just read some of the article again and wonder why it isn't better. I think he lacks brilliance, lacks entirely the zest that makes your writing magnificent. If you wrote about Brooklyn Bridge I would have a great desire to see it, but in his writing of it I would just let it alone. He does not add to the bridge as you would." Wolfe's hallmark was this creative additive, his imagination bursting into every pocket of his being and alchemizing his subject matter.

Once more Perkins was pressing him for the novel, and since it was going to be difficult to cram the overgrown manuscript into one volume, Wolfe now decided on the reverse tactic of expanding a single episode to book length. He narrowed his focus to a train journey home during the Boom, with detailed characterizations of some of the passengers, and called it *K-19*—the number of the Pullman on the New York to Asheville express. Cheered by the success of his two novellas, he wrote *K-19* at the record clip of three to five thousand words a day, and Scribners announced it for the coming autumn. But when Perkins read the 200,000-word manuscript the end of June, he found it thin and slapdash and persuaded Wolfe to shelve it. The blow was softened somewhat by the praises soon being showered on *The Web of Earth* in the August *Scribner's,* the longest piece ever printed in a single issue of that magazine. Meanwhile *A Portrait of Bascom Hawke,* which Perkins had entered without telling Wolfe, tied for first place in Scribners' $5,000-prize short-novel contest, and Wolfe was overjoyed. Not only had the fifteen hundred contestants included such worthies as Edith Wharton and Sherwood Anderson, but the $2,500 windfall seemed like picking up gold in the streets.

For with his royalties exhausted and his next book still in limbo, his finances were problematical. High-paying magazines like *Collier's* and *Cosmopolitan* had asked him for material, but he felt helpless about meeting their specifications and the same applied to Hollywood, which lately had been smiling in his direction. When a scriptwriter he knew urged him to come out and fill his coffers, Wolfe answered that though he was full of ideas which might be adapted to the movies, "they are of no use whatever to me until I can get them woven in, somehow, into the color and vision of my own life. . . ." He had to bumble ahead as the spirit moved him, but he *was* interested, and one day he lunched with "a very elegant, highly perfumed, and fancy talking Hollywood lady"—an agent—with whom he had been corresponding for months. There had been "feelers," then "nibbles," then very mysteriously she was engaged in a "dicker"—would he accept this, would he accept that? His mouth watering at the huge sums being bandied about, he imagined himself in a Hollywood palazzo, with a butler and a private limousine. When he and the agent met for lunch, he said with small exaggeration that he was down to his last ten dollars and couldn't afford the fare to the Coast, but she told him not to worry, that everything was settled—well, practically settled. "If you can just hitchhike your way out there, I've made an appointment for you to see a man who—"

Meanwhile he struggled on with his proliferating, amoebalike manuscript, visiting Montreal for a few days in August, and in October taking a quick trip to Bermuda, which he hated. Though he wrote scene after scene and his characters multiplied into the hundreds, it seemed to him that he had put down only a fraction of what he wanted to say. It was now a question of subduing or being devoured by "this nine-headed monster of a book," as he called it. He was afraid that he wouldn't live long enough to complete it, that to do so would require the energy of a dozen lives.

Through it all Perkins held him to his task. "I had for a friend," Wolfe said later, "a man of immense and patient wisdom and gentle but unyielding fortitude. . . . I did not give in because he would not let me give in." (Perkins was to liken his own role at this time to that of a man trying to hang onto the fin of a plunging whale.) In January, 1933, Wolfe accompanied Perkins on a trip to Johns Hopkins where the latter was being treated for his deafness, and afterwards they went on to Washington to visit Mabel. During the journey Perkins decided that Wolfe's main problem was how to begin, and he urged the simple expedient, which Wolfe had been resisting, of resuming the story of Eugene where he had dropped it in *Look Homeward, Angel*. When Wolfe went back to work from this perspective, the narrative began to cohere and what he had written thus far fell into place.

Since his retreat to Brooklyn, his personal isolation had been growing and he sometimes spoke of Perkins as his only friend, yet he was closer than ever to humanity in the large. During rush hours he would duck into Grand Central, and stand there head and shoulders above the throng, absorbing its hum and movement. He delighted in the way the grand concourse "took all the hard and driven clamor of the street, the ugly swarm and fury of the crowd and composed it in its calm and beneficent embrace, its immortal quietudes of space and time. It took man out of the driven and confused bewilderment of the dusty moment, and it cast over him its enchantment of eternity." He soaked up the medley of human types, the kaleidoscope of colors and textures, the cries of greeting, the sharp farewells, and the unctuous reassurances of the porters. Nor was it the station alone that held him, but his vision of what was transpiring beyond the gates, where the great continental locomotives of the New York Central and the New York, New Haven & Hartford slid out of their berths with their tons of lighted cars.

Another favorite haunt was the wholesale markets off West Street. Unwinding after a night's work, he would go there in the small hours when the trucks and drays were bringing in the produce and dim shapes moved among the stalls piled high with fruits and vegetables. In his swaying raincoat and shabby felt hat, he would wander through the acreage of sheds with slow, countryman's stride, savoring the odor of soil thick around him, his ears tuned to the shouts of the drivers and grocery boys. The markets in Paris were supposed to be so wonderful, but it seemed to him that Les Halles had nothing on this. He also frequented the docks where he mingled with the hoi polloi, and he liked to go into bars and listen to the natural, expressive talk of those whose tongues had been loosened by a little or too much. He once remarked that Sinclair Lewis had sacrificed a lot in leaving low life behind him. "When you enter a saloon," said Wolfe, "and feel that wet bar under your hand, you've got something." Lewis had had it in his day but now regarded it as beneath his dignity.

Nothing was beneath Wolfe's. He lay open to all manner of sordidness and suffering. During the desperate winter of 1932–33 he would go down into the public latrine opposite New York City Hall on cold nights when it was jammed with the homeless. Some were the old men one finds in any metropolis—"all rags and bags and long white hair and bushy beards stained dirty yellow," Wolfe remembered, "wearing tattered overcoats in the cavernous pockets of which they had carefully stored away all the little rubbish they lived on and spent their days collecting in the street—the crusts of bread, old bones with rancid shreds of meat still clinging to them, and dozens of cigarette butts." Some were Bowery bums "fumed with drink or drugs or half-insane with 'smoke.'" But most were the flotsam of the Depression—decent young and middle-aged men with careworn faces who huddled together in this squalid meeting place and fought over the open doorless stools, which they wanted more for rest than for necessity. One night in a subway corridor, after watching a group of these derelicts curled up on newspapers, Wolfe said to his companions as they walked away how appalling, how wicked it was that human beings should come to this, that there was no place for them in society.

Till now he had shown little interest in politics, but the summer of 1932 he sat up all night listening to the Democratic Convention on the radio, and the fall election concerned him deeply. He wanted Roosevelt to win, if only to insure the repeal of the Eighteenth Amendment, though he was skeptical of the Democrat's ability to find a quick cure for the Depression. In March he joined his mother in Washington for the inauguration, having urged her to buy a reserved seat and let him pay for it. As she had neglected to do so, he edged her through the crowd and got her up into a chair which he held in place, staring at her back while she watched the parade. That spring and summer he went on several jaunts through Pennsylvania Dutch country with Fred, now a Westinghouse salesman based in Harrisburg. The fat farmland with its huge barns and powerful horses and air of abundance stirred memories of his father who still had relatives living in York Springs, near storied Gettysburg. In July, Tom and Fred, accompanied by Max Perkins, tramped over the battlefield where seventy years earlier almost to the day their great uncles, George Penland and Bacchus Westall, had fought under Lee.

Wolfe was solvent once again, after running very low. On the basis of a pile of manuscript submitted to Scribners in April he had signed a contract with them and with his English publisher and had pocketed $1,500 in advances. He had also sold three stories to *Scribner's Magazine* early in the year—mood pieces on night, death, loneliness, and wandering—rough poetic gleanings from his work in progress. One of them brought a letter from Percy Mackaye, the poet-dramatist then living in the mountains near Asheville. Of "The Train and the City" Mackaye wrote Wolfe, "It is as if I had seen the tallest and tranquillest of these mountains (which I watch, evenings, against the west-light, from our porch) stir majestically on one bent arm, and reach the other to pluck up the straightest & primevalest black-oak for a fountain-pen, and begin furiously, like a roaring millrace, to inscribe a new-world Genesis on fresh tablets of rock, with the live sap of pent centuries—quick & bursting with potency, yet sharp-pointed and controlled by the mastering, organic grip of imagination." Wolfe was pleased, especially when Perkins remarked in his laconic way that you only had to meet Mackaye to know he was *somebody*.

Wolfe had been in Brooklyn two and a half years, but his life there seemed to stretch back through centuries. The summer of 1932 he had moved to an apartment a few doors up the street, and in October, 1933, he moved again to 5 Montague Terrace, still on the Heights. His unfinished book had assumed the proportions of a nightmare from which there was no issue. In his sleep his mind would go on functioning with what he called "a kind of horrible, comatose intelligence" and he was wracked by dreams like the following: Passing along a twilit street, he came on a crowd gathering before one of the rich little shops one finds in European towns. With a sudden feeling of nausea he realized that the objects in the brightly lit windows were candies, glacéed fruits, and pastries oozing with whipped cream. He did not know why these delicacies should repel him until, thrusting his way through the crowd, he beheld the sight he had dreaded all along. A man lay dead on the pavement. He had died of madness and it was as if an explosive had burst inside him, giving his face and head a huge hydrocephalic appearance, though one could see that in life he had been a handsome and lovable person. The spectacle reminded Wolfe of medical museums where the relics of aborted and unnatural births are kept in jars.[9]

Often he dreamed of familiar faces that looked at him in silence because he had wasted his time and allowed his life to rot. He knew that he would never again sleep the sweet sleep of childhood, "that one bright cell in brain or heart or memory would blaze on forever" and "that no anodyne of food or drink or friendship, travel, sport or women could ever quench it." At last he knew the cost of being a writer; he saw what happens to a man who makes the writer's life his own.

Early in December Perkins summoned Wolfe to his office and told him the book was done. Wolfe was amazed; though he had driven himself almost to the breaking point, the end as he envisioned it was not in sight. But Perkins assured him that the book was finished whatever he might think and told him to collect the manuscript in its proper sequence. Just before Christmas Wolfe delivered it to Perkins, estimating its length at over a million words. (In reality it was more like 700,000—still five or six times the length of the average novel.) Wolfe compared his relief to that of a drowning man who at the last gasp of his dying effort suddenly feels the earth beneath him. With the draft of his book in Perkins' hands his spirit was borne up by the greatest triumph he had ever known, and he felt equal to anything—even the stupendous job of revision which lay ahead.

Meanwhile Aline had re-entered his life in an unexpected fashion. Not that she had entirely left it, for since their agonized parting two years before he had phoned her several times in the middle of the night at the Hotel Gotham where the Bernsteins had an apartment. Once she had gotten a call from the men's room of the Plaza —"There's a fellow here by the name of Wolfe, he's drunk, and he says he won't leave unless you come and get him"—and under these trying circumstances she had seen him again. She had written him occasional letters, doubting that he read them, but unable to restrain herself since her feeling for him was still the great reality in her life. "Everything else," she wrote him, "is a shadow, and a dream to be slept through. . . . This whole relation of ours to each other, which was like the sun itself, do you ever think of it any more?"

When *The Web of Earth* was published in *Scribner's,* she wrote him that like all his work it had affected her deeply and then went on to criticize it: "Now let me say something about your stories, Tom—listen carefully to what I am saying. You are a great writer, great in your scope and expressiveness. But you are going wrong, you are taking on instead of losing your fault. You are covering yourself with a mass of words that are a fungus growth, I could have killed you for what you did with the last one. Do you remember I always told you not to be fancy? Well, you are heading in that direction, away from the golden core of what you have to say. You could have told that story in two-thirds the words, and it would have been a finer work. Even your mother's diffuseness could have been expressed. You make her often very tiresome and I know that was not your intention. . . . I wish your editors would let me give them some advice."

She added that she had been doing some writing herself to "help me through this tragic end of my life that should really be so fine," and in December, 1933, at her own expense, she published *Three Blue Suits*, the manuscript of which she had sent Wolfe for comment, but he hadn't replied. He had thought these stories—one of them clearly about him—were only exercises, and when they appeared, he wrote her to congratulate her on their quality and then to take issue with some of her interpretations. He said she had pictured him as an unmitigated dreamer who wanted to gaze out the window and have his books magically appear on paper, when she knew perfectly well how he slaved. Having compared her manuscript with the published book, he said that he had never been able to do a piece of writing "so free from revision and the necessity of change, cut and rewrite as your own pages are. I don't know if you have ever seen one of my pages when I get through with it, or after I get through with the proofs—but it looks like a map of No Man's Land in Flanders." (Something of an exaggeration: though capable of painstaking revision, Wolfe also released material which was practically first draft.) But he spoke with authority when he added, "I think you have done some very fine writing in your stories on Mr. Froehlich and Eugene, but I think you would have done better if you had worked harder. By work in an artist's life I do not mean eight hours a day or fourteen hours a day or all the different things you get accomplished. I mean an integrity of purpose, a spiritual intensity, and a final expenditure of energy that most people in the world have no conception of."

For the first time he was learning what it felt like to be portrayed in thin fictional disguise, and he admitted that it would make him more careful than ever to be fair and comprehensive in what he wrote about others. Still, he did not think he had ever stacked the cards to justify himself, and in her account of their affair Aline had shown him heartlessly deserting her to go on a Guggenheim Fellowship while suppressing certain relevant facts: the difference in their ages, for example, and that she was married and had no intention of leaving her family—also that she had means, while he must support himself, and the Guggenheim had meant freedom to write. By not going all out, Wolfe felt that Aline had damaged and sentimentalized her tale.

She answered that she did not think her portrait unjust, that the indolent dreamer was part of him but "not all by a million." As for his poverty, at the time described in the story his book had begun to sell and Scribners had offered him a generous advance. Wolfe had no long-term security, however, and about the more serious obstacles of her marriage and the difference in their ages she had nothing to say. Instead she fell back on her old plaint that he had deserted her when she was down (down, really, *because* he had deserted her) after she had struggled so hard for his success.

Wolfe's conduct was sometimes hard to justify, but as Perkins once remarked he was "a truly great man and not a petty one" and when his passions led him astray, he was ashamed of it afterwards. Early in their friendship Perkins had said in a moment of exasperation, "Tom, there are ten thousand devils in you, but there is also an archangel." How to make the most of this archangel was now the central concern of Perkins' packed professional life.

W. O. and Julia in 1900

2. Tom at nine months

3. Aged eight

4. AND 5. Asheville about 1900. The building on the hilltop in the center is the old Battery Park Hotel, demolished in 1925 when the hill was razed. The dome at the right is the old Courthouse on Court Square, later Pack Square where W. O. had his marble shop (opposite page).

6. The Old Kentucky Home in 1908—W. O., Ben (?), Julia, Mabel, Tom

7. Tom at sixteen

8. W. O. in his sixties

9. Margaret Roberts at twenty-five

10. Tom as "Buck Gavin"

11. Clara Paul

2. Tom and Kenneth
Raisbeck at Harvard

13. George Pierce Baker

14. Aline Bernstein

15. Publicity shot for *Look Homeward, Angel*

16. Maxwell Perkins

18.   Central City, Colorado, August 10, 1935

19.   Aline

20. Julia and Tom on the porch of the Old Kentucky Home, May, 1937

21. The Wolfes—Tom, Effie, Julia, Mabel, Frank, Fred

22. The cabin at Oteen

23. From *The October Fair* manuscript

24. AND 25. During a newspaper interview
in Denver, May, 1938

26. Louise Perkins, Aline Bernstein, Maxwell Perkins, Lee Simonson

27. Tom

28. Max

9. Crater Lake, Oregon, June, 1938

30. Tom at Olympia, Washington, July 2, 1938, four days before the onset of his fatal illness

8 · TRIUMPH

THOUGH not yet fifty, the man who had commandeered Wolfe's manuscript was widely regarded as the dean of his calling—a kind of Prospero among editors. Awed glances would follow when he slipped into the Scribner Book Store and stood at the fiction counter with hands on lapels, scrutinizing the offerings of rival publishers. At such moments his clear blue eye and meditative, withdrawn expression brought to mind Yankee lighthouse keepers, sailors, and farmers—the type of man who lives austerely and alone through sensitivity and choice—while his hat jammed down so that it rested on his ears added a substantiating touch of quirky defiance. The cashier would be hoping he'd recognize her and give her one of his lovely, sheepish smiles. When she had asked him for a job, he had said there weren't any in the editorial department but she could try the book store downstairs. He doesn't look at her, however, nor at anyone else, the truth being that despite his hat he is in terror lest a customer mistake him for one of the store personnel. His attention is riveted on the new book jackets, and having found several that he likes, he takes the books off the rack, nods shyly to the clerk who has been eying him from a respectful distance, and vanishes through the side door that leads to the elevator. Stopping on the floor below his office, he hands the books to the art editor, asking her perhaps, "Now why can't we have something along these lines for the new Fitzgerald?" Or, more typically, he leaves them on her desk in silent reproach.

So too, with authors, he makes his points with a minimum of talk. When he invites one of them to "tea" (his term for downing several martinis before catching the 6:02 for New Canaan), he may go through the entire occasion with barely a remark. Yet his silence, charged with the judgments and awareness of a superior intelligence, is positive, instructive, and helpful to the author, who finds his dilemmas unravelling as he discusses them in the presence of this quizzically interested man with the telepathic glance and the comprehension deeper than words. If the author is depressed or licking his wounds, Perkins may not say anything, but his hurt is visible in the flicker of his sensitive, beautifully moulded mouth as he fingers his glass. When he speaks—briefly and not always in agreement—his views coming after so much silence have an added weight and force. He never stoops to smartness, glibness, or the cheap satisfaction of showing people up. Everything he says comes out of the top drawer, his standards and his sense of tradition being coupled with an openness, a receptivity, a fundamental bigness and lack of bias.

When holding forth as he sometimes does—for in Perkins there is a lawyer, an Evarts, who likes to argue points—he will discuss current events or American history or some neglected book (Hardy's *The Dynasts*, for instance), avoiding the work of the author he is with, though it is the reason for their get-together. At some point, however, he may inquire innocently, "What do you make of the theory that you fall in love with your wife over and over?" and reflecting on it next day, the author grasps its relevance and is perhaps able to finish the chapter that is holding him up. For despite a knack amounting almost to genius of visualizing the ideal book the author has in mind, Perkins has a horror of forcing his hand. He looks on himself as a catalyst who initiates trains of thought that enable the author to solve his problems in his own way. In artistic matters better too little said than too much, and where possible let that little dawn as a revelation from within.

Through such scruple and adroitness Perkins had risen to the top of his profession. There were other excellent editors, to be sure, but none who combined his cultural quality with his fine point and touch, none who responded with such subtlety and exactness to a wide variety of challenges. His instinctual, unfailingly personal approach resembled that of a wise mother. The books that passed through his hands were never ends in themselves but steps toward the full realization of a particular talent. Having sized up his author, Perkins *felt* whether or not the stuff was there, and though sometimes mistaken, how usually right he was in his conviction that so-and-so would make his mark, if not with this book, then with the next, or the next after that! At times he sounded more like an obstetrician than an editor. "That woman has two books in her," he would say, "and it will be very bad for her if they aren't written," or again, "It's there inside him all right, but it's going to be the devil getting it out." Though boundlessly sympathetic with the agonies of creation, he regarded such distress as inevitable, fruitful, and roughly proportional to the value of the work. Meanwhile he was tolerant of his authors' misdemeanors and stood by them in their scrapes, pointing out that some of the greatest literature had been written by "rascals," as he called them—by the Marlowes and the Villons whose crowded emotions kept them in constant hot water.

Not that Perkins was solely or even principally concerned with the production of masterpieces. Publishing was a business after all, and a book's potential sales had to be considered. He respected sound workmanship of the popular, less durable sort, and fostered the narrative gift wherever he found it, yet he was always on the lookout for the extraordinary talent capable of producing great art: that was the quest that kept him boyish and gave him his strange, glinting quality of a fawn caught in a briar bush. And of the many fine writers he had added to the Scribner list over the years, none had excited him more or aroused higher expectations than Fitzgerald, Hemingway, and Wolfe.

Just now Fitzgerald was in eclipse. He hadn't published a book for eight years, and because his stories kept cropping up in *The Saturday Evening Post* it was thought by serious writers that he had sunk into the popular class, or, as the phrase went, "sold out to the slicks." Perkins hoped that his new novel, at long last completed and soon to be published, would silence his detractors. Recently Perkins had gone to Baltimore to read the still-chaotic manuscript under non-too-favorable circumstances, with Fitzgerald handing him Tom Collinses every few minutes, and pulling out his favorite parts to read aloud. Even so, Perkins had satisfied himself that *Tender Is the Night* was a beautiful book, less perfect and gemlike than *Gatsby*, but magically evocative and full of a poignant understanding. Private misfortunes had mellowed Fitzgerald and added new subtlety and depth to his shorthand of the heart.

Why, then, his aura of defeat? Why, at thirty-seven, with his superb talent, did he talk like a has-been, conceding the superiority of Hemingway who was now in Africa on his first safari? Hemingway had followed up the triumph of *A Farewell to Arms* with more brilliant short stories and a treatise on bullfighting, *Death in the Afternoon*. Now and again he would issue Perkins not so much an invitation as a command to join him in some remote spot, and Perkins would tell his secretary, "Remember, for me this is work," though the tales he brought back with him didn't sound that way. In January, 1929, when Hemingway completed the manuscript of *Farewell* in Key West, he had written Perkins that he couldn't have it unless he called for it in person, and on his arrival Hemingway and several companions had spirited Perkins off to the Dry Tortugas —a group of tiny keys on one of which they were stranded by a series of northers. Supplies ran low, and though he had never before fired on anything alive, "Maxie Dead-Pan Perkins," as Hemingway dubbed him, had great success in shooting the gauldings which, together with the fish they caught, were their principal diet. When the weather finally cleared, a yacht rode into the harbor, and Hemingway's party looked so seedy bobbing alongside in their rowboat that the owner was cool until Perkins inquired about the stock market. That broke the ice, and they were asked on board for a lavish meal, and so liberally plied with the best French wines that

Perkins thought the Dry Tortugas should be renamed after their visit.

Another time he had received an urgent summons from Hemingway to shoot ducks with him in Arkansas where Perkins was routed out of bed each morning before daybreak, but he enjoyed himself even so. The White River where they hunted had a powdering of snow on its steep banks that reminded Perkins of the rivers in the Civil War illustrations of *Harper's Weekly*, and the woods behind the banks were not the usual second growth, but widely spaced trees through which he imagined horsemen riding at full gallop. Once, returning to the houseboat where they spent the nights, they heard a terrible racket and around the bend came a paddle-wheel steamer with tall twin funnels pouring out smoke, and for a moment Perkins was back in the world of *Huckleberry Finn*. After dinner in the evenings he and Hemingway conversed over highballs, and Perkins wrote a friend that Hemingway was "wonderful company. In a wild time he's done some mighty evil things, but I never knew anyone who was naturally decenter than he is."[1]

More a man grown, more responsible and self-reliant than Fitzgerald or Wolfe, Hemingway needed Perkins the least of the three, as Wolfe needed him the most. Indeed it is hard to see how Wolfe could have gone on without the editorial assistance and moral support (the latter especially) which Perkins so unstintingly gave him. A deep affection had grown up between them. Wolfe quite frankly looked on Perkins as a second father, and Perkins, after taking Wolfe on as a professional challenge, had become a part of that enormous life from which it was so hard to disentangle yourself once you got involved. Not that Perkins wanted to. The severe, drilled New Englander was fascinated by the obstreperous Southerner, and for Perkins the discovery of such a talent had been like stumbling on a large diamond—no less thrilling for being a rough one that needed considerable cutting and polishing.

By now Fitzgerald and Hemingway, youthful as they were, had been around so long that they seemed like the Old Guard, while Wolfe was still coming on. He belonged to the future, and Perkins took pride in his American spirit. Whereas Hemingway's two novels and Fitzgerald's new one had European backgrounds, Wolfe, though familiar with Europe, was committed to the native scene which by virtue of his huge projection, his giant reach, he seemed born to describe. If only he could acquire some of Hemingway's discipline and control! In January, 1933, when Wolfe's confusion over his novel was at its peak, Perkins had taken the two of them to lunch—the only time they would ever meet. No artists could have been more different in style and method, but Hemingway had been struck by the force and originality of *Look Homeward, Angel*—in his lingo Wolfe was no jackal, but someone who killed by himself —while Wolfe, perhaps for the very reason that his nature impelled him to a copious outpouring, admired the other's "superb concision." "[Hemingway]," he had written in a review of *A Farewell to Arms*, "says one thing and suggests ten more: his words not only pull their own weight in a sentence, they also pull a very rich weight of profound and moving association and inference."[2]

Capable of great tact and gentleness and fond of the advisory role, Hemingway hit it off with Wolfe and threw an oblique yet helpful light on his problems. It was shortly afterwards that Wolfe succeeded in getting his novel on the tracks, and Perkins thought the conversation with Hemingway had contributed.

Despite his seeming assurance, Perkins had taken Wolfe's manuscript away from him with deep misgiving, weighing the unprecedented step for several months before putting it through. Wolfe's health and sanity had been a prime consideration; by the fall of 1933 he was so hectically overwrought that Perkins feared he would crack if he worked on the book much longer. Then too, it was getting bigger and more unmanageable all the time, though Perkins felt confident of his own ability to shape it. Perhaps because he himself had such a keen sense of form, he put a premium on other attributes, such as passion, vividness, and authenticity.[3] He looked for writing that sprang from the depths of the author's mind and heart and that drew its inspiration directly from life, instead of echoing other books as so much fiction tended to do. Above all, he looked for the touch of the poet, which Wolfe had to an exceptional degree.

The manuscript he had given Perkins covered the life of Eugene Gant from his departure for Harvard through his affair with Esther Jack (Aline Bernstein), and Perkins' first move was to divide it roughly in two. He then persuaded Wolfe to save the love story for a later volume and concentrate on the earlier part, which needed cutting in some places and development in others. Perkins cut while Wolfe developed, a process which one observer likened to bailing a boat with water pouring in at the seams; if Perkins sometimes seized the oars and appeared to row too frantically for shore, it was to prevent them from sinking altogether. It would have been easier to do the trimming after Wolfe had finished adding, but knowing his propensity for adding ad infinitum, Perkins wanted to control that part of the operation as well. He had made up his mind that it was to Wolfe's—not to mention Scribners'—advantage to get the manuscript between covers as soon as possible. Then the creative log jam would be broken, and the other books Wolfe had in him would flow unhindered. Thus Perkins put aside his usual scruples about staying in the background and took matters more firmly into his own hands than ever before.[4]

Wolfe's Brooklyn flat where he began the final work on *Time and the River* (the *Of* was added later) had the underfurnished look of all his habitations, as though he were only camping there while his spirit roamed abroad. Each morning when the girl who did his typing came in around eleven, he would just have gotten up and be priming himself with quantities of black coffee from his acrid, smoky, graniteware pot. Instead of percolating it, he boiled it, adding fresh grounds to the old ones until they choked the spout—at which point he emptied the pot and began anew. The typist would find him pacing back and forth with a cup in one hand and in the other the first of an unending chain of cigarettes, which dangled from his lips as he wrote, or smoked unheeded in a butt-filled ashtray. Before getting down to his labors there had to be some human interchange. Wolfe must pour out his latest difficulty with friend or foe, publisher or landlord, not simply to get it off his chest but to salt it away for possible literary use. The typist listened eagerly, for though he talked in the same rambling, circuitous way that he wrote, any subject he mentioned came instantly to life. Having exhausted the trials of the moment, he would pass on to some incident from his nocturnal wanderings. He might, for instance, tell of returning to his apartment house at 4 A.M. and hearing desperate sobs as he was getting out his key. Then he had noticed a milk wagon drawn up to the curb; the driver was leaning against his horse and crying with an arm thrown over the animal's neck. Wolfe had felt an impulse to say, "Look, brother—can I do anything?" but he had turned away and gone in. When the typist asked him why, he seemed troubled. "I don't know—" he said, with that concentrated drive to express his exact feelings, "I just decided it was something personal between him and his horse."

Or he might describe a harrowing subway ride, acting it out so vividly that the typist felt like a bystander. It was dawn, and he had been coming home weary and a little drunk, sitting dully among the stupefied human leftovers of the night. Gradually he had become aware that a huge Negro was staring at him. The man rose and moved closer, making obscene gestures and mouthing silent rebukes. He seemed to resent Wolfe's appearance, his very existence. Uneasiness growing to quiet terror, Wolfe wondered if this were some maniac who had singled him out as the object of a blind hatred. Or did he recognize Wolfe as a Southerner and hold him responsible for the maltreatment of his race? When Wolfe got up to leave, the Negro got up too, and as he stood by the door waiting for the train to stop, he felt the stranger's breath on his neck. Then the man spoke: "Mister, your fly is open." Wolfe could wring the last ounce of juice and humor from a situation like this.

Abruptly his outpouring would cease, and he would be cross-examining the typist, for either he talked or she satisfied his curiosity —that, she had learned, was conversation with Thomas Wolfe. He listened to her with the delicacy of a high-precision instrument, savoring all that she said and all that she didn't say, his shifting expressions showing that he was filling in the background, adding depth and color to whatever she described. His curiosity about people was insatiable: if she mentioned a cross-eyed man who had lived on a neighboring farm when she was a girl, Wolfe would ask her enough minutiae about him to fill a book. Finally, as a warm-up for what he planned to write that day, he would begin reminiscing about "this friend of mine" or "a pitiful old duck I knew"—using their real names interchangeably with the fictitious ones he had assigned them. About this time the phone might ring and standing at the mantel Wolfe would say, "Yes, yes, Max—we're getting down to it right now. . . . Oh, Max, I'll have the little girl with me when I come in this afternoon—I haven't paid her this week."

He was slow to begin, often spending an hour or two in such preliminaries, but once under way he was indestructible. He would draw up a chair to his heavy oaken writing table, light yet another cigarette, choose a stub pencil from the coffee can in which he kept them, purse his mouth for concentration, and then for several hours, almost without pause, the unnumbered manila sheets covered with his onrushing scrawl would fall to the floor as if blown by a fan, while the typist scurried to and fro to gather them up, not daring to ask about words she couldn't read since Wolfe grew annoyed at the slightest interruption. There were moments when he puffed at the cigarette stuck to his lower lip and squinted at the ceiling through the spiralling smoke, the pencil poised over the yellow sheet looking like a jackstraw in his giant hand. Sometimes, after brief reflection, he would crumple up the page and begin anew, but this was rare. The copy he would take to Scribners at the end of the afternoon was largely first draft, with only an occasional word crossed out or changed. And yet in a way it wasn't first draft at all, or rather it was as thoroughly digested as if he had written it a dozen times. Before putting a subject on paper Wolfe revolved it in his mind till he had seen it in every light and extracted the last shred of meaning. Often he had told it on a number of occasions, which for him were like practice runs.

His conference with Perkins was scheduled for 4:30, and if he wrote much beyond that hour, the phone would ring again, and Wolfe would say, "Why, why, we're stepping out the door this minute, Max," but then he would dash off a few more pages before putting on his pulpy hat and shapeless topcoat and stuffing the new copy in his briefcase. Meanwhile, in his corner office overlooking Fifth Avenue, Perkins would be winding up a busy day. He might be standing with thumbs hooked in the armholes of his vest repeating, "I'd say . . . I'd say . . . I'd say," as he framed the opening sentence of the letter he was about to dictate. (He liked it when the typed draft had a few mistakes, so that he could correct them in his handwriting and give it a more personal air.) Or he might be leafing through a manuscript so rapidly that he seemed to be counting the pages instead of reading them, but his verdict of "This

189

won't do" or "We must have this" would be judicious and final, his authority having grown to the point where it could almost be said that Perkins *was* Scribners. Brownell had died in 1928 and Charles Scribner II in 1930, and in matters of literary judgment the new chief, Charles Scribner III, trusted Perkins implicitly. His responsibilities were vast, yet no matter how tense or tiring the day had been, he always seemed to be waiting for the moment when Wolfe, overcoat flying, stalked into the office stammering his apologies for being late.

There followed a brief hurly-burly while Wolfe unloaded whatever joy or sorrow was in the forefront of his consciousness. Getting him to settle down was sometimes more onerous than the work itself. Then, with a hawklike concentration punctuated by an occasional sniff, Perkins would read the fresh material, seldom taking issue with a word or a sentence. Wolfe's style was Wolfe's style, his unique way of saying things, and not to be tampered with. Instead, Perkins bent his energies—as he had with *Look Homeward, Angel,* only now the task was far greater—on getting Wolfe to eliminate certain paragraphs, scenes, or chapters. "Tom, this is good," he would say, "this is excellent, but in view of your over-all plan, don't you think it would be better if you cut from here to there?" Twisting and agonizing in his chair as in the days of the 47 Workshop, Wolfe would say, "No, Goddamn it!" and "To hell with it!" and finally agree, perhaps with the provision that he be allowed to write a transitional sentence—whereupon he would go into the next office and toss off a transitional sentence of several thousand words, which again had to be fought over. There were times when they glowered at each other for as long as twenty minutes without saying a word. To break the tension, Perkins might fumble at his breast pocket with a trick he had of pulling out not the pack but a single cigarette, which he meditatively lit. Or, on his scratch pad he would doodle a profile of Napoleon in tri-cornered hat, or of Mark Twain with a corn-cob pipe. During one of these armed truces Wolfe's restless glance wandered to the corner where Perkins had hung his coat beside a rattlesnake skin with seven rattles—a gift from Marjorie Kinnan Rawlings. With a gleam in his eye Wolfe pointed to the skin and said, "Aha—the portrait of an editor!" Another time when they were arguing over a cut, which admittedly contained some of the best writing Wolfe had ever done, he said, "Well then, will you take the responsibility?" "I have simply got to take it," Perkins replied. "And what's more I'll be blamed either way."

Recalling these sessions a year later, Wolfe wrote, "My spirit quivered at the bloody execution. My soul recoiled before the carnage of so many lovely things cut out, upon which my heart was set. But it had to be done, and we did it." And for excellent reasons. To cite one example, in the opening scene Eugene was standing on the platform of the Altamont railroad station with several members of his family who were seeing him off for Harvard. The scene as Wolfe originally wrote it ran to thirty thousand words, but since the act of waiting for a train involves a suspense that can't be maintained over such a span, Perkins got him to reduce it by two-thirds. In another case, Helen Gant left her husband's car and went into her mother's house and kept calling to the impatient man every time he honked his horn, "All right—all right—I'll be out in five minutes." Those five minutes lengthened into four hours while Helen, her mother, and her two brothers discussed the lives and histories of everyone in town. Wolfe was particularly proud of this dialogue for its "utter naturalness, the flood tide river of it all," but it amounted to some eighty thousand words—a novel in itself—and Perkins finally convinced him that nearly all of it should go.

Yet in his role of hatchet man Perkins was wisely flexible and pragmatic. When Wolfe came to the point in the narrative where Eugene's father dies, Perkins said that since the boy was away at Harvard, Wolfe need only tell of his distress and of his return for the funeral—a matter of a few thousand words. Wolfe agreed, and next day he brought in thousands of words about the life of the doctor who attended Gant during his last illness. Good as it was, Perkins said it had no place in a book seen through the eyes of Eugene. Wolfe acquiesced, but next day he came back with more thousands of words about Eugene's sister and her thoughts while shopping in Altamont shortly before her father's death. "How in God's name will you ever get this book done?" Perkins erupted. "You've spent the last two days on complete irrelevancies!" Wolfe was penitent—from now on he would write only what was needed —but next day he brought in a long sequence about Gant's final illness, and suddenly Perkins realized that the whole digression was too fine to let go. It was wrong and yet it was right, and Wolfe went on to complete one of his great set pieces, the death of Gant, which ranks with the death of Ben in *Look Homeward, Angel*. (After Wolfe's own death, Edgar Lee Masters would write Mabel, "I read the other day again in the chapter in *Of Time and the River* dealing with the death of Stoneman Gant. It is one of the most moving and beautiful things in literature. There are numberless touches in it showing that his eye penetrated to secrets, to understandings that are hidden from all except those gifted with the eye of imagination. He was a poet, and that word does not confine itself to writers of verse, but to all those who see into secrets and whose hearts respond with music.")

That winter and spring, evening after evening, Sundays and holidays included, Perkins gave several hours to the manuscript and brooked no interruptions. Once when there were voices in the corridor, Wolfe went out to investigate, and after a moment Perkins called, "Who's out there? Who wants you?"

Wolfe called back the name of one of the junior editors and his wife, a couple with whom he was friendly.

"Tell them to go sit in the water closet," growled Perkins.

By June they had shifted to an after-dinner schedule, working from eight to ten and then repairing to the "Chatham Walk," the outdoor café of the Hotel Chatham which reminded Wolfe of "Paris walled in with forty-story skyscrapers." There they were joined several times by Struthers Burt, another Scribner author, who later recalled "the languid air and the languid smells in which the street lights and the lamps of the café floated like round electric fish in the depths of a tropic ocean. Tom would come striding in like a giant who has dined well on human flesh but always a little cross and pettish with the childish crossness of a giant. Behind him would be Max, white and utterly exhausted. Max was of average height, but he looked small on those hot June nights and sparse like a dry-point etching." The previous fall the Perkinses had moved from New Canaan to a house in Turtle Bay, and on leaving the Chatham, Wolfe would walk Perkins home to 246 East Forty-ninth Street and go on talking there until Perkins went out, as was his custom, for an early edition of the morning paper. Then Perkins would finally get rid of Wolfe, who roamed the city for several more hours before turning in. He made no distinction between night and day, unless it was to favor the night when he gathered much of his material.

Lunching with Wolfe and Fitzgerald that summer, Perkins said, "You tell Tom to cut something and a great hand comes over and slowly crosses out a word, but you tell him to improve it, to add to it, and the words just flow"—whereupon Fitzgerald observed that he had never cut anything out of a book that he later regretted. In July the first half of *Of Time and the River* went to the printer, none too soon from the point of view of Wolfe's finances. He was making large inroads on his Scribner advance, and early that year he had been turned down when he applied for another Guggenheim. During 1934, he sold five more stories, or rather excerpts from his manuscript, to *Scribner's Magazine,* but an agent who had undertaken to market his stuff elsewhere made only one sale and that for a piddling sum, the main trouble being that Wolfe's "stories" far exceeded the usual five-thousand-word limit.

With his book under control, he was giving more rein to his wanderlust. In May he had spent a week at a home for defective children run by his friend Catherine Brett at Dingman's Ferry in a wild corner of Pennsylvania. One of his most attractive traits was his compassion for the handicapped, whether deaf, blind, paralytic, or otherwise shortchanged in life's lottery. At the Brett School he ate his meals with the "children" aged twelve to thirty, afterwards writing Fred that "the first time you see and talk to [them] is pretty bad—it gives you a sick feeling." But he projected himself into their world and laughed when one of them, on being introduced, said, "How do you do, Mr. Wolfe? My father took me to the circus once to see a giant." In September he spent two weeks at the Chicago World's Fair, and in October he visited "Welbourne," a pre-Civil War mansion in Middleburg, Virginia, that belonged to some friends of the Perkinses. On one of the window panes were Jeb Stuart's initials, which the Gallant Pelham had scratched with his diamond ring while waiting for his horse to be brought to the door, and five miles away was the Manassas battlefield. Deep-seated emotions welling up in him, Wolfe wrote his hostess after his return to Brooklyn, "There is an enormous age and sadness in Virginia—a grand kind of death—I always felt it, even when all I did was ride across the state at night in a train—it's the way the earth looks, the fields and the woods and in the great hush and fall of evening light."

The past few years he had seen a good deal of his old college friend, John Terry—likewise a bachelor living in Brooklyn. A wheezing, Woollcottean figure of a glandular obesity, Terry, like Wolfe, was untidy and unpunctual, an endless talker, a colossal eater, and a tireless explorer of New York. One day Terry, who taught English at N.Y.U., got Wolfe to attend his class in creative writing. During the reading of a story, Wolfe sat pensively brooding, his set jaw resting on a firmly closed fist, and when it was over, he said under his breath to the student beside him, "You know, John invites me to these affairs and then expects me to offer all kinds of suggestions. It is wonderful, but I don't know what to say." He looked worried. A moment later, however, he rose with magnificent diffidence and gave a brilliant and kindly analysis of what he had just heard. Beneath his bulk and celebrity he seemed a touchingly gentle person, reluctant to dash the hopes of these would-be authors.

In August, when the galleys of his novel had begun coming back from the printer, he had sat with them in the Scribner library dreaming of cuts he would like to restore and making so few corrections that John Hall Wheelock had to take over the proofreading. Before he went to the World's Fair, Wolfe had filled all the gaps in his narrative, but he planned further additions, which Perkins forestalled by sending the last half to press during Wolfe's absence. On his return he was outraged. He must have six more months, he said, but Perkins finally persuaded him that the important thing was to publish this book, imperfect though it might be, and get on with the next one.

During his year-long tug of war with Perkins, Wolfe had fluctuated between angry rebellion and almost slavish subservience. "God knows what I would do without him," he had written a friend in February. "I told him the other day that when this book comes out, he could assert it was the only book he had ever written. I think he has pulled me right out of the swamp just by main strength and serene determination." When the proofreading was finished and the novel a *fait accompli,* Wolfe poured out his gratitude in a three-page dedicatory preface to Perkins, which the latter never saw but heard about from Wheelock. He at once wrote Wolfe urging him to omit it. "Nothing could give me greater pleasure or greater pride as an editor than that the book of the writer I have most greatly admired should be dedicated to me if it were sincerely done. But you cannot, and should not, try to change your conviction that I have deformed your book, or at least prevented it from coming to perfection." Perkins added that working on Wolfe's writings, "however it has turned out, for good or bad, has been the greatest pleasure for all its pain, and the most interesting episode of my editorial life." Wolfe then reduced the dedication to the tribute to Perkins, his "dauntless and unshaken friend," that actually appeared in *Of Time and the River,* and in thanking him, Perkins wrote that he was sorry their struggles of the past year were over and that he liked to think they might "go through another such war together."

Early in January, 1935, Wolfe's mother came to visit him, and one evening they had John Terry for dinner. Wolfe bought an eight-pound porterhouse steak, of which his mother only wanted to cook two pounds, saying the whole thing was enough to last them a week, but Wolfe prevailed in his characteristic desire "to cook it all and enjoy it right now." Surveying his nicked, unmatching china with shrewd, falcon eyes, Julia knowingly pursed her lips and said it was high time he got himself some decent tableware, but he brushed it aside as they sat down to a plenteous Southern repast of big red sliced tomatoes, green beans, cabbage, potatoes, hot biscuits, coffee, and rare, juicy steak. Tom was happy that night, talking and eating with excited relish, now and then slapping his thigh and breaking into the great *wha whas* of his books, and at the height of his merriment, rounding his lips and emitting high-pitched *whees* that blotted out all other sounds. Julia was gay also, her muted laughter consisting of long-continued *heh hehs,* and from time to time both would pause to wipe the tears from their eyes.

The following month, when young Sanderson Vanderbilt came to the apartment to interview Wolfe for the *Herald Tribune,* he found the author in a less jovial mood. Wolfe was wary of reporters, who as a tribe seemed more interested in his size than in his work, but with his novel coming out March 8th Scribners had persuaded him that a little advance publicity would do no harm. Wolfe, who was out when Vanderbilt arrived, had left a note telling him to make himself at home, which he proceeded to do. He inspected the legendary refrigerator, whose usefulness as a standing desk has been exaggerated, though Wolfe did occasionally write on it. The bridge lamp in the corner lacked both shade and bulb, and beside the hastily made bed in the adjoining room was an old green alarm clock which only ran when lying on its face. Vanderbilt made a note of the unpaid telephone bill for $17.18, but the *pièce de résistance* was a copy of *Of Time and the River* in which Wolfe had corrected the manifold errors resulting from his negligence with the proofs. Vanderbilt listed some of them for the edification of his readers: "elemental" has gotten printed instead of "eternal," "numerous" instead of "murmurous," "moist" instead of "most," "sweet" instead of "secret."

A taxi door slammed, and presently Wolfe barged in with—as Vanderbilt would begin his piece—"a good two inches of blue shirt separating the bottom of his rumpled vest from the top of his unpressed pants." Apologizing for his tardiness and brushing the cigarette ashes from his suit, Wolfe sat down to a discussion of his projected cycle of six novels which would cover the last hundred and fifty years in America; two were now in print and two others largely done. "I hope the whole thing will be kind of like a plant," Vanderbilt quoted him as saying. "Now don't make that sound kind of fancy. Sort of like a plant that's had a lot of roots in it. . . . I've been learning about writing like hell in the last four years. You might say I've worked like hell. I've got to write five million words, but you fix it up if it sounds like boasting because, damn it, I need some money and I want to sell this book." At the conclusion of the interview Vanderbilt had Wolfe running his fingers through his disordered hair and crying, "I'm a nut!"

The published article, which made Wolfe seem like a deranged bumpkin, angered him and increased his desire to be out of the country when *Of Time and the River* appeared. He had written a friend that he was going to Europe as "part of the freight on a freighter," but at the last minute he booked passage on the *Ile de France,* sailing March 2nd. He was giving up his Brooklyn apartment where he had struggled to produce something and which had a dead feeling now that the struggle was over. On the eve of his departure, he left his 5′×2′×1½′ wooden packing case of manuscript in Perkins' house in Turtle Bay, and as he and Perkins and the cab driver were setting it down in the front hall, Wolfe asked the driver his name. "Lucky," he replied; it was an Americanization of some Italian name. "Lucky!" cried Wolfe, seizing his hand. It seemed a good omen, and they all three shook hands.

Next morning, as he was leaving his hotel with suitcases and assorted packages, a handful of unopened mail, and an extra pair of shoes laced together and slung over his shoulder, he remembered his overdue laundry and went to the phone to ask about it. Half in and half out of the booth, he pled, cajoled, and finally lost his temper, filling the hotel lobby with his invective, which ended in a polite request that the laundryman stick the laundry in a very personal and obviously inadequate part of his anatomy. A group of astonished spectators had gathered round, but it was so real they couldn't help laughing. No sooner had Wolfe hung up than he turned to the friend who was with him and began reproaching himself for talking that way to the poor laundryman who had a cough and looked tubercular; Wolfe need only imagine such a thing for the man to be practically dead. Then he went to the front desk to get the money he had left with the cashier. Having signed the receipt, he peered through the grille and said jestingly, "Better keep that, my girl—it will be valuable someday."

At the boat half a dozen friends were waiting to see him off, and when he landed at Le Havre after a stormy crossing, *Of Time and the River* was out and being reviewed.

Because of his intimate involvement with it, no one had a keener sense of the book's shortcomings than Perkins. He had written Wolfe's agent that it would "contain many too many adjectives, and much repetition of a sort, and too much loud pedalling. Those are faults that Tom won't dispense with as yet." But Perkins thought that the virtues of this 912-page leviathan far outweighed its defects, and he hoped that the criticisms it received would impel Wolfe to a sterner discipline.

Wolfe's virtues, as Perkins conceived them, began with the splendor of his prose, which ran the gamut from sharp, tiny sensitivity to bulky grandeur and which, without denying the grosser aspects of reality, transcended them by giving them a shimmer and a sheen. Back of the style was a unique vision—an urge to body forth the whole of America which only Whitman could rival. "[Wolfe] was wrestling," wrote Perkins after his death, "as no artist in Europe would have to, with the material of literature—a great country not yet revealed to its own people. It was not as with the English artists who revealed England to Englishmen through generations, each one accepting what was true from his predecessors, in gradual accretion, through centuries. Tom knew to the uttermost meaning the literature of other lands and that they were not the literature of America. He knew that the light and color of America were different; that the smells and sounds, its people, and all the structure and dimensions of our continent were unlike anything before. It was with this that he was struggling, and it was that struggle alone that, in a large sense, governed all he did. . . .

"No one so loved this nation, and yet no one denounced it more bitterly—its injustice and violence and waste and inequality. He seemed at times to hate it—but it was the hatred that comes from love."

The previous summer Wolfe had been visiting friends in Rutherford, New Jersey, when after midnight he decided to take the milk train back to New York. His friends accompanied him to the station, and Wolfe was striding along with his head back, watching the moths dance around the lights and listening to the creak of the insects, when suddenly they came to the deserted one-room shack silhouetted in the moonlight with the rails running by like silver ribbons. "Look!" cried Wolfe, his eyes catching fire. "All over the country there are little stations like this, with a tree—there's a factory with a siding for loading freight. Look at the rails. Here!" He made his friends kneel down and feel the vibrations of the oncoming train. Then stepping over to the factory: "Come along, I'll show you how you should write. See these walls. Feel them. You can't write except you feel them. Think of the color. They are yellow. They are *faded* yellow. The moon is shining all over this eastern part of America. It *will* be shining," he said.

Look Homeward, Angel had been a North Carolina book, but in

Of Time and the River he widened his canvas, as in the hymn to October:

"The ripe, the golden month has come again, and in Virginia the chinkapins are falling. Frost sharps the middle music of the seasons, and all things living on the earth turn home again. The country is so big you cannot say the country has the same October. In Maine, the frost comes sharp and quick as driven nails, just for a week or so the woods, all of the bright and bitter leaves, flare up: the maples turn a blazing bitter red, and other leaves turn yellow like a living light, falling about you as you walk the woods, falling about you like small pieces of the sun so that you cannot say where sunlight shakes and flutters on the ground, and where the leaves.

"Meanwhile the Palisades are melting in massed molten colors, the season swings along the nation, and a little later in the South dense woodings on the hill begin to glow and soften, and when they smell the burning wood-smoke in Ohio children say: 'I'll bet that there's a forest fire in Michigan.' And the mountaineer goes hunting down in North Carolina, he stays out late with mournful flop-eared hounds, a rind of moon comes up across the rude life of the hills: what do his friends say to him when he stays out late? Full of hoarse innocence and laughter, they will say: 'Mister, yore ole woman's goin' to whup ye if ye don't go home.'

"Oh, return, return!

"October is the richest of the seasons: the fields are cut, the granaries are full, the bins are loaded to the brim with fatness, and from the cider-press the rich brown oozings of the York Imperials run. The bee bores to the belly of the grape, the fly gets old and fat and blue, he buzzes loud, crawls slow, creeps heavily to death on sill and ceiling, the sun goes down in blood and pollen across the bronzed and mown fields of old October.

"The corn is shocked: it sticks out in hard yellow rows upon dried ears, fit for great red barns in Pennsylvania, and the big stained teeth of crunching horses. The indolent hooves kick swiftly at the boards, the barn is sweet with hay and leather, wood and apples— this, and the clean dry crunching of the teeth is all: the sweat, the labor and the plow is over. The late pears mellow on a sunny shelf: smoked hams hang to the warped barn rafters; the pantry shelves are loaded with 300 jars of fruit. Meanwhile the leaves are turning, turning, up in Maine, the chestnut burrs plop thickly to earth in gusts of wind, and in Virginia the chinkapins are falling."

For Wolfe, this was only a beginning. "I will go out West," he wrote in *Of Time and the River*, "where States are square: Oh, I will go to Boise, and Helena and Albuquerque. I will go to Montana and the two Dakotas and the unknown places." He would ransack the continent and fill his books with its colors though it killed him.

The reception of *Of Time and the River* was more or less what Perkins had anticipated. The critics complained of Wolfe's overwriting, his hyperthyroid emotionalism, his "adolescent" gropings and questionings. For all Perkins' efforts the book was imperfectly shaped and full of loose ends, elaborately drawn characters dropping from view with the suddenness of the animals in *Alice in Wonderland*. And yet it had an eloquence, a magnificence. As J. B. Priestley said later, Wolfe was "one of the rare big chaps . . . one of those great sprawling writers whose work you can easily correct, but whose virtues lie beyond your pains." Bewildering, unclassifiable, he loomed in the literary heavens like some vast nebula, wanting much in form but packing terrific power, and for all his rhetoric he had substance, a closeness to life.

> You praise the firm restraint with which they write—
> I'm with you there, of course:
> They use the snaffle and the curb all right,
> But where's the bloody horse?[5]

With Wolfe there wasn't much doubt of the animal's existence.

Of Time and the River was the literary sensation of 1935, sweeping its author to fame with big sales and excited reviews.

As he waited for the news three thousand miles away, Wolfe sank into a psychotic depression. He was painfully conscious of the book's failings and feared the worst from the critics. From Le Havre he went to Paris where he spent three days drinking and roaming the streets before getting up the courage to read the cable at American Express which Perkins had promised to send on publication day. It said, MAGNIFICENT REVIEWS. SOMEWHAT CRITICAL IN

WAYS EXPECTED. FULL OF GREATEST PRAISE—which Wolfe interpreted
as Perkins' gentle way of telling him the book was a flop.

The next three days were largely a blank in his memory, though
in his pocket notebook he logged his drinks during one twelve-hour
period: "Arose at one o'clock. (1) Whiskey at Adega bar (13F) at
2–3:00—*Two* or *three* amer picons at Regence 3:30–4:20—2 (or
3?) fines at Café de La Paix at 5:30.—(?)—Resolved to take nothing
more—got into taxi and went to Mrs. Beach (had impulse to take
drink before seeing her)—saw her. . . . Went to Mrs. Massey's
(who called this morning at 10 or 11—I was in a strange ship (?)
dizzy state and answered foolishly)—drove from there to Lipp, had
cervelles and (1) beer—from there to Pruniers (oysters and (1)
glass cognac)—from there to hotel where slept 3 hrs.—and now out
to Regence and next place—where (3) fines."

As he later wrote Perkins of this period, he felt as if he were "on
the back of some immense rackety engine which was running wild
and over which I had no more control than a fly." One morning
when he returned to his hotel at dawn and tried to get some sleep,
he seemed "to disintegrate into at least six people—I was in bed and
suddenly it seemed these other shapes of myself were moving *out*
of me—all around me—one of them touched me by the arm—another
was talking in my ear—others walking around the room—and suddenly I would come to with a terrific jerk and all of them would
rush back into me again." Finally he cabled Perkins for the truth,
and the answer was, GRAND EXCITED RECEPTION IN REVIEWS. TALKED
OF EVERYWHERE AS TRULY GREAT BOOK. ALL COMPARISONS WITH GREAT-
EST WRITERS. ENJOY YOURSELF WITH LIGHT HEART.

This convinced him, but when he went to England ten days later
he was still on edge. His English editor, A. S. Frere, met him at
Folkestone, and they drove to Frere's house in Kent overlooking
the Romney Marshes. After a walk through woods and fields and
a splendid roast beef dinner, Wolfe began to feel his old self again,
and that evening the Freres drove him to a London hotel where he
had his first good rest in weeks. Next day they found him a "service
flat" in Mayfair with "a valet like Ruggles of Red Gap," he wrote
John Terry, "and a clean and pretty maid who wakes you up in the
morning with news that breakfast is served in the sitting room—and
then a merry table, ham and eggs, grilled sausages, kippers, toast

and marmalade, a big pot of tea—it's too grand for me, but it's got me eating and sleeping again with some regularity and that's worth a good deal." Frere's wife took him to one of the best tailors for a complete outfitting, and he and Frere dined at a pub where they had "a mug of 'audit ale'—can't describe it adequately here except to say that after one mug you feel thoroughly, beautifully and completely audited—[and] a wonderful creature known as grilled herring that just melts right away the minute you put it in your mouth —and rump steak which was the rumpiest, steakiest, juiciest, thickest and best I'd ever tasted—oh I've done them a grievous wrong about their food."[6]

One day Wolfe lunched with Hugh Walpole, who lived in the Lake District and spoke of his London flat as "a little place to come to when he happened to be in town"—said little place, overlooking Green Park in Piccadilly, consisting of several magnificent rooms crowded with Renoir paintings, Egyptian sculptures, Max Beerbohm drawings, and huge Chinese figures in jade and amber, and containing a library of nothing but first editions, many of them inscribed by their authors. "Well, that's success for you," Wolfe wrote Terry, "success from every pore of his vigorous, ruddy, cheerful personality." Walpole invited Wolfe for another meal, after consulting his little black book full of engagements as Maugham had him do in his satire of Walpole, *Cakes and Ale.* It seemed to Wolfe that Walpole had sold out so completely to success, comfort, and "getting on" that he was no longer capable of attempting an important work—the labor of writing having become the necessary though tedious adjunct to the more pleasant occupation of being a successful popular novelist. Ruffled by criticisms of his recent books, Walpole told Wolfe never to accept the opinion of unsuccessful people about anything—which seemed to have some truth in it until Wolfe reflected that it was often dangerous to accept the opinion of successful people too.

At home, *Of Time and the River* was leaping up the best-seller list, and though he rejoiced over the money this would bring him, Wolfe began to worry about the stigma of cheap popularization that attached to best sellers. As he wrote Perkins, he still felt "a sense of irremediable loss—at the thought of what another six months would have done to that book—how much more whole and perfect it would have been. Then there would have been no criticisms of its episodic character—for, by God, in purpose and spirit, that book was not episodic but a living whole and I could have made it so—the whole inwrought, inweaving sense of time and of man's past conjoined forever to each living present moment of his life could have been manifest—the thing that I *must* and *will* get into the whole thing somehow."[7]

The third week of April he left London thinking he would visit Germany, where blocked royalties were waiting to be spent, and then perhaps go on to Russia. "I am now planning a monumental work in three volumes on The Success of Russian Communism," he kidded Perkins, "and following the example of some of my American colleagues, I figure I shall need at least a week in Russia to gather the necessary material." After rusticating for ten days in the small towns of Norfolk County, where he discovered a "real, blunt and good England" he hadn't known before, he took a boat from Harwich for the Hook of Holland. In Amsterdam his solitude began to oppress him. Though he had come abroad to escape the furor of publication, when he boarded the train for Berlin on May 4th he was "exhausted and sickened and fed up to the roots of my soul with . . . being *alone*. I am tired of myself . . . I am surfeited."

Relief was imminent. News of his triumph had spread to Germany where he was already esteemed as the author of *Look Homeward, Angel*. In 1933, the excellent German translation of that novel had been acclaimed by the serious critics, no less a figure than Hermann Hesse calling it "the most powerful piece of work from contemporary America with which I am familiar." Berlin now threw itself at the feet of the great American *dichter*. "I have heard it said," he would presently be writing Perkins, "that Lord Byron awoke one morning at twenty-four to find himself famous. Well, I arrived in Berlin one night, when I was thirty-four, and got up next morning and went to American Express and for the last two weeks at least I have been famous in Berlin." Like Marlowe's Tamburlaine he found it "passing great to be a king, and ride in triumph through Persepolis. . . . By day there was the shining and the sapphire air, the horse chestnut trees, the singing sparkle of exultant life that swept through me across the town, so that at noon among the great crowds thronging the Kurfürstendamm, I also was a part of the green faery of the great Tiergarten park, and thence unto all crystal sparkles of Berlin, until I seemed to share it all, and all of it to be in me, as but a single, shining and exultant drop of water reflects and shares, and is a part of the million, million scallop shells of dancing light, and every lapping wave, and every white sail on the surface of the Wann See."

His guide in this northern paradise was Martha Dodd—the petite, intellectual daughter of Ambassador William E. Dodd, himself a North Carolinean and a former history professor at the University of Chicago. Enamored of Wolfe's writing, Martha made a beeline for him as soon as she reached Berlin, and thereafter he was a fixture at the embassy. A German observer later recalled his first appearance there—"the dark, imposing head towering above all the guests, the almost coquettishly deferential modesty of the giant who was soon the center of the party, and who was blushingly putting himself out to say something friendly all the time and to brush aside any compliments." The might and music of his personality exalted everyone he met; striding the streets with head aloft and his body full of lumbering rhythm, he personified the freedom and promise of America. For the first time since Hitler's rise to power the Romanische Café, a former gathering place of artists and intellectuals, showed signs of life. People began shyly to enter it for a glimpse of Wolfe holding forth, and going back to his room at the Hotel Am Zoo he would find it full of flowers which women had sent him in his absence. The newspapers published articles about him, and a waggish press photographer snapped a picture of him with a policeman under his arm. Basking in appreciation, flooded with affectionate good will, he was happy as a child. Accompanying a German friend to his house one night, Wolfe folded the thick Sunday edition of the *Berliner Tageblatt* which he had in his hand and threw it with the sure aim of his route days across the street into his friend's garden, listening for the slap and then laughing like a youngster whose trick has come off.

With Martha Dodd and a few others he journeyed to Weimar where he saw Goethe's garden house and the famous saddle chair he sat in when writing; also the laboratories and workshops where he did his experiments, and the crypt where he and Schiller were buried side by side. Wolfe loved German culture and the warmth

and kindness of the people, and certainly the Nazi regime had in-
stilled a new hope, but there was a taint in the atmosphere. Wolfe
had felt it in Berlin as "something half-heard, half-suspected, coming
from afar, a few flung seeds of golden music upon the air, the sudden music of tootling fifes, and suddenly, the solid, liquid smack
of booted feet, and young brown faces shaded under steel goose-
stepping by beneath the green arcades of the Kurfürstendamm, the
army lorries rolling past, each crowded with regimented rows of
young, formal, helmeted, armfolded, ramrodded bodies, and laughter, laughter in the crowd, and laughter rippling like a wave across
the terraces of great cafés, and bubbling like wine sparkles from
the lips of all the pretty women. . . ." Motoring across Germany,
he felt it again in the pleading of an eye, the terror of a look, the
swift concealment of a fear. "This is one of the loveliest towns,"
he wrote on a postcard from Weimar, "one of the most beautiful
countries—yes, and the people too the friendliest—but there are
other things, too, I cannot cheer for."[8]

After five weeks in Germany, he went to Copenhagen to recuperate and then, "crammed to the gills with *kultur, küche,* and
antiquity," he sailed from Bremerhaven on the *Bremen* June 30th.
Landing in New York on a blazing Fourth of July, he was met by
a flock of reporters and by Perkins, who took him to lunch at a
floating restaurant in the East River off Fifty-second Street. Tanned,
glowing with success, and glad to be home, Wolfe looked troubled
when he spoke of the atmosphere in Germany, of the thing which
had prompted him to glance over his shoulder all the time. He and
Perkins were finishing their meal when Scott Fitzgerald came in
unexpectedly and sat at their table for a moment. Pale, tentative,
and unwell, he seemed like a shade beside the ebullient Wolfe.
That evening towards sunset, Wolfe and Perkins went to the roof
of the St. George Hotel in Brooklyn, and looking across at the near-
far splendor of Manhattan, gazing down on all the kingdoms of the
world with his friend at his side, Wolfe was filled with an ecstasy
he had never known and would never know again.

Later, as they strolled across Manhattan carrying their coats because of the heat, they passed the loft where *Look Homeward,*

Angel had been written, and Wolfe insisted that Perkins go up and see it. When no one answered their knock, Perkins suggested they climb the fire escape "to the nest where the eaglet had mewed his mighty youth." And for once the impeccable Perkins was guilty of housebreaking.

9 · FAME

THE America Wolfe came back to was pulling out of the Depression which, for all its suffering, had seemed to him a necessary moral shakedown, a return to the bedrock of toil and endurance. Though unemployment was still rife, thanks to government controls (some would have said despite them) production had been rising. Huey Long and Father Coughlin were at the height of their unsavory appeal, but Roosevelt had hammered through reforms—the WPA, the Wagner Act, a "soak the rich" tax bill—which would spike the guns of the demagogues. That summer Dizzy Dean was baseball, Shirley Temple was box office, and Clifford Odets ruled Broadway with *Waiting for Lefty* and *Awake and Sing!* The cow mildness of his expression belied the fistic deadliness of the young Negro sensation, Joe Louis, who had recently paralyzed Carnera in the sixth. On her maiden voyage in June the *Normandie* had broken the trans-

Atlantic speed record, and the year would end in the saxaphone blare of "The Music Goes Round and Round."

Wolfe's first delightful duty on his return was to cope with his mountain of fan mail at Scribners. Perkins said he had never known anything to equal it—that Wolfe opened people's eyes to "the richness of the world" and "they worship him for it, in gratitude."[1] There were hundreds of letters from men and women in every walk of life, many of them saying they had never written an author before and didn't expect a reply but had to vent their enthusiasm. A note from Sherwood Anderson, whom Wolfe admired and wanted to meet, confessed that after closing *Of Time and the River,* he—Anderson—knew why he could never write a novel. Wolfe wrote James Boyd that it was wonderful to be "a little famous . . . and if it makes a difference to me or my work, except to make it better, please come up here to New York and kick me in the pants the whole way from Scribners to the Battery." Far from giving him a swelled head, success had humbled him and steeled him to greater effort; he was "going to hit this next book like a locomotive," he told Boyd. So happy he couldn't contain himself, he would emerge now and then from the Scribner library, where he and a typist were working on his correspondence, and wander beatifically around the office, talking to secretaries, the receptionist, the elevator man, anyone who would listen.

Since their exchange about her book of stories, Wolfe had heard several times from Aline, whose letters suggested a deepening despair. The other side of her zest for life was a capacity for suffering which he had been conscious of from the earliest days of their love, when a look of brooding melancholy had sometimes suffused her eager, merry face. Her depression had reached the point where she couldn't work, and in June, 1934, she had written him from a sanitarium "where I do not need to keep up a face, I can crumple up and cry or howl when the pain takes me, and need not worry about it making other people uncomfortable." A few months later she was recuperating in Carmel, California, whose "mighty hills" and "great wooded valleys like the inside of a Cathedral" reminded her of Wolfe, and she commended it to him for his future travels. He hadn't answered for fear of arousing false hopes, but on the eve of his departure for Europe he had sent her a copy of his book, neutrally inscribed "For Aline from Tom." Then at the end, where she made her appearance as "Esther" with whom Eugene falls in love on sight, he had inked a line in the margin and written "my dear."

Soon afterwards Aline had begun corresponding with Perkins (whom oddly she had never met) about her concern over Wolfe's next novel, for if he continued the saga of Eugene Gant, he would necessarily deal with their affair. At first she took the position that she didn't care what he said about *her*—"he long ago entered the final stronghold of my being, and whatever I have of love, goodness, and beautiful perception passed from me to him"—but she was worried by what he might say about her family, who had all stood by her "when Tom had almost wrecked my bright soul and loving heart." She wouldn't have them traduced, no matter what means she took to prevent it, and her implied threat of a suit was sharpened by a prejudice against Perkins, whom she suspected of having influenced Wolfe to leave her. When Wolfe had asked his advice, Perkins had merely said that in view of the difference in their ages he didn't see how the relationship could last—feeling privately that it shouldn't be dragged out if Wolfe wanted to end it, and that all this emotionalism was bad for his work. He had admitted as much to Aline when she called on him at his office in June, and at the end of their interview, when he held out his hand, she had put hers behind her back, saying, "I regard you as my enemy." Meanwhile, in a letter to Wolfe she had shifted her ground somewhat. Granting that when they were lovers she had gladly told him all she knew, she asked him—now that he had deserted her—to stop using her material. She was doing a book about her girlhood, and she didn't want their life together—her property, as well as his—paraded in public. She herself was writing about it, however, and ironically her version of their affair was destined to be published before his![2]

In the back of her mind there was still the hope of a reconciliation —perhaps fame had mellowed him—and after he had been home a week without calling her, she arranged to be in the Chatham Bar at the cocktail hour when Perkins habitually stopped there. Sure enough, Perkins came in with Wolfe, who rushed over to Aline as soon as he saw her, and the three of them adjourned to Scribners where they could talk more freely. At one point Wolfe and Perkins left the room to discuss something in private, and on their return they were horrified to see Aline putting a vial of pills to her mouth. Wolfe knocked it out of her hand, and she collapsed in his arms. A doctor who was summoned counted the pills, phoned the pharmacy that had put up the prescription, and ascertained that none had been taken.

Two weeks later Wolfe went West, and when he got back in September, Aline had come to terms with herself. Out of old habit she would help him furnish his new apartment, ordering a king-sized bed at Macy's and advising him against Venetian blinds because "under the most skillful pulling they always get out of order, and you know how *ept* your hands are at managing material things." The few letters she wrote him thereafter were affectionate without bitterness. She saw him rarely but was grateful for every chance to converse with the most congenial spirit she had ever known. "Your welfare and happiness and success," she wrote him, "are always the dearest things in the world to me, the same as [that of] my own children."

What saved her in the end was her religion of work and the irrepressible love of life which had attracted Wolfe in the first place. She had pursued him beyond the point of losing her dignity, almost to self-destruction. She admitted that she was selfish and had wanted a lot, but she had given a lot in return, and her crowning joy, after helping him rise, would have been to share his glory. In a way her position would be easier after his death when her memories of what they had known—"an actual companionship," she wrote Mabel, "that was divine"—were unencumbered by a sense of what she was missing in the moment. She and Perkins would end up fast friends, united in their feeling for Wolfe, who had hurt them in somewhat the same way. "I've started work at Vassar—" Aline would be writing Perkins the fall of 1945 of her course in stage-designing, "hundreds of young women with fine, strong faces, all kinds of faces, and it gave me a pang when I saw my classes to think of what they all have in store for themselves, such wallops as they are going to have to take and nothing can save them; but our old colored cook used to tell me that trouble makes us strong."

When Wolfe came back from Germany, he was not only the author of a critically acclaimed best seller with sales of 40,000 the first year, his name had burgeoned in the magazines as well. In the month of June alone, stories by him had appeared in *Scribner's, Harper's Bazaar, The Modern Monthly, The North American Review, Esquire,* and *The New Yorker,* and before the year was out he would hit *Cosmopolitan, Vanity Fair,* and the *The Saturday Review.* Invited to participate as a "visiting novelist" at the University of Colorado Writers' Conference in Boulder, he jumped at the excuse to see the West with expenses paid.

He left New York July 27th, stopping in Greeley to speak at the Colorado State Teacher's College and reaching Boulder July 31st, where he was immediately pressed into service as part of a panel addressing an audience of several hundred. For one who had been celebrated for his undergraduate oratory, Wolfe was strangely tongue-tied. Swaying to and fro like a chained elephant, he made several attempts before getting out "Ladies and gentlemen," and went on to describe his embarrassment on being asked to explain to a group of writers how he did his writing. He really didn't know, he hadn't analyzed it—all this very hesitatingly and ponderously. Next day when he tip-toed into a poetry workshop on large, creaking shoes, the students stopped listening to the lecturer and gaped at the tall, rumpled barrel of a man as he looked around for a seat, his eyes bright and curious as a child's, the long hair which curled behind his ears giving him a faintly cherubic aspect. He slipped into a chair at the side of the room, and when the lecturer introduced him at the end of the hour, he grinned at everyone in silence. In another class, where he held the floor, he read aloud the description of the horse in "Venus and Adonis"—

> Round-hoof'd, short-jointed, fetlocks shag and long,
> Broad breast, full eye, small head, and nostril wide,
> High crest, short ears, straight legs, and passing strong,
> Thin mane, thick tail, broad buttock, tender hide:

—going on for several stanzas and breaking off suddenly with, "what I mean, that, that . . . well, THAT is a HORSE!" in a tone that brought the house down. His accompanying shrug expressed more clearly than words, "It's an effect worth trying for, so read as much of this sort of thing as you can find, but how can I, how can you, how can anyone hope to equal it? It's impossible, but go ahead and try."

The conference director had given Wolfe some of the more promising novel manuscripts to go over and discuss with their authors, and Wolfe recommended three of them to Scribners for an immediate reading. But more valuable than his technical advice was the sense he gave his students that nothing is trivial, that the conversation with the cook that morning or the spray of blossom in the garden are matters of importance, causes for wonder—though even Wolfe's capacity for wonder had limits. One night at a party when he was summoned out of doors to witness a phenomenon, he came back puzzled. "Do you know what that man wanted to show me?" he said. "Every number on his speedometer stands at three—the miles travelled today, the total number of miles. Well, hell, it's gotta happen sometime!"

He took his job seriously; he was interested, available, and eager to please. In the presence of Robert Penn Warren, who had severely criticized *Of Time and the River,* he said in the nicest way that there was one review of his book which had been by no means favorable, but that he had learned from it and appreciated it. As one observer recalled, Wolfe was "not so much lionized as adored. There seemed to reside in him such an intensity of living experience, along with the honesty and humility." Students trailed him around the campus, and over drinks he was mountainous, voluble, and warm, smashing down his fist with an incontrovertible "By God, this is on me!" if someone else tried to pick up the tab. He was the despair of his hostesses, however, for becoming engrossed at one party, he would forget about the next, though fifty guests were awaiting his arrival to sit down to dinner.

The climax of the conference was his evening address to a capacity crowd of seven hundred. Unlike the preceding addresses on such topics as "What is a Short Story?" "The Recent Southern Novel," and "What Poetry Thinks," Wolfe's was nakedly, almost embarrassingly personal. Before leaving New York he had prepared a speech of seventy-four typewritten pages about the composition of *Of Time and the River,* from which he departed somewhat once he got rolling. He conquered his audience at the start by putting himself on their level; he said he wasn't a professional writer or even a skilled writer, but just a writer on his way to discovering the avenues appropriate for him, and that he would try to tell them some of the things he had learned. When he paused at the end of an hour, apologizing for his verbosity and offering to stop, the audience shouted him on, and for another forty minutes he kept them on the edge of their seats with his ability to communicate his own travail. And then, at the reception afterwards, there he was moving among them with outstretched hand, saying, "I'm Tom Wolfe—who are you?"

When the conference broke up, he took an auto trip with the poet Tom Ferril and his wife, who drove him to the reconstructed gold-mining town of Central City and showed him the location of the "Blossom Rock" which had started the gold rush of '59. They traversed the Platte canyon country to Shaffers Crossing, a hangout of the bandits lying in wait for the gold trains, and then, skirting the northern side of Pikes Peak, they went down Ute Pass, the trail used by the buffaloes and Indians coming up from the plains. At Colorado Springs Wolfe was met by a former teaching associate at N.Y.U., who drove him across the desert of New Mexico to Santa Fe.

There, at a lunch in his honor, he fell in with two young society women who happened to be driving north that day and offered to drop him at Mabel Dodge Luhan's in Taos. This literary head-hunter and the genius-collector—the former paramour of John Reed and close friend of D. H. Lawrence—had written him a specially gratifying letter about *Of Time and the River,* and had asked him to visit her on his Western trip. Phoning ahead, he promised to arrive in time for a 6:30 supper, but he and the two young women sat drinking Tom Collinses till late afternoon. Then they were driving along the Rio Grande which glowed metallically in the waning light, with Wolfe pouring out his love of the West. "I feel as if I'd been born here," he said, "come up through the earth here." As they entered a village with high adobe walls surrounding the church, Wolfe asked them to stop so he could climb the wall. "I hate scenery unless I can do something with it," he explained, but having gotten out, he thought better of it and instead drew a bottle of gin from his tousled luggage and they all had a drink before pressing on.

On the Taos plateau, where it had been raining, they stopped again to sit on the running board and breathe the aroma of wet sage. Wolfe thought the wild and beautiful scenery demanded a big toast, a real libation to the glory of it, and he went on toasting and libating all the way in to the Taos pueblo. He was already an hour late at Mrs. Luhan's, but his companions decided he must sober up before meeting her, so he called her on the wall phone of a café where they stopped for something to eat. "Mabel!" he roared in his throaty, resonant voice. "Sorry, I'm late!" Pause. "Well, can I bring along two whores who're with me? You'll like 'em!" Mrs. Luhan evidently hung up, for the next thing they knew Wolfe was flashing the operator, sputtering indignantly, and calling for vengeance in his best Edwin Booth manner. Everyone was listening and laughing, and as he went back to his table a woman shouted, "That's telling 'em, Big Boy!" Presently a man came over and said, "You're famous—who are you?" "Anthony Adverse," Wolfe replied. Word got around, heads turned in his direction, and a few people brought him magazines and papers which he duly autographed "Anthony Adverse." It was 9:30 when they got to Mrs. Luhan's, with Wolfe still far from sober.

Mrs. Luhan had posted a man with a torch who led them along the twisting road to her casa, but she herself had retired, leaving Ina Cassidy, a talented and spirited lady in her sixties, to open the door. Mrs. Cassidy invited them into the living room where Wolfe settled himself in one richly upholstered chair and put his feet on another. Informed that Mrs. Luhan had gone to bed, he expostulated that this was no way to treat a guest, that she had pursued him, and that he was used to having women stay up all night to meet him. When Mrs. Cassidy reproved him for not behaving like a gentleman, he said she was drunk and would feel differently about it in the morning. Mrs. Cassidy told the two young women—they were friends of hers—to leave, she would take care of Wolfe, she said, but no sooner were they in their car than Wolfe, shouting imprecations at his absent hostess, rushed out to join them. No flare guided them as they drove away from the house in which all the lights appeared to be lit. Wolfe was comparing Mrs. Luhan to a big fat spider ready to pounce on any celebrity, but he had been flattered by the invitation to her web, and this ambivalence had no doubt brought on the dramatics.[3]

Perkins thought Wolfe should be heading back. "Don't go and stretch your travels out too long," he wrote. ". . . I feel nervous about your being there in the vicinity of Mabel Dodge Luhan." Having come this far, however, Wolfe was determined to see the coast, and he assured Perkins that "in the end, we shall not lose by it." On his way to California he was accosted by a college professor in the Albuquerque railroad station, and Wolfe suggested they meet in the smoker after dinner. In the dining car the professor, sitting several tables away with his family, was fascinated by Wolfe's absorption in his food. Ranging over his plate, he brought to mind some great bear, some marvellous gorilla, the way he stuffed things in; shreds of macaroni dripped from his mouth as he drank with one hand and signalled the waiter with the other to bring him a second planked steak. Later, over highballs, he told the professor about writing his books—a repeat of his Boulder lecture with new roman candles of word association and imagery. He seemed naïvely pleased by his reception at the conference. "They all seemed to know who I was," he said.

In Hollywood, friends took him to M-G-M, where he asked for an introduction to Jean Harlow who was on the set at the time. Though she had never heard of him, she warmed as story editor Sam Marx explained who he was. Wolfe spent the rest of the day watching her, drove off the lot that evening in her limousine, and came back with her next morning to watch some more. When Marx offered him a $1,500-a-week contract, he declined, though not from any scruple about prostituting his talent. As he later remarked, if Hollywood wanted to prostitute him by buying one of his books for the movies, his position was that of the Belgian virgin the night the Germans took the town: "When do the atrocities begin?" But lucrative scriptwriting didn't tempt him because his own work was so overwhelmingly important to him.

A week later he was in Palo Alto visiting a doctor he had met on the *Bremen,* and one afternoon they went to Big Basin, a grove of giant redwoods near Santa Cruz. When Wolfe got out of the car to put his arms around one of the trees, he found he could only embrace a tiny segment of the trunk. Then he lay down on the thick carpet of needles and looked up through the branches, and the doctor remembered it as the one time he ever saw Wolfe hushed. On his way east the middle of September, he stopped in St. Louis to visit the house where his brother Grover had died in 1904, and a reporter who interviewed him discovered him "in shirt-sleeves, his bulky trousers upheld by galluses which could safely be used to tie up a fair-sized yawl, his black hair roached back but resisting the process." Wolfe told the reporter that at last he had "gotten some celebrity and a bit of money, and it would be silly to say I don't enjoy it. I like it so much that I'm going to work all the harder to get more money and more celebrity."

Back in New York he took a three-room apartment at 865 First Avenue on the fourteenth floor overlooking the East River, whose flashing tides and traffic of boats delighted his eye. Perkins lived two blocks away on Forty-ninth Street, and for the moment Wolfe had everything, or seemed to: fame, financial security, good health, plenty to do, and an eager public awaiting his next book.

Picture him that autumn, just turned thirty-five, as he barges up Fifth Avenue at an arm-swinging gait between a walk and a run, his head rearing above the other pedestrians, his look of intensity suggesting that something magnificently important or infinitely tragic is about to happen. Suddenly he wheels and strides into Scribners as if assailing a fort. The onlooker, not knowing what this imperial figure was up to, wouldn't necessarily have taken him for an author. With his cast of a country person who has gotten a little polish somewhere, he might have been associated with the performing arts—say, the assistant manager of a circus—or he could have passed for an engineer supervising the construction of a large dam. What impressed you when you met him was his simplicity and directness: here, you knew, was a man used to shifting large loads and one who faced life with a joyous abandon, trusting his instincts and reactions and finding them good. This self-acceptance, reinforced by a glowing vitality, gave his every word the integrity of gospel. Natural and intensely personal, he was no sooner introduced than he would be pouring out his thoughts and feelings—especially his feelings—with the confidingness of a child at the kitchen table.

When he entered a room full of people, he could still it with his presence, and when he began to talk in his sympathetic, heavyish, cadenced baritone (not quite as deep as you might have expected from a man of his hugeness) all that he said seemed to flow from some bubbling-over, incandescent source. Telling a story was for him a creative act and often the prelude to writing it. He would get high on a subject and go on and on, with the words spurting out of him, rolling down his sleeves, popping from his trouser cuffs—precise, pictorial words used a little differently than you had ever heard them used before and arousing sentiments you didn't know you possessed. When he came to the funny part, he would roll his eyes and look sly, though he didn't go out of his way for laughs; the humor was incidental to his rough-and-tumble narration. A practiced mimic, he would take off the botanist he had met on an English train who claimed to be "fairly sure of himself with the grahsses but rather shy with the sedges" and make him so real you felt he was there in the room. Or, puffing out his cheeks, he would parody a portly Municher reaching for slabs of sausage and cheese and swilling beer, while denouncing American materialism. "All you Americans think about is filling your bellies! No history, no culture, no refinement . . . glub-glub." Pulling his hat down over his ears, he was Max Perkins to a T, and tears would come to his eyes as he impersonated the members of his family caught up in some ancient woe. "It was tragic, tragic," he would say. Then shaking his head and beginning to laugh: "But it had its grotesque aspects too."

Occasionally a listener would grow impatient with what seemed to him a sort of road-company Whitmanese. "There's nothing like the smell of fresh-sawed pine boards," Wolfe would proclaim, as if he were the first to discover it, and sometimes another writer or artist might wish that Wolfe would simmer down and give *his* dynamic creativity a chance. But on the whole the egocentricity was made palatable by its innocence. Wolfe talked, after all, not about himself, but about his experiences, about the river of life flowing past him, and he did it with such relish that his audience hung on his words. Though he rolled over you, he wasn't a juggernaut, for he hadn't any spikes. His face in repose was enormously gentle.

He had grown rather stout, with even a hint of jowls, but he still looked the poet, especially in profile. The mop of hair sweeping back from his domed forehead and curling in untidy tendrils was more leonine than ever, and the tip-tilted nose seemed as always a trifle small and delicate for the rest of the face. His dark, penetrating eye had a defensive, somewhat haunted quality. In the midst of conversation he would suddenly stare off into space, and then you knew he had it, the thing—whatever it was—came alive inside him, to issue presently in a spate of words, his pouting underlip trembling with emotion. A moment later, his humor breaking through, that petulant mouth would widen into the warmest and most winning of smiles—a grin from ear to ear, turning up in the left-hand corner and as full of fun as a boy's before he reaches the self-conscious stage.

Much lionized and sought after, he was going out a lot, and as usual one took him on his own terms. A friend stopping by to drive him to some festivity would find him hard at work, and though Wolfe promised to be through in a moment, he might go on writing for another hour, after which, like a plane cutting down for a landing, he would pace the apartment talking of what he had written and reading some of it aloud. Late for one party, he would stay doubly long to make up for it, thus compounding his tardiness at the next. Invited for eight o'clock dinner, he might not show up until midnight, and then it would be dawn before you got rid of him. Ever his homespun self, he would bring his battered portmanteau with a bit of underwear protruding into a Park Avenue salon and place it in plain view so he wouldn't forget it when he left to catch his train. Once he came to a cocktail party with an atomizer which he put on the floor beside him. Reaching for it presently, he said, "I hope you all won't mind if I do this—I've got a cold and it seems to help," and everyone watched happily as he sprayed his nostrils.

He was certainly old shoe, and yet somehow the final impression he created was that of an easy, *uneasy* man, chafing physically and mentally at the restraints of our too small, too careful world. "Tom was always," said Mrs. Max Perkins after his death, "held down by some kind of bonds, wasn't he? The shortness of a path, the smallness of a room, or the lack of space in people's motives." He was built on a different scale, like some visitor from Mars: though you expected him to be big, you were never quite prepared for the enormity of his broad-shouldered, long-limbed, six-and-a-half-foot frame which had now expanded to a girthy two hundred and fifty pounds. The hostess leading him to a chair would be thinking, "Will it hold this time or will it give?" and when he made one of his normal gestures in a crowded living room, you expected half a dozen people to fall down.[4] After a meal which seemed ample by ordinary standards, you knew from a certain meek, downtrodden atmosphere that Wolfe hadn't had enough, and his capacity for drink was such that if you were wise you put a bottle of Scotch and a pitcher of water by his chair, so that he could replenish as often as he liked without interrupting his talk.

After the long layoff, he was having difficulty getting back into the traces. When he sat down to it, he found he had gone stale on *The October Fair,* the withheld portion of the *Of Time and the River* manuscript covering his affair with Aline, and instead he went to work on the other partially written novel in his series of six, *The Hills Beyond Pentland*, which dug into family history. He spent most of the fall on a prologue for it which he called "The Book of Night"—roving glimpses of the American continent after dark, the sort of rhapsodic impressionism he loved to do.

More accessible than he had been in Brooklyn, he was plagued —despite an unlisted number—by people he scarcely knew calling him up and ringing his doorbell at all hours. Wishing he saw something of those he really cared about, he decided shortly before Christmas to give a dinner for his North Carolina friends then living in New York. There were four couples and John Terry, and Wolfe had expected to buy all the food, but to his surprise each of the wives brought something along—chickens prepared for frying, or biscuits ready to bake. Wolfe's party manner was the more engaging for being a little gauche and unaccustomed; as the women went about the cooking, he kept getting in their way—officious and eager to please. "Tom," laughed one of them, "everything about you begins with 'g.' You're greedy, you have a gargantuan appetite, you're gay, you're grim, when you talk you're a gushing waterfall." And having gotten in her licks, she added, "You're also great!"

With his cracked, miscellaneous china and his silver mostly of ten-cent-store origin, places were set at his writing table and two card tables borrowed for the occasion. Finally they sat down to eat in a glow of good fellowship, and afterwards the men settled back to smoke and reminisce while the women over Tom's protest —leave it for the cleaning woman, he said—washed the dishes and tidied up the kitchen. At the height of the evening he reached up with a black crayon and scrawled across the ceiling, "Merry Christmas to all my friends and love from Tom," and one of the wives, climbing on her husband's shoulders, responded in lipstick, "Same to you." Towards midnight the guests began to leave, Wolfe wishing them effusive farewells and begging them with a sorrowful look to come back soon. The company had dwindled to John Terry and the Mack Gorhams, who were congratulating him on the party's success, when the doorbell rang.

"Who on earth is that?" said Wolfe, going to the door.

In the hallway a buxom, rather attractive woman stood smiling at him. She was swaying a little as though she too had been celebrating. Wolfe looked at her inquiringly.

"Oh, Mr. Wolfe," she said, "I live in the next apartment. I've seen you going up and down in the elevator, and though I have never spoken to you I feel very close to you."

Wolfe glanced back at his friends in wordless appeal.

"The elevator man told me that you've been having a party," the woman went on. "It's after midnight, I know you feel like some bacon and eggs, and I cook the best bacon and eggs." She reached up and put her hand on his tall shoulder. "You must let me cook you some bacon and eggs."

"It's awfully nice of you," said Wolfe, heading her off, "but I couldn't possibly. We've just had a big feast and I'm full of fried chicken."

"Well, let's don't stand here in the doorway," she chided. "My name is ——. Can't I come in and meet your friends?"

Wolfe introduced her with obvious reluctance. He offered her a chair and brought her a drink which she gulped as she began talking volubly about practically nothing.

"My God, my God, who's this?" said Wolfe when the bell rang again.

He opened the door on a small, dapper young man who was obviously feeling no pain. To everyone's surprise Wolfe asked him in and introduced him as the crime editor of a New York publishing house. They had met a few nights before when some people Wolfe had known in Hollywood had phoned Max Perkins at 3 A.M. for his address. They had come straight to his apartment, waked him, and insisted he go out with them, the crime editor being one of the party. These explanations were interrupted by gurgling noises. The crime editor had knocked over the gallon jug of wine on the table, and it was making a puddle on the rug underneath. Wolfe lunged to retrieve it, and the young man, trying to get there first, made a wild grab that sent the wine whirling over the floor. This amused the buxom woman, whose laughter attracted the young man's attention; he sat down at her feet and began making passes at her, which she blearily fended off. Wolfe called him to order and when he paid no heed, Wolfe picked him up bodily and placed him on a straight chair where he teetered precariously.

"I don't know who this lady is," said Wolfe, "but as long as she is my guest, you have got to respect her."

At which point the lady and the Gorhams decided to go, leaving Wolfe and Terry to cope with the crime editor.

"John," Wolfe pleaded, "will you help me get this drunk home? I never saw him until two nights ago, and if I don't get rid of him he'll pester me for no telling how long."

With one of them propping him on each side, they walked the young man to his apartment house six blocks away through newly fallen snow. The cold seemed to revive him, and when they got to his door he insisted they come in and see his place. In the living room he picked up an automatic lying on the table and began twirling it on his forefinger.

"Greatest pistol in the world," he said. "Shoots seven times without stopping."

Wolfe and Terry eyed each other in consternation. There was no way of knowing whether the safety catch was on.

"Don't you want to look at it, Tom?"

Wolfe accepted it with relief and suggested they have some black coffee to sober up. While the young man was in the kitchen putting the water on the flame, Wolfe hid the automatic behind a row of books, but on his return the young man picked up another one they hadn't noticed. When Wolfe asked to see it, he surrendered it meekly and sank into a chair where he was soon asleep. Turning off the stove, Wolfe and Terry left.[5]

Fame had its drawbacks. Wolfe's inherent loneliness and his thirst for human contact made him an easy target for time-wasters and bores. A well-known figure around New York, he was quickly recognizable because of his size and impact, and he wouldn't have been in a night club very long before the grinning bandleader struck up "Who's Afraid of the Big Bad Wolf?" That fall a cartoon in *The New Yorker* showed a disheveled giant berating a mild runt at a cocktail party while one woman said to another, "He looks a little like Thomas Wolfe, and he certainly makes the most of it." A subsequent item in that magazine's "Talk of the Town" told of Wolfe being joined in the elevator of his apartment house by a lady with a police dog that began jumping all over him. When he pushed the dog away, the lady said, "Wolfe! you great, obnoxious beast!" Wounded, the author had "spent the rest of the day wandering along the waterfront in the rain, bumping into warehouses and brooding like a character in one of his novels." The matter was cleared up when the elevator man told him the police dog's name was Wolf—"which, when you say it fast, sounds pretty much like 'Wolfe.' The lady, Mrs. Sabine Baring-Gould, was bawling out the dog and not the novelist whom, as a matter of fact, she rather admires."

She among many. The women were after him. "Will Triton ever blow his wreathed horn," one wrote him, "or Tom call me at Lex 2-8126?" And another, with wily sophistication: "I know that you have no intention of coming to the party tonight, and it is just as well—I saw the horror in your eye when I said it was a costume affair—which it has now turned out to be with a vengeance. . . . But anyway, all that was just an excuse, a pretext to see you again. Will you lunch with me one day soon? You will? Well then, let's say Monday or Tuesday the 26th or 27th—just to put it far enough off to make excuses rather difficult for you to think up." And still another, *ex post facto*: "I had a great impulse this afternoon to send you a telegram with a few foolish words which only we would understand, but thought better of it as I do not know the circumstances of your private life, and would not want to disrupt any smooth-going situation which may mean much to you. Last night was so divinely perfect, every minute of it, that when I think of it little shivers of excitement and pleasure and tenderness run through me. It was sweet lying in your arms for hours. You are so kind and gentle, along with your deep passion which is so strong and so *direct* and so thrillingly relentless."

Wolfe's mixture of boyishness, virility, and renown appealed to a wide spectrum of women, from out-and-out sensation-mongers to bluestockings who had read his books and whose husbands seemed blue milk by comparison. There were some, too, who wanted primarily to mother him, for it was impossible to conceive of him sewing on a button, hanging a picture, or preparing the simplest food. Yet those who became involved had a bad time of it. "He was," said one of them, "intolerable and wonderful and talked like an angel and was a real son-of-a-bitch." He could be charming all evening only to phone his companion after taking her home and accuse her of pursuing him and trading on his name.[6] Or, half-drunk, he might inform her that he had spit blood and was having a hemorrhage, and hypochondriac that he was, he probably believed it. "You know I'm going to die of T.B.," he would add in a sepulchral tone. His drinking had increased, as it always did when his work was troubling him. In the trough of one of his manic-depressive cycles, he would decide that his talent was deserting him or that he wouldn't live long enough to get down all that he had to say, and clutching his head he would hurl himself around the room like one distraught and almost insane, and then, coming out of it, he would beg the woman who was with him to stand by him, not to leave him. "Put your arms around me and tell me I'm all right."

Women were a solace, but disliking their guile and possessiveness, he preferred on the whole the company of men. Once when Max Eastman and Sherwood Anderson were saying in his presence that they were most themselves when talking to women, Wolfe hotly demurred. He was, however, strongly sexed and uninhibited in his expression of it. If he met a girl at a cocktail party and sensed her availability, he was quite capable of taking her into another room and making love to her, and later in the evening—when someone pointed her out—of asking, "Who's she?" He was familiar with what he called "the coarse appeasement of the brothel," and yet at the same time he had a wistful longing for domesticity and was always asking friends if they wouldn't find him some nice girl to marry, half-aware that no woman could assuage his loneliness or contain his lawlessness.[7]

After reading everything in sight while he was finding himself, he had cut down on new reading since hitting his stride, though he constantly reread the English poets and his favorite parts of the Bible—Job, Psalms, Proverbs, Ecclesiastes, The Song of Solomon, and Isaiah. Some of the other books he went back to for refreshment were *War and Peace, Anna Karenina, The Brothers Karamazov, Moll Flanders, Leaves of Grass,* Joyce's *Ulysses,* Burton's *Anatomy of Melancholy,* and *Moby Dick,* the last of which he had first read in 1930 to find out why the critics compared him with Melville. They had also likened him to Whitman, of whom he had read comparatively little before *Look Homeward, Angel,* though since then Whitman had become a standby. As he confined himself to books like these when immersed in his own writing, his burst of miscellaneous reading that fall and winter was a sign that his work was languishing.[8] On the back of an envelope postmarked February 21, 1936, he listed the following as recently read, at least in part: Carlyle's *Past and Present,* Dickens' *Tale of Two Cities,* Shakespeare's *Henry V,* Twain's *Life on the Mississippi,* Whitman's *Specimen Days in America,* Pepys' *Diary,* Thackeray's *Book of Snobs* and *Paris Sketchbook,* Tolstoy's *Resurrection,* Browning's *The Ring and the Book,* Maurice Baring's *Collected Sketches,* Beard's *Rise of American Civilization,* and—reflecting his perennial interest in the Civil War—General Gordon's *Reminiscences,* Abner Doubleday's *Chancellorsville and Gettysburg,* and J. F. C. Fuller's *Grant and Lee.* The only staples he mentioned were *The Oxford Book of English Verse* and *The World Almanac,* whose "wonderful, hard and certain figures" on everything imaginable he loved to contemplate.

Unable to recapture the mood in which he had conceived his series of six novels covering the last hundred and fifty years, he was casting about for a new approach and began to ponder an objective, satiric novel with an author as its protagonist. "Someday," he had remarked in 1932, "I think I will write a book about what happens to a fellow who writes a book." To rescue it from autobiography he would give it the legendary quality of *Don Quixote, Gulliver's Travels,* and *Candide*; with a like detachment he would show an innocent venturing into the world and striking his shins on hard reality. He would use as his epigraph these words from *War and Peace*: "Prince Andrei . . . turned away. . . . His heart was full of melancholy. It was all so strange, so unlike what he had anticipated." In March, he discussed the idea with Perkins who snapped his fingers and told him to go ahead; Perkins said he had always known that Wolfe would have to write such a book and that he was the only one who could. Giving it the working title of *The Vision of Spangler's Paul* (Spangler's Spring was a site on the Gettysburg battlefield near his father's birthplace), Wolfe began it on St. Patrick's Day and the book went swiftly ahead. In May, Perkins wrote a friend that Wolfe was "working hard and God knows what the result will be, but I suspect it will be the end of me. A worse struggle than *Of Time and the River* unless he changes publishers first."[9] The third and last of his great creative cycles had begun.

By midsummer he felt sufficiently launched to take a vacation in Germany. *Of Time and the River* had just been published there and handsomely reviewed, and his blocked royalties had gone on accumulating. Sailing on the *Europa* July 23rd, he went straight to Berlin where he renewed his friendship with the Dodds at the embassy and was feted by his *bon vivant* publisher, Ernst Rowohlt. The Olympics were taking place, but the games themselves seemed only a pretext for demonstrations of Nazi might. Wolfe saw Hitler in his shining limousine drive slowly along "the tremendous banner-laden ways" walled with troops, and "something like a wind across a field of wheat was shaken through the crowd." Since his visit the previous summer, the international climate had darkened. Germany had occupied the Rhineland, Mussolini had subdued Ethiopia, and Fascist-backed rebellion had broken out in Spain.

One afternoon at the games, when Jesse Owens sprinted to a spectacular victory, Wolfe was sitting in the diplomatic box with the Dodds, and he let out such a whoop that Hitler turned in his seat and peered down, as if to locate the miscreant. "Owens was black as tar," Wolfe said later, his attitude towards the Negro being the benevolent superiority of the Old South, "but what the hell, it was our team, and I thought he was wonderful. I was proud of him, so I yelled." When Wolfe was interviewed by the *Berliner Tageblatt,* the reporter brought along a woman artist to draw his picture, and something passed between her and Wolfe the minute she entered the room. A ruddy-cheeked Valkyrie with a shining braid of hair wound round her head, Thea Voelcker was thirty, divorced, and beautifully proportioned, though almost as tall for a woman as Wolfe was for a man.

He persuaded her to go away with him to the Austrian Tyrol, and in the village of Alpbach, amid the sounds of hobnailed boots on gravel and water splashing in troughs and cows drinking, they lived their brief idyl. Across the valley was the 8,000-foot Galtenberg which Wolfe climbed one morning all by himself, later boasting to Perkins that it made his "New England mountains look like toadstools." He spent the evening carousing with the farmers who came to the hotel to drink the pale-red native wine and dance to Tyrolean harp and zither music. Wolfe was happy at first, and then, as with most of his affairs, this one degenerated into bitterness and vituperation, although Thea was deeply in love, and the letters she wrote him after his return to America showed rare understanding. "Dear, honest, delicate, sensitive man," she called him, despite the fact that in their quarrels he had been "harder and more pitiless than a revenging god." She saw him as belonging in the company of the great, solitary, and—in the self-abnegating sense—religious artists like Beethoven and Van Gogh, whose work had been accomplished at the cost of their everyday happiness. But so far Wolfe had failed to achieve their resignation. He was two people: a greedy, dionysiac youth and a seer "as old as the world." He seemed afraid that curbing the youth would diminish the seer, but she believed, on the contrary, that it would be the making of him, by channelling all his strength into his work.[10]

From the Tyrol Wolfe went to Munich for a few days, then back to Berlin. The Nazi oppression had tightened since his last visit. The summer before he had met a German of an old family distinguished for its scholarship, who had talked with him in a café till three one morning about his hatred of the Nazis, and had they been overheard the German would have been shot. Now Wolfe lunched with this man in his apartment high up between the thick walls of a great house in Berlin. There were geraniums on the window sill and the windows were open, but the city noises seemed remote. The man had resumed his condemnation of the regime when suddenly he noticed the windows, and like someone shutting himself away from a pestilence, he sprang to his feet, closed and locked them, and in a trembling voice reviled his wife for her carelessness. She tried to calm him, insisting there was no danger this far above the street, but on the verge of hysteria he said that in these times no one could be sure about anything.

On another occasion Wolfe was told that a little man wanted to see him. The man had previously been employed by Wolfe's publisher, and when Wolfe asked to have him invited to a party, the publisher said it was impossible, that during the past year this man and all others like him had been discharged from their jobs, for he was a Jew. It would be unwise to meet him in public, but if Wolfe wanted to see him, a private meeting could be arranged. "And so I met him in secrecy in a room one afternoon," Wolfe later recalled. "And this little man came in, and I had known him before, not very well, and now, what was there to say? He was a little scrap of a man, not more than five feet tall, and he had always been a shabby-looking little man, and now I saw him and remembered he was wearing the same shabby little suit that he had always worn, except that now his shabby little suit was frayed and patched, and his collar was clean, but he had turned it, and it had the mottled look that collars have when people launder them themselves. He wore a shoestring of a tie, and his neck and Adam's apple were as thin and stringy as gristle, and his eyes were like sunk comets in his face. His little claw-like hands were cold as fish and trembled when he talked; and all that I can remember that he said to me, shaking his head upon that gristle of a neck, was, 'Sir—sir—the world is very sad, sir; the world is very sad.'"[11]

Despite the Nazis, Wolfe retained an affection for the German people which they reciprocated. The reporter for the *Berliner Tageblatt* had written that, in type, Wolfe resembled a South German peasant and that his head brought to mind certain drawings by Albrecht Dürer. His writings, too, eloquently translated by the poet Hans Schiebelhuth, seemed inherently German in their blend of earthiness and mysticism, their romantic, declamatory fullness.

Perhaps for the very reason that Wolfe's friends were mostly anti-Nazis trying to make him see the light, he gave the regime the benefit of the doubt. In his notebook he listed its pros and cons: "For: Physical Clean-ness, Healthy People, Effective Relief, A Concentration of Natural Energy. Against: Repression of Free Speech, a Cult of Insular Superiority, with this A Need For Insular Domination." And there remained his old ambivalence about the Jews. "I don't like Jews," he wrote in his notes of the journey, "and if most of the people that I know would tell the truth about their feelings, I wonder how many of them would be able to say that they liked Jews."

But then as he was leaving the country in September, he caught a glimpse of the Nazi terror which crystallized his feelings once and for all. There were four other passengers in his train compartment —one of them a dour, suspicious little man whom Wolfe instantly disliked, though as the trip progressed and they all became acquainted, Wolfe decided that old Fuss-and-Fidget wasn't so bad, that beneath his crusty exterior he was really rather nice. At the border town of Aachen, Wolfe left his car to watch them change engines, and on his return he found the passageway full of people whose "feeding silence" indicated a crisis. Something fateful was occurring in his compartment behind the drawn shades. Just then the door opened and a burly uniformed man with sprouting mustaches came out, climbed clumsily down to the platform, and signalled excitedly to a colleague. Wolfe began to tremble with that hatred of the police which had caused him to run amuck in the South Carolina jail. He wanted to smash this fat-necked, shaven-headed official and kick his lumbering buttocks.

As the officers re-entered the compartment, Wolfe saw two others inside, and Fuss-and-Fidget sat huddled up facing them. As Wolfe later described it, "his face was white and pasty. It looked greasy as if it were covered with a salve of cold, fat sweat. Under his long nose his mouth was trembling in a horrible attempt at a smile. And in the very posture of the two men as they bent over him and questioned him there was something revolting and unclean." Again the door was shut, the awful stillness prevailed, and Wolfe was told by one of the others in his compartment that the little man—a Jew— had been apprehended trying to smuggle his savings out of the country. Then the officers were coming out with the little man be-tween them. One of them carried his suitcase, and as they herded him down to the platform, Wolfe could hear him protesting "in a voice that had a kind of anguished lilt in it . . . that the whole thing could be explained, that it was an absurd mistake." As the train pulled out, he stopped pleading long enough to raise his terror-stricken eyes and look directly at Wolfe, who felt guilty and ashamed, knowing that he was saying farewell "not to some pathetic stranger . . . but to mankind; not to some nameless cipher out of life, but to the fading image of a brother's face."

In Paris, where Wolfe spent a week before sailing, he wrote the incident with every detail fresh in his mind, intending it as one of the adventures of Spangler's Paul, though the piece was destined for a career independent of the novel.

10 · MAX

In contrast to "Tom, the far-wanderer," as Perkins called him (borrowing an epithet from *Look Homeward, Angel*), Perkins himself was a stay-at-home of inflexible routine. He had been abroad only once—a business trip to London in 1927—and his occasional jaunts with Hemingway came under the heading of business also. Out-and-out vacations he looked down on. "Why?" he would chaff the secretary who put in for one. "To get rested from what?—you haven't done anything." And he would hand the editor going on his honeymoon a batch of manuscript with the comment that the layoff should give him plenty of time to read. "Blessed is he who has found his work," said old Carlyle; "let him ask no other blessedness" —which summed up Perkins completely. The man was his job to a rare degree, and he shut himself away in it more and more as his deafness abstracted him from the world around him. His infirmity had grown quite marked, though he stubbornly made light of it and refused to wear a hearing aid, claiming that his chief difficulty was the way people mumbled; if only they would enunciate clearly like so-and-so, he said, little realizing that so-and-so was yelling.[1] As for his other crotchet of wearing his hat in the office, it was so much a part of him that no one gave it a thought. Once when a lady visitor, coming to see him for the first time, apologized for interrupting him as he was about to leave, he took off his hat, looked at it, and put it back on again.

He lunched every day at Cherio's on Fifty-third Street east of Madison, for though he belonged to several clubs in the vicinity, he disliked their atmosphere of men playing dominoes and dozing behind newspapers, and rarely used them. His bond with Cherio, a small, twinkling Italian who always waited on him in person, went back four years to the time when Cherio had returned a five dollar bill which was thought to have dropped from Perkins' pocket. "After that," said Cherio, "there is something between us, a troost. He is really the kind of gentleman which is really few in the world." On a wall of the restaurant next to a picture of Lake Como (Cherio's birthplace) was a sixty-five-pound sailfish which Perkins had caught with Hemingway, and the round table by the door was reserved in perpetuity for the editor and his guests, usually authors or members of the book world. In these genial surroundings with the jig of the cocktail shaker constantly emanating from the bar at the other end of the room, Perkins had his dry martini, breast of guinea hen, and black coffee; he would pick out a dish that suited him and order it meal after meal. If by mistake others were seated at his table, he didn't make a fuss but went straight to the bar, as on the occasion when he and Struthers Burt found a pair of young women sitting there. "People at my table," murmured Perkins, leading Burt to the bar where they had the two cocktails with which they always celebrated their reunions. Afterwards he took Burt to his table and introduced him to the interlopers, or rather recalled them to memory. They were Perkins' daughters!

"Women—" he was sometimes heard to mutter as he emerged from one of his long silences. His misogyny was largely a pose and a talking point, for he delighted in womanly graces, and surrounded by his five attractive daughters to whom he was so devoted, he seemed well-off without the hoped-for son. (In the end he had gotten to telling people that "in our family we always drown the boys.") Nevertheless, his prejudice was not without a grain of conviction; generally speaking, he regarded the weaker sex as precisely that. Lacking the truth and integrity of men, they seemed to him frivolous, unreliable, and all too ready to marry as the easy way out. "She won't do anything," he would say of some promising girl, "she's just a female—she wants to play around," and if things went wrong at the office, he was quick to assume that a woman employee was at the bottom of it. He complained of the way his women authors—an impressive roster[2]—chopped up their proofs, and when Fitzgerald did it with the galleys of *Tender Is the Night*, Perkins remarked, "It's the feminine instinct in the man that makes him behave that way." He shook his head at the endless primping and listening to the phonograph in his all-female establishment, and when a phone call interrupted his reading of a manuscript to his wife and daughters, he would throw it on the floor shouting, "Hell's bells, nobody cares about anything worthwhile in this place!" A moment later he would pick it up again. "But just listen to this. . . ."

His marriage, an intense love-match at the start, hadn't been entirely serene in the long run. He and Louise were both strong-willed and somewhat eccentric, and his ascetic restraint clashing with her more effusive and pleasure-loving disposition had made it seem—to overstate the case—a little like the union of a Scotch professor and a midinette. Louise was fey and romantic and craved gaiety and attention, while Max was socially indifferent; he lived on another plane, from which he descended now and then to escort her to dinners and balls where it seemed to him that nothing intelligent ever got said. Sometimes she went to parties alone, while Max stayed behind pretending he didn't care—but he did. To her great chagrin he had held her to her promise that she wouldn't go on the professional stage after their marriage, though he encouraged her writing talent and some of her poems and stories had been published in *Scribner's* and other magazines. Disappointed that she hadn't done more in this line, he blamed it on the flightiness and indiscipline of her sex.

On her father's death in 1929 Louise had come into a large inheritance which Perkins managed with a shrewdness that delighted his broker; instead of taking his capital gains to offset his losses, he invariably sold the losing stocks and let the gains run, for with authors and securities alike he believed in growth. Though he constantly overtipped and sometimes lent or gave his own money to needy writers, he was as thrifty by nature as Louise was extravagant. She had wanted the house in Turtle Bay, which from Max's standpoint was suffocatingly overdecorated. Another bone of contention was her interest in Catholicism, which would presently lead to her becoming a convert. Not that Perkins was irreligious. A God-fearing man and a better Christian than most in his ethics, he hadn't gone to church since college—he said it was always so stuffy in there and he got more religion out of doors—but he once remarked that "all people of a deep nature *are* religious truly, even if not technically."[3] Louise's Catholicism, however, struck him as theatrical and exaggerated; broad-gauged though he was, it offended his innate conservatism and propriety. When she spoke of Luther as a drunken monk who had run off with a nun, Perkins —though his temper was Erasmian and he didn't much care for Luther—would protest that it wasn't that way at all. "Just try it, Max! Just try it!" Louise would say of her new-found faith, and Max would growl back, "Have you ever tried Buddha?"

His escape from domestic friction was the drug of his work, for he had no hobbies to speak of except walking in the country. His culture was narrowly literary—his interest in art, for example, being more or less confined to the work of his authors like John Thomason and Will James who drew their own illustrations. The theater left him cold, male ballet dancers actively embarrassed him, and once when he was dragged to a symphony concert, he said to his daughters at the end, "Don't clap—they might start again." His musical favorites were cowboy ballads and military items like "The Marine Hymn," "Marching Through Georgia," and especially "Taps," which brought back his days on the Mexican border. Movies bored him except for newsreels; once he got one of his daughters to accompany him to *The Charge of the Light Brigade* and stationed her where she could see the film while he waited in the lobby. When the charge began, she called him, and when it was over, they left.

During Wolfe's visit to Germany, Perkins had been saddened by Hemingway's public and uncalled-for chastisement of Fitzgerald. Harshly competitive, Hemingway was noted for his attacks on other authors. The year before, in his hunting book *Green Hills of Africa*, he had given Wolfe a cuff which Perkins secretly approved, thinking Wolfe might learn from it. "Writers are forged in injustice as a sword is forged," Hemingway had written. "I wondered if it would make a writer of him, give him the necessary shock to cut the overflow of words and give him a sense of proportion, if they sent Tom Wolfe to Siberia or to the Dry Tortugas. Maybe it would and maybe it wouldn't. He seemed sad, really, like Carnera." Wolfe was in Copenhagen when another publisher, hoping to pry him away from Scribners, had sent him this barb, and in a postcard to Perkins Wolfe had called Hemingway "the Big Big He Man and Fighter With Words who can't take it"—referring no doubt to Hemingway's outrage when Max Eastman in an article and Gertrude Stein in her autobiography had twitted his stance of hypermasculinity. But though he fumed in private, Wolfe had continued to hold Hemingway the artist in high esteem, praising his work and speaking confidently of his future in an interview a few months later.[4]

By now a reaction had set in against Hemingway, who hadn't published a novel since 1929 and whose recent non-fiction betrayed a vein of ranting self-indulgence. It didn't worry Perkins; he believed Hemingway to be undergoing a metamorphosis which would surely lead to a new creative burst. In Perkins' eyes, Hemingway and Wolfe were still the two big bulls in the Scribner paddock, though they stood aloof and did not communicate save through their editor who tactfully let each know what the other was accomplishing. On his rare appearances at Scribners, Hemingway seemed a bit blustery and haughty compared to Wolfe, who fraternized with the underlings and was "Tom" to everyone almost immediately. Wolfe's egotism had the spontaneity of a geyser, while Hemingway's partook of a studious, self-watchful reserve.

But to return to Hemingway and Fitzgerald, since the failure of *Tender Is the Night* in 1934, Fitzgerald had entered a dark valley of the soul which made it increasingly hard for Perkins to get through to him and help him. Fitzgerald had a Catholic, confessional strain, and lately he had published three pieces in *Esquire* which analyzed in harrowing detail his nervous and psychological breakdown, or "crack-up." His friends deplored his self-exposure, and some had privately rebuked him, but no one was more disgusted than Hemingway, who wrote Perkins that it was so miserable, this whining in public—a writer could be a coward but at least he should be a writer—nevertheless, it made him feel badly and he wished he could help.

His method of doing so was curious indeed. In his story, "The Snows of Kilimanjaro," in the August *Esquire,* he had the hero musing, "He remembered poor Scott Fitzgerald and his romantic awe of [the rich] and how he had started a story once that began, 'The very rich are different from you and me,' and how someone had said to Scott, 'Yes, they have more money.' But that was not humorous to Scott. He thought they were a special glamorous race and when he found they weren't it wrecked him just as much as any other thing that wrecked him." Crushed and humiliated, Fitzgerald had written a measured letter asking Hemingway please to lay off him in print. "If I choose to write *de profundis* sometimes it doesn't mean I want friends praying aloud over my corpse."

Deeply loyal to both Hemingway and Fitzgerald, Perkins had sided unequivocally with Fitzgerald, who had done everything in his power to promote Hemingway in the early days, and whose printed references to him had been nothing but the highest praise. Perkins wrote Fitzgerald that he resented Hemingway's action and was still more emphatic in a letter to Elizabeth Lemmon: "Wasn't that reference to Scott in [Hemingway's] splendid story otherwise, contemptible, and more so because [Hemingway] said, 'I am getting to know the rich,' and Molly Colum said—we were at lunch together —'The only difference between the rich and other people is that the rich have more money.'"[5] Hemingway, the original straight man as it seemed to him, had thus shifted the onus to Fitzgerald through the unorthodox device of bringing real names into a piece of fiction.

Fitzgerald had yet to reach his nadir, which occurred that September when *The New York Post* interviewed him on his fortieth birthday. Barely recovered from a shoulder injury which had kept him in a plaster cast for six weeks, he was in no condition to receive anyone, but the reporter prevailed on him and Fitzgerald thought the occasion had gone pleasantly enough until he saw the front-page article which, with due attention to the nurse's rationing him his drinks, described how "the poet-prophet of post-war neurotics" had spent his birthday "as he spends all his days—trying to come back from the other side of Paradise, the hell of despondency in which he has writhed for the last couple of years." The article's appearance coincided with Wolfe's return from Germany, and he was furious, especially as he had met the owner of the paper, who prided himself on his liberalism and was forever deriding Hearst's vicious and unprincipled methods. If Fitzgerald was bent on professional suicide, Wolfe thought it dastardly of others to help.

A few days later one of Perkins' daughters was married in New Canaan, and Louise Perkins asked a mutual friend to see that Wolfe came to the wedding clean, sober, and on time. Wolfe met the friend in Grand Central with his hair newly cut, his suit pressed, and his shoes shined, but without a tie. Unable to decide which one he should wear, he had stuffed a bunch of them in his pocket and chose one at leisure during the trip. He and the friend sat in the middle of the church, and in the hush that followed the ceremony Wolfe announced in his rich, carrying voice, "You didn't tell me my hat-band stank of sweat."

Wolfe was back in the Perkinses' lives all right.

Since moving to First Avenue two blocks from the Perkinses, Wolfe had been virtually a member of their household. He dropped in whenever he felt like it, and though Perkins welcomed the intrusions as a breath of masculine fresh air, they were less pleasing to the rest of the family. Least of all to the youngest daughter, eleven-year-old Nancy, who was terrified of Wolfe and exasperated by the way he fiddled with things at meals. Once when she was beside him, a great white hand had encircled her butter plate and had kept twirling it so she couldn't get at it, but she was too timid to protest. Wolfe would sit with his elbow on the table and his cheek resting on his palm, his other hand toying with his glass and his dark eyes staring fixedly before him as he monologued on and on. Sometimes when he had had a lot to drink, he would shout at Perkins and blame him for this and that in a tone that outraged Nancy, who one day found the courage to say, "Don't you speak that way to my father!" "It's all right, Duck—it's all right," said

Perkins, laughing and patting her hand, but she went on glaring at Wolfe and had a moment of triumph when he not only stopped talking but actually seemed ashamed.

"Tom at his very worst," according to Perkins, was the time he came to dinner with the American wife of a Hungarian count; she had just had an eye removed and it was her first night out of the hospital. Perkins had foreseen that the countess's international society manner of taking everything lightly would irritate Wolfe, who in such company was apt to become a snob in reverse, boasting that his father was "just a working man, a stonecutter," but as the countess admired writers and wrote some herself, Louise had invited Wolfe to meet her over Max's protest. Having had a few bracers before he arrived, Wolfe began by announcing that his grandfather was a rabbi, but instead of the anti-Semitic reaction he had anticipated, the countess seemed interested and tried to draw him out on the subject. At dinner he launched a tirade to the effect that she was no better than anyone else, getting up at one point to take off his coat "from the best tailor in London" and exhibit its lion-and-unicorn label. He said he didn't care if she *did* have only one eye, he was as good as she was any day. The countess controlled herself admirably, and when she left, Perkins for once lost his temper with Wolfe, who on the countess's next visit brought flowers and stammered a formal apology.

His genuine contrition made him easy to forgive, yet among Perkins' friends there was a feeling that he was devoting entirely too much time to this unruly giant from the raw part of the South. The strain was aging him, for it had reached the point where Wolfe went to Perkins with everything. He would phone to say that a girl had been sick in his apartment—how could he get her out?—and Perkins was supposed to deal with it. Or he would insist that Perkins join him for a drink at some impossible hour and be offended if Perkins refused, Perkins knowing from bitter experience that a quiet drink with Wolfe had explosive possibilities. Apropos of nothing he might take a dislike to some man at the other end of the bar who seemed perfectly harmless. "Yeah, but he's a grey-looking man, and I *hate* grey-looking men," Wolfe would rumble on, and his imagination catching hold, he would adduce further unpleasant characteristics until it was all Perkins could do to prevent him from picking a fight with the innocent offender.

As Struthers Burt remarked, Perkins vis-à-vis Wolfe was not merely an editor but a species of elephant trainer. No one would have done as much for him, nor would Perkins have done it for anyone else, and let it be added in extenuation of Wolfe that Perkins enjoyed—or at least gave every indication of wanting—the responsibility. Perkins had a fatherly affection for Wolfe, who seemed to him at once the greatest talent and the most lost soul he had ever dealt with. Besides which, Wolfe was now an extremely valuable publishing property, and Perkins hoped their friendship would offset Wolfe's mounting dissatisfaction with Scribners.

It had flared up the previous April in connection with the royalties on *The Story of a Novel,* an enlarged and polished version of Wolfe's Boulder speech which Scribners was bringing out as a small book. When Perkins and Wolfe first discussed it, they had agreed the book should sell for a dollar or less to widen its readership among students and apprentice authors, and for the sake of the low price Wolfe had accepted a reduced royalty—or so he thought when he signed the contract. Later the sales department had set the price at $1.50, and when Wolfe discovered it on the eve of publication, he had written Perkins a letter accusing Scribners of sharp practice. While he didn't question their right to raise the price, he thought that since they had done so, he should receive his customary fifteen percent royalty. "If you make use of a business advantage in this way," said he, rattling the sword, "don't you think I would be justified in making use of a business advantage, too, if one came my way?" He referred to the efforts of other publishers to lure him away from Scribners, which heretofore he had instantly rebuffed. To keep the peace, Perkins wrote Wolfe acceding to his demands but adding that he had been mistaken in thinking that the reduced royalty was geared to price. Because of their relatively greater cost of production, small books necessitated a reduced royalty. In his letter Wolfe had also harked back to the $1,200 he had been charged for excess corrections on the proofs of *Of Time and the River,* pointing out that most of the corrections had been made by Scribners—to which Perkins replied unanswerably that, had Wolfe corrected the proofs himself, the excess charges would have been still greater.

Even before he got Perkins' reply, Wolfe had relented. He accepted the reduced royalty, adding that life was too short to quarrel about such matters and that "all the damn contracts in the world don't mean as much to me as your friendship means."

A month later he and Perkins had differed again, this time over the settlement of a suit filed by Madeleine Boyd. Back in 1932 Wolfe had dismissed her as his agent for withholding the advance on the German edition of *Look Homeward, Angel*. According to Perkins, Mrs. Boyd had "a very complicated though perhaps valid explanation"; making allowances for female negligence, he thought her technically but not morally at fault, and in any case she had done Wolfe the outstanding service of interesting Scribners in *O Lost*. She had accepted her dismissal, but after the success of *Of Time and the River* she had claimed that her original agreement with Wolfe entitled her to a commission on all his work. Her flimsy case had only a nuisance value and in the out-of-court settlement she relinquished her claims for $500, plus $150 which Wolfe was persuaded to give her because she was poor and ill. Wolfe, however, thought Perkins' attitude excessively lenient and complained thereafter of his "fond tenderness for women."

These wrangles, as Perkins had come to realize, were only the symptoms of a deeper malaise. Slowly, subconsciously, Wolfe had reached the point of resenting his dependence on Perkins and on Scribners, which for the past seven years had been his second home. He dropped by at all hours of the day, "just visiting" as people do down South, and he had even been known to spend the night there, sprawled in an armchair in the library with his feet on the directors' table. Scribners was his post office and his bank as well, with the cashier doling out his royalties in small sums as if it were an allowance. Sometimes Wolfe complained to friends that he was a grown man capable of handling his own affairs and that Scribners treated him like an idiot, but if you sympathized he would backtrack, "Now don't you interfere. They are fine, honest people and they're doing all they can to help me. Or are they? How do I know?" Half serious, half in jest, he would say to Perkins, "Goddamn you, why do you keep my money? I'm a Communist!" for Wolfe had grown increasingly radical, while Perkins, a Democrat before the New Deal, distrusted Roosevelt's concentration of power and voted for Landon in 1936. Identifying himself with the workers, Wolfe accused Perkins of being the reactionary guardian of inherited means, and Perkins slyly jabbed back. At lunch one day when Wolfe had ordered frogs' legs and a vintage wine and was grumbling as he often did about the writer's hard lot, Perkins said, "It's too bad about you, Tom, really. Have some more frogs' legs. Is the wine all right?" Wolfe saw the irony and had to laugh.

In December, 1935, he had declared his financial independence by opening a bank account, but the root of the trouble was artistic. The extravagant dedication in *Of Time and the River*, reinforced by his remarks in *The Story of a Novel*, not to mention his unthinking exaggerations at cocktail parties, had spread the notion that he couldn't function as a writer without Perkins at his elbow. In his essay, "Genius Is Not Enough," ostensibly a review of *The Story of a Novel*, Bernard De Voto had levelled this charge pointblank. De Voto was unduly patronizing, for Wolfe's "genius" was sufficient to make his fiction endure, while De Voto's would perish for lack of it, but considering the Wolfe bandwagon at the time, De Voto's outspokenness had required a certain audacity.

"One indispensable part of the artist," wrote De Voto, "has existed not in Mr. Wolfe but in Maxwell Perkins. Such organizing faculty and such critical intelligence as has been applied to [*Of Time and the River*] have come not from inside the artist, not from the artist's feeling for form and esthetic integrity, but from the offices of Charles Scribner's Sons. For five years the artist pours out words 'like burning lava from a volcano'—with little or no idea what their purpose is, which book they belong in, what the relation of part to part is, what is organic and what irrelevant, or what emphasis or coloration in the completed work of art is being served by the job at hand. Then Mr. Perkins decides these questions—from without, and by a process to which rumor applies the word 'assembly.' . . . Worse still, the artist goes on writing till Mr. Perkins tells him that the novel is finished. But the end of a novel is, properly, dictated by the internal pressure, osmosis, metabolism—what you will—of the novel itself, of which only the novelist can have first-hand knowledge. There comes a point where the necessities of the book are satisfied, where its organic processes have reached completion. It is hard to see how awareness of that point can manifest itself at an editor's desk—and harder still to trust the integrity of a work of art in which not the artist but the publisher has determined where the true ends and the false begins."6

At the time Wolfe took it manfully. "I am not trying to laugh it off," he had written a sympathizer, "but it didn't hurt me, it doesn't rankle, I have no vengeful feelings; in the end I may even get some good from it. The main thing is I am working like a horse and I don't see how anyone, not even Mr. De Voto, is going to do anything about that." Deep down, however, it *did* rankle. After De Voto's thrust Wolfe felt the need of proving his artistic autonomy, while expecting from Scribners an absolute and continuous moral support which no longer seemed forthcoming. Though Perkins had encouraged him to begin *The Vision of Spangler's Paul*, there had been no talk of a contract, and Perkins showed comparatively little interest in its progress. Wolfe thought he knew why.

As part of his new novel, he had begun to write about a publishing house called James Rodney and Sons, easily recognizable as Scribners. From some of this material he had fashioned a short story which he hoped to sell to a magazine, and his agent, Elizabeth Nowell, had showed it to Perkins to test his reaction. For years Perkins had been telling his colleagues, "When Tom gets around to writing about us—look out!" and now the time had come. Wolfe had laid bare the private lives of Scribner personnel whom Perkins had freely discussed during their long intimacy, and Perkins felt responsible. It didn't matter that much of Wolfe's information had come to him through his own eyes and ears during seven years of haunting the Scribner building and hobnobbing with everyone from Charles Scribner himself to the shipping boys in the basement. Perkins shouldered the blame, confessing to Miss Nowell that he would feel it his duty to resign if Wolfe published his exposé.

Perkins asked Miss Nowell not to repeat his attitude to Wolfe, but in her alarm she did so, and Wolfe's answer was: "When we published *Look Homeward, Angel*, Max thought it was all right, fine, for me to write about those people—all that mattered was to do the best possible job. But now it's getting close to home and his attitude changes. He seems to think that while it was all right to write about those humble folk down in North Carolina, his own fine friends at Scribners are a special race. Well, it's just too bad because I'm going to write what I please and as I please, and no one is going to stop me." Miss Nowell finally persuaded him to modify the story so that the characters couldn't be identified, and while Wolfe was abroad, she had resubmitted it to Perkins, who now objected on artistic grounds. He said the revised story would harm no one except Wolfe, that it wasn't up to his standard. On Wolfe's return they had it out. "Maybe it isn't the best story I've written," Wolfe said, "but it isn't the worst one either. No, Max, you just want to suppress it because you think I'm writing about Scribners and to you that's sacrilege." The argument worked around to Perkins saying he would publish Wolfe's book no matter how it treated Scribners and then resign. Wolfe accused Perkins of behaving like a martyr; he said Charles Scribner wouldn't accept the resignation, and that in any case, he, Wolfe, would leave Scribners first and simply not be there to be resigned about. The following week he wrote Perkins' secretary to forward his mail to 865 First Avenue, as much as to say that he would no longer be dropping in at Scribners unless urgent business required it.

Very soon it did. The last straw in this crumbling relationship was a suit filed by Marjorie Dorman, Wolfe's former landlady at 40 Verandah Place, who claimed that she had been libelously portrayed as the Mad Maude Whittaker of "No Door" in Wolfe's volume of short stories *From Death to Morning*. Wolfe had said that her father and her two sisters were "all touched with the same madness," and the Dorman family was suing Wolfe and Scribners for $125,000. Wolfe blamed Scribners for getting him into it on the grounds that they had been intimidated by Mrs. Bernstein to postpone the publication of *The October Fair*,[7] which had caused Walter Winchell to say in his column that Wolfe was delaying publication of his latest novel for fear of libel suits—which in turn had given the Dormans the idea of suing. Scribners quite naturally saw it the other way around: Wolfe's recklessness had implicated them. Although in his contract, he had guaranteed that *From Death to Morning* contained no libel and that Scribners would be held blameless in any such proceeding, the firm agreed to split the cost of the suit provided that Wolfe cooperated with them in retaining first-rate legal counsel. Scribners' attorney was by no means sure that the case could be won in court, and when the Dormans began fishing for a settlement, it seemed cheaper and quicker to negotiate—a prime consideration being that law suits kept Wolfe in a frenzy and impeded his work. Because his fiction was so open to libel, Scribners was also afraid lest the publicity of a trial stir up suits in other quarters. He finally agreed to a settlement wherein his half of the cost and damages was $2,745.05 which Scribners considered a victory in view of the sum the Dormans had been asking, but Wolfe considered it an outrage. He was now convinced that libel suits were "part of a great organized national industry of shaking-down . . . and the only way to stop it is to fight it, because it lives by threats and flourishes on submission."

The settlement with the Dormans was reached in mid-February, 1937. Three months earlier when the suit had barely begun, Wolfe had asked Perkins for a formal letter saying that he, Wolfe, had discharged all his obligations to Scribners and that no further agreement existed between them. Perkins had complied but added in a covering note, "This is to say that on my part there has been no 'severance.' I can't express certain kinds of feelings very comfortably, but you must realize what my feelings are towards you. Ever since *Look Homeward, Angel* your work has been the foremost interest in my life, and I have never doubted for your future on any grounds except, at times, on those of your being able to control the vast mass of material you have accumulated and have to form into books. You seem to think I have tried to control you. I only did that when you asked my help and then I did the best I could. It all seems very confusing to me, but whatever the result, I hope you don't mean it to keep us from seeing each other, or that you won't come to our house."[8]

Wolfe had Christmas dinner with the Perkinses, and then, needing a break (he estimated that since his return from Germany he had written a quarter of a million words), he headed for New Orleans which he had last visited with his mother when he was nine. He told a friend that he was hoping "to sleep solid for about a week," but as soon as word got around that he was staying at the Roosevelt Hotel, there was no rest for him in that colorful and hospitable city. At eight one morning, after carousing all night in the French Quarter, he asked the young reporter he was with to show him the Mississippi, so they drove to the foot of Audubon Park where they stood on the levee and surveyed the sweep of the river beyond the willows. After a moment of silence, Wolfe plucked up some grass and let the wind carry it from his hand.

"That's America," he said, "and that's some river."

"Shucks," said the reporter, "you should see it at high water."

Wolfe charmed everyone with his stammering uncertainty and his modesty about his writing, which cropped up in such phrases as "if I become an established writer" and "if my work is ever recognized" and "when I learn to write." On January 10th when he strolled into Arnaud's with his big, full-knotted tie slightly askew, people turned to stare at him and the waiters were more than usually attentive. A man at a nearby table heard Wolfe say that this was to be his last meal in New Orleans and that he wanted to make a little occasion of it. He ordered shrimp remoulade, bouillabaisse, and a Graves, and while it was being prepared he chatted with the waiter about Sherry's and Lüchow's in New York. The eavesdropper had now paid his bill, and on his way out he got up his courage to speak to Wolfe, who graciously invited him to sit down while he ate. The conversation turned to other writers. Had Wolfe read anything by Jesse Stuart? Yes, a couple of stories—he had met the boy, and it looked as if he might have the stuff all right. What about Saroyan? Wolfe said it was awfully easy for dried-up little people who had never written anything to laugh at Saroyan, but pretty soon Saroyan was going to have to take his writing and get Bill Saroyan out of it. Saroyan would be all right someday, he'd go places if only he would get that fellow Saroyan out of his writing. He'd written Bill a letter about it once and never mailed it.

After New Orleans Wolfe went to Biloxi to recuperate and then to Atlanta to spend a few nights with a college friend, Garland Porter. Dinner the first evening was typical North Carolina fare: fried chicken, snap beans cooked with a slab of streak-of-fat-streak-of-lean, candied yams, fruit salad, and plenty of biscuits and gravy. Wolfe's chair was nearest the kitchen door, and when the cook came in she served him first, then worked her way around the table to Porter, his wife and three children, Wolfe using the interim to good advantage. When the cook passed him on her way out, he would look up and catch her eye and she would serve him again. "You've got to excuse me," he told the Porters, "but this is the first real meal I've had in years—this is the kind of food I was raised on." After dinner, when he and Porter were standing on the edge of the terrace which rose a foot or so above the lawn, Porter's seven-year-old boy came over to Wolfe, and his eyes, on a level with Wolfe's knees, were full of amazement as they travelled upward.

"It's all right, Buddy," said Wolfe. "I just grew that way. I'm not on stilts." He turned to Porter, laughing. "Looked like he was afraid I would fall off."

Later that evening when Porter asked him how he had felt after the world acclaimed him, Wolfe said it had given him "a hell of a kick." He rose and began pacing the room as he often did when excited. "A lot of people had laughed at me, had called me a crazy lout. I felt damn good showing them up. But I had to dig like hell, and I still have to dig."

When Porter expressed his admiration for *Of Time and the River* and backed it up with specific references, Wolfe said, "Damned if I don't believe you've read the book. Very few people have ever waded through it." He picked up Porter's copy and riffled the pages musingly.

The previous year the North Carolina Literary and Historical Society had invited Wolfe to speak at their December meeting, which had made him feel for the first time since the publication of *Look Homeward, Angel* that he might be *persona grata* in his home state. He had planned to visit Asheville on his way North, but because of a misunderstanding with his family over the phone, he decided to go back by way of Chapel Hill. He hadn't been there since graduation, and the university had burgeoned in his absence. Approaching it, he remarked to the alumni secretary who had met him in Raleigh that it seemed as if they were entering West Philadelphia, and as they turned into the campus proper, Wolfe said, "Would you mind if I got out? I just want to feel the place." He walked over to the Old Well, which was now a drinking fountain and not a well at all. "Finest water in the world," he said after taking a drink. "I always loved this place." Then he had to go down to Patterson's, which had changed its name to the Pritchard-Lloyd Drug Store, for a "dope" as Coca-Colas were called in his undergraduate days.

When it got around that Wolfe would meet with Professor Phillips Russell's creative-writing class, a hundred or more showed up, and Wolfe, flushed and sweating, came stumbling in half an hour late with a hoarse mutter of apology. Fidgeting with his coat buttons, he whispered to Russell almost pleadingly before turning towards the audience, which he photographed with one long stare—then dropping his head, he began drawing arcs with his feet. "I-I thought I was coming to sit in on this class. I-I-I didn't. . . . Wh-when I was here, there weren't th-this many in the whole school." He seemed scared, and friendly laughter greeting one of his remarks, he looked up with a grateful smile, warming every face with his eyes' glow. He said how good it was to be back and how much he had forgotten. "The color of our Carolina clay. I hadn't remembered it was so red. And the dogwood and the broom sage. . . ." As he paced to and fro, his hands were never still, now coursing through his hair, now digging deep in his pockets. Yes indeed, the campus certainly had changed! "Why, when I was here all this part below Old South was nothing but blackberry thicket. Why God a-mighty. . . ." And on he talked about the old days, his every gesture and his warm brown eyes pleading for understanding and forgiveness. "I'm sorry the people in western North Carolina didn't like my first book, and I hope someday to write one they'll like. I say that from my heart. Before too long I plan to come back here and settle down. I'll probably be married then," he added with a wink.

During his three-day visit he had several talks with his mentor, Horace Williams, whose mind "still flashed like a rapier," Wolfe said afterwards, though Williams was seventy-six and had retired. His students had been his life for half a century, and Wolfe pitied the old man's loneliness as he brooded in his study dominated by the busts of Greek philosophers. Williams had reservations about Wolfe which the latter wasn't aware of. Later that year Williams remarked to a contemporary of Wolfe's, "Tom hasn't grown since Chapel Hill—he is a babbling brook." It was typical of Williams to disparage someone in the limelight, but also Williams, a crabbed and indifferent stylist, had no use for what he called "the literary mind." Nor—if he had read it, which seems likely—would he have appreciated his own portrait as Vergil Weldon in *Look Homeward, Angel*, where Wolfe dismissed the word-juggling which Williams palmed off as philosophy, while rapturously praising the man himself. Babbling brook Wolfe may have seemed, but he had not only grown since leaving Chapel Hill, he had outgrown Williams after absorbing what the master had to give him: chiefly his ruggedness, his idiosyncrasy, and his determination "to make his life prevail," a phrase of Williams' which Wolfe often used.

After Chapel Hill he spent several days in Warrenton, North Carolina, with Billy Polk, one of his Harvard roommates, who was a grandnephew of the President. Polk's sister, when Wolfe came to her house for a meal, never forgot his picking up a photograph of her son—how wonderful it was to see him give a thing his full attention, the really noble look of his fine head as he did so. Later when he turned the same scrutiny on a Currier and Ives print, an abundant still life, she thought to herself, "That is what he loves, the abundance, and he sees its stilted, bound, meticulously arranged charm. He wouldn't want to own it, but he likes it from the bluest flower to the last strawberry and the little bee flying above."

During Wolfe's Southern trip his relations with Scribners had deteriorated still further, and his legal difficulties had multiplied. Two years earlier he had gotten involved with a youth of twenty-one whom we shall call "Francis O'Reilly"; for a commission he had sold several of Wolfe's published manuscripts. Wolfe had welcomed the extra revenue, but subsequently O'Reilly had become so aggressive about asking for more manuscripts that Wolfe had broken with him. O'Reilly had then accused Wolfe of breach of contract and of gravely damaging his career as a rare-book and autograph agent. Wolfe had tried to settle the matter amicably through O'Reilly's family, who were friends of his, but when O'Reilly persisted in demanding $500 for the return of the unsold manuscripts in his possession, Wolfe had brought suit against him. While Wolfe was in New Orleans, his lawyer had written him that O'Reilly was threatening to join forces with the Dormans whose suit was still pending, to stir up additional suits in North Carolina, and to make public "salacious material" which he claimed to have found in the manuscripts. The lawyer had suggested Wolfe's immediate return to cope with these new developments.

Wolfe's first reaction had been to write Perkins in a vein of drink-exacerbated self-pity reminiscent of old Gant: "I have come [to New Orleans] for a rest of which I was in desperate need; [the lawyer's] amazing letter has caused me the most intense distress; I have been hounded by this shameful business for a year and a half now—and it has got to stop! I am an honorable man and an artist—and the cursed thing now is that my work and talent are being destroyed. [The lawyer] says he got my address here from you. In the name of God, knowing the state of my health and the utter exhaustion I was in when I left New York, how could you do it?

"Max, I have begun to lose faith in your power to stick or to help when a man is in danger. I know now that I must fight this whole horrible business out alone—the whole vicious complex of slander, blackmail, theft and parasitic infamy that usually destroys the artist under this accursed and rotten system that now exists in America. You are going to get out from under when you see me threatened with calamity—but, in the name of God, in the name of all the faith and devotion and unquestioning belief I have in you—if you cannot help me, for Christ's sake do not add your own influence to those who are now trying to destroy me. Under *no* conditions, save the death or serious illness of a member of my family, give my address hereafter to anyone. Before I come back to that black and vicious horror again, I must restore myself. I shall fight to the end, but for Christ's sake have the manhood now not to aid in the attack until I can try to mend a little in energy and health."

Wolfe was further incensed because Perkins, who at the outset had urged him to take uncompromising legal action against O'Reilly, was now recommending that Wolfe pay him off and be done with it. From Perkins' standpoint, the primary object was the advancement of Wolfe's work, which worry over the O'Reilly suit was clearly obstructing, but interpreting Perkins' reversal as timidity, Wolfe now mailed a letter written before he left New York—a sort of full-dress apologia for the break with Scribners. It began by answering De Voto's charge that Wolfe was unable to write his books without Perkins' critical and technical assistance. Wolfe pointed out that *Look Homeward, Angel* had been finished to the last comma without a word of criticism or advice from anyone, and that the changes made under Perkins' supervision were almost entirely cuts with a view to reducing the already existing book to a more publishable form. With *Of Time and the River* the process had been much the same "although the finality of completion was not so marked because . . . I was working in a more experimental, individual fashion and dealing with the problem of how to shape and bring into articulate form a giant mass of raw material, whose proportions almost defeated me." There were other skilled editors, Wolfe said, who might have given him the necessary technical help. Perkins' great contribution, for which Wolfe would always be grateful, had been his unflinching moral support and his profound and sensitive understanding.

Wolfe then outlined the temperamental differences between them. He spoke of himself as a "Revolutionary," and of Perkins as a "Conservative." In retrospect he believed that though Perkins had enjoyed publishing *Look Homeward, Angel,* he had also been alarmed by it and had hoped that the years would temper Wolfe to "a greater conservatism, a milder intensity, a more decorous moderation." But if Perkins expected him to conservatize simply because he was getting fat and had a few dollars in the bank, Perkins was mistaken. From now on Wolfe was going to write as he pleased, and no one would cut what he wrote unless he wanted it. "I have at last discovered my own America, I believe I have found my language, I think I know my way. And I shall wreak out my vision of this life, this way, this world and this America, to the top of my bent, to the height of my ability, but with an unswerving devotion, integrity, and purity of purpose that shall not be menaced, altered, or weakened by anyone."

Wolfe charged Perkins with allowing his judgment to be swayed by apprehension over what Wolfe might say about Scribners. He repeated his old claim that he was neither more nor less autobiographical than other serious fiction writers, all of whom, from Tolstoy on down, necessarily began with their own experience. "As you know very well, I don't 'write about' people: I create living characters of my own—a whole universe of my own creation. And any character I create is so unmistakably my own that anyone familiar with my work would know instantly it was my own, even if it had no title and no name." In any case, no "paltry, personal, social apprehension" should come between the artist and his material. Fearing that Aline Bernstein would make trouble, Scribners had postponed the publication of *The October Fair* until Wolfe had gone stale on it and turned to other things. He couldn't continue in this vague "well now, you go ahead for the present—we'll wait and see how it all turns out" manner. He needed a guarantee that whatever he felt like writing would be published just as he wrote it.

In response to these grievances Perkins had written, "What a task you've put me to, to search myself—in whom I'm not so very much interested any more—and give you an adequate answer." He re-affirmed his belief that the book belongs to the author, who should make of it exactly what he wants. "But my impression was that you asked my help, that you wanted it. And it is my impression too that the changes were not forced on you (you're not very forcible, Tom, nor I very forceful) but were argued over, often for hours." Undesired assistance certainly wouldn't be thrust on him. Nor did Perkins hope the years would make him more conservative, but only that they would give him greater control of his talent. As for guarantees, Perkins said that apart from unavoidable "physical and legal limitations" (he was thinking of the length of Wolfe's manuscripts and the libelous passages they might contain), Scribners would publish anything he wrote. And then in mild rebuke, "Tom, you ought not to say some of the things you do—that I find your sufferings amusing and don't take them seriously. . . . I do try to turn your mind from them and to arouse your humor, because to spend dreadful hours brooding over them, and in denunciation and abuse on account of them, seems to be only to aggravate them. It does no good."

In conclusion, Perkins said he had never known anyone with whom he was in such complete agreement on fundamentals as he was with Wolfe, and that there was mighty little in his letter which he didn't wholly accept, "and what I did not, I perfectly well understood. There were places in it that made me angry, but it was a fine letter, a fine writer's statement of his beliefs, as fine as any I ever saw, and though I have vanities enough, as many as most, it gave me pleasure too—that which comes from hearing brave and sincere beliefs, uttered with sincerity and nobility."

The impartial observer, reading the exchange, cannot help missing on Wolfe's side a more sympathetic awareness of what Perkins was going through. Obsessed with his own dilemmas, Wolfe seemed to forget that Perkins was also a beleaguered mortal who tossed on his pillow at night. And after all, there was much to be said in Scribners' favor; had not their enterprise and imagination launched Wolfe, who had seemed almost cringing when he first appeared in their office and who, Luciferlike, was turning against them now? But if Perkins felt any indignation, he swallowed it, seeking instead to throw the light of pure reason on the conflict, with the magnanimity of one who knows he is dealing with a demonic type.

For Perkins comprehended, better than anyone ever had or would, the pathos of this great lonely misfit paradoxically crossed with Everyman, whose intensities became self-lacerating when deflected from his work. Obviously Wolfe was guilt-ridden over the break with Scribners, which in the last analysis Perkins accepted as just and inevitable. Aline once spoke of Wolfe's "advancement from one thing to another within himself, the mighty stride of his changes, and his cruel and relentless disentanglement from all that bound him." Till now he had always leaned on some omniscient arbiter, with whom sooner or later it was necessary to break in order to go on developing according to his own laws. Margaret Roberts, George Pierce Baker, Aline Bernstein, and Max Perkins had been the principal ones, and in turning away from them, Wolfe's "cruelty" was that of a force of nature purifying itself; floods and erupting volcanoes do not ask permission of the villages in their path. And so, though profoundly hurt, Perkins spoke approvingly of what he called "Tom's instinctive and manly determination to free all his bonds and stand up alone."[9]

It was only in his editorial capacity that Wolfe considered Perkins a baneful influence. Wolfe wanted them to remain friends, and after his return to New York the end of January, he went on seeing Perkins who hoped the breach could be healed, though he grew weary of discussing it. "All right, Tom," he said finally, "if you have to leave Scribners, go ahead and leave, but for heaven's sake stop talking about it!" One evening when Wolfe and Perkins were dining with a group at Cherio's, a member of the party who hadn't met Wolfe before said, "Oh, now I know who you are—I read Bernard De Voto's article about you in *The Saturday Review*." Other ill-considered remarks were made about his relations with

Scribners, and when the dinner broke up, Wolfe was left alone with Perkins in a state of murderous intoxication. As they rose to go, Wolfe threatened to knock Perkins down and stood there swinging his arms in preparation. Perkins tried to cajole him out of it, but seeing he couldn't, he said that if they must fight they ought to do it outside. He followed Wolfe to the street, thinking that only a miracle could prevent a catastrophe that everyone would regret. The miracle occurred. Simultaneously a group emerged from the restaurant next door, and one of them, a tall handsome brunette unknown to Wolfe, ran up to him and threw her arms around him, exclaiming, "This is what I came to New York to see!" Talking to her, he forgot his rage.[10]

Despite his law suits and his troubles with Scribners, Wolfe had been unusually productive since his return from Germany. He had gotten into the habit of dictating his first drafts—the natural outcome of a life-long practice of telling his stories before he wrote them. Unlike Hemingway and Fitzgerald, who felt that relating what they intended to write took the bloom off it, Wolfe—whose art was more in the oral, the folk tradition—thought that his stories improved with each retelling. "The third time around they are masterpieces," he had quipped in his notes. The manuscript of his novel was growing apace, and he was back at writing short stories because the Dorman suit had given him a deficit with Scribners, and despite a few thousand dollars in the bank, he was fretting about money. During the first half of 1937 he sold two stories to *The New Yorker* and one apiece to *Harper's Bazaar, Redbook, Scribner's, The American Mercury,* and *The Saturday Evening Post.* The last, "The Child by Tiger," brought him $1,200, the highest price he ever received. This account of a crazed Negro who goes on a shooting spree and is hunted and killed by a white mob was also one of his best tales. Though it derived from an actual occurrence in Asheville in 1906, Wolfe had recreated it to expose the cruelty and blood-lust in the hearts of all men, white as well as black.

Another fine story, completed during the fall, was "I Have a Thing to Tell You," serialized in *The New Republic* in March, 1937. In September when Wolfe had written the first draft of this indictment of Nazi Germany, climaxed by the capture of the Jew who had been his travelling companion, he had realized that if it were published he could never go back to Germany. The Jew had asked Wolfe to take some of his pocket money to get it past the inspectors, and Wolfe still had the little handful of two-mark pieces when he got to New York. He didn't like to touch it, saying that this blood-money was greasy with its owner's agony and sweat, but it lay on his table a long time, and glancing at it he would pucker his mouth with pity and rapidly and repeatedly shake his head, too moved for words. Wolfe was not, and never could be, a propagandist. An artist first and last, he had conceived the story in simple, human terms, and yet in the taut atmosphere of 1937 its political import was unmistakable. Wolfe was through with Germany as long as the Nazis ruled. He had gone abroad on the *Europa* free of charge, having agreed to send them a travel article for the company's magazine, but on his return to New York he reimbursed them for his passage, explaining that his present convictions did not permit him to write a suitable piece.

His greatness was his merciless exposure of the tangle of good and evil in us all, nor did he spare himself. In "I Have a Thing to Tell You" he showed that even the anti-Nazi Germans who were his friends harbored anti-Semitic feelings which made the whole rotten system possible, and in condemning their anti-Semitism he was condemning his own. His story was a reluctant adieu to the country he had loved best after America, and hence the wrench at the end—one of his great flash utterances, prophetic of man's brotherhood and instinct with his own mortality:

"To that old Master, now, to wizard Faust, old father of the ancient and swarm-haunted mind of man, to that old German land with all the measure of its truth, its glory, beauty, magic and its ruin—to that dark land, to that old ancient earth that I have loved so long—I said farewell.

"I have a thing to tell you:

"Something has spoken to me in the night, burning the tapers of the waning year; something has spoken in the night; and told me I shall die, I know not where. Losing the earth we know for greater knowing, losing the life we have for greater life, and leaving the friends we loved for greater loving, men find a land more kind than home, more large than earth.

"Whereon the pillars of this earth are founded, toward which the spirits of the nations draw, toward which the conscience of the world is tending—a wind is rising, and the rivers flow."[11]

11 · PROMISES

Cut off from Germany, his mythic and adopted homeland, and at odds with Perkins and Scribners, Wolfe thought it was time to renew his connection with Asheville, where he hadn't shown his face since *Look Homeward, Angel* appeared. As he planned someday to write a book about a common soldier during the Civil War, he took a bus from Gettysburg the last week of April and loafed down the Shenandoah Valley where Stonewall Jackson had so brilliantly campaigned. The scent of rain and apple blossoms was in the air as he poked around Winchester, the birthplace of his great great grandfather Westall, and then, after stops in Roanoke and Bristol, he pushed on through the mountains to Burnsville, North Carolina, near which his mother had spent her girlhood. He looked up Julia's father's half-brother, John Westall, who lived in a remote cabin and who gave him an eye-witness account of the Battle of Chickamauga

255

which he promptly made into a short story. The afternoon of May 3rd he slipped into Asheville unheralded, to spend his first night in almost eight years at the Old Kentucky Home.

The initial outrage over *Look Homeward, Angel* had subsided; nowadays more people were resentful because Wolfe had left them out of the book than because he had put them in. He was ready to concede that the ignorance, intemperance, and hypersensitivity of youth had caused him to write certain things he regretted. It was all right, he would tell you, to call a man a horse thief, but you shouldn't give his street address and telephone number, and in some cases he had practically done that. When a North Carolinian he chanced to meet in Washington a few years after the publication of *Look Homeward* had said, "Tom, you really gave 'em Hail Columbia in that book you put out," he had replied, "Well, I had a lotta hurt—I just got to writing and I couldn't stop." But now the emotions underlying *Look Homeward,* including an incidental bitterness, had been exorcised, and his deepest impulse was to get back into the fold and make amends.

Mabel and Ralph Wheaton were once more living in Asheville, and the morning after his arrival Tom was sitting over coffee at their breakfast table when the reporters came in. He said how grand it was to be back again and that despite all the new construction he felt perfectly at home—"You can't change the mountains." Meanwhile, at his mother's the phone kept ringing, and when he returned, friends were queued up to meet him—all so glad to see him, all hoping he would stay a while. "Sure," they said, "there was a lot of talk at first—some were pretty mad about the book—I guess you heard about it—but hell, that's all over now—it's all forgotten." Nevertheless, on being told that one of his Westall cousins was downstairs, Wolfe asked with a sardonic smile, "Is he armed?" Wherever he went on the street, groups clustered around as he held court with still a country air about him for all his cosmopolitan travels. "You don't remember me," someone would say, and with unerring recall Wolfe would answer, "Sure I do—we had the same paper route one summer," or "Didn't you run on the high-school track team?"

His homecoming would hardly have been complete without a session at the Robertses. The previous spring when Mrs. Roberts and her husband had visited New York, she had written Wolfe suggesting they get together, though it was clear that she hadn't forgotten *Look Homeward, Angel.* "I am wondering," she had said, "if you still think all you did to us and others whom you hurt so dreadfully was kind, or necessary, or wise. . . . Mr. Roberts has at no time tried to influence me not to answer your letter. He has left me absolutely free. It would really have been worth your while to have observed the fineness in the man through the whole unhappy business. But you knew him many years intimately and saw only a snob, a pedant, a dullard, and, what seemed worse than anything to me, a man who was brutal to a frail wife. (No human being could ever have been more gentle, more considerate than he has been to me in every relation of life.) . . . But because we are so near to you that fine happy old memories keep coming to the surface: because your letters reread moved me more deeply than I know how to tell you; because of that sprawling signature on the back of [*The Story of a Novel*]; because Buddie and Margaret [her children] think that I should have appreciated your power and beauty and squelched the personal, should have allowed the artist in you to predominate over the friend in you—because of all these things, but above all because wounded to the quick as I, and we, were, I have never forgotten to love you at all times, from the time when you were twelve to now and to rejoice in your success, I have been angry and hurt, but I have felt that sometime as you grew older, you would, with your powers, learn how to go up and on without treading down others as you did us—and through it all I have loved you and, of course, because I did love you, resented more and suffered more because of what you did to the others I love."

In his answer Wolfe had said how glad he was to hear from Mrs. Roberts after all these years. He wanted to see her and her husband and would discuss some of the points in her letter "if you think it will make for clarification and better understanding, but if it causes greater pain and confusion in the lives or hearts of anyone, I'd rather not say anything. . . . I know I have done things that I ought not to have done, and left undone things that I should have done, but my hope and faith is that I grow a little in knowledge and experience and in understanding all the time, and that I shall, accordingly, do better in the future." When Mrs. Roberts answered that they would behave just as they always had, letting the chips fall where they may, Wolfe was apprehensive and didn't go to see them. In Asheville, however, an intermediary brought them together, and their friendship was renewed almost as if there had been no break. By tacit agreement the moral insolubles of *Look Homeward, Angel* were simply not discussed.

Next to Wolfe himself, the chief beneficiary of his triumphal return was his mother, who at seventy-seven seemed to him the most fearless and independent soul he had ever known. He had watched her stand up under crushing blows with no suggestion of giving in—with no idea that there was anything to do but live through them. Proud of Tom's achievement, she took it in her stride, for in her own estimation she had always belonged with the best. A few years back she had written him about her dreams: "I have always travelled in my sleep, met many strangers and somehow always people on a high social plane, never had the least feeling of inferiority complex, seemed natural and at home with any and all. The other night I was at dinner someplace, and President Hoover was opposite me, I talked with him, asked his opinion of several things and it seemed nothing out of the ordinary, he seemed so quiet and sociable. . . . I am always high-minded, goes to prove in earlier life I was ambitious, wanted to be at the top of everything, common people or anything cheap disgusted me but circumstances of life caused me to live not my life but a substitute."

Having a famous son, therefore, seemed perfectly in keeping.

One day, Julia, Mabel, and Fred (now a salesman for the Bluebird Ice Cream Company in Spartanburg, South Carolina) drove Tom over to Tennessee and left him in Newport with a young admirer, James Stokely, who had heard that Wolfe was planning to rent a cabin for the summer and wanted to show him one. At the restaurant where he and Stokely lunched, Wolfe listened to the conversations around him and copied snatches of them on his paper napkin, and later, as they drove through the countryside, he quizzed Stokely about the farms—when the crops were harvested, the yield per acre, the ratio of corn to tobacco, and so forth. He seemed a man in a fierce hurry to find out about everything. At one point he asked Stokely, "How's the woman situation around here? I like 'em with plenty of meat on 'em." On May 15th, the day he left Asheville for

New York, he wrote a piece for *The Citizen Times* describing how, during his years of exile, he had longed to go home and explain himself, but now that he was back, what was there to say? "I think there is nothing—save the knowledge of our glance. I think there is nothing—save the silent and unspoken conscience in us now that needs no speech but silence, because we know what we know, we have what we have, we are what we are."

He had decided against the Newport cabin in favor of one at Oteen six miles north of Asheville, which he would occupy the beginning of July. In New York, meanwhile, he put the finishing touches on some short stories to build up his bank account, and one night he took Perkins and Marjorie Kinnan Rawlings—a keen admirer of his work who had been anxious to meet him—on a tour of the markets. Afterwards, Mrs. Rawlings wrote Perkins of Wolfe "plowing his way among the vegetables in a drizzle of rain at four o'clock in the morning, while you and I followed like pieces broken off from a meteor in transit." She said she wouldn't have started the argument about suicide in the Chinese restaurant had she known that Wolfe would take it so personally. She had always thought suicide "a delightful abstraction for discussion," but Wolfe got it into his head that she was urging him to do it, and at the top of his lungs he had refused "even to satisfy my publishers"—this with a glare at Perkins. Another evening a friend walking down First Avenue after a thunderstorm to join Wolfe for dinner glanced up to see him high over the city, leaning on his window sash and smoking as he took in the beauty of the sudden clearing at sunset—the "clean glory" of the scene, as he spoke of it when his friend entered. Again the conversation worked around to death. Wolfe asked the friend if he had ever seen a man die, and when the friend said he had, Wolfe wanted to know all the details. "Did he give any sign of—of—anything? I suppose not. I suppose no one ever really has."

Like other talented young men from the hinterland, Wolfe had come to New York seeking love and fame and had enjoyed a measure of both. Instead of the city's turbulence, he now craved a serenity which had always eluded him—wherefore he was going home "to set a spell and think things over." Since the publication of *Look Homeward, Angel* he had been living, working, and adventuring at high pressure, and he needed a period of repose to digest his experiences. He wished he had rented a cabin a little further from Asheville, where there would be fewer distractions. "If people could only understand," he wrote a friend down there, "that when you tell them you have to work, you mean it, but that also you don't mean you want to be left utterly alone. I certainly hope this doesn't happen to me either." Privacy and companionship, solitude and a flow of life around him—determined for once to achieve a proper blending of these opposites, Wolfe nailed the lid on his packing case of manuscript and headed for Asheville the end of June.

His log cabin—commodious if somewhat primitive, it had neither electricity nor hot water—nestled among the trees on a tabletop hill a ten-minute walk through the woods from the main road. In this asylum the only reminders of civilization were the whistles of the trains going past in the azalea bottoms, and occasional gusts of music from an amusement park three-quarters of a mile away. "If I can't write here," Wolfe told his landlord, Max Whitson, the day of his arrival, "I can't write anywhere." Whitson had found a lanky Negro to act as Wolfe's houseboy and cook, and when the three of them drove to the settlement of Oteen for supplies, Wolfe—who knew nothing about housekeeping though he had always lived alone—wanted to buy everything in sight. In the grocery store a good-looking blonde—a little high from drinking beer—eyed Wolfe as he came in and brazenly exclaimed to the woman who was with her, "My God, what a big man!" Sidling up to him while he was making his purchases, she said, "I'd like to take you home with me, big man. I got a cottage over here in the woods and an outdoor furnace—what do you say we cook some steaks?" Wolfe made an excuse, observing to Whitson as they drove back to the cabin, "Women have changed a lot since I lived in Asheville. Now you have to drive them away with a stick, and if they come to my place that's just what I'll do." He was eager to get to work, and next day he hired a stenographer to take dictation. When Whitson asked whether she was satisfactory, Wolfe said, "She's no stenographer at all. She's a champion swimmer and has cups to prove it. She can't even spell. Do you suppose she's trying to frame up on me?" He lived in horror of additional law suits. "I've been sued so many times," he told Whitson, "that I don't feel at home unless a bunch of lawyers are sitting on

my doorstep. At first they sued me for a few thousand, but now if
it's under a hundred thousand, I'm insulted."

No sooner was he settled than the locusts descended. That summer people said, "Let's go out and see Tom Wolfe" as one might
say, "Let's go to the zoo." Those he knew slightly accompanied by
those he knew not at all turned up at any time of day or night for
their "glimpse of the beast of the Apocalypse in his lair," as he spoke
of it in letters. Though he grumbled about not getting his work done,
he was pleased by his popularity and reluctant to turn away his
guests, and sat on the porch swapping stories with them and drinking the corn liquor they often brought along.

The first time he asked a group of friends and their wives to dinner, it was five o'clock and the chickens they were to eat still roamed
the yard when Ed, the houseboy, drew up in a taxi and ordered
Wolfe to pay his fare. Ed was drunk again after a day in town, and
Wolfe, who had bad luck with servants that summer, chose this
juncture to fire him. Happily, the grocery boy who had brought the
chickens was persuaded to kill and cook them, and a succulent
aroma floated through the woods when the first guests arrived.
Wolfe went out to greet them radiating warmth and affection, for
the occasion satisfied a deep longing in him. During dinner his eyes
with their trust of a St. Bernard turned sorrowful at the mention of
certain Ashevilleans who had been ruined by the Crash. "That's bad
—that's terrible," he would say, shaking his head; he was never one
to gloat over others' misfortunes no matter how lofty they had been.
After coffee he went to his writing table to autograph books while
his friends leaned over his shoulder and asked him to say this and
that. These were men he had grown up with and—in pursuit of his
demon—grown far beyond, and now they were fawning over him a
little, and he was trying to bridge the gap. Suddenly he reached for
a roll of toilet paper reposing on a corner of the table and wrote on a
section of it, "I love you all." "Is that what you want me to put in
every book?" he laughed, tossing aside the mock inscription which
one of those present retrieved and later framed.

Society people, who a decade earlier wouldn't have known he
existed, were begging him to come for dinner and meet their friends.
Sometimes he went and acquitted himself graciously, answering
questions that led nowhere and autographing books bought for the

sole purpose of having them autographed, but the look on his face said, "How do I get out of here?" At one of these affairs he was rescued by a young couple who had just graduated from Chapel Hill and were devotees of his writing. When they asked him what he would like to do, he asked them what they would do if he weren't there, and when they told him, he said with puppylike eagerness, "Let me go with you then. Do you mind? Would you be good enough to let me join you?" So they took him to the Open Pines, where there were outdoor tables and you danced and drank beer. In a listening mood, Wolfe hung on the words of the young couple and their friends who gathered round. "Is that a fact!" he would say. "Imagine that! Do you really think so? How come you feel that way?"—his overwhelming desire to know being mixed with ingenuous apologies for asking so many questions.

Behind his monolithic façade he still seemed to be groping for a happiness denied him by his gifts. Poetry seethed within him because he had found no peace, because he kept butting his head against—what? A stone, a leaf, a door, a *wall*. "You felt like patting him," said a woman who met him that summer, "and telling him it was going to be all right if he would just try not to suffer so much." He talked of getting married and as usual asked others if they couldn't find him a nice girl, and he gazed bemusedly at his friends' babies whose hands were like little pink feathers resting in his huge one. "Lordy, look at that!" he would say. (Wolfe's hands, though in scale with the rest of him, were conspicuously those of an artist; long-fingered and tapering, with shapely nails, and in some of their gestures—the way they picked up a flower or touched a woman's hair—expressive of great gentleness and delicacy.)

The last week of July, Wolfe was surprised to hear from Scott Fitzgerald, for despite a mutual respect and the bond with Perkins, they had seldom corresponded or sought each other out. As men and as artists they were of utterly different mold.

By nature attentive to dress and address, Fitzgerald couldn't help being put off by Wolfe's uncouthness and disorder, by his tendency to spray you when he talked and a trick he had of stirring his drink with a long, middle finger, and Wolfe's delicate antennae had sensed the reservation. After their first meeting the summer of 1930,

Wolfe had written Perkins, "When I am with someone like Scott, I feel that I am morose and sullen—and violent in my speech and movement part of the time. Later, I feel that I have repelled them." He exaggerated; Fitzgerald was writing Perkins simultaneously that he had "liked [Wolfe] enormously," and yet on both sides there *was* a temperamental rub. In Wolfe's eyes Fitzgerald smacked of gilded youth and the spoiled rich he wrote about and was rumored to consort with. Once when Fitzgerald had stopped to see Wolfe and Perkins at the Chatham Bar, he had excused himself after forty minutes because he had a taxi waiting, and Wolfe was appalled by such heedless extravagance. "That's not funny—it really isn't," he would say when relating the incident. To Wolfe, Fitzgerald was an illustration of the perils of early success. At twenty-three he had sold a novel and gotten his by-line in *The Saturday Evening Post*—terrific inflation—and then the girl he wanted but didn't seem to be getting had fallen into his arms—more inflation—and after *This Side of Paradise* became a best seller it seemed he could do no wrong. Hemingway had undergone a more rigorous apprenticeship before touching fame at twenty-six, and Wolfe began to be grateful that he had struggled in obscurity till he was twenty-nine. He did feel, however, that the critics had been unfair to *Tender Is the Night*, that despite its flaws it not only went deeper than Fitzgerald's other books but contained his best writing, and what was unusual for Wolfe—so absorbed in his own work that he seldom thought of anyone else's—he had written Fitzgerald saying so. A year later Fitzgerald had done Wolfe a good turn when he visited the Asheville Public Library and found that none of Wolfe's writings were on the shelves, because of the animosity they had aroused. Fitzgerald had immediately bought two copies of *Look Homeward, Angel* and donated them to the library, thus lifting the unofficial ban on Wolfe's work. While in Asheville the spring of 1937, Wolfe had visited Fitzgerald in Tryon, sensing the latter's need of friendship and encouragement as he tried to get back on his feet after his "crack-up."

They wished each other well, and yet artistically the gap between them had steadily widened. Generously admiring of new talent, Fitzgerald had written Perkins after reading *Look Homeward, Angel*, "You have a great find in him—what he'll do is incalculable. He has a deeper culture than Ernest [Hemingway] and more vitality, if he is slightly less of a poet that goes with the immense surface he wants to cover. Also he lacks Ernest's quality of a stick hardened in the fire—he is more susceptible to the world. John Bishop told me he needed advice about cutting, etc., but after reading his book I thought that was nonsense. He strikes me as a man who should be let alone as to length, if he has to be published in five volumes."

Of Time and the River had qualified Fitzgerald's enthusiasm. Admitting that "nothing [Wolfe] did could be undistinguished in its way," Fitzgerald told a friend that he was disappointed by "the gawky and profuse way in which [Wolfe] handled his material."[1] "There are fine things in it," he wrote Perkins, "and I loved reading it, and I am delighted that it's a wow, and it may be a bridge for something finer. I simply feel a certain disappointment which I would, on no account, want Tom to know about, for, responding as he does to criticism, I know it would make us life-long enemies and we might do untold needless damage to each other, so please be careful how you quote me." A month later Wolfe's story, "His Father's Earth," which seemed an epitome of all his sins, had brought Fitzgerald's criticism to a boil.[2] "He who has such infinite power of suggestion and delicacy has absolutely no right to glut people on whole meals of caviar. I hope to Christ he isn't taking all these emasculated paeans to his vitality very seriously. I'd hate to see such an exquisite talent turn into one of those muscle-bound and useless giants seen in a circus. Athletes have got to learn their games; they shouldn't just be content to tense their muscles, and if they do they suddenly find when called upon to bring off a necessary effect they are simply liable to hurl the shot into the crowd and not break any records at all. . . . The lyrical value of Eugene Gant's love affair with the universe—is that going to last through a whole saga? God, I wish he could discipline himself and really plan a novel."

Perkins, who saw the justice of Fitzgerald's strictures, had answered that it would be a grand thing if sometime Fitzgerald would talk to Wolfe, but as for Perkins himself, "Even if one had an utterly free hand instead of being subject to constant abuse (Goddamned Harvard English, grovelling at the feet of Henry James, etc.), it would be a matter of editing inside sentences, and that would be a dangerous business.[3] But gradually criticism, and age too, may make an impression."

Though he wasn't an envious man, Fitzgerald in his present obscurity and neglect couldn't help feeling a little annoyed by all the attention Perkins had been lavishing on Wolfe. (Hemingway's pique was equally apparent; he referred to Wolfe ironically as Perkins' "world genius" and "writer of world masterpieces," and recently when Perkins had expressed reservations about Hemingway's new novel *To Have and Have Not*, Hemingway had broken off his angry rebuttal with, "Hell, let Tom Wolfe write for you then!") Wolfe seemed coddled to Fitzgerald, though the real point at issue was Wolfe's disregard of the novel form, and the summer of 1937 Fitzgerald found the courage to speak his mind. His affairs had taken a turn for the better. After six months on the wagon he had signed a lucrative contract with M-G-M and had gone to Hollywood, where he immediately fell in love with movie columnist Sheilah Graham. He was feeling his oats for the first time in years, but realizing that he was taking his life in his hands, he headed his letter to Wolfe, "Pure Impulse, U.S.A., 1937," and then went on to plead for the necessity of Wolfe's cultivating "an alter ego, a more conscious artist in you. Hasn't it occurred to you that such qualities as pleasantness or grief, exuberance or cynicism, can become a plague in others? That often people who live at a high pitch don't get their way emotionally at the important moment because it doesn't stand out in relief? . . . The novel of selected incidents has this to be said: that the great writer like Flaubert has consciously left out the stuff that Bill or Joe (in this case, Zola) will come along and say presently. He will say only the things that he alone sees. So *Madame Bovary* becomes eternal while Zola already rocks with age.

"Repression itself has a value, as with a poet who struggles for the necessary rhyme and achieves accidentally a new word association that would not have come by any mental or even flow of consciousness process. 'The [Ode to a] Nightingale' is full of that.

"To a talent like mine of narrow scope there is not that problem. I must put everything in to have enough and even then I often haven't got enough.[4]

"That, in brief, is my case against you, if it can be called that when I admire you so much and think your talent is unmatchable in this or any other country."

Ever touchy, if less morbidly so than in times past, Wolfe decided to wade in with both hands. With sardonic relish, he answered that the "unexpected loquaciousness" of Fitzgerald's letter had struck him all of a heap. "I was surprised to hear from you but I don't know that I can truthfully say I was delighted. Your bouquet arrived smelling sweetly of roses but cunningly concealing several large-sized brickbats. Not that I resented them. My resenter got pretty tough years ago; like everybody else I have at times been accused of 'resenting criticism' and although I have never been one of those boys who break out in a hearty and delighted laugh when someone tells them everything they write is lousy and agree enthusiastically, I think I have taken as many plain and fancy varieties as any American citizen of my own age now living. I have not always smiled and murmured pleasantly 'How true,' but I have listened to it all, tried to profit from it where and when I could, and perhaps been helped by it a little. . . .

"I have read your letter several times and I've got to admit it doesn't seem to mean much. . . . I may be wrong but all I can get out of it is that you think I'd be a good writer if I were an altogether different writer from the writer that I am.

"This may be true but I don't see what I'm going to do about it, and I don't think you can show me. And I don't see what Flaubert and Zola have to do with it, or what I have to do with them. I wonder if you really think they have anything to do with it, or if it is just something you heard in college or read in a book somewhere. This either-or kind of criticism seems to me to be so meaningless. It looks so knowing and imposing but there is nothing in it. Why does it follow that if a man writes a book that is not like *Madame Bovary* it is inevitably like Zola? I may be dumb but I can't see this. You say that *Madame Bovary* becomes eternal while Zola already rocks with age. Well this may be true—but if it is true isn't it true because *Madame Bovary* may be a great book and those that Zola wrote may not be great ones? Wouldn't it also be true to say that *Don Quixote* or *Pickwick* or *Tristram Shandy* 'becomes eternal' while already Mr. Galsworthy 'rocks with age.' I think it is true to say this and it doesn't leave much of your argument, does it? For your argument is based simply upon one *way*, one *method* instead of another. And have you ever noticed how often it turns out that what a man is really doing is simply rationalizing his own way of doing something, the way he has to do it, the way given him by his talent and his nature, into the only inevitable and right way of doing everything—a sort of classic and eternal art form handed down by Apollo from Olympus without which and beyond which there is nothing? Now you have your way of doing something and I have mine, there are a lot of ways, but you are honestly mistaken in thinking that there is a 'way.'

"I suppose I would agree with you in what you say about 'the novel of selected incidents' so far as it means anything. I say so far as it means anything because every novel, of course, is a novel of selected incidents. There are no novels of unselected incidents. You couldn't write about the inside of a telephone booth without selecting. You could fill a novel of a thousand pages with a description of a single room and yet your incidents would be selected. And I have mentioned *Don Quixote* and *Pickwick* and *The Brothers Karamazov* and *Tristram Shandy* to you in contrast to *The Silver Spoon* or *The White Monkey* [by Galsworthy] as examples of books that have become 'immortal' and that *boil* and *pour*. Just remember that although *Madame Bovary* in your opinion may be a great book, *Tristram Shandy is* indubitably a great book and that it is great for quite different reasons. It is great because it *boils* and *pours*—for the *unselected* quality of its selection. You say that the great writer like Flaubert has consciously left out the stuff that Bill or Joe will come along presently and put in. Well, don't forget, Scott, that a great writer is not only a leaver-outer but also a putter-inner, and that Shakespeare and Cervantes and Dostoyevsky were great putter-inners—greater putter-inners, in fact, than taker-outers—and will be remembered for what they put in—remembered, I venture to say, as long as Monsieur Flaubert will be remembered for what he left out."[5]

The letter continued for several pages ("unselective, you see, as usual," said Wolfe at the end), but the above was the gist of it. Though he confessed his desire to be a more restrained artist, using "such talent as I have . . . more cleanly, more surely, and to better purpose," the high precision novel *à la* Flaubert lay outside the capabilities and indeed the ambitions of this sprawling, teeming, life-saturated author whose strengths were more those of a Dickens or a Rabelais, or of Flaubert's opposite number, Balzac. Wolfe had to write as he did in broad strokes; only by a process of slather and daub, by slowly masticating his subject and revolving it in every light, could he speak the truth that was in him. As Perkins said later, his bodily size symbolized a disproportion in other respects. Artistically he needed plenty of room to move around in, though Perkins thought that at bottom he *did* have a sense of form which would have been apparent had he lived to complete his huge design. But unlike Fitzgerald, who began a novel with elaborate outlines, charts, and diagrams, Wolfe gave little thought to such scaffolding, concentrating instead on what he had to say and trusting that each emotion or episode, when fully explored, would reveal a shapeliness of its own.

Wolfe saw nothing sacrosanct in the novel form. Sometimes he spoke of his books as "novels" but more often simply as "books," and if pressed as to whether he was writing novels or something else with a name yet to be invented, he would probably have said the latter.[6] What did occupy him—and passionately—was whether his writing rang clear and true, whether it said what he wanted it to say, whether his readers would be moved by it and would put his book down thinking, "Yes, that's the way life is." As for the solipsism Fitzgerald had objected to in his letter to Perkins, though Wolfe never escaped the cockpit of himself, his was hardly a narrow or myopic self-centeredness. His cycloramic gaze swept the universe, and his feeling for the protoplasm of existence was akin to that of the Russian masters, who in his estimation outshone Flaubert. Making the case for Wolfe immediately after his death, the editor and critic V. F. Calverton wrote Perkins, "Tom was not the perfectly disciplined writer Hemingway is, not the clever, astute writer Scott [Fitzgerald] was and still is . . . but he was more. He was undisciplined, unrestrained, unreserved in his writing, but he had more in the guts of it than Hemingway and Scott combined. . . . Tom was closer to the earth-source of life, closer to the chthonic element, closer to death and life than any writer, without exception, in our generation."

A poet above all, Wolfe was most himself in the fits and blazes of his inspiration when an occult power streamed through him, and his life had been a struggle to maintain the purity of his poetic vision.[7] On the one hand, he had the poet's sure grasp of actuality, a marvelous thickness of specification, a way of choosing his words and calculating his effects to appeal to all of the senses; on the other, he had a poet's awareness of the mystery that lies beyond the circle of our knowledge and experience. Wolfe was a poet of remembrance, of the hauntings of childhood and the tricks of time, of the poignancy of the moment with its freight of immortal longings. Acknowledging this poet-nature, Fitzgerald was to write Perkins, "The more valuable parts of Tom were the more lyrical parts or, rather, those moments when his lyricism was best combined with his powers of observation—those fine blends such as the trip up the Hudson in *Of Time and the River*." And in an essay written the last year of his life Fitzgerald would call Wolfe's early death "a grievous loss. With Hemingway, Dos Passos, Wilder and Faulkner he was one of a group of talents for fiction such as rarely appears in a single hatching."[8]

That summer Wolfe's oldest brother, Frank, had drifted in from the West and was staying at the Old Kentucky Home. Sensitive about his portrayal as the dissolute Steve in *Look Homeward, Angel,* Frank asked Tom why he had been so hard on him, and letting him down easy, Tom asked Frank if he had ever read *The Virginian.* Frank said he had. "Well, you remember Trampas, don't you?" Tom said. "Trampas was the villain and without Trampas there would have been no book. You were my Trampas, Frank." As a rule Tom visited his mother in the evening after Frank had gone to bed, but once he came in when she was trying to get Frank to eat some solid food. He had developed a constriction of the esophagus which made swallowing extremely difficult, and watching his brother's efforts, Tom remarked with sudden brutality, "Why don't you just kill yourself, Frank—drink enough to kill yourself? You don't amount to anything."

"So I know," said Frank. "I don't amount to a thing."

Julia tried to intercede, but Tom went on: "You drink—don't do anything but drink—you never tried to make anything out of yourself. I do try. I drink, too, but I try to do something else besides. Why don't you die?"

"Well, I don't know," said Frank. "Maybe I will sometime."[9]

Wolfe was working, when he worked, on his novella *The Party at Jack's* which would become a major episode in *You Can't Go Home*

Again, but finding it hard to concentrate in Asheville he was already thinking of returning to New York. The middle of August he was summoned to a trial in Burnsville where he had stopped on his way South in May. In that picturesque mountain town where red-faced, cracked-fingered farmers in slouch hats sat by the steps of the seedy courthouse eying strangers malignantly, Wolfe had seen a man shot at and a week later the man was killed. Wolfe relished the drama of the trial and got off, he thought, fairly easily compared to some of the witnesses, although the defense lawyer in his final plea denounced Wolfe as the author of "an obscene and infamous book which held up his family, kinfolk, and town to public odium."

As the summer wore on, he became increasingly bored and disgruntled with the visitors who trooped to his cabin and squandered his time. He took refuge at the Weavers'; old Dr. Weaver was one of Asheville's most respected citizens, and his daughter, Tot, a fading, witty blonde some years older than Wolfe, had won his devotion with an enthusiastic letter about *Look Homeward, Angel* when Asheville's animus against it was most intense. The last week of August he stopped living at the cabin and took a room at the Battery Park Hotel where women left their keys for him as though he were a matinee idol, but he was skilled at not getting involved. "The old biddies," he would say, shrugging it off. One day Fred came up from Spartanburg, and over a drink in his hotel room Tom told of his fatigue, of the impossibility of doing his work at the cabin, and of his having to return to New York, though he didn't want to stay there either. Suddenly he tapped his brother on the knee and asked with utter seriousness, "Fred, do you think I'm going to die?"

"Merciful God, yes, you're going to die!" Fred exploded. "And so am I! But what the hell has come over you? By the law of averages you should outlive me. I'm six years older than you."

Tom mentioned a scare he had had that spring. After recovering from what he thought was a touch of flu, his fever had hung on and he had gone to a doctor. He never told anyone exactly what the doctor had found and no record of the examination exists, but it seems likely that X rays were taken and that they revealed an old tubercular scar on his right upper lobe. At the time Wolfe was heard to say that "there's something wrong with my lung," and he was sufficiently worried to draw a new will, naming his mother as chief beneficiary, and Perkins and a college classmate living in New York as co-executors.[10] He now admitted to Fred that the doctor had urged him to slow down, which had perhaps been another reason for renting the cabin at Oteen.

But though his health concerned him, he didn't mend his ways. One afternoon that summer a newspaperman named Bright Padgitt was in a restaurant opposite the Langren Hotel when Wolfe came in and joined him, explaining that he had spent the night at the hotel to get away from the annoyances at the cabin. He asked for an empty glass and a glass of water, and taking a pint of whisky from his pocket, he filled the empty glass and drank it down as if it were a mild red wine—without making a face, Padgitt remembered, though he looked a bit stoic at the finish. He then drank half the water as a chaser. After talking to Padgitt a while, he said he'd better be getting back to Oteen, and having poured the rest of the pint except for an inch at the bottom, he drank it off, finished the water, and set out on foot for the cabin six miles away. It was drizzling, and he had no hat or coat. Wolfe lived carelessly, and carelessness can kill.

One of his last days in Asheville, he ran into Reeves Rutledge at the drugstore. Rutledge had lived across the street when they were boys, and Wolfe used to slip into the Rutledge's back yard and steal cherries, while Rutledge would invade the lot next door to the Wolfes' and steal apples. When they weren't telling on each other, they were having rock fights, and as they reminisced, Wolfe said, "Why the hell I left you out of my book I don't know, but I guess we just fought too much, and I didn't want to fight you again." They laughed, and tossing off his coke, Wolfe said, "Goodbye, Reeves—I won't be seeing you any more."

He left Asheville September 5th without notifying the Robertses, of whom he had seen very little during the summer. One day Mrs. Roberts had called on him with a young couple from Tennessee who were ardent fans of his, and later she wrote that on this "gleaming" occasion she had felt his "power of mind and spirit more vividly than ever, except of course [than in] the wonderful days of your boyhood and young manhood when, it seemed to me, there was none like you. . . ." In her heart she always came back to the lad she had discovered and nurtured, and when she spoke of his days at the North State Fitting School, of her straightening his tie and pulling him together, the look of tenderness that crossed her face was as intense as when she spoke of her own children. With Wolfe the man, the awe-inspiring world celebrity, she felt a slight constraint, nor was she at liberty to say what she thought. After his death she would confide that the only time she had ever really been mad at him—*Look Homeward, Angel* having hurt rather than angered her—was the summer of 1937. Never had she been so conscious of his powers, and she couldn't bear to see him burn himself out and "butcher his genius with liquor."[11]

From Asheville he went north through the mountains to Bristol, Virginia, where he spent several days with Anne Armstrong, whom he had met in April on his journey South. Mrs. Armstrong, a widow of sixty-five, had with no previous experience become a Wall Street executive when her husband suffered reverses in middle life. She was also the author of two novels and a number of popular articles on big business. Wolfe liked her spacious guest cabin, with a little mountain river rushing past the door. "A man can breathe here," he said, reaching up and swinging from a rafter with boyish glee. He ate his meals at Mrs. Armstrong's house halfway up the wooded slope, and she took pains to provide such dishes as he, a Southerner living in the North, would most enjoy: green beans cooked with bacon, country ham and fried chicken, corn pone, and hot biscuits that *were* hot. Mrs. Armstrong's blend of culture, horse sense, and sympathy made her the perfect listener as Wolfe recounted his woes, from the summer in Asheville ("I found that being forgiven was almost worse than being damned—have you ever had just too much hospitality?") to his desire to settle down and raise a family, to his bewilderment about finding a new publisher, since in his mind the break with Scribners was now complete.

He talked a great deal about literature and "with complete unpretentiousness," Mrs. Armstrong remembered, "without the slightest pontifical touch. Never, in fact, have I known anyone who had himself been a professor and so wholly escaped professorial blight." She noted some odd gaps in his reading; among the books under his arm as he started down the hill to his cabin one night were George Moore's *Hail and Farewell* and Turgenev's *Fathers and Sons*, neither of which he knew. Once he picked up her collection of

Longfellow, saying that it was fatuous for people to laugh at Longfellow, that his work contained much that was lovely and worth preserving. Then he read aloud "My Lost Youth," simply and with deep feeling when he came to the refrain,

> A boy's will is the wind's will,
> And the thoughts of youth are long, long thoughts.

He, of course, had been that boy.

On another occasion, as he was surveying Mrs. Armstrong's library, he squared himself and said, "Those kids I've been playing around with this summer think they have a good time. God, no one knows what a good time is who hasn't known the adventure of great books!" His story, "The Child by Tiger," had just come out in *The Saturday Evening Post,* and Mrs. Armstrong remembered the "quick lift of his eyes and slight stare" with which he met a visitor's inquiry as to whether he had written down in writing for *The Post.* "I always," he said, "write as well as I can." On September 8th Mrs. Armstrong drove him the forty miles to Marion where he was to spend a night with Sherwood Anderson, and during the trip the conversation turned to authors' names. Wolfe spoke of his own as a gift from heaven: "Thomas Wolfe—that was a good running start for a writer, wasn't it?" Then he went over a long list of ludicrous names he had been fortunate enough to escape.

Although Sherwood Anderson of *Winesburg, Ohio* fame had by this time written himself out, Wolfe revered his early achievement and coupled him with Twain and Whitman as a writer of poetic vision who had "plowed another deep furrow in the American earth, revealed to us another beauty that we knew was there but that no one else had spoken." A folksy, heavy-set man with warm eyes the color of iodine, Anderson spun his yarns with his elbows planted on the table, his chin in the air, and a cigarette held loosely and awkwardly in his curved right hand. Pausing now and then, he would look down to wipe away an imaginary crumb with flattened palm, and then looking up again, he would continue his tale in a grave, sweet drawl. His sincerity invited confidences—not that Wolfe needed such invitations—and Anderson listened patiently while Wolfe spilled his troubles. "A flood, a continent, but . . . generous and full of fine feeling," Anderson later described Wolfe in a letter to Perkins, amending it in his diary to "generous & big in every way, but a good deal the great child."

Despite the impasse with Scribners, as recently as August 22nd Wolfe had thought of sending *The Party at Jack's* to Perkins for an opinion as to whether it might stand alone as a book. The same week, however, another attack by Bernard De Voto in *The Saturday Review* had triggered his first steps toward finding a new publisher. One morning over long distance he had offered himself to five firms without being taken up on it, part of the trouble being that it was hard to believe a writer of Wolfe's standing would change publishers so unceremoniously. How could one be sure that the booming voice which said, "My name is Wolfe—would you be interested in publishing me?" *was* the best-selling author, and not some impostor? At Harpers he was connected by mistake with the editor of *Harper's Magazine* who said that if Wolfe would send him something he'd be glad to read it, and Wolfe, thinking that he was talking to a book editor, construed it as a lack of interest in his work. Harcourt, Brace was noncommittal because their close ties with Scribners made them reluctant to steal Wolfe and fully conscious of the headache of publishing him. Though an editor at Knopf expressed a desire to meet him and discuss his future plans, Wolfe later decided not to get involved with them because Alfred Knopf was a friend of Aline and her publisher as well.

On his return to New York the middle of September, he gave up his First Avenue apartment, and during the next six weeks he lived in various hotels, keeping his whereabouts a secret and telling people to communicate with him through his agent, Elizabeth Nowell. Of an old New England family, this breezy, talky, tartly smiling young woman was a blend of tomboy heartiness and sentimental, mothering warmth. She had known Wolfe from his earliest days at Scribners when she had been a reader for the magazine, and during the past three years, as his agent, she had given him helpful suggestions about adapting his stories for popular consumption. Since he regarded them as a means of making money and rewrote them the way he wanted them for incorporation in the novels which were his pride, his relations with Miss Nowell had been largely free of the tensions which had grown up between him and Perkins, although at times even she came under his displeasure. He would call her a leech sucking unearned commissions out of him, and in the thick of his difficulties with Scribners he had said to her, "Of course for all I know you may be a tool of the Scribner interests." Fiercely protective and completely dedicated, Miss Nowell handled Wolfe with easy camaraderie. He called her "Nowell" and she called him "Wolfe," varying it with "Hey, sweetheart" or "Listen, you big bastard," and as formerly with Perkins, he went to her with all his problems. Once when a girl who was after him tried to get a reaction by pretending she was pregnant, he said, "Why don't you telephone Miss Nowell? She's my agent. She takes care of everything for me."

As the weeks went by without a publishing offer, he began to feel that no one wanted him, but instead of making further overtures he withdrew into himself. Finally, in mid-October, there came a letter from Robert Linscott of Houghton Mifflin inquiring into the rumors of his dissatisfaction with Scribners and suggesting they meet. The sequel points up the cumbrousness of Wolfe's dealings—his almost pathological suspicion, combined with his painful honesty and his horror of hurting people's feelings. He answered Linscott that the severance with Scribners, involving "deep and complicated differences," was "one of the most grievous and sorrowful experiences of my whole life," but that he could "honorably talk about these things now." When they met, Wolfe agreed to show Linscott the manuscript of *The October Fair* then reposing in a Brooklyn warehouse. Linscott suggested that Wolfe bring it to Houghton Mifflin's New York office where he could sort and assemble it, and soon afterwards Wolfe appeared with a packing case and nine smaller containers. As Wolfe was leaving, Linscott handed him a letter of receipt which said among other things that because they had no fireproof safe Houghton Mifflin was holding the manuscript at Wolfe's risk. No one else would have objected to this routine disclaimer, but with his hatred of legalism and his distrust of publishers Wolfe began fuming, "Jesus, these people persuade me to take my manuscript out of storage where it was safe, and now they say they won't be responsible if anything happens to it." Worse still, though he and Linscott were on a first-name basis, the letter began, "Dear Wolfe." "You cannot talk to a man over the dinner table and a drink," wrote Wolfe in his unmailed reply, "about your belief and interest and enthusiasm for his work, and how your organization supports and upholds such people in failure or success, and then talk about who is to take the risk or whose responsibility is whose when he brings his property into your office and entrusts it to your care. I do not say that either set of chips is wrong but you've got to play one or the other." A few days later he reclaimed his manuscript and took it to his hotel.

As he glanced through this draft of *The October Fair,* written five to seven years earlier at the height of his troubles with Aline, he became increasingly reluctant to show it to Linscott until he had revised it, and Houghton Mifflin policy forbade Linscott from offering an advance until he had seen a publishable manuscript. Pacing his hotel room, Wolfe complained to Miss Nowell, "Houghton Mifflin says it's years since they've 'moved towards a publishing alliance' with greater anticipation, but I can't see that we're moving towards anything at all!" Meanwhile, an old friend of Miss Nowell's, Edward Aswell of Harpers, had entered the picture. Wolfe had asked her not to mention his troubles to Aswell because of Harpers' rebuff over the long-distance phone, but on hearing from Bernard De Voto of all people that Wolfe was leaving Scribners, Aswell checked with Miss Nowell who arranged a meeting, and although as a junior editor he wasn't authorized to make commitments on his own, he offered Wolfe a $10,000 advance on his next book, sight unseen. Wolfe needed the money, but even more he needed the faith which the money represented. "If Aswell really believes what he said about me," Wolfe told Miss Nowell, "and he must believe it, or he wouldn't have said it the way he did—" Breaking off, he pursed his mouth and shook his head as was his wont when profoundly moved. "Well anyway, if Aswell does believe all that . . ."

Luckily for Aswell, his superiors approved his high-handed offer, and the following week the rapprochement was solidified when Wolfe had dinner at the apartment of Eugene Saxton, Harpers' editor-in-chief. Also on hand were Cass Canfield (president of the firm), Aswell, and a third editor who couldn't hold his liquor. After the brandy they settled themselves in the living room before the fire, and Wolfe began telling the story of his life, with the others throwing out occasional questions. From time to time the bibulous editor would struggle to his feet and teeter across the room to where Aswell was sitting and whisper in a drunken roar, "He"—meaning Wolfe—"is the most Goddamned honest man I ever heard talk." It got to be embarrassing because it happened so often, but it aptly expressed the reaction of Wolfe's audience who, losing track of the time, were startled when the clock in a nearby insurance building struck 5 A.M.

Obviously Wolfe's next move was to accept the Harper offer, and yet because of his friendship with Linscott he deliberated another five weeks. To complicate matters, Doubleday had entered the bidding, saying they would match anyone else's advance, so Wolfe had several delicious alternatives to ponder. Houghton Mifflin got the *coup de grâce* when one of Linscott's associates told Miss Nowell that much as they wanted Wolfe, they were worried by the prospect of editing his books and managing his affairs, and would therefore like to retain her as an editorial consultant in charge of Thomas Wolfe. When she passed on this information, Wolfe said disgustedly, "Here I've been dealing with these people for the past month only to find they're afraid of me." Nevertheless, when Linscott offered him a $10,000 advance the first week of December, conditional upon the reading and acceptance of *The October Fair,* he couldn't bring himself to decline. "Damn it all, I *like* Bob Linscott," he told Miss Nowell. "There's something *fine* about him, he looks like the young Abe Lincoln, and I really think he is my friend. And his wife just died, and I hate to spoil his Christmas." It wasn't till December 18 that Wolfe finally phoned Aswell to say he was going with Harpers.

Invited to spend Christmas with the Aswells in Chappaqua, Wolfe missed the afternoon train which he and Aswell had agreed to catch, nor was he on the next one after that. Aswell met trains for a while, and then began phoning Wolfe's favorite haunts, finally locating him in a bar with Elizabeth Nowell. "He's going from one bar to another, celebrating," she told Aswell, "but don't worry, I'm following, and I'll see he gets out there." (What Aswell didn't realize was that Wolfe had gotten the impression that Aswell wanted to show him off to his house guests, and as usual Wolfe was reluctant to cooperate.) Towards midnight Miss Nowell phoned that Wolfe was on his way, and Aswell went to meet him expecting the worst, but as Wolfe avalanched down to the platform full of sheep-faced apologies, he was steady on his feet and one wouldn't have known he had been pub-crawling save for the enormous, woolly toy dog which he held by the tail—a gift for Aswell's small son. In the course of the evening the dog's wrappings had come off and its tail hung by a few threads, but under the tree it went, and the boy got it next day.

Wolfe later described it as the most enjoyable Christmas since his childhood. There was no accident about it, Aswell's wife Mary Lou having looked up the description of Christmas in *Look Homeward, Angel* and having gotten all the things Wolfe had been accustomed to as a boy. As they sat down to eat, he commented on the fact that there were thirteen at the table. One of the other guests had made the cranberry sauce, and after telling her how much he liked it "with those whole cranberries all mushed up in it," Wolfe said disarmingly, "Can you make good lemon meringue pie? 'Cause if you can I'll marry you." In the midst of dessert Mary Lou asked him if it was all right to tell, and he said yes, so champagne was produced and Mary Lou announced that Wolfe was signing with Harpers, and everyone had tears in their eyes. Wolfe was solidly attached to Aswell, a Southerner from Nashville six days his junior, of whom he had written Fred, "The man thinks I am the best writer in the country—which he is wrong about—and he thinks I am going to get better, which I think he is right about. At any rate, I feel I am leaving the greatest editor in America, and a man of genius to boot, and maybe this young man Aswell is none of these, but I am playing a hunch—I feel he is a good man, and an able man, and if anybody has got this much faith in me I'll kill myself if I have to to live up to it."

With his dread of the irrevocable Wolfe put off signing the contract until December 31st, the last possible day if he wanted to receive part of his advance in 1937 and thus reduce his income tax. When the technicalities had been completed, he wrote Mary Lou of his "strangely empty and hollow feeling" now that he was committed. "But I guess it is good for a man to get that hollow empty feeling, the sense of absolute loneliness and new beginning at different times throughout his life. It's not the hollowness of death, but a living kind of hollowness: a new world is before me now. . . ."

Wolfe hadn't seen Perkins since June. Until the actual signing with Harpers, Perkins had kept hoping that Wolfe would exhaust his hurling-rocks, me-against-the-world tempestuousness and come back to Scribners, and now that the break was official Perkins talked of nothing else when he lunched with other writers who knew Wolfe, as if seeking every possible explanation. But he analyzed it without bitterness, knowing how difficult this desperate tearing himself loose had been for a man of Wolfe's innate probity and loyalty.[12] In November, when Fred had written Perkins for news of Tom, Perkins had answered that Tom "has turned his back on me and on Scribners, so I haven't seen him at all, though I would like to very much." Fred forwarded the letter to Tom, who then wrote Perkins a tract rehashing their differences, ending with, "I am your friend, Max, and that is why I wrote this letter—to tell you so. If I wrote so much else here that the main thing was obscured— the only damn one that matters—that I am your friend and want you to be mine—please take this last line as being what I wanted to say the whole way through." And Perkins replied, "I am your friend and always will be. . . . I told Fred truly too when I said I did not understand about [the break]. I don't, but that need make no difference between us, and I won't let it on my side. . . . Anyhow, I'm glad to have seen your handwriting again."

In February, 1938, when Wolfe's suit against Francis O'Reilly— the agent who wouldn't return his manuscripts—came up for a hearing in Jersey City, Perkins was glad, and indeed eager, to testify in Wolfe's behalf. "The more I have to do with lawyers," Wolfe had said in a letter the previous year, "the more I feel as if I had been compelled to take a voyage down a sewer in a glass-bottomed boat,"[13] but he was determined to bring O'Reilly to heel, and appealed to Perkins and others for support as if humanity itself were at stake. In court O'Reilly was easily vanquished. Wolfe had an almost air-tight case and gave "an overwhelming impression of sincerity and dignity," according to Perkins, who touched Wolfe to the quick when he took the stand wearing a hearing aid for the first time in his life. Afterwards, on the ferry back to New York, Wolfe said, "What do you suppose was in those pages of mine which

[O'Reilly] claims he burned because of their filthy and pornographic nature?" With an impish grin he added, "I wish I could see them now. I may never again sink low enough to achieve such heights of obscenity and what a loss to *belles lettres*!" He and Perkins had a triumphal lunch at Cherio's, and Perkins always regretted that one of the other witnesses came along, it being the last time Wolfe and Perkins ever saw each other.

Since late October Wolfe had been living at the Chelsea on West Twenty-third Street, a bohemian hostelry famed for such former occupants as O. Henry and Mark Twain. When he had appeared prospecting for a room, Edgar Lee Masters had urged him to stay and had vouched for him at the desk. They enjoyed each other's company, for although the author of *Spoon River Anthology* worked in cameos while Wolfe worked in frescoes, they had a common love of the American adventure. Wolfe also made friends with a resident pulp writer, Fred MacIsaac, and his diminutive wife Violet. She had never heard of Wolfe and was totally unprepared when her husband ushered the stammering giant with the uncombed hair to their table in the hotel restaurant. Before the evening was over, she had given him her comb—he said he had lost his— and was biting her tongue to keep from suggesting that she sew the loose button on his coat. On a later occasion she asked him if he would autograph one of his books were she to buy it. He looked at her sternly and said, "Would you really read my book? It's six hundred pages—I got a bit garrulous." When she assured him that she would, he rushed out to the neighboring bookstore and came back with a copy of *Look Homeward, Angel* which he signed for her saying, "Violet, I don't think you are an intellectual woman, but you sure have great understanding." Once she gave a cocktail party, and seeing her in a hostess gown for the first time, Wolfe remarked, "Gosh, Violet, I'd like to have you served up on toast!" She responded by going to the piano and playing a dreamy Schumann number she thought he would like, but when it was over he said, "Can't you play something fast?" so she gave up and banged out "Dixie."

Wolfe's eighth-floor corner suite at the Chelsea—a foyer, bedroom, living room, office, and bath—had his usual atmosphere of hard labor and few creature comforts. In the center of the living room were two large packing cases, wherein crisp white sheets typed yesterday mingled with archaic, dog-eared manuscripts and the miscellaneous jottings Wolfe accumulated lest their precious alignment of words never be arrived at again. He had the writer's mania, also, for saving letters, photos, mementos—anything capable of striking a glimmer from his spirit. In these high-ceilinged, airless quarters, rank with the smell of unemptied ashtrays, his day began at eleven when his secretary arrived, and after she left at six he would go on working till hunger sent him down the street to Cavanaugh's for a couple of thick steaks. He had a special table in the rear of the restaurant where he would sit with his back to the wall and watch the other diners. Afterwards, he would go for a walk, or stop at the Chelsea Bar to gossip with the bartender and listen to the girl with the accordion. Tiring of this, he would drift into the lobby and strike up a conversation with another guest or the night clerk or the elevator boy. One evening when his nerves were frayed and the switchboard operator called him "Toots," he complained of her familiarity to the manager who said he'd be glad to fire her, whereupon Wolfe with characteristic ambivalence got mad at the manager for persecuting the help. Towards midnight he returned to his room where he often worked some more before collapsing into a troubled sleep.

Aside from Elizabeth Nowell, Ed Aswell and those at the hotel, he saw hardly anyone and his unopened mail accumulated on the mantel. "If you don't open 'em," he once remarked, "you don't have to answer 'em, and it doesn't make much difference anyway." His friendship with John Terry had cooled because Terry, still on good terms with Francis O'Reilly's family, had been in an ambiguous position during the trial. Wolfe tolerated no middle ground: you were for him or against him, ally or enemy. "And I thought he was my friend!" he was always saying of some supposed turncoat, whereupon Miss Nowell would jolly him, "Oh now, Wolfe, that isn't so—nobody's trying to do you in." The recent publication of Aline Bernstein's novel, *The Journey Down*, had depressed him. To his mind this version of their affair made her seem too much the victim and ingenue, but he went on speaking of her as the "biggest" woman he had ever known, and was sure he would never love that way again.

In December he quarreled with Sherwood Anderson, then visiting New York. Wolfe, Anderson, and his wife Eleanor had attended a dinner party where someone had spoken of the Southern propensity for smearing liberals on other grounds than their liberalism. In corroboration Mrs. Anderson, who had recently been in North Carolina, said she had heard it rumored that Wolfe was Jewish. Jumping to his feet, he called the imputation outrageous, while Anderson and the others defended Mrs. Anderson and accused Wolfe of anti-Semitism for taking offense. At the end of the evening Wolfe made up with the Andersons, but the incident left a bad taste, and several weeks later Anderson wrote Wolfe that he hoped their "queer row" was forgotten. Before receiving the letter, Wolfe ran into Anderson in a hotel lobby. Wolfe's publishing dilemma was still unresolved, and having done little during the past week except drink and brood, he was now inspired to tell Anderson off (a favorite pastime of his generation of authors, Faulkner and Hemingway having done so already). Wolfe said that though *Winesburg* had been a revelation to him and his contemporaries, Anderson had let them down since and that "this business of sitting around and talking, naked, on parlor sofas"—as in *Many Marriages*—was no good. Next day Wolfe got a note from Anderson: "When I wrote you yesterday, suggesting that you have dinner with me Tuesday evening, I had no notion how you felt. As you have expressed such a hearty desire to chuck our acquaintance—why not?"

Wolfe wrote, but did not mail, an apology in which he attributed his flare-up to his publishing worries. However, on their original difference, the Jewish question, he stood his ground: "I just can't agree that it is something that should not be taken seriously, because it seems to me the implications not only to myself, but to a lot of obscure decent people [Wolfe's relatives] are pretty serious, and whether you will agree with my point of view or not, you must have understanding enough to see that such a thing would affect them pretty tragically in so many of the fundamental relations of life and their marital relations, their social and business relations, and so on. And I think also it would affect me pretty seriously too. I have been mighty fortunate as a writer, people have said some mighty fine things about me. I don't know whether they were right or not, or whether it means anything, but apparently a lot of people have thought I was a pretty American sort of writer, and what I did was indigenous to this country. I hope this is true. At any rate, I am pretty proud of it, and I would like to live up to it, and I say this honestly without a word or thought of prejudice towards any people, any race, or any creed."

For all his bearishness and seclusion, Wolfe was a commanding figure that winter of 1938, and his prestige had political overtones. His demotic flavor, his rough-hewn, down-to-earth appeal meshed with the social consciousness of the period, and what more eloquent indictment of Fascism than his *New Republic* serial, "I Have a Thing to Tell You?" Proud of the working-class element in his background, he wrote with deep feeling of the poor and the oppressed, and believed in the necessity of what he called "a radical transformation of capitalist society." Nevertheless, despite the arguments with Perkins in which he had played the devil's advocate, he was impervious to Marxism. Not only did he grasp the fundamental antithesis of art and propaganda, but he had been repelled by the intellectual opportunists who began spouting *Das Kapital* as soon as it became fashionable. Instead of writing manifestoes and discussing Marx at cocktail parties, Wolfe had studied the Depression at first hand in his wanderings across the city. Later, when the Marxists began stumping for Loyalist Spain, he said, "The miseries at home, I suppose, are not romantic enough, not noble enough, and above all, oh dear yes, not ideological enough." At a symposium on social responsibility during the Boulder Writers' Conference he had defined it as the responsibility to do an honest piece of work. Thus when Edgar Lee Masters' son asked him to join in picketing the French consulate in behalf of the Spanish Loyalists, Wolfe begged off. "I just can't do it," he said, "you've got to count me out on things like that," meaning that though he sympathized with the cause, his work came first.

His pen, however, was in the service of justice and humanity, and that winter he gave the impoverished *New Masses* a satire of business ethics which he could have sold elsewhere for a good price. Nor did his political quietism spring from blindness or indifference. When Frieda Kirchwey of *The Nation* asked him for a statement on

"How to Keep Out of War," he sent her an attack on isolationism, calling it "a King Canute-Christian Science kind of word, which says, there is no sickness, there is no death; or if there is, let us ignore them." Though he hoped with so many others that war could be avoided, he thought it increasingly clear that armed aggression would have to be met with armed resistance, and that sooner or later the democracies must fight.

He had arrived at a new maturity of outlook, an embattled resignation. "Man was born," the protagonist of *You Can't Go Home Again* tells his editor, Foxhall Edwards, "to live, to suffer, and to die, and what befalls him is a tragic lot. There is no denying this in the final end. *But we must, dear Fox, deny it all along the way.*" The summer in Asheville had crystallized his view that, in a phrase he specially liked, you can't go home again: can't go back to your childhood, the town of your birth, the father you have lost, romantic love, dreams of fame and glory, or any of the other "solacements of time and memory." His home from now on would be the future and the work he had carved out for himself, which he hoped would reflect an ever-widening objectivity and a shrinking self-concern. A man may wander the earth in search of a father when actually he is seeking his own manhood, waiting for the moment when he becomes self-starting, self-reliant, self-conquering, self-governing, becomes a man himself and no longer needs a father. Had Wolfe reached this point by 1938? He thought so.

His big book, *The Vision of Spangler's Paul*, had changed its title to *The Life and Adventures of Bondsman Doak* when he signed with Harpers in December, and more recently the hero had become George Webber whom Wolfe considered an objective creation, though he was really a prowling, squinting, simian mutation of Eugene Gant. Wandering in and out of the little office where his secretary typed and took dictation, Wolfe mimicked the characters he was bringing to life with his dark eyes fanatically blazing. Now and then he would lean on the chest of drawers near her typewriter and gaze out the window, as he reached unthinkingly for one of her cigarettes. (The first few times he had asked permission, but after that he just took them.) He had grown so heavy that he scarcely seemed related to the knife blade of a young man he had been, but underneath the excess weight was a skeleton of force, a

covered hardness, just as a genuine strength underlay the rodomon-
tade in his style. He wore reading glasses now, and a bald spot had
appeared on his crown. The unhealthy darkness under his eyes
bespoke high tension and exhaustion, and a girl who saw something
of him that year noticed he was feverish at times, though any mention of doctors or illness made him angry. Once when she suggested
he take an aspirin, his reply was to walk across Brooklyn Bridge and
back in a sleety rainstorm.

He was working longer hours than ever before, and a friend who
came in when his door was ajar and surprised him at his writing
table—sweaty, unkempt, muttering, and chain-smoking as he filled
the yellow second sheets with his butcherly scrawl and pushed them
to the floor—came away with the impression of an abattoir. He wrote
with an animal fury reminiscent of that other prodigious toiler, Balzac. Both were slaves of their gift, of a tormenting drive to people
the void and both had a zest for life, a greedy innocence which
heightened the discomfort of their self-willed confinement. Balzac's
contemporary, Gautier, has described "those nightly battles from
which he emerged broken but triumphant. The fire having gone out
and the room being chilly, his head would smoke and his body would
exhale a visible mist like the bodies of horses in winter." Had the
Chelsea been unheated, one could imagine the same thing happening to Wolfe.[14]

With the coming of spring, his spirits lifted. He would plunge out
of his hotel singing "Rosalie" or "Heigh-ho" from *Snow White and
the Seven Dwarfs,* lustily if none too accurately. He bought the
newspaper now to keep up with the Yankees and probably saw
the first of the half-dozen or so games he took in every year. Baseball excited him as the most American of sports, and in January he
had gone to a baseball dinner with sportswriter, Arthur Mann. During one of the speeches Wolfe was contemplating Ruth, Gehrig,
Foxx, Honus Wagner, and other surrounding greats when the waiter
came by for tips. Mann put a dollar in the plate, and at the waiter's
second nudge Wolfe looked at it blankly and said, "No, it's not mine."
Mann whispered that the waiter wanted a gratuity. "Oh—oh, yes,"
said Wolfe, and to the waiter, "I'm sorry, sir." Jabbing his hand into
one pocket of his tuxedo and then the other, he produced a check-

book and fumbled for a fountain pen, which of course he didn't have. "How much shall I give him?" he asked Mann, who by this time had put in another dollar, and with a red-faced mutter of thanks Wolfe went back to studying his heroes.

He had been asked to address a literary banquet at Purdue on May 19th, and feeling the need of a layoff, he had accepted. He knew he wasn't a speaker, but as he told a friend, "I can d-do a hell of a lot of stuttering for th-three hundred dollars." After Purdue he would visit the Pacific Northwest which he had never seen, and be back early in June for the final assault on his manuscript.

On May 6th he wrote Aswell of his conviction that his book had reached "the same state of articulation" as *Of Time and the River* when he delivered it to Perkins in December, 1933. He reasoned by analogy that he would need a year to finish it, though he didn't regard *Of Time and the River* as an unbreakable precedent; he was simply trying to give Aswell some idea of "the magnitude of the task before us." Feeling sure of what he was after, he thought it best to proceed without assistance until he had brought the book "to a further state of development and completion." But he suggested, somewhat hesitantly, that it might be the moment for Aswell to begin reading the manuscript and learning his way around it. Wolfe likened his going ahead without editing to Aswell's small son learning to walk, and he said what a comfort it was to know that patient and unstinting help would be forthcoming when he needed it. Had Wolfe lived, it seems likely that Aswell's role, though less crucial than Perkins' because of Wolfe's greater confidence and maturity, would still have been a large one.[15]

The next ten days were spent ordering the manuscript and writing transitions. Wolfe had a miraculous sense of just where everything was in the packing cases which appeared so chaotic. Once when the phone rang, it was Martha Dodd, the ambassador's daughter who had shown him around Berlin. "Well, if you're having the Budapest String Quartet, what do you want *me* for?" said Wolfe, remarking after he had hung up to the person who was with him, "Goddamn it—a cocktail party for share-croppers!" The evening of his departure he worked till half an hour before train time, while the man who ran the Chelsea Bar and Grill packed his suitcases and decided which shirts, socks, and ties should accompany him on his journey.

Next morning he wrote his baseball friend, Arthur Mann, "We are just leaving Middletown (Muncie, Ind.) U.S.A.— Do you know what this country is like— It's like a big fat hog—flat, fat, green and fertile— For 300 miles I've never seen such lushness, such fatness, such fertility— It's very wonderful and I'm proud of it—but I'm glad I came from the mountains where we were poor and [illegible]— You need mountain people too—I think m't'n people and sea people think and feel harder, deeper—somehow more imaginatively and intuitively—The point is the West is America but not all of America is the West— Excuse the jitters of my pencil-ship— It's not me—it's the Southwestern Limited— I'd've written you anyway in an hour or two from Indianapolis—but I just wanted to see if I could do it at 72 per hour— Did I sleep last night? Say—I haven't missed a house, a barn, a horse, a hog, a cow, or a plowed field since we left Buffalo— I'm dog-tired but I feel swell— I put through a big job and completed it—and feel *completed*. I'm going a few thousand miles further and raise hell—Whee!—"

12 · DEPARTURE

Wolfe's Purdue speech was another resumé of his creative odyssey, not unlike *The Story of a Novel* but with greater emphasis on world events, on how the Depression and his visits to Nazi Germany had changed his views and brought him nearer "the common heart of man." Though he stammered a good deal at the start, he quickly won his audience with his naturalness and verve as he stood at the microphone occasionally sawing the air with a heavy arm. Next day he insisted that several Purdue professors and their wives accompany him to Chicago and help him spend the money he had earned. At the Brookfield Zoo he was disappointed because he couldn't find a baboon with as colorful a rump as one remembered from his boyhood: "It was like a rainbow." He smiled when a man looking at the giraffes said, "Oh, but you know they're highly exaggerated," and a colored woman calling to her companions, "Heah some mo' bea's ovah heah" caused him to remark, "Isn't this a great country!"

Not always. No one had written more scathingly than he of its cheapness and dreariness, of "the wasteland horror of its little shops, hot dog stands, grease and food emporiums," of the debasement of the original dream. "We've got to *loathe* America, as we loathe ourselves," he had said in his notes. . . . "We've got to face the total horror of our self-betrayal."[1] Yet he had also prophesied, "I believe that we are lost in America, but I believe we shall be found. . . . I think the true discovery of America is before us. I think the true fulfillment of our spirit, of our people, of our mighty and immortal land, is yet to come." And after a rundown of various national types he had written, "So then to every man his chance—to every man, regardless of his birth, his shining golden opportunity—to every man the right to live, to work, to be himself, and to become whatever thing his manhood and his vision can combine to make him—this, seeker, is the promise of America."

On May 23rd he left Chicago on the *Burlington Zephyr*, his first streamlined train, and stroking its aluminum flanks, he spoke of the bar at either end and told the friend who was seeing him off that he doubted whether he'd be able to drink them both dry before he got to Colorado. In Denver, the Ferrils whom he had met at the Boulder Writers' Conference rounded up a group of his former acquaintances, and he greeted them all by their first names, going on to inquire about their children and to recall tiny incidents from three years before. "An elephant never forgets," he said. After a week in Denver he headed for the coast, lingering a while in Portland and then in Seattle, where he looked up his Westall kin—the descendants of Julia's half-brother Bacchus, who had gone West in the Nineties.

Back in Portland he and two other men set out June 21st on a giant sweep of the national parks. Ed Miller, a feature writer for *The Portland Oregonian* and Ray Conway, manager of the Oregon State Motor Association, wanted to demonstrate for the benefit of prospective tourists that twelve parks could be visited in two weeks, and Wolfe jumped at the chance to go with them. Starting late, they had to omit one park, but in thirteen days they travelled 4,662 miles, their record being 693 miles the third day—at the end of which Wolfe and Miller ganged up on Conway and told him the whole idea was insane. They held to their schedule, however, Wolfe coming down like molasses every morning and folding into the cream-white Ford sedan with the official AAA emblazoned on its sides. With knees wide-spread and arms akimbo, he took up the whole back seat, while the other two sat in front and alternated at the wheel.

The first day they crossed "the great line of the Cascades with their snow-spired sentinels, Hood, Adams, [and] Jefferson," Wolfe wrote in his notes of the trip—then up and up to Crater Lake, "the great crater fading coldly in incredible cold light." Mt. Shasta dominated the second morning—"Mt. Shasta all the time—always Mt. Shasta—and at last the town named Weed (with divine felicity)." At Yosemite they ran into "1200 little shop girls and stenogs and new-weds and school teachers and boys—all, God bless their little lives, necking, dancing, kissing, feeling, and embracing in the great darkness of the giant redwood trees—all laughing and getting loved tonight—and the sound of the dark gigantic fall of water." Thence down "the vertebrae of the Sierras" to Sequoia where, legs apart, feet firm, and body rotating, hands on hips and a cigarette lolling in the corner of his mouth, Wolfe was contemplating a redwood thousands of years old when a tourist with a radio shouted, "Joe Louis knocked out Schmeling in the first round!"

Next day they sped across the Mojave Desert "through fried hills —cupreous, ferrous and denuded as slag heaps" to the town of Needles (106 in the shade and 120 out of it). It was almost night when they reached the Grand Canyon, which Wolfe described as "a fathomless darkness peered at from the very edge of hell with abysmal starlight—almost unseen—just fathomlessly there." (In conversation as well as in notes he referred to the Grand Canyon as "old Gorgooby" and "the big Gorgooby," and when Conway asked him why, he said he didn't know, he had never heard the word before, but it seemed to describe what the canyon meant to him.) Next morning he was "wakened at four or thereabouts by deer grazing, and by its hard small feet outside of window." Northward now to Mormon country: at first "the dusty little Mormon villages—blazing and blistered in the hot dry heat" and then the "full fat land of Canaan," and the town of Richfield, symbolically named.

In Jackson, Wyoming, one of the sunburned toughs at the gas station said to Wolfe, "My God, if I was as big as you I'd go around knocking people down just for the fun of it." At Yellowstone he waited with the crowd for "the vast bouquet of Old Faithful . . . the hot boiling overslopping of the pot, and then the vast hot plume of steam and water—the people watching—Middle-America watching . . . the tons of water falling and the hot plume dipping." He sent Hamilton Basso a postcard of the geyser, inscribing it, "Portrait of the author at the two million word point," and Basso's comment was, "It sort of looks like Tom too." One afternoon, as the white Ford sped through Montana, a transcontinental freight of the Northern Pacific blasted towards them up the grade—"the interminable freight cars climbing past and suddenly—the tops of the great train lined with clusters of hoboes—a hundred of them—some sprawled out, sitting, others erect, some stretched out on their backs lazily inviting the luminous American weather, and the mountain ranges all around, the glacial green of Clarks Fork just beyond—and the 'bos roll past across America silently regarding us—the pity, terror, strangeness, and magnificence of it all."

Then Glacier Park and a day of lakes, and Grand Coulee Dam, and finally Mt. Rainier, the Great Cloudmaster and giant of them all. Facing "its perilous overwhelming majesty . . . its tremendous shoulders, the long terrific sweeps of its hackling ridges, we stood trying to get its scale, and this impossible because there was nothing but Mountain—a universe of mountain, a continent of mountain . . . to compare mountain to." The next day, July 2nd, they lunched at a famous seafood restaurant in Olympia where Wolfe had "a shrimp cocktail of tiny Puget Sound shrimp" followed by "a delicious pan roast of the small but succulent Puget Sound oysters, the whole cooked in with crab meat in a delicious pungent sauce and spread on toast." And then, after the delays "of men with some sadness in their heart avoiding farewells," Wolfe said goodbye to his companions and watched the white Ford flash away with "a curiously hollow feeling."

A few hours later he took the bus to Seattle where he found a telegram from Aswell calling his manuscript—which Aswell was in the process of reading—MAGNIFICENT IN SCOPE AND DESIGN WITH SOME OF THE BEST WRITING YOU HAVE DONE. Though eager to go back and finish it, he first wanted to expand the notes of his Western trip while the impressions were fresh in his mind. The breakneck journey had left him restless and keyed up, and Tuesday, July 5th, he decided to go up to Vancouver on the coastal steamer, *Princess Kathleen*. They stopped for the night at Victoria, and when they continued next day Wolfe fell in with another passenger who appeared to be suffering from a bad cold. This "poor shivering wretch," as Wolfe later described him, had a flask from which they both drank[2]—as a result of which, or of his lingering on deck in a stiff gale to watch the island scenery, or of the two combined, Wolfe caught a cold and stayed in bed next morning trying to throw it off. By afternoon he had a fever, a severe cough, and pains in his chest and back, but reluctant to leave Vancouver without seeing more of it, he toured the city for several hours in a hack before catching the evening train for Seattle. When he boarded it, he was shaking so badly that the porter settled him on a leather sofa in the club car with a blanket wrapped around him.

Friday he phoned the Stevenses, his best friends in Seattle, to say he had returned with a touch of grippe. (A public-relations officer for the West Coast Lumberman's Association, Jim Stevens was also a popular authority on Paul Bunyan.) Saturday night a professor at the University of Washington had planned a cocktail party in Wolfe's honor and he arrived late, after phoning the Stevenses to consider whether he should go at all. Though wild-looking and obviously cold-ridden, he carried it off, talked and ate a lot, and was among the last to leave. Sunday the Stevenses phoned to find out if his cough had improved: it was worse, and when he asked about a cough remedy someone had mentioned at the party, Mrs. Stevens told him he needed a doctor, not a cough remedy. Monday he phoned Mrs. Stevens and said, "I've got to yell 'calf rope'—I'm afraid I'm pretty sick," whereupon she made arrangements to have him examined by Dr. E. C. Ruge, who had pulled her husband through two bad cases of influenza.

Ruge diagnosed Wolfe's illness as pneumonia and ordered him to the hospital. A general practitioner who of recent years had been specializing in psychiatry, Ruge had a private sanitarium twelve miles north of Seattle, and Wolfe chose to go there so as to be under the surveillance of this doctor who was a friend of his friends. Rest and quiet were prescribed, and he was less likely to be disturbed by visitors at Firlawns than in one of the city hospitals. Firlawns had no X-ray equipment, but that was perfectly agreeable to Wolfe, who dreaded X rays, and as yet Ruge did not suspect T.B. His first night at the sanitarium Wolfe's temperature soared to 105. Three days later it was down to 100, and the pneumonia crisis had been passed, though a blood test and a clinical study revealed an infection with its nidus in the upper lobe of his right lung. He seemed to be overcoming it, however, and a lung specialist who examined him found nothing to report, which may have been the basis for Wolfe's cable to Aswell on or about July 15th, DOCTORS SAY I'M OUT OF DANGER NOW.

He was not an easy patient. Mrs. Stevens wrote Elizabeth Nowell that she had "never seen anyone who took illness with swifter-changing moods and every one of them colossal—positively acrobatic." Wolfe had been hospitalized only once before—after his injuries at the *Oktoberfest*—and he seemed to consider it a disgrace. What would those fellows he had toured the parks with think of him? Besides, with all the work he had to do there wasn't time to be sick. The expense worried him, and each consultation with a specialist sent him into a tail-spin. Meanwhile, Ruge had suggested that Fred come to Seattle to take the responsibility off the Stevenses. He arrived July 23rd, and the Stevenses accompanied him to the sanitarium, where they found Tom lying on a cot under a Douglas fir with the dappled sunshine and shade sprinkling down on him. His nurse was with him, and when Tom saw the visitors approaching he threw up his hand very weakly, Fred thought, in response to their wave.

"What are you doing here?" Tom asked Fred. "You found out I was sick, didn't you? They think I'm pretty sick, don't they?"

"I did find out you'd been a little sick," answered Fred, who had been cautioned not to say anything to agitate his brother. "But I'm on a month's vacation, and I thought I'd like to see the country out here."

"You're lying, Fred. You came to see me."

"Oh no, Tom, not altogether. I've got a whole month, and I needed a good rest."

Though Tom grew increasingly tractable, his recovery was slow and erratic. Good days when his appetite picked up and his strength seemed to be returning were followed by listless ones, and the low-grade fever hung on. Ruge was perplexed, and on August 6th he transferred Tom to the Providence Hospital in Seattle for X rays and extensive lab tests. The tests came back negative, but the X ray showed a large area of consolidation in the upper lobe of the right lung, which Ruge and the radiologist diagnosed as an old tubercular lesion recently reactivated. In a consultation with four other doctors they were overruled; the aforementioned lung specialist found no evidence of T.B., and "pneumonia with delayed reaction" or "unresolved pneumonia" was now the diagnosis.

In Portland two months earlier, when Wolfe had heard that Scribner salesmen were circulating derogatory tales about him, he had leapt to the conclusion that Perkins was behind it. Soon afterwards Miss Nowell had written him of lunching with Perkins, who had seemed old and tired and had asked repeatedly and wistfully about Wolfe. "I'm sorry about M.P.," Wolfe had answered. . . . "Please— *please* don't tell him . . . anything about me, if you can avoid it. For six years he was my friend—I thought the best one I ever had —and then, a little over two years ago he turned against me. . . . It's almost as if he were praying for my failure. . . . I don't think he *consciously* wants me to fail or come to grief, but it's almost as if *unconsciously,* by some kind of *wishful* desire, he wants me to come to grief, as a kind of sop to his pride and his unyielding conviction that he is right in everything—the tragic flaw in his character that keeps him from admitting that he has wronged anybody or made a mistake."[3]

Perkins knew nothing of this exchange, nor did he hear of Wolfe's illness till he was thought to be out of danger and slowly recuperating. Then Perkins wanted to write him but hesitated to do so lest it stir Tom up when he ought to be relaxing—a state he had never achieved in all the years Perkins had known him. Finally Perkins sent Tom a letter in Fred's care, telling Fred to show it to Tom at his discretion. It was a chatty letter, calm and full of friendly concern. Perkins told of his having moved back to the house in New Canaan and of his being "once more a commuter, as I was born, and always should have been. . . . Louise has become somewhat of a landscape gardener, and we have hemlocks in front and at the side of the house. And she has made a sort of an 18th century grove around a diminutive fish pond created from an old washtub painted blue. I could not see how it could turn out well, but it really did. It would make you think of those grottos and groves that Horace

Walpole used to write letters about such as Pope indulged in. Then our place not being large enough for a deer park, she thought she would improve the landscape with a couple of kids. I mean real kids. And she bought them somewhere on the Merritt Highway, but they did not turn out very well in the end. They are not very clean animals, and so she took them back just after I had got quite attached to them."

Perkins spoke of his second grandson—"a very fierce-looking baby who might well bring trouble to the world," said he hopefully, "with the nose and chin of a Caesar, and flat ears—and red hair!" His artist son-in-law was doing a portrait of Aline Bernstein's daughter, and business was looking up, what with Marjorie Kinnan Rawlings' *The Yearling* topping the best-seller list. "All the people hereabouts [at Scribners] are just as you used to know them," he concluded, "though Weber has grown a little heavier, and all of them were mightily concerned about your illness. But honestly, Tom, it may well be the best thing that has ever happened to you, for it will give you a fresh start after a good rest."

When Fred received the letter on August 12th, he read it aloud to Tom who wanted to answer it at once although forbidden to write. He was so insistent, however, that Fred smuggled in some hospital notepaper on which Tom traced the following in a feeble hand:

"Dear Max:

"I'm sneaking this against orders—but 'I've got a hunch'—and I wanted to write these words to you.

"I've made a long voyage and been to a strange country, and I've seen the dark man very close; and I don't think I was too much afraid of him, but so much of mortality still clings to me—I wanted most desperately to live and still do, and I thought about you all 1000 times, and wanted to see you all again, and there was the impossible anguish and regret of all the work I had not done, of all the work I had to do—and I know now I'm just a grain of dust, and I feel as if a great window has been opened on life I did not know about before—and if I come through this, I hope to God I am a better man, and in some strange way I can't explain, I know I am a deeper and a wiser one. If I get on my feet and out of here, it will be months before I head back, but if I get on my feet, I'll come back.

"Whatever happens—I had this 'hunch' and wanted to write you and tell you, no matter what happens or has happened, I shall always think of you and feel about you the way it was that 4th of July day 3 yrs. ago when you met me at the boat, and we went out on the café on the river and had a drink and later went on top of the tall building, and all the strangeness and the glory and the power of life and of the city were below.

"Yours always,
"Tom"

The letter sent a chill through Perkins. He told his secretary that Tom must be very sick to write that way, but in his reply he covered his alarm, emphasizing that by really resting now Tom would be gaining time rather than losing it.

After's Wolfe's death Mrs. Roberts wrote in her copy of *Look Homeward, Angel* some lines from Edwin Arlington Robinson's "Ben Jonson Entertains a Man from Stratford." The man, of course, was Shakespeare, and the words seemed doubly fitting when she recalled Tom's prize-winning school essay on "Shakespeare, the Man."

> And you have known him from his origin,
> You tell me; and a most uncommon urchin
> He must have been to those few seeing ones—
> A trifle terrifying, I dare say,
> Discovering a world with his man's eyes,
> Quite as another lad might see some finches,
> If he looked hard and had an eye for nature. . . .
> The churning out of all those blood-fed lines,
> The nights of many schemes and little sleep,
> The full brain hammered hot with too much thinking,
> The vexed heart over-worn with too much aching,—
> This weary jangling of conjoined affairs
> Made out of elements that have no end,
> And all confused at once, I understand,
> Is not what makes a man to live forever.
> Oh no, not now! He'll not be going now. . . .
> He'll not be going yet. There's too much yet
> Unsung within the man.

But he *was* going, and in his heart he must have known it and was perhaps trying to intimate it to Perkins when he spoke of his "hunch." "It is not strange," Marjorie Kinnan Rawlings wrote Perkins later, "that so vibrant and sentient a personality as Tom knew or guessed that he had come to the great wall. He must have felt far beyond most of us that withdrawing of the cosmic force from his individual unit of life."

Wolfe was familiar with death. Grover's passing, the loss of his college roommate Edmund Burdick, Ben's Sophoclean agony, and his father's long decline—these early experiences had brought it home to him, while his spitting blood at Harvard had heightened his consciousness of his own mortality and quickened his desire to do something overwhelming and death-destroying with the life he had. In the anthology of English verse he had used in his teaching at N.Y.U. so many of the underlinings relate to death, burial, and the swiftness of time. The phrases "when I'm dead and buried" and "I've got to hurry" were often on his lips, and if friends told him not to be ridiculous, that he had years and years ahead of him, he would say, "No, I've got to hurry to get it all down. They say I'll write myself out, but I won't live that long."

The evening of the day he wrote Perkins, his temperature rose to 103 and his headaches began. During the ensuing week he was frequently nauseated and had trouble sleeping. It was thought that the strain of writing the letter and of too many visitors had caused the relapse, which brought Fred's dissatisfaction with Dr. Ruge to a head. From the start there had been a clash of temperaments between the touchy, secretive Ruge and the garrulous, excitable Fred, who on August 20th transferred his brother to the care of Dr. Charles Watts. A leading internist, Watts had for several weeks been a consultant on the case and had concurred in the diagnosis of unresolved pneumonia. A second set of X rays on August 17th showed that the area of consolidation had shrunk to the size of an egg, and after Watts took over, Tom's temperature dropped to almost normal and his appetite improved, though the headaches remained. But as the doctors reassured Fred, one had to expect these fluctuations; Tom's unremitting labors followed by the fatiguing travel had worn him down and lowered his resistance. Shaking her head over his self-neglect, Elizabeth Nowell wrote him that she just plain wanted to tie him to her apron strings and see that he led a regular life, instead of driving himself and driving himself and then wasting an equal amount of time wandering around on trains looking for "peace" and "rest" and never finding it.

As Fred had to go back to his job, Mabel came out to relieve him. The hub and nexus of the family, Mabel at forty-eight was the most like Tom in appearance, with her warm, dark eyes, and her strong, rounded features, and the big swinging movements of her body. She resembled him, too, in her gruff, outspoken friendliness and in her independence—her determination to do what she wanted when she wanted with no outside interference. She had left behind a husband who was critically ill, and Tom seemed comparatively hale when she reached Seattle August 24th. "You look fine, honey—" she told him, "rested and everything," but he answered, "I've got these headaches, Mabel, I've got these terrible headaches."

He had to have Dilaudid to dim the pain enough to be able to sleep, though on August 26th a third X ray showed the spot on his lung to be no larger than a quarter. About this time a young, attractive registered nurse named Annie Laurie Crawford, who came from Asheville and was doing advanced work in nursing education at the University of Washington, befriended Tom and Mabel and began taking exclusive care of him. "Sit down and let me chatter at you," he would tell her, going on to describe one of the national parks, or the English beauties of Victoria which he was glad to have seen even if it had resulted in his catching pneumonia. In the back of his mind there was always some doubt about his illness, he craved reassurance, yet Annie Laurie couldn't bring herself to reassure him superficially: she felt the need to allow him to be scared. Speaking of his work, he remarked several times that if he lived—it was always "if I get through this"—he would produce something worthy of the acclaim he had received. He didn't feel he had quite justified it to date; the star for which he was reaching had always just eluded him. Because he disliked their suggestion of invalidism, he sent the flowers he received to the children's ward, but one day Annie Laurie brought him a red amaryllis whose brightness so cheered him that he kept it, Mabel moving it to whichever side of the bed he was turned towards.

With Mabel, Tom discussed that perennial Wolfe topic—food— and the good times they had had, and Palo Alto where he planned to stay with a doctor friend during his convalescence. As Mabel said later, his fury had ceased and he seemed kindly disposed towards everyone, even those he had formerly disliked and "all the little dribble people who came out of the alleys and shacks when he and I were young. . . . That's what fooled me with his condition. I never saw anyone so relaxed, balanced, forgiving, considering the furious, unhappy man he had been for eighteen or twenty years." Wolfe's talent was ruthless and assertive, but the man underneath was humble and kind, and with his talent in abeyance, the man emerged more and more.[4]

He had once described himself to Perkins as "a religious and believing person"[5]—not, of course, in the orthodox sense. Like many romantics, he belonged to a race of lost believers wandering the earth, the yearning and mysticism in their work being to some extent a religious residue. Wolfe lived in what could be called the area of the absence of God, acutely feeling the lack. His powerful unrest brings to mind Augustine's words, "Thou hast made us for Thyself, O God, and our hearts are restless till they find their rest in Thee." Having soaked himself in the Old Testament, he had absorbed not only its rhythms but some of its attitudes—above all, its respect for righteousness, for the simple and undevious heart. One of his favorite passages in literature was Alyosha's speech at the funeral of the little boy in *The Brothers Karamazov*.[6] "My dear children," says Alyosha, "perhaps you won't understand what I am saying to you, because I often speak very unintelligibly, but you'll remember it all the same and will agree with my words sometimes. You must know that there is nothing higher and stronger and more wholesome and good for life in the future than some good memory, especially of childhood, of home. People talk to you a great deal about your education, but some good, sacred memory, preserved from childhood, is perhaps the best education. If a man carries many such memories with him into life, he is safe to the end of his days, and if one has only one good memory left in one's heart, even that may sometime be the means of saving us."

The end of August, Dr. Watts left Seattle to attend a medical conference, saying that on his return he would probably be able to release Wolfe and treat him as an out-patient until he got his legs sufficiently to go to Palo Alto. Wolfe was on fire with anticipation, for he not only longed to escape the hospital but felt that if they let him go it would prove beyond question that he was getting well. He asked Mabel to rent an apartment for them at the Spring Apartment Hotel, which had caught his fancy two months earlier when he was looking for a place to expand the notes of his Western journey. "Get a nice one," he told her, "with plenty of room. This is no time to be parsimonious. Parsimony has killed more people than you'll ever know." Mabel engaged a top-floor suite with cream-colored furnishings and the last word in electric kitchens, which she stocked with some of the items they had talked about: pickled peaches, flour for hot biscuits, apple sauce, golden bantam corn, string beans, vegetable soup, loin lamb chops, and porterhouse steaks. Tom still had his appetite, and it was Wolfe doctrine that if one could "eat hearty" he was going to be all right. At Tom's request she bought an earthenware pot to make tea in, because he hated "those darn little tea balls" they gave him in the hospital.

Dr. Watts returned September 3rd, and the next morning, a Sunday, Mabel went to the hospital at ten to pack Tom's belongings preparatory to moving him to the hotel. Watts came in around noon, laughing when Tom made fun of his having to be "released." "I thought you released prisoners from the penitentiary," he said.

Suddenly turning professional, Watts said, "Tom, I've been looking at your chart, and I see you've still got those headaches. That medicine I gave you didn't do much good, did it?"

"Not much—I haven't felt much relief. Dr. Watts, I notice that when I get up and sit on the side of the bed and hang my feet over on this ottoman my head stops aching, but when I lie down, it aches."

"Well, listen," said the doctor, "I've been meaning to look into your eyes with an ophthalmoscope. It'll only take a minute."

"Oh my God!" said Wolfe. "I hope you don't find a tumor."

"Of course you don't have a tumor!" Mabel rebuked him. "You're perfectly all right. It's just the hospital that's giving you these headaches . . . staying in here . . . this air . . . the smell of things."

She left the room as she always did when Tom was being examined. Sitting in the sun parlor, she saw Watts return with the ophthalmoscope, and a few minutes later she was walking back towards Tom's door when the doctor came out.

"Oh, Mrs. Wheaton," he said. "I want to talk to you." There was a moment's hesitation. "Now you know this has been no ordinary case of pneumonia. I've just examined Tom's eyes and it looks to me as if there's a choked disc there. I want you to have Miss Crawford here in the morning for another set of X rays, and I'm bringing a good eye man. I've told Tom he will have to stay overnight. You and Miss Crawford be here at nine."

Mabel was thinking what she would say to Tom when Annie Laurie appeared and they went in together. His Sunday dinner, the best meal of the week, had just arrived, but Tom was staring into space with moody preoccupation. He hardly spoke to Annie Laurie, of whom he was very fond. Instead, turning to Mabel, he held up a bluish capsule an inch long and said, "I'm taking horse medicine now—this is a horse pill for headache." He swallowed it and began to eat in silence, ignoring their efforts to break the gloom.

Finally Mabel said, "Now listen, Tom, there's no use brooding because you have to stay here till tomorrow. I'm going to leave Annie Laurie with you while I have my dinner, but I'll be back and I'll stay with you tonight until they *put* me out. And tomorrow we're going out of here if I have to pack up and take you myself."

He looked at her with childlike belief.

"You'll get behind 'em, won't you, Mabel? You'll get behind 'em."

Late in the day she was writing letters at her hotel when Annie Laurie phoned.

"Oh, Mabel, did Tom seem all right when you were here this morning?"

"Why, perfectly. What's the matter?"

"I don't think he's known a thing all afternoon. He's been acting so strangely. I wish you'd come over here as soon as you can."

Mabel hurried to the hospital, and as she approached Tom's second-floor room she saw him standing outside the door in his blue pajamas. He was looking up and down the hall, and catching sight of her, he raised his hand in friendly greeting.

"Hello, Mabel! How did you get here? Did you come by plane?"

"No, Tom, I came on the streetcar."

"Now, Mabel, I don't want you riding that streetcar. You know fifty people in this town with automobiles. They ought to be riding you around. Henry Westall"—a favorite cousin in Asheville, who went in for stylish cars—"where's he? Henry, Mabel—where's Henry?"

"You're tired, honey," she said, taking his arm. "You've been up too long. Lie down and let me rub your head with witch hazel."

She had bought him a bottle of Three Star Hennessy with which to make hot toddies, and she noticed that some of it had been poured into two used glasses on the bureau.

"Good," she said. "You've had a drink. Who had one with you?"

"Oh, I don't know, I don't know, Mabel, I don't know. So many of 'em have been passing in front of me all afternoon. So many of 'em have been here."

She soaked his head with witch hazel until it looked as if he'd been under a shower, and then she rubbed and rubbed to ease the incessant throb. After a while she went down the hall and asked the Catholic sister in charge of the nurses whether Tom had had any visitors that afternoon. The sister assured her that no one had been in the room except Annie Laurie.

"Then what on earth have you been giving him?" said Mabel, thinking that the medication had affected his mind.

She stayed with him that evening as long as they would let her, and before she left she exacted a promise from the night nurse to watch him and see he didn't step through the window in his unbalanced state.

Next morning when he returned from his X rays in a wheel chair, Mabel said, "Well, honey, they didn't hurt you, did they? It was all right, wasn't it?"

"Oh yes," he replied, "but they gave me some of that brown stuff that always makes me sick and I swallowed it." (She later learned that they had given him nothing.) He fell into bed exhausted, while the doctors gathered solemnly to break the news. It was either a tumor or an abscess of the brain, they told Mabel, and Tom must be taken at once to the best brain surgeon in the country, Dr. Walter Dandy at Johns Hopkins.

Tom's heart was still set on going to the apartment, and Watts saw no harm in his staying there until the arrangements for the journey were complete. One of their Seattle relatives, Lonnie Harris, had offered to chauffeur them from the hospital, and leaning on

Harris' arm, Tom walked out with smiling eyes and his battered hat on his head. When Mabel, who had been held up a moment, got to the car, she asked Tom why he wasn't sitting in the front where he could see better.

"We're out, Mabel!" said he, grinning. "That's all that counts— we're out at last!"

So as not to attract attention, they entered the Spring Apartment Hotel by the rear door, which involved a long walk to the elevator, and Tom's knees were buckling when he reached it. Seeing his condition, the elevator man shot them up to their seventh-floor apartment where Tom flopped across the large double bed which had been set up for him in the living room. Mabel and Annie Laurie at once began preparing a lavish meal, and when it was ready they settled him by a window overlooking Puget Sound. He was fascinated by the small aluminum boat which plied back and forth between Seattle and the Bremerton Navy Yard. "You picked well this time, Mabel," he kept saying, "you picked a nice place, this is a fine hotel," forgetting that it was he who had first discovered it. During the meal he seemed happy and excited, though towards the end he was so tired that Mabel had to feed him.

Unwilling to accept the grim diagnosis, she had asked Dr. George Swift, a brain specialist recommended by Harpers, to stop by their apartment that evening and examine Tom. A distinguished, white-haired gentleman with a kind, smiling face, Dr. Swift, on being introduced, told Tom he had heard a great deal about him.

"And I've heard a great deal about you too," Tom replied.

"The Harpers people are very fond of you," Swift went on. "They called me when you first took sick, but I didn't want to step in after you'd gotten a doctor. They think a lot of you, Tom. They think you're a great person."

"And they think an awful lot of you, Dr. Swift. You're a great person yourself."

Swift, who had been watching Wolfe intently, now said, "Tom, with your permission I'd like to examine you. Do you object?"

Tom assured him that he didn't, and Swift took out an ophthalmoscope, talking calmly all the while.

"Don't you think we have beautiful flowers out here, Mrs. Wheaton?" He nodded at a jardiniere of gladiolas sent by one of Tom's admirers. Looking in Tom's eyes, he said "Mmmm-hmmm" without the least change of expression, and then began taking Tom's reflexes. Tom answered correctly when asked which part of his leg was being tapped by the little mallet.

"How old are you, Tom?" the doctor asked suddenly.

Tom told him.

"Where is your mother?"

Mabel half-rose in her seat, but Tom answered straightforwardly that she was back home in Asheville.

"What do you want to go to California for?"

Tom said he had a friend in Palo Alto, Dr. Russel Lee, with whom he was going to stay during his convalescence.

After a few more questions Swift said, "Tom, I want to talk to you man to man."

Mabel jumped up and grasped the doctor's arm, but he remained smiling, unruffled.

"Now Mrs. Wheaton, you stand back. Tom is a big man, and he can take this. Tom, don't let anybody tell you that you are well. You are very, very ill. You owe it to yourself, to the people who read your books, and to those who love you to get well. You and your sister should have left tonight." He was deadly serious now. "You must leave on the first train you can get for Johns Hopkins. You must go where there are a dozen men who can find out what the trouble is, why you are having these headaches, and you must go at once."

Mabel had run out of the apartment crying, and Dr. Swift went after her.

"Keep your chin up, girl," he said. "You've got a big job to do. I'm sorry. I'm *very* sorry. He's *desperately* ill." When she continued to sob hysterically, he said, "Girl, be a fatalist. Get him across the country, and *if* it happens, then you have done *all* you can, all anyone can do." (Swift himself was to die of a heart attack three months later while hauling a Christmas tree.)

Mabel asked him to speak to her mother over long distance, and when she got Julia on the wire Mabel was crying so hard that Swift took the receiver from her hand and said, "Now, Mrs. Wolfe, your daughter here is younger than you and a little emotional. She's all to pieces at the moment. But *Tom's* going to be all right. She's leaving with him tomorrow. There's a little trouble, but it'll be fixed up *all* right when he gets to Johns Hopkins. So, Mrs. Wolfe, you compose yourself. You get ready to come out this way and meet them. You meet them as far this way as you can."

Tom, Mabel, and Annie Laurie left Seattle on the *Olympian* at 10:30 the next night, Tuesday, September 6th. Pushed through the lobby of the Spring Apartment Hotel in a wheel chair, Tom hardly noticed the cluster of University of Washington students who had been standing vigil for a glimpse of him. His eyes were glazed, but he bid an affectionate farewell to the Stevenses who had come to see him off. Dr. Swift and Dr. Watts were at the station, Watts carrying his wife's copy of *Look Homeward, Angel* which Wolfe, in one of his expansive moods, had insisted he autograph. Having asked her first name and jotted a brief inscription, Wolfe said he would come back to Seattle for an autographing party when his new book appeared.

The doctors had warned that he might go into convulsions, and if his illness seemed to be taking that turn they were to detrain at St. Paul, Minnesota, and proceed by ambulance to the Mayo Clinic in Rochester. Annie Laurie had been instructed to keep him "snowed under" with morphine, but he didn't like to take it, and the pain and pressure were now so acute that the drug had little effect. He seemed to get more relief from cold towel applications and from having his forehead and the back of his neck massaged, and Mabel and Annie Laurie did it for him by the hour. The door was open between their adjoining compartments (Mabel and Annie Laurie in one, Tom in the other), and the first night, after giving him a shot and getting him settled, the women went to sleep. At 2 A.M. they were awakened by light streaming in and Tom's deep voice saying, "Hello, Mabel." His pajama-clad figure loomed in the corridor doorway. With him were a porter and a conductor, who said he had walked through seven cars back to the observation platform looking for a telegraph office so he could send a telegram. To prevent such an occurrence, Mabel had piled their luggage against his outside door, but he had burst the barricade.

During the rest of the journey he was quiet and had a surprisingly good appetite. When Mabel brought him the menu from the diner, he would order steak or roast beef and eat it with relish. To lull his fears she had said they were going to Palo Alto as originally planned, and in his confused state he seemed to believe it, but as they neared Chicago where their mother was to meet them she had to tell him they were headed East.

"Now it wouldn't surprise me," she said, "if Momma was in Chicago when we get there. That wouldn't worry you too much, would it?"

Tom winked at Annie Laurie. "If she looks too bad," he said, "we just won't speak to her."

Julia was at Union Station when the train pulled in early Friday morning. Two months previous Fred had phoned her to say that Tom was ill in Seattle, and her first reaction, she later recalled, was, "Tom's going to die, Tom's going to die." When Fred had phoned soon afterwards to say he had a message, she had asked, "Oh, is he dead?" but Fred had reported him better. Since then the news had been increasingly hopeful until the thunderbolt of his departure for Hopkins.

In Chicago Tom was to spend the lay-over of several hours in the station hospital, and he insisted on being fully dressed and consented to a wheel chair only when promised that no reporters would be present. He had a horror of being photographed or written about in his weakened state. He had just gotten off the train and was sitting in the chair with his hat on when Julia came up and put her hand on his shoulder.

"Do you know who this is?" Mabel asked him.

Tom looked up and smiled.

"Why, it's Mrs. Julia Wolfe of the Old Kentucky Home."

That was the way she introduced herself to strangers, and Tom sometimes teased her about it, and Julia was encouraged, thinking that if he could banter he mustn't be as sick as they said. When they left Chicago, Annie Laurie gave him a shot, and he subsided into a lethargy from which he roused himself now and then to ask, "Momma, are you all right? You all right, Momma?" She had brought with her from Asheville some grapes and some choice peaches which she peeled and fed him. He smiled at her remarks and seemed to understand, but initiated none himself. When she asked if his lung hurt, he said no, that he hadn't any pain in his body, only in his head. She didn't think he looked too badly, except for his complexion and a slight bulging of the eyes. Once when he whistled a bar of music, his eyes seemed suddenly larger and he closed them. Another time he locked himself in the washroom and couldn't remember how to get out, but Annie Laurie was able to explain it through the door, and when he emerged he said, "Something's wrong with my head—it's screwy somehow—my head's screwy."

They got to Baltimore early Saturday morning, and lying in a stretcher on his way to the ambulance, Tom asked Mabel where they were taking him. She told him they were going to Johns Hopkins to find out what was causing his headaches. "Well, Mabel," he replied, "your ideas about Johns Hopkins may be all right, but I've got my ideas." And a moment later: "I need a rest. I'm awfully tired, and I need a rest."

The whole family had come to know the Hopkins when W.O. was going there for radium treatments during his Seven Years' War with cancer, and Tom's aversion to it had blazed forth in *Of Time and the River*:

"The great engine of the hospital, with all its secret, sinister, and inhuman perfections, together with its clean and sterile smells which seemed to blot out the smell of rotting death around one, became a hateful presage of man's destined end. Suddenly, one got an image of his own death in such a place as this—of all that death had come to be—and the image of that death was somehow shameful. It was an image of a death without man's ancient pains and old gaunt aging—an image of death drugged and stupefied out of its ancient terror and stern dignities—of a shameful death that went out softly, dully in anesthetized oblivion, with the fading smell of chemicals on man's final breath."

Despite his despondency at being back in the hospital, Wolfe ordered a large lunch, with a tall glass of gelatin and whipped cream for dessert, and when he had finished it, a girl with a tray of ice cream appeared in the doorway, and he topped off with a dish of that. Mabel kept telling herself that no one with such an appetite could have anything seriously the matter with him. She was summoned to the phone to speak to Ed Aswell who had just arrived from New York and said he'd be over in a minute. Back in Tom's room she told him she had good news for him, but he eyed her suspiciously.

"Now, Mabel, is it *really* good this time?"

When he heard that Aswell was coming, his whole mood changed, his spirit and intelligence quickened, and as Aswell entered, he lifted himself on one elbow and put out a great hand, saying, "Ed, it's wonderful to see you. How are you, how are you?"

Aswell said *he* was all right. How was Tom?

"Oh these terrible headaches. I don't know what causes them, but maybe they'll find out."

Aswell said he hoped so, and then sitting down by the bed, he told Wolfe that he had read every word of his manuscript, that it was magnificent, and that Harpers was jubilant.

"Oh, *thank you*, Ed," said Wolfe, with flooding gratitude. "It's so good of you to come to me."

They went on talking and Wolfe was perfectly lucid until suddenly he stopped in mid-sentence, and it seemed to Aswell as though a shade had been drawn on a scene he was looking at. Wolfe sat there, not staring wildly—just blank—and then the shade went up, and he resumed the sentence where he had left off. Presently Dr. Dandy and his assistants came in, and Aswell, Mabel, and Julia withdrew to the waiting room until the doctor reappeared and beckoned to them.

"I want to tell you about your son and brother," said Dandy. "He's desperately ill, and I doubt if anything can be done for him." He paused, considered. "Now if it's cancer, the case is hopeless. And if it's multiple tuberculosis—oh, there's nothing we can do. There's only one chance: if it's an abscess or a tumor, and then a great deal depends on where it is. If it's back here"—he put his fingers to the base of his skull—"there may be some hope."

"What are his chances?" asked Mabel.

"Ninety-five percent against him," said Dandy evenly. "But if he had only one chance in a million, he has the right to that chance."

Julia was for waiting till Fred came up from South Carolina before letting Dandy proceed, but Mabel talked her out of it. Dandy recommended an immediate trephining to decrease the pressure on the brain and facilitate X rays.

Back in the sick room Dandy said, "Tom, with your permission

I'd like to do a little work on you—just bore a little hole in your head right back here. You won't even feel it, and it will relieve your headache."

Tom looked fearful.

"You're not going to bore clean through, are you?"

"Oh, no, no, no. Just through the bony shell."

Julia, who had been standing beside Tom and petting him like a child, bent down and kissed him.

"And I get that too," he said, smiling up at her.

When they performed the trephining that afternoon, the pressure was so great that intracranial fluid spurted out into the room. For a time Wolfe's headache subsided. "They've fixed it," he told Aswell joyfully, but meanwhile Dandy had diagnosed the trouble as tuberculosis of the brain. The only shred of hope was that instead of being diffused, it had localized in a single, removable tuberculoma.

Sunday Tom rested in Marburg Building while friends and relatives hovered nearby in the waiting room down the hall. Fred had arrived early that morning, and he and Mabel seesawed between hope and panic, but Julia never lost her composure or raised her unceasing voice. Aswell had gone back to New York to break the news to Harpers, and Elizabeth Nowell had taken his place. Sunday evening, in response to an urgent wire from Fred, Perkins arrived but didn't let Tom know he was there. The silent friend of Tom's spirit, he spent the night sitting quietly with the others. Aline Bernstein had wanted to come too, but Perkins had dissuaded her, afraid that her presence might upset Tom on the eve of his ordeal.

Monday morning they watched him go by on the way to the operating room, his long white-swathed form motionless and comatose. When they had waited for what seemed an eternity, Annie Laurie, who had been taken off the case but was allowed to watch the operation, came running towards them in tears.

"He didn't operate," she said. "They opened Tom's skull, and Dr. Dandy took one look and laid down his scalpel."

Dandy in white suit and cap was close behind, glistening like a prize fighter.

"The case is hopeless," he said. "He has miliary tuberculosis of the brain. It's simply covered with tubercles."

As Dandy later diagnosed it, Wolfe at some time in his youth had contracted a tuberculosis of the lung which had cured itself, but the encapsulated lesion had been reopened by the pneumonia, and the tubercle bacilli entering the bloodstream had been carried to the brain. Dandy said he might live another six weeks, and they could make him fairly comfortable. It would be better, however, if he died from the shock of the operation, as might occur within the next three days.

The family were allowed to visit him for a minute or two at a time. When Fred went in at six that evening, he was shocked by Tom's appearance: his head was swathed in bandages and only the whites of his eyes were showing, except for a narrow crescent of pupil at the top. (The nurse explained that Tom could see and that the eyes would return to normal in a few days.) Fred patted him on the shoulder and called him a good soldier, and Tom told of a dream he had had: he and Fred were riding through the country in a shiny black limousine, they were all dressed up, and wherever they went they had a big feed. Tuesday morning Dandy told Fred, "Go up and see him. The improvement is wonderful. He's looking so much better and his eyes are coming back. I don't want to raise any false hopes, but twelve years ago I operated on a man for the same thing Tom has—we called it brain fever then. I went in and gave up, but a month later he was getting better, and in fifty days he was well. Nature had dried up the tubercles. Of course his case wasn't half as bad as Tom's."

Tuesday afternoon Tom sank into a coma. Pneumonia set in, and they gave him a transfusion in a last effort to stave off the end. For a day and a half he lay with eyes shut, stertorously breathing through half-opened mouth, the great vitality ebbing, the mighty engine running down. At 6:30 Thursday morning he died so suddenly and serenely that there wasn't time to call the family to his side.

It was a shining day. Across the globe, Neville Chamberlain had just landed at the Munich airport for his peace meeting with Hitler at Berchtesgaden that afternoon. But in Baltimore something had gone out of the universe. There was a rent in nature, a hole against the sky.

They laid him out, rouged and powdered, against the crinkly undertaker's satin, with an ill-fitting toupee on his shaven head. The fifty pounds he had lost during his illness added to the air of unreality. Aswell and Miss Nowell were at the station next afternoon to see the Wolfes off for Asheville. The train came in, the family boarded, and the grey metal coffin was trundled towards the baggage car. One of the strapping Negroes who eased it in danced back a few steps immediately afterwards with a fending-off gesture of both hands which Wolfe would have appreciated and recorded— a gesture of protest at the coffin's size mixed with a superstitious dread of its contents. As the train pulled out, Aswell took Miss Nowell by the arm and pointed to a window placard which said "K-19." It was the pullman designation Wolfe had used as the title of his abandoned novel.

Asheville stood at attention for the funeral of her honored son, her world-famed prodigal. The First Presbyterian Church was packed, and they sang lusty hymns. The presiding minister, old Dr. Campbell who had known Tom from Sunday School days, considered him a heretic and had been outraged by *Look Homeward, Angel*, so his task wasn't easy, but he performed it with dignity. At one point he quoted from the prologue of *Of Time and the River*: "Where shall the weary rest? When shall the lonely of heart come home? What doors are open for the wanderer? And which of us shall find his Father, know His face, and in what place, and in what time, and in what land?" It suited the minister's purpose to read "Father" and "His" as though they began with capitals, and Mrs. Roberts in the back of the church could hardly refrain from crying out, "Not capitals! No capitals there!" Wolfe's grandeur of spirit needed no false embellishments.

As the procession wound through the business district on the way to the Riverside Cemetery, people lined the sidewalk and men bared their heads. Carrying the heavy coffin from the hearse up the little embankment to the Wolfe lot, the pallbearers cut the turf with their shoes. Tom had once described this spot where he now joined Grover, Ben, and his father. "Around them in the cemetery the air brooded with a lazy drowsy warmth. There was the cry of sweet-singing birds again, the sudden thrumming bullet noises in undergrowth and leaf, and the sharp cricketing stitch of afternoon, the broken, lazy sounds from far away, a voice in the wind, a boy's shout, a cry, the sound of a bell, as well as all the drowsy fragrance of a thousand warm intoxicating odors—the resinous smell of pine, and the smells of grass and warm sweet clover. It was all as it had always been. . . . And now he heard his mother's voice again: 'And you'll come back!' he heard her saying. 'There's no better or more beautiful place than in these mountains, boy—and someday you'll come back again,' she cried with all the invincible faith and hopefulness of her strong heart."

Max Perkins was an honorary pallbearer, but instead of coming to the graveside he stood by himself in a nearby clump of trees, aloof from the other mourners. Since Tom's death a line from *Lear* had been running through his head: "He hates him that would upon the rack of this tough world stretch him out longer." As he afterwards wrote Mabel, "Isn't there something in thinking, as I have so often thought, that Tom is no longer in the midst of the terrific struggle that he was almost continually in? It was as if some obligation had been imposed upon him and that he was compelled to struggle always to fulfill it. It was the obligation of genius, but now Tom is out of the tempest that was most of his life because of this compulsion. We have lost by it, and terribly, but he is at least in peace."

Wolfe's last letter to Perkins had been like a sudden ray of sunlight illuminating the landscape after an electrical storm, and self-effacing though he was, Perkins would send a copy of it to Fitzgerald, Sherwood Anderson, Mrs. Rawlings, and a few others, identifying it proudly as the last thing Tom ever wrote.

"You and Aline made Tom," one of Perkins' colleagues at Scribners had remarked.

"No," said Perkins, "Tom had the wit to find us."

Appendix

NOTES AND REFERENCES

ONLY THOSE heretofore *unpublished* quotations which would be hard to locate in the tangle of Wolfe's papers have been documented. The following abbreviations have been used: TW for Thomas Wolfe; MP for Maxwell Perkins; HCL for Harvard College Library; UNCL for University of North Carolina Library; CSS for the files of Charles Scribner's Sons.

CHAPTER ONE

1. "As a matter of fact," wrote Perkins long afterwards, "I think the percentage of very good books—the really notable books—that are declined is higher than the percentage of really competent mediocrities. The reason is that the books of the greatest talent are almost always full of trouble, and difficult, and they do not conform to the usual standards. They are often strange. They are different, as were *This Side of Paradise* and *Look Homeward, Angel*." MP to Alice D. Bond, July 17, 1944, CSS.

2. TW's middle name, Clayton, came from William Clayton Bowman, a clergyman friend of T. C. Westall who had been much admired by Julia Wolfe in her girlhood.

3. Julia's handwritten memories in the "Clover Farm" notebook, UNCL.

4. Julia left four detailed descriptions of this dream: (1) letter to TW, Jan. 8, 1933, HCL; (2) letter to Henry Westall, Jan. 10, 1944, HCL; (3) "Clover Farm" notebook, UNCL; (4) a recorded interview, UNCL. And she alluded to it in a newspaper interview the year she died: "I don't believe our spirit, or soul, or whatever we are, who lives in the body of flesh, wears out or grows old—only the body, and we will inherit that mortal house until it becomes an unfit dwelling place; then the silver cord is severed and we go to our ethereal home—for a more progressive life—but it is up to us, like life here, how fast we progress. This is my religion and has been since I was seventeen years old." *The Charlotte Observer*, Feb. 18, 1945.

5. This account of their courtship is drawn chiefly from Hayden Norwood, *The Marble Man's Wife*, pp. 17–21, with a few touches from Mabel Wheaton Wolfe, *Thomas Wolfe and His Family*, pp. 27–29.

6. Be it remembered that Wolfe wrote autobiographical fiction, not literal autobiography, and it is wrong to equate his fiction with his life. But in places fact and fiction come together, or come together so nearly, that the distinction is minute, and when I interchange the two it is in my opinion one of these places.

7. TW to Julia, Aug. 14, 1924, UNCL.

8. The quotations in this paragraph are from TW's letter to Margaret Roberts, July 8, 1927, HCL.

9. The angel on the jacket of this volume has been authenticated as the one described by TW in *Look Homeward, Angel*, pp. 267 and 618. Imported from Italy and made of Carrara marble, it was sold by W. O. Wolfe in 1906 and marks the grave of a minister's wife in the Oakdale Cemetery in Hendersonville, twenty miles from Asheville. (See "Hendersonville Monument Identified as Thomas Wolfe's 'Angel,'" *The Asheville Citizen*, Nov. 21, 1949.)

10. See William F. Kennedy, "Economic Ideas in Contemporary Literature—the Novels of Thomas Wolfe," *Southern Economic Journal*, July, 1953. Kennedy got his estimates of assets and income from *Look Homeward, Angel*, and Fred Wolfe questions their accuracy. Mr. Wolfe believes that at this time the assets were more like $60,000 and the income $7,500, but by Asheville standards they would still have been prosperous.

11. From a letter of Margaret Roberts to her daughter Margaret, Oct., 1938.

12. Bound typescript of *O Lost*, Part II, p. 521, HCL.

13. Julia, however, was the family disciplinarian: when the children misbehaved, it was she who cut a hickory switch and tanned them across the legs.

14. Wolfe's early agnosticism is partially explained in a note written while he was at Harvard, HCL 46AM–7(22–b). It was, how-

ever, the reluctant agnosticism of a natural believer. In the early Thirties he would write, "I do not think that I have believed in God for fifteen years. Sometimes it seems that I never believed in him save when I was a little child, saying my prayers, mechanically, at night. Yet, I think a man is a fool to exult in the loss of God. When I first dared say to myself that God was not an old man with a beard I felt proud and free. It was a mark of the childish sophistication that existed in America at that time that a person who held to a belief in the Man-God was supposed to be mentally inferior. But that is not true. Some of the subtlest and profoundest of this earth's spirits have believed in Him. The reason we do not believe is not because we have grown wise but because the power to believe is not in us." HCL 46AM–7(46)(2).

15.   *O Lost* typescript, Part II, p. 624.

CHAPTER TWO

1.   Prof. George M. McKie. Told me by his daughter, Elizabeth McKie.

2.   "A nice young boy here, the son of my landlady, has a crush on me," Clara Paul wrote her sister from the Old Kentucky Home. "He hopes to become a writer. He has right much talent, I think. The most trivial thing he says sounds like poetry. Of course I told him right away that I was engaged. I explained that I could never return his feeling. I was real sorry for him. But he seemed to understand. He'll get over it, I feel sure. He is little more than a child and doesn't seem much older than our Ray."

3.   TW to Walter Bonime, Sept. 30, 1927, HCL.

4.   Twenty years later Wolfe would paint an uncomplimentary picture of Graham as Hunter Griswold McCoy, president of Pine Rock College, in *The Web and the Rock*, pp. 202–05.

5.   When Terry died in 1953, he had gathered a good deal of material but had written only a few sketches towards a biography.

6.   Wolfe's classmate, Pulitzer Prize dramatist Paul Green, got his start under Koch.

7. Although this course doesn't appear on the transcript of Wolfe's college record, two people—Benjamin Cone and Rachel Field —have circumstantial memories of his being in it, and his copy of *All's Well That Ends Well* has the pasted-in vocabulary sheets which Koch demanded of his students. He probably began the course and changed to something else because he disliked the survey approach.

8. The Horace Williams-Edwin Greenlaw antithesis is also described in the *O Lost* typescript, Part III, pp. 980–83, and in a fragment about Professor Weldon, 46AM–7(21).

CHAPTER THREE

1. HCL 46AM–7(46)(1).

2. HCL 46AM–7(46)(1).

3. "The Grocer's Daughter" in "A Passage to England," HCL 46AM–7(23).

4. HCL 46AM–7(47)(1), p. 174.

5. HCL 46AM–7(46)(1).

6. Eight fragments of plays, HCL 46AM–7(21).

7. HCL 46AM–7(22–b).

8. HCL 46AM–7(46)(2). Wolfe was anti-academic but not anti-intellectual. "Coleridge's experiences," he would write in 1932, "came mainly from the pages of books and Joseph Conrad's experiences came mainly from the decks of ships, but can anyone tell you that one form of experience is less real and less personal than another, or that Coleridge's books had less reality for him than Conrad's ships . . . ?"

9. Wolfe's imaginary meeting with Shakespeare occurs in 46AM–7(46)(2).

10. TW to George Pierce Baker, summer of 1922, UNCL.

11. Eight fragments of plays, HCL 46AM–7(21).

CHAPTER FOUR

1. Looking back on this period in the early Thirties, Wolfe would write, "Considering we were the kind of people I have described, my people acted toward me . . . with a tolerance, liberality and understanding which I will never forget and which now seems wonderful to me." HCL 46AM–7(46)(1).

2. The previous August, Baker had discouraged Wolfe's going abroad, and Wolfe made much of this inconsistency. But in August *Welcome* had had commercial possibilities and Wolfe seemed about to break in as a playwright.

3. Told me by Mrs. J. H. Riddle.

4. Though Wolfe called the Albert "sterile," it was clean and the service was good. It wasn't the cheapest way to live. His room cost him $12 a week when he could have had a cold-water flat or chipped in with other instructors on a rented apartment for about $15 a month.

5. TW to Mrs. Roberts, quoted in her unpublished recollections.

6. Wolfe probably did not know this. I learned it from Mrs. Barry.

7. TW to Mrs. Hortense Pattison, summer, 1925.

CHAPTER FIVE

1. HCL 46AM–7(22–e).

2. Told me by Jack Westall to whom Wolfe had told it.

3. The authoritative document here is Aline Bernstein's description of the occasion in her letter of Sept. 20, 1926, to TW, written less than a year after the event.

4. Told me by Agnes Morgan.

5. HCL 46AM–7(22–e).

6. HCL 46AM–7(22–e).

7. Wolfe sometimes referred to *Look Homeward, Angel* as his "*Ulysses* book." For an aping of Joycean rhythms and effects, see the description of Mrs. Thelma Jarvis in Chapter 24, which begins, "Seated alone, with thick brown eyes above her straw regardant. . . ." But in the end Wolfe was not uncritical of Joyce. In the Thirties he would describe *Ulysses* as "a work whose greatest fault is really the finical preciseness of a Jesuitical logic and whose greatest weakness is the sterile perfection of its planned design." HCL 46AM–7(46)(2). This opinion echoes Richard Aldington's review of *Look Homeward, Angel* in *The Referee*, June 6, 1930. Wrote Aldington: "Whereas *Ulysses* is intellectual, minutely planned, static, and *au fond* life hating, *Look Homeward, Angel* is the product of an immense exuberance, organic in its form, kinetic, and drenched with the love of life." For further criticism of *Ulysses*, see TW's *Letters*, pp. 585–86.

8. "Christmas Week, 1924," HCL 46AM–7(46)(2).

9. Pocket notebook #2.

10. HCL 46AM–7(30)(3).

CHAPTER SIX

1. As first president of the New York Bar Association, Evarts had instituted legal reforms which struck at the corruption of the Tweed Ring. Not tall but lean and dignified like his grandson who somewhat resembled him, he had a high-browed, large-nosed, strong-chinned intellectual face and an over-all cast of tenacity and frail force. "I pride myself," he once remarked to Henry Adams, "on my success in doing not the things I like to do but the things I don't like to do"—sounding like his father, Jeremiah Evarts, who had fought the saloons and the Sunday mails while editing *The Panoplist*, the best religious journal in the land.

2. A composer and conductor as well, Charles Callaghan Perkins was for many years the president of Boston's Handel and Haydn Society, and he had given the city of Boston Crawford's statue of Beethoven, the first statue of any sort of artist to be erected in this country.

3. When he was eight, he and his brother had another august
    encounter. Benjamin Harrison, touring the country with his
    retinue, descended on Senator Evarts, and there was a large
    reception, in the course of which Edward and Max were herded
    through a forest of skirts and trouser legs and introduced to a
    small man with a pouter-pigeon chest overspread by a white
    beard. Shaking hands with them, the President said in a deep,
    booming voice, "Well, I suppose you boys are good Republicans
    too." A general silence had accompanied the President's words,
    and now that silence lengthened horribly. Max's father, the
    black sheep of the family, was a Mugwump who had voted for
    Cleveland, but Max didn't want to offend the President, so he
    made no reply. Finally Edward spoke up. "No, we are not—we
    are Democrats," he said very decidedly, and there was a great
    burst of laughter to which the President himself contributed.

4. A few times Max summered in Newport where he remembered
    the old sailing frigates the Navy used for training and a Revo-
    lutionary fort called "The Dumplings" on a bluff overlooking
    the harbor.

5. His favorite professor was Charles Townsend Copeland. Widely
    read without being a scholar in the ordinary sense, this crusty
    little down-easter made fun of what he called "the Ph.D. death
    rattle." Literary vivisection was not for him; rather, with his
    actor's flair for reading aloud, he aimed to pour the master-
    pieces alive and whole into the hearts of his students, and in
    their compositions the quality most likely to win his hard-earned
    praise was a Kiplingesque vividness, the complete resurrection
    of a moment of experience.

6. Once a lucky tip enabled him to beat the town with the story
    of the S.S. *Republic* collision off Nantucket Light, but his great-
    est triumph occurred when he volunteered to accompany auto-
    mobile racer George Robertson during an attempt to break the
    record of the Vanderbilt Speedway on Long Island. Perkins
    substituted for the "mechanician" in Locomobile No. 16 as it
    whizzed over the twenty-three-and-a-half-mile course at just
    under seventy miles an hour, and according to his write-up in
    The Times, with the wind forcing him back in his seat and
    "the million rattling explosions of the engine" in his ears, he
    felt as if he were running into the teeth of a tornado. Before
    they set out, Robertson—a twenty-two-year-old daredevil who

had recently killed a bystander when his car crashed through a fence—assured Perkins there was nothing to worry about. "I'm not going to break my neck to kill you," he quipped, but as they screeched through culverts and careened around curves Perkins wasn't so sure. Nevertheless, at the finish, with the danger behind him, he felt a sudden regret and sinking of his spirits.

7.   In his off-hours he read the *Odyssey* while his tentmates played poker, and at dusk, when he took his post as corporal of the guard on a house-high pile of alfalfa bales, he readily imagined that he was looking out over the plains of Troy. In the half-light the rows of tents and tethered horses against the jagged mountain background seemed Homeric. "Whatever they may *say*," he wrote Louise, "the men here love this life—they sing, groups of them, as they go up to feed their horses; and a man must be happy indeed to sing at [6 A.M.]".

8.   Perkins' views on censorship were those of the founding fathers and of the Enlightenment. "The function of a publisher in society," he wrote, "is to furnish a means by which anyone of a certain level of intelligence and abilities can express his views. A publisher should not be, as such, a partisan, however strongly partisan he may be as an individual. If he allows his partisanship to govern him in his choice of books, he is a traitor to the public. He is supposed to furnish a forum for the free play of the intellect, in so far as he possibly can. That is the whole American theory—that opinions can be given a means of full expression, and that the public, hearing all of them and considering them, will eventually approximate a right conclusion. Every profession has its own particular code of ethics, its own morality, that its members must adhere to or they betray it. And a primary element in the morality of the publisher is that he shall not let his own personal views obstruct the way for the expression of counter-views." (Perkins, *Letters*, pp. 244–45.) In defense of a Scribner book criticized for its salacity, Perkins wrote, "It often puzzles me when people think that matters connected with sex should be suppressed. Sex itself cannot be suppressed, and the efforts to do it, it seems to me, generally result in greater damage than it can do itself. After all, it was not an invention of man, but of God. We are not to blame for it. We are to blame, perhaps, for the abuse of it, but that usually

comes from ignorance, which results from suppression and censorship. The way to kill germs and maggots is to bring them into the open, where they are recognized for what they are. It is when they are allowed to propagate under stones and in darkness that they can grow strong and more harmful." (Perkins, *Letters*, pp. 300–01.) Countering the charge that writers introduced salaciousness to make their books sell, Perkins wrote, "A true writer never wants to introduce that element. He does it because his book is a revelation of life—and life should be revealed as it is—and he generally hates it just as much as any genteel reader or censor, and generally much more, for he is bound to be a sensitive person if he is a true writer." (Perkins, *Letters*, p. 281.) Wolfe seemed to agree. To James Mandel, the N.Y.U. student who did his typing the spring of 1929, he remarked, "Pornographic books are inexcusable unless they illustrate life as a creative force. Books that are written merely to illustrate the grime and grease of sex are disgusting." (*Thomas Wolfe at Washington Square*, p. 97.)

9. Winters he sledded with them wearing his "balaclava helmet," a knitted affair that completely covered his head and neck, and during their illnesses he was tenderly solicitous and called them "Ducky." When one of them said she wished she could see a a house burn down, he stuffed an old dollhouse with paper and lit it in the fireplace, and flames shot out the windows and the roof caved in. Sometimes he showed them the galley proofs he brought back with him in the evening (it was glamorous having a father who dealt with famous authors—almost like having a mother who was an opera star), and if they jumbled the sheets he would chide them for being like "kittens with a ball of wool."

10. His probing curiosity about peoples' thoughts and habits was sometimes embarrassing. In the Scribner elevator he would crane and peer so aggressively at the titles of the books the girl employees had with them that a colleague said he wouldn't be surprised to see Max get a punch in the nose. Out driving with his daughters one evening, he came on a couple walking by the side of the road and followed slowly behind, holding them in the headlights while he explained from the artist's point of view the difference between the way a man and a woman walk. His daughters begged him to go on and stop annoying

the bewildered pair, but he paid no attention. He was too engrossed in how to represent this nuance.

11.   "Eugene" in *Three Blue Suits*. This story is patently autobiographical, and for convenience' sake I have used the characters' real names.

12.   MP to Elizabeth Lemmon, Sept. 5, 1929.

13.   To cite an example of the way Perkins persuaded Wolfe to cut for taste and for poetic effect—the far more rigid literary code of that day entering into it as well—here is the description of Eugene Gant losing his virginity in a brothel his first term at college as Wolfe originally wrote it (*O Lost*, Part III, pp. 661–62). Only the italicized words appear in *Look Homeward, Angel*.

" 'Let's get started,' she said. 'Where's my money?' "

"*He thrust two crumpled* dollar *bills into her hand.* She went over and lay upon the bed. He tore off his tie and collar with blind fingers, and removed his coat and vest. *Then he lay down beside her. He trembled uncontrollably.* [In *Look Homeward, Angel* "uncontrollably" was changed to "unnerved and impotent."] *Passion was extinct in him.* The woman worked patiently upon his cold body, chafing him with her broad hands, warming his fingers in her breasts, and, gathering his thin figure into the wide cradle of her thighs, flowing rhythmically around him. After a time she said, in a kindly troubled voice:

" 'What's the matter, son? Ain't you never had a woman before?'

" 'No,' he said.

"But his chattering flesh warmed slowly: his young strength responded mechanically in spite of his weary heart. He closed his eyes, trying desperately to evoke once more some fragment of a lost vision, to weave, in the presence of this eclipsing horror, some new restoring loveliness. He felt a bitter shame before this woman because of his sorry show of impotence: he strove desperately with her, blotting out his mind in travail, and achieving a moment of oblivion, as his senses drowned, and his life rushed from his limbs. Spent, he lay for a moment in her huge uncouth embrace, then got blindly up and turned away from her squat wipings. *The massed coals caved in the hearth. The bright lost wonder died* away, leaving a cinder of mean wisdom.

"Stolid, the woman rose. 'You took a hell of a time,' she said."

14. TW to D. L. Jackson, Sept. 24, 1929, HCL.

15. In retrospect, Wolfe was dissatisfied with the portrait of Eugene. "I believe the character of the hero was the weakest and least convincing one in the whole book, because he had been derived not only from experience but [was] colored a good deal by the romantic aestheticism of the period." (Purdue speech, May, 1938.) Olin Dows remarked to me that he had found Wolfe more curious, grotesque, and interesting than Eugene, who seemed a somewhat romanticized and sentimentalized version of the author.

16. When asked about the autobiographical content of Wolfe's fiction, Perkins replied, "The writings of every great novelist are in some considerable degree autobiographical. He always creates out of what is seen, and in fact, the best novels of almost every great novelist, like *David Copperfield, Pendennis,* Tolstoi's *War and Peace,* etc., are very close indeed to autobiography, but everything in them is different from what it really was, has been transmuted in passing through the imagination of the writer. It is this way with Thomas Wolfe. None of the people are literally as he presents them, nor are any of the happenings. They are the basis out of which he creates a world. Wolfe's books certainly are more autobiographical than *David Copperfield* but the difference is only one in degree." (MP to Laurence Greene, CSS.)

17. Amplifying the "digested in my spirit" in a letter to Mrs. Roberts after *Look Homeward, Angel* appeared, Wolfe wrote, "All creation is to me fabulous . . . the world of my creation is a fabulous world . . . experience comes into me from all points, is digested and absorbed into me until it becomes a part of me, and . . . the world I create is *always inside* me, and never *outside* me, and . . . what reality I can give to what I create comes only from *within.*"

18. TW to Mrs. Roberts, HCL 63M–152.

19. "One may begin by hating them, when he writes about them," Wolfe confessed, "but as he goes on he comes to have a kind of loving tenderness for them: 'Ah, you bastard,' he will whisper tenderly at length, 'you bastard! What a beautiful, complete, and perfect specimen you were!'—and from the moment that

he feels this, he can never hate that man again." HCL 46AM–12(10).

20. Undated TW fragment to Mrs. Roberts, HCL 46AM–14, 15.

21. HCL 46AM–7(30)(1).

22. MP to William Wisdom, June 7, 1943, UNCL.

23. HCL 46AM–7(30)(2).

CHAPTER SEVEN

1. Fitzgerald's unpublished essay, "My Generation."

2. TW to MP, Jan. 7, 1931, CSS.

3. HCL 46AM–7(46)(1).

4. TW to Aline Bernstein, summer of 1928.

5. *Rock Me, Julie,* 1929. It folded after several performances.

6. Unpublished essay on Wolfe and Fitzgerald by David Randall.

7. This account of the confrontation between Julia Wolfe and Aline Bernstein is based principally on Julia's recorded interview, UNCL. Julia also discussed the matter with Nancy C. Wylie of Winnsboro, S.C., who showed me her write-up of what Julia told her.

8. The severest critic of Wolfe's anti-Semitism was Aline Bernstein who had suffered from it the most. "He hated us like poison—" she wrote Elizabeth Nowell after his death, "it was a twist in him that made me loathe him at times." But among those I questioned on the subject, the majority minimized it. "I do not remember him making an anti-Semitic crack," said Hamilton Basso who saw a good deal of Wolfe during his last few years. Prof. Boris Gamzue, who taught with him at N.Y.U., said that Wolfe's "was not a deep anti-Semitism—rather he seemed to be working off the irritation of the moment, some dissatisfaction within himself." Belinda Jelliffe, who knew him extremely well, said that his "mild anti-Semitism was Southern small town." Younghill Kang, who taught with him at N.Y.U.: "Wolfe was not anti-Semitic. The portrait of Abe Jones was typical of his

attitude; while satirizing Abe, he brought out his humanity." A Jewish girl who had a brief affair with him in 1929: "Wolfe was not deeply anti-Semitic—he carried over a little bias from his home town perhaps." Writer Beverly Smith, a good friend of Wolfe in the early Thirties: "Wolfe was not anti-Semitic, or rather his anti-Semitism, if it could be called that, was more the irritation of the moment." Coley Taylor, teacher: "Since he has been wrongly accused of being anti-Semitic, I think it should be said that Wolfe was a great admirer of his Jewish students at N.Y.U. for their intelligence, their eagerness to learn and their aptitude and penetration in study. He often expressed this in conversation—their hunger for life and learning, and their amiability and enthusiasm."

Wolfe denied his anti-Semitism in letters to two readers who criticized him for it. (TW, *Letters,* pp. 417 and 561.) And Perkins wrote a critic of the anti-Semitism in *Of Time and the River,* "The author has no anti-Semitic leanings, rather the the contrary. He numbers Jews among his best friends. . . . There are hard things said about Jews in *Of Time and the River.* There are also very many fine things said about them, and certainly the Christians in the book are unfavorably represented to at least an equal degree. The race which suffers most in Mr. Wolfe's representation of it is the Irish, but they have not as yet made any protest, nor do we expect one from them." (MP to Simon Pearl, April 20, 1935, CSS.)

9. This dream is recorded in TW's pocket notebook for Feb., 1931. I cite it here to show how he was haunted by dreams of madness.

CHAPTER EIGHT

1. MP to Elizabeth Lemmon, Dec. 25, 1932.

2. Fragment of an unpublished review, HCL 46AM-7(70-h).

3. With specific reference to *The History of Rome Hanks* by William Stanley Pennell, Perkins wrote, "As for form, I know that is wanting, but there were reasons peculiar to the case which made its full achievement impossible. And it has other things that are far less common. Anyhow, I am glad I was never much good in college because a number of the books that I

have been peculiarly concerned in publishing would probably have got turned down by us as well as they were by other publishers because they lacked form." MP to Marjorie Kinnan Rawlings, Oct. 17, 1944, CSS.

4. It has been argued that at this point Perkins went too far, that without his aid Wolfe would somehow have resolved his problems and been the better for it, that with Perkins to lean on and pick up after him, he unconsciously indulged his worst traits. But I remain of the opinion that, all things considered, the Perkins alliance was fortunate and necessary.

5. Roy Campbell, "On Some South African Novelists."

6. TW to John Terry, March 28, 1935, UNCL.

7. Though Wolfe accepted full responsibility for errors in wording and proofreading, he added, "I was not ready to read proof, I was not through *writing.*"

8. TW to Betsy Hatch Hill, May, 1935.

CHAPTER NINE

1. MP to Elizabeth Lemmon, July 12, 1935.

2. Beatrice Hinkle, the psychiatrist, had encouraged Aline to write about Wolfe as therapy.

3. For the details of Wolfe's visit to Mabel Dodge Luhan I am indebted to the two ladies who accompanied him, Mrs. Joseph McKibbin and Mrs. Bradley Saunders (then Sallie Faxon).

4. Wolfe was frightened by antiques, by the spindle-legged Colonial and Louis Quinze chairs which had a way of becoming unglued in overheated apartments and were thus somewhat rickety to begin with. Once when he was asked out to dinner, his hostess settled him in an ample wing chair which he proclaimed the most comfortable he had ever sat in. Next day it was delivered to his apartment, wrapped in brown paper, with a note from the hostess explaining that she wanted him to have it. Greatly agitated, Wolfe phoned a mutual friend to ask if he had been gauche in admiring it, if his hostess had thought he was hinting, but his friend reassured him that it was simply

the generous act of an understanding person. After which, he went around describing it as one of the most wonderful things that had ever happened to him—"People just don't give me chairs," he said.

5. This episode is based on an unpublished reminiscence by Terry, UNCL.

6. Wolfe's constant suspicion that women were trading on him is implicit in the following letter, written him by the mother of two boys: "Tom, the Revelator: You were kind to call me. Thanks. The boys are coming to town on Saturday. I'd like you to see them. In making this suggestion I am *not* acting as a spy for Eastman, Winchell, Stalin, Polly Adler, Mr. O.O.O. or or any groups or other individuals. I am *not* trying to get your signature or have you shake hands with the boys so they can say they have shaken hands with you. I am *not* trying to get you interested in my family in a guileful female manner. I do want the boys to meet you because I think you are a great man. I do want you to meet the boys because I trust your ability not to 'miss' people and I do want your word on the two of them. Have I touched them in the sad manner you indicated?"

7. Wolfe understood the redemptive power of love, as indicated by this unpublished fragment: "I believe in love, the savior and redeemer of the universe. I believe in the true and faithful hearts of women, and I believe that without their love, our lives are lost and desolate, and our work sterile. I believe in the bitter pangs of the lover, I believe in all the agony of the mind, the dark madness of the lover's soul, I believe in all the bitter words love marks our lives with." HCL 46AM–7(32)(2).

8. The fall of 1935 Wolfe had been disheartened by the reception of his first book of stories, *From Death to Morning*. The critics had complained that he shouted too much and would soon wear the edges off words like "immense" and "terrible" and that the stories were formless and undisciplined.

9. MP to Elizabeth Lemmon, May 29, 1936.

10. Thea Voelcker married a German who was killed in World War II and she subsequently committed suicide. The following excerpts from a letter she wrote Perkins in September, 1938, on

hearing of Wolfe's death, help to explain why: "Every personal grief has to disappear in the grand grief that a poet like him died. . . . He knew he would die very soon, how painful was his fear to die before he had done his work. . . . I am already destroyed by him, in him, I don't lament it. . . . I didn't like to understand that he was without charity, but I had to understand it, and I did: For the work he had to do everything that it could grow. Every hindrance he had to finish the minute it was no more utile. . . . Tom was the splendid glory of my life, he was my finishing and every fulfillment of which I had to wait for. I didn't love him as a passion from a woman to a man, I loved him how you love the deepest, holiest desire of the own heart, I loved him with a might of faith and love, how perhaps it is too great to exist in the world. Perhaps must surely this holy love, this accomplished total compromiseless love has to be tragic because the world isn't total. This love had to break down. And I had to break down. You break down in the love of Tom, or you never loved him. (Wasn't she [Aline Bernstein] dying too, whom he loved ten years, she costed me ten years of my life, he said so bitterly.) There is only one highest mountain in the world, one highest measure. Tom was my highest mountain. When you have reached your highest point and you cannot stay there you must fall down, there is no other way. You cannot go back in a smaller life. Nothing more is to compare to the world you have seen, and for this you are lost for everything that meets you.

"When I saw him he was in a state of agony . . . crashes from one violent state into the other, possessed devils, meeting deadly; or tormented, trembling, vibrating creature, that helpless makes responsible the outer world for his pain; destroying, raging man who with cold amusement—but always with the own torment—ruined other persons. And humble instrument, pious child, who begged the father for strength to work. In one night, Mr. Perkins, when he came to me drunk, frenzy, aggressive like never, vomiting, nearly crazy for agony, from which he believed he would never in his life have an end, the poor, poor man; in this night he prayed. He prayed, Mr. Perkins, and in this tired, exhausted, humble and urgent (*dragend*) prayer to the father, in this silent, urgently imploring prayer for the work, that he prayed after a flood of raging eruptions, scornful laughters, in which I want to die, in this prayer I learned to

330

know him entirely and since this prayer I served him and his work without any personal wish. I knew I never should demand anything and that I had not right to do it. I never, not any time, demanded everything for me, Mr. Perkins. (Maybe if I should have done it, if I had forced him it would have been better.) There, I thought, was only to do one thing: Let him do the work. And do everything for him that another person could do. . . .

"I never more can love. I want to die. I love death. If I can have once more a destination, it is death. Not a feeble death."

11. TW to Donald Ogden Stewart, Feb., 1938, HCL.

CHAPTER TEN

1. Perkins' deafness was the common form known as otosclerosis—a calcification of the bones of the middle ear which can now be cured by surgery. The disease causes noise and ringing in the ears, and Perkins said that in his case it was like the chirping of birds, and he found it very trying. In a crowded bar or restaurant, the background noises seemed to obliterate the noise in his ears, and he could actually hear better.

2. Perkins' women authors included Taylor Caldwell, Marcia Davenport, Caroline Gordon, Nancy Hale, Marjorie Kinnan Rawlings and Christine Weston.

3. MP to his daughter, Bertha, June 10, 1927.

4. Interview with May Cameron, *The New York Evening Post*, May 14, 1936. In this interview Wolfe also expressed his admiration for Faulkner, whose *Sanctuary, The Sound and the Fury* and *As I Lay Dying* he had read.

5. MP to Elizabeth Lemmon, Aug. 16, 1936.

6. A month later Carl Van Doren described Perkins' role as follows: "Thomas Wolfe is his own river and Max Perkins is his levee. There have been floods along this river for years, when the water did not know where its banks were and poured itself in gigantic torrents over the land, unable to stop and blindly wondering where to go. A stupid engineer might have tried to dam the river. Maxwell Perkins, wise and shrewd, was satisfied

to throw up levees here and there, helping the water find its direction until it settled to its proper channel and swept magnificently to sea. There is *Of Time and the River* as a joint monument to the river and the engineer." *New York Herald Tribune Book Review*, May 17, 1936, p. 5.

7. This was a half-truth. Though Mrs. Bernstein's threats had worried Scribners, *The October Fair* (that is, the second half of the *Of Time and the River* manuscript) had been set aside in January, 1934, with Wolfe's approval while he got the first half into publishable shape. When he came back to it in his own good time the fall of 1935, he found he had lost interest in it.

8. Belinda Jelliffe, who came from North Carolina and knew Wolfe and Perkins intimately and was married to the psychiatrist Smith Ely Jelliffe, had an interesting psychiatric explanation of Wolfe's conflict with Scribners. She maintained that Scribners had taken the place of his family—with all his love for them, his fear of disapproval, and his frustrated desire to be free. "Can't you see that you've got to have a fight with Tom," she told Perkins, "a real emotional disturbance, and then make up? His own pattern of life is established upon that procedure and his personality demands and needs it. He has not learned to handle his love for you, his real gratitude to you and Scribners. He is still a child and he hates you all because you are simply his family all over again. . . . I know this is true because I have come into this building with him many times and observed his dread, his childish fear of disapproval, his fury at his inability to be free. You have got to understand this and handle him differently." Looking off in the distance with a patient desire to see, Perkins answered, "Belinda, I'll never understand people from Asheville. I cannot fight Tom, nor you." "Unless you fight him," she warned, "you will lose him, and, what is really beyond bearing, he will lose you." "No," said Perkins smiling, "he can never lose me no matter what happens." (Belinda Jelliffe, unpublished memoir of Wolfe and Perkins.)

9. MP to Marjorie Kinnan Rawlings, Feb. 9, 1938, CSS.

10. Wolfe's portrait of the editor, Foxhall Edwards, in *You Can't Go Home Again*, in so far as it is a portrait of Perkins, exaggerates his guile. Perkins was reserved and detached, he kept his own

council, but there was nothing the least bit shifty or dishonest about him.

11. There is a different version of this passage at the end of *You Can't Go Home Again*, amended by editor Edward Aswell to fit the context.

CHAPTER ELEVEN

1. Unpublished Fitzgerald letter to Mrs. Bayard Turnbull, May 15, 1935.

2. *The Modern Monthly*, April, 1935. In *The Letters of F. Scott Fitzgerald* I mistakenly identified the story which triggered Fitzgerald's criticism as "Circus at Dawn," which appeared in *The Modern Monthly* of March, 1935.

3. Charles Angoff, who "edited inside sentences" when he cut Wolfe's story "Boom Town" from 25,000 to 9,000 words for *The American Mercury* in 1934, later decided that he had been wrong to do so. "A good editor," said Angoff, "should never forget that there are two basic styles in writing: the opulent and the parsimonious. Dreiser, Zola, Balzac, Melville wrote in the opulent manner. Edgar Saltus, Willa Cather, Hemingway wrote in the parsimonious manner. . . . My edited version of 'Boom Town' is a piece of carpentry. It is neat and swift and polished. But it is not genuine Wolfe. His original had a flow and a richness and a thunderous impact that my version hasn't got. But doesn't Wolfe indulge in repetition? I used to think that he did, but I haven't been so sure for years. He builds, he seldom repeats, and even when he repeats he often enriches." *The Southwest Review*, Winter, 1963.

4. The four preceding sentences are published here for the first time. When I was editing Fitzgerald's *Letters*, I was unable to locate the original of this one.

5. Of this letter Wolfe wrote Hamilton Basso a few days later: "I let him have it with both barrels when I answered him, and I hope the experience will do him good. I know he will understand I wasn't a bit sore and enjoyed writing a letter and a chance of ribbing him a little. He has come out apparently as a

classical selectionist. . . . Anyway I had some fun and I know Scott won't mind it."

6.   See Edward Aswell, "A Note on Thomas Wolfe" in *The Hills Beyond.*

7.   Wolfe once confessed that a poet "is what I should most like to be and what, it seems to me, every man who ever wrote would want to be, if he could." HCL 46AM-7(70-g).

8.   "My Generation."

9.   And yet it was Tom who that summer arranged to have Frank X-rayed. Frank's son, Dietz, who was present, remembered Tom's great concern and his relief on learning from the doctor that although Frank had severe rheumatoid arthritis, there was no malignancy.

10.   In his previous will, drawn shortly after the publication of *Look Homeward, Angel,* Wolfe had made his mother and Aline Bernstein equal beneficiaries.

11.   After he left, they resumed their correspondence. He enlisted her aid with some research he was doing on Asheville during the Depression, and when he wrote her about it, he slipped into his old confiding vein. One of his very last letters was to her, telling of Harpers' enthusiasm for the manuscript he had left in their hands and of his determination to perfect it and justify their belief in him.

12.   "Tom did show unkindness to people," said Perkins later, "but he didn't mean to do it. He was in torment so much of the time on account of his being so sensitive a person and so distracted about his work, etc., that he was sometimes cruel and unjust. But he hated those things. There was no man who loved the good more than Tom." MP to William Wisdom, July 27, 1939.

13.   TW to Norman Holmes Pearson, March 5, 1937.

14.   Wolfe's similarity to Balzac has been remarked upon by those who knew him. See, for example, Mary Colum, *Forum,* Nov., 1939, p. 227, and Robert Raynolds, *Thomas Wolfe: Memoir of a Friendship,* p. 66. In both there was physical disproportion: as Wolfe suffered from his height and bulk, so Balzac suffered from his short-coupledness, his basset legs being absurdly short for

his large torso. Both had a superabundance of animal spirits, an acute sense of smell, a tendency to jet saliva when they spoke, unruly manes of hair, turned-up noses, sensual mouths and dark, inquisitorial eyes. Night workers and excessive coffee-drinkers, both were provincials who came to the metropolis seeking love and fame, and both were formed by much older mistresses. Both were visionaries with a realistic veneer.

15. Wolfe's life ends in the enormous question, "What if he had lived?" Was he on the threshold of an artistic breakthrough when he died? Had he been allowed his three score years and ten, would he have cut a substantially greater figure?

Though conscious of the frailty of such hypothetical deduction, I am inclined to say "No." Of course an artist of Wolfe's stature is a loss at any age, and poet that he was, his premature death surely deprived us of some magnificent bursts. With his German background one wonders too what miracles the Second World War might have wrought in his consciousness, especially if—as correspondent or observer—he had gotten near the scenes of conflict. Although he had skimmed the cream, he would doubtless have fashioned more books from his past experiences, but not, I would hazard the guess, essentially different ones from those we know. As a novelist, Wolfe was uniquely dependent on what he had seen and known, on the world as it impinged on his superb sensory equipment. To an unusual degree he was the center of his universe, his assumption being that what had happened to him was so vitally important that he could make it important to others, and in large measure he succeeded. He began with himself, but the rings emanating from his intensely personal vision lapped the farthest shore. And had he recovered from his last illness, his compassionate range would have been further increased by his brush with "the dark man"—his realization, as he wrote Perkins, that he was "just a grain of dust."

Nevertheless, the resolve after *Of Time and the River* to write a more objective, less autobiographical type of fiction was not as simple as it seemed. One doesn't change his nature by decree. The letters of Wolfe's last year, though they show a wider concern and more humor about himself, are in their viewpoint hardly less self-centered than before; they are Wolfe unburdening his mind and spirit with the same minimal interest in the person he is addressing. George Webber, the protagonist of the two posthumous novels whom he considered an objective creation without a trace of "Eugene Gantiness," was still a transparent likeness of Wolfe himself. And though these books—which, incidentally, should not be judged too critically since he planned to spend another year on the manuscript—are on the whole more leanly and tersely written, the change is not altogether for the good. The first third of *The Web and the Rock,* a recapitulation of his boyhood, contains some of his most controlled, detached and "mature" prose, yet many prefer the lyrical extravagance of *Look Homeward, Angel.* Wolfe died young, it is true—three weeks before his thirty-eighth birthday—but there had been time to show what he had. At this age Faulkner, Hemingway and Fitzgerald had done most of the work on which their reputation rests.

Viewed with the hindsight of three decades, Wolfe's life completes a circle, returns on itself. He had uttered his cry, which was also the cry of a continent. And perhaps in the beauty and fury of his writing was implicit the early death which he had long foreseen and dimly foretold in "I Have a Thing to Tell You."

In a letter of sympathy to Mabel, Edgar Lee Masters was to write, "We can lament that Tom did not have time to say all that was in him, but neither did Keats or Shelley. Something fashions the story and whether it be the finished or the *un*finished picture, at last it takes its place as the picture and seems not *un*fitting. . . . And in spite of everything you have the consolation, you and your mother and the family, that he, in his brief years, went ahead with the swiftness that marks men of genius, and left a name for you and America to treasure."

CHAPTER TWELVE

1. HCL 46AM–7(70–aa).

2. In her biography of Wolfe, Elizabeth Nowell states that it was he who had the bottle of whisky and offered "the poor shivering wretch" a drink, but I have come to the opposite conclusion on the following evidence: (1) On July 18, 1938, a week after Tom entered Firlawns Sanitarium, his doctor, E. C. Ruge, wrote Fred a letter summarizing Tom's illness, which included the remark, "On his trip by boat to Vancouver he met a gentle-

man who had influenza and this man was asking different people for a drink. Tom gave him a drink out of his bottle and it is possible could have contracted it in this way." (2) In 1958, however, Ruge wrote Miss Nowell that Tom had told him in effect, "I was going to Vancouver on the boat. I met a fellow passenger who had a bad cold. He took a drink out of a bottle and offered me a drink. I drank out of the bottle. I believe I got his cold." (3) In 1958 Bessie Fisk, Tom's nurse at Firlawns, wrote Miss Nowell that she remembered taking dictation on a letter from Tom to Fred (now lost) in which Tom said "having made the acquaintance of a fellow passenger, he had been induced to imbibe from the flask which the man had on his hip." The last two items overrule the first because Tom was very sick his first week at Firlawns and in telling Ruge the story he could have garbled it, or Ruge could have misunderstood him. Thereafter, he and Ruge had many talks, so that in the end Ruge must have gotten the correct version which he told Miss Nowell in 1958. It is backed by the nurse's testimony.

3. When Perkins saw this letter for the first time in 1945, he wrote Miss Nowell, "Were you capable of believing—I know Tom could believe anything when his imagination got working—that we would instruct our salesmen to damage him? Besides, we should betray our profession and everything we believe in, if we tried to injure a great talent. It's incredible that even Tom could believe that. It is possible that some of the men were so aggrieved at Tom's leaving us that they expressed derogatory opinions of him as a man. Very likely they did. . . . But you must know that I never said much of anything about the whole matter, and that when pressed, I spoke in Tom's defense."

4. "The artist must be a good man," Wolfe had written in his notes, "or some sort of a good man: if the man is no good, then the art is no good." HCL 46AM–7(32)(3). See also the Robert Raynolds memoir, pp. 147–48.

5. TW to MP, Jan. 7, 1931, CSS.

6. Raynolds memoir, p. 146.

SOURCES AND ACKNOWLEDGMENTS

I REMEMBER my first contact with the writing of Thomas Wolfe. The spring of 1943 I was on an old four-piper convoying tankers to the Caribbean, and going off watch in the sunny afternoons, I would settle myself far forward on the gently swinging, browsing fo'c'sle of that pencil-like ship where, flicked by spray that instantly dried, I would lose myself in the cadences of *You Can't Go Home Again*. This novel was perhaps a good place for the unwitting biographer to dig in, because here one meets the characters modelled on Max Perkins and Aline Bernstein, those twin engines that got Wolfe's heavy plane off the ground. From *You Can't Go Home Again* I followed his saga back through *The Web and the Rock*, losing my momentum somewhere in the mazes of *Of Time and the River*; it wasn't till I began this biography that I read *Look Homeward, Angel* which I had merely picked at before. But in 1945, in *The Crack-Up*, I came across Wolfe's free-swinging letter to Fitzgerald in which he firmly, humorously and commonsensically shrugged off the Flaubertian yoke, and it seemed to me then, as it seems to me now, that Wolfe said the last word in that classic debate.

When I decided to write his life, I was fortunate to be living in Cambridge near the bulk of his papers, which had been bought and donated to Harvard by William B. Wisdom. A few doors up the street from me was George Pierce Baker's former abode, and looking out my window I have been warmed by the thought that forty-five years ago Wolfe's gaunt shape might have been seen hurrying past, en route to a conference with his drama professor. I have familiarized myself with the other locales that colored his spirit, and I have questioned everyone I could find who knew him and those close to him. Before listing the many people who shared their memories with me, I would like to thank them one and all for their patient, courteous and friendly assistance which has made this book possible.

I am grateful to the following for information on Wolfe's family and his life in Asheville (in a few instances those I shall name did not know Wolfe but someone else in the story): Charles Abergast, Mrs. D. W. Allen, Wade Allison, Walter Bearden, Harry Blomberg, Mrs. Henry Boehm, Hilda Westall Bottomley, Belknap Bourne, Mr. and Mrs. Sanford Brown, Robert Bunn, Sam Cathey, John Cheesborough, Philip Cocke, William Cocke, Robert H. Cooke, Roy Dock, Dr. Ollie Donnahoe,

Rev. Norvin C. Duncan, Mrs. T. O. Ferguson, Hal U. Fisher, Samuel Fisher, Anne Ferril Folsom, Mrs. Henry Fuller, E. C. Goldberg, Gray Gorham, Elaine Westall Gould, Fannie Gross, Allen Hall, Mrs. Leon Hall, Herschel Harkins, Henry Harris, Mrs. Sadler Hayes, Frank Hill, Junius Horner, Max Israel, J. Y. Jordan, Charles Lee, Marguerite Lewis, Louis Lipinsky, Mr. and Mrs. Charles Malone, John W. Martin, Mrs. George McCoy, C. R. McIntire, J. B. McIntosh, Albert McLean, Betty Anne Mills, Irwin Monk, Blair Moore, Ed O'Donnell, Martha Wrenshall Osborne, Bright Padgitt, Marjorie Pearson, Nettie Perkinson, Seth Perkinson, Mr. and Mrs. Thomas Polsky, Claude Ramsey, Hiden Ramsey, Mrs. W. E. Reid, Miss Margaret Roberts, Paul Rockwell, Reid Russell, Lavon Sarafian, Mr. and Mrs. Holmes Sawyer, Grace Scruggs, Virginia Sevier, Mrs. Harold Shuttles, Inez Sorrells, Mrs. Lillian Taft, Mr. and Mrs. Charles Tennent, French Toms, Edith Vanderhooven, Mr. and Mrs. Thomas Wallis, Kester Walton, Mrs. Eugene Ward, Charles Westall, Jack Westall, Ralph Wheaton, Mrs. Edward White, Lenore Powell Whitfield, A. A. Wilkinson, Fred Wolfe, Louise Wolfe, Dr. R. Dietz Wolfe, Julian Woodcock, Mrs. Charles Wrenshall, Nancy C. Wylie.

On Wolfe at Chapel Hill: Dr. William Banks Anderson, W. P. Andrews, John Lee Aycock, Lexine Baird, H. G. Baity, C. Dale Beers, Dr. W. R. Berryhill, LeGette Blythe, B. C. Brown, Cordelia Camp, Prof. and Mrs. D. D. Carroll, Lenoir Chambers, Albert Coates, Frederick Cohn, Richard G. Coker, Mrs. W. C. Coker, James Coleman, Benjamin Cone, Dr. Joseph L. Cook, Jonathan Daniels, Mrs. Lola Paul Dawson, W. E. Debnam, J. E. Dowd, Carl Durham, Dr. Watt Eagle, Clement Eaton, Mrs. Willard Goforth Eybers, Rachel Freeman, Frank Porter Graham, Daniel Grant, Mr. and Mrs. Paul Green, Mrs. MacFayden Hall, Dr. Robert Harden, Charles Hazlehurst, Phillip Hettleman, Luther Hodges, Mrs. Harold Hodgkinson, Mrs. Richard Hogue, Robert B. House, James Howell, Carl Hyatt, Alfred H. Iseley, Edgar B. Jenkins, Claude R. Joyner, John Kerr, Minnie Sparrow Keyes, John Lasley, Mr. and Mrs. Harry Latshaw, Mrs. Sturgis Leavitt, William F. Lewis, Bryce Little, Lewis MacBrayer, Ernest MacKie, Dougald MacMillan, Dr. J. Donald MacRae, Hunter Martin, Mrs. Fred McCall, Nathan Mobley, Dr. Clement R. Monroe, Frederick Moore, Jerome Pence, Garland Porter, C. Percy Powell, William E. Price, Gary Pritchard, J. A. Pritchett, Frank O. Ray, Oren Roberts, Dr. R. A. Ross, Moses Rountree, Mrs. Armistead Sapp, Arnold Schiffman, Howard Sharpe, Carlyle Shepard, H. B. Simpson, B. W. Sipe, R. Hobart Southern, J. F. Spainhour, E. M. Spencer, Mr. and Mrs. Corydon Spruill, W. W. Stout, Tyre Taylor, Mary Thornton, Richard Thornton, Folger Townsend, Donnell VanNoppen, Hilton West,

SOURCES AND ACKNOWLEDGMENTS

Louis R. Wilson, Thomas Wilson, Dr. W. G. Wilson, Jr., Richard L. Young.

On Wolfe at Harvard: Philip Barber, Mrs. Philip Barry, Bernard Barton, Harry Behn, Mrs. Charles Bolster, Richmond Bond, M. A. Braswell, John Mason Brown, Patrel R. Buck, William Calvert, Henry Fisk Carlton, F. V. Casey, Grant Code, Frederic L. Day, Olin Dows, W. Ney Evans, Marjorie Fairbanks, Sydney Fairbanks, William Gaston, Edward P. Goodnow, Robert L. Gump, Doris Halman, William E. Harris, Val Hennessee, Marvin T. Herrick, Eleanor Hinkley, Charles S. Howard, Donald Keyes, Edward Kiernan, T. Skinner Kittrell, Henry LaFarge, Mrs. John R. Little, John Lodge, Robert Lord, John McAndrew, Donald McCandless, Eugene McCarthy, David McCord, Paul McElroy, Elizabeth McKie, W. N. Morse, Donald Oenslager, Leon Pearson, Laura Plonk, Nell V. Raisbeck, Fred N. Robinson, Mrs. Howard Sachs, Dorothy Sands, Edgar Scott, George Seldes, Mrs. Arthur Sherrill, Betty Smith, Royall Snow, Alice Howard Spaulding, Mr. and Mrs. William Tanner, Mrs. Henry F. Thoma, Weston Thomas, Lydia Walker, Mrs. W. L. Wiley.

On Wolfe at N.Y.U.: Edwin Berry Burgum, Harold Calo, Oscar Cargill, Bruce Carpenter, Harry Charriper, Leo Denslow, Gerald Doyle, Dr. M. Martin Finder, Vardis Fisher, Boris Gamzue, Joseph R. Gangemi, Rose Gilbert, Aaron Glickstein, Hans Gottlieb, Helen Gude, Paul Haines, Richard Hertzberg, Jules Kabat, Abraham Kadanoff, Younghill Kang, Abraham Katsh, Milton Kirschman, Julius Kraman, Herman Licht, Mabel Eggleston Locke, Vernon Loggins, Dorothy A. Lord, Walter MacKellar, James Mandel, Frank H. McCloskey, Samuel Middlebrook, Edward Norwalk, Paul Osborn, Thomas Clark Pollock, Desmond Powell, S. Ravitz, Albert Schnitzer, Irving Shakin, Harry Shaw, Arthur ("Abe") Smith, William York Tindall, John Varney, William W. Watt, Dudley Wynn, Alexander Zamschnick, Rabbi Nathan Zelizer.

On Wolfe at various times and in various places during the Twenties and Thirties: Ernest H. Abernethy, Ruth Aley, Mrs. Sherwood Anderson, Benjamin Appel, Mary Louise Aswell, Grady Bailey, Caroline Bancroft, LeBaron Barker, Mrs. John S. Barrows, Mrs. George Bartlett, Hamilton Basso, Mrs. Clayton Bates, Gweneth Beam, Rita Romilly Benson, Mrs. Jonathan Bingham, Mrs. Watson K. Blair, Dr. Walter Bonime, Mrs. James Boyd, Madeleine Boyd, Joseph Brewer, Emily Bridgers, Mrs. Robert Briffault, Ernest Briggs, Jack Bronson, Cleanth Brooks, Paul Brooks, Roger Burlingame, Whit Burnett, John M. Burns, Mrs. Struthers Burt, Louise Bushnell, Helen Butler, G. C. Buzby, Lila Fisher Caldwell, Gwen Jassinoff Campbell, Melville Cane, Cass Canfield, Cleveland Chase, Mrs. Paul Child, V. L. O. Chittick, Mrs. Albert Coates, Joseph W. Cohen, Marjorie

Cohn, Padraic Colum, Charles Cooke, Joseph Cotten, Malcolm Cowley, Ramona Herdman Craddock, Annie Laurie Crawford, Oliver Crawley, Robert Cross, Minna Curtiss, Nancy Cushman, Clifton Daniel, Eula Daniels, Whitney Darrow, Alfred Dashiell, Edward Davison, Mrs. Clarence Day, David DeJong, Laura Delano, Elizabeth DeVoy, Byron Dexter, Robert Disraeli, Mrs. Tracy Dows, Dorothy Gardner Durfee, Philip Duschnes, Max Eastman, Morris Ernst, Mr. and Mrs. Thomas Hornsby Ferril, William H. Fitzpatrick, Kimball Flaccus, Sue Flanagan, Martha Foley, Muriel Francis, A. S. Frere, David Gambrell, Anne M. Garges, Charles Garside, Mary Polk Gibbs, Mr. and Mrs. Walter Gilkyson, Mrs. Frank Gledhill, Mrs. Bernard Glemser, Mr. and Mrs. Mack Gorham, James Gray, Alec Hammerslough, Helen Washburn Harden, R. P. Harriss, Henry Hart, Prof. and Mrs. Henry M. Hart, Rupert Hart-Davis, Mildred Hartshorn, Josephine Herbst, Claire Zyve Hertz, Greta Hilb, Mr. and Mrs. Arthur Hill, Mr. and Mrs. Clayton Hoagland, Mrs. Terence Holliday, Harriet Hoppe, Paul Horgan, Jessica M. Hunt, Katherine Gauss Jackson, Louise Wright Jackson, Belinda Jelliffe, Spud Johnson, Mr. and Mrs. Lombard Jones, Isidor Kaufman, William S. Knickerbocker, Mrs. Alfred Knopf, Ann Mulfinger Koran, Irene Breslin Krebs, Dr. Elsie K. La Roe, F. Marion Law, Jr., Margaret Leach, H. M. Ledig-Rowohlt, Dr. Russel Lee, Florence Lehv, Max Lerner, Robert Linscott, Harold Loeb, Harlan Logan, Ina Lowthorp, Ferdinand Lundberg, Mrs. Peter Lynch, Thomas MacGreevy, Mrs. J. Donald MacRae, Mr. and Mrs. Arthur Mann, Sam Marx, Dexter Masters, Mrs. Edgar Lee Masters, William Maxwell, Mrs. Joseph McKibbin, Nina Melville, Thora Meredith, Wallace Meyer, Toni Milford, Cornelius Mitchell, Henry Allen Moe, Agnes Morgan, August Mosca, Henry A. Murray, Grace Naismith, John U. Nef, Charles Norman, Paul O'Neil, Mr. and Mrs. Gene Otto, C. A. Pearce, Norman Holmes Pearson, Virgilia Peterson, Richard C. Pettigrew, Frances Phillips, Ann Pinchot, Mr. and Mrs. William Platt, James Poling, Mrs. William T. Polk, Rush Ray, Robert Raynolds, Ruth Rich, Charles Richardson, Mrs. J. H. Riddle, Verna Britt Roberts, Dolly Robinson, James Grafton Rogers, Carol Mae Russell, Phillips Russell, Mrs. Bradley Saunders, J. Maryon Saunders, Joel Sayre, George Schieffelin, Franz Schoenberner, Mrs. Charles Scribner III, Marjorie Allen Seiffert, Evelyn Shattuck, Irwin Shaw, Arthur Sheekman, Mr. and Mrs. Beverly Smith, Catharine Brett Spencer, Ray Staples, Marion Starkey, Martha Dodd Stern, Leonie Sterner, George Stevens, Mr. and Mrs. James Stokely, George Stoney, Allene Talmey, Coley Taylor, Nathan R. Teitel, Virgil Thompson, Mrs. James Thurber, Margaret Dows Thyberg, Alice

Davis Tibbetts, Frank Tilson, Mrs. Alexis Tiranoff, Dr. Cornelius Traeger, Mrs. Ben Tuttle, Dr. Willard Van Dyke, Henry Volkening, Thomas Walsh, Mrs. Donald Warman, Janice Warnke, Robert Penn Warren, Dr. William E. Watts, Mrs. Leon Wavle, William Weber, Nat Werner, William Westall, John Hall Wheelock, Katharine S. White, Mrs. Frank Wigglesworth, Charles W. Wilcox, Mr. and Mrs. Whit Wilder, Ralph Williams, Mr. and Mrs. Ronald Lee Wilson, William B. Wisdom, Edgar Wolfe, Francis Wolle, Elizabeth Youngstrom.

On Maxwell Perkins (in some cases these people also knew Wolfe or others in the story): Conrad Aiken, Roger Baldwin, Nona Bell, Elizabeth Cox Bigelow, Charles Breasted, Erskine Caldwell, Curtis W. Cate, Mrs. Archibald Cox, Marcia Davenport, August Derleth, Effingham Evarts, Dr. Helen Evarts, Dr. Josephine Evarts, Richard C. Evarts, Waldo Frank, Dr. and Mrs. John Frothingham, Martha Gellhorn, Caroline Gordon, Douglas Gorsline, Elizabeth Gorsline, Emmett Gowen, Richard Gregg, Nancy Hale, Marian Ives, Mrs. Reid Jorgenson, Mrs. Robert King, Mrs. Alexander Ladd, Mr. and Mrs. Harold Landon, Elizabeth Lemmon, Burroughs Mitchell, Mrs. O. F. Muench, Walter Oakman, Ann Chittenden O'Meara, Mrs. George Owen, Waldo Peirce, Edward Perkins, Louis Perkins, Mrs. Maxwell Perkins, Dawn Powell, Lucien Price, John Reynolds, William L. Savage, John C. Scammell, Herman Scheying, Charles Scribner, Jr., A. C. Sedgwick, Al Seria, Chard Powers Smith, Mrs. Robert Terrell, Eva Browne Tweedy, Mrs. Guy Walker, Theodore Weeks.

On Aline Bernstein (in some cases these people also knew Wolfe or others in the story): Herbert Andrews, Horace Armistead, Alice Beer, S. N. Behrman, Marc Blitzstein, Mrs. Peter Cusick, Ethel Frankau, Lillian Hellman, Josephine Howell, Arthur Kober, Louis Kronenberger, Mrs. Lawrence Langner, Robert Lewis, Aline MacMahon, Elmer Rice, Emeline Roche, Herman Shumlin, Mrs. Harold Sterner, Carl Van Vechten, Polaire Weisman, Claire Weiss, Russell Wright.

Of the many valuable books on Wolfe, the two most important for my purposes were *Thomas Wolfe* by Elizabeth Nowell and *The Window of Memory* by Richard S. Kennedy. There is a wealth of published reminiscences, far too many to list here, but I would single out as being of unusual interest Anne W. Armstrong, "As I Saw Thomas Wolfe," *Arizona Quarterly*, Spring, 1946; Edward Aswell, "A Note on Thomas Wolfe," *The Hills Beyond;* Maxwell Perkins, "Scribners and Thomas Wolfe," *Carolina Magazine*, October, 1938; Maxwell Perkins, "Thomas Wolfe," *Wings*, October, 1939; Maxwell Perkins, "Thomas Wolfe," *Harvard Library Bulletin*, Autumn, 1947; Desmond Powell, "Of

Thomas Wolfe," *Arizona Quarterly*, Spring, 1945; Robert Raynolds, *Thomas Wolfe: Memoir of a Friendship*; and Henry Volkening, "Penance No More," *Virginia Quarterly*, Spring, 1939. Particularly good on Max Perkins are Struthers Burt, "Catalyst for Genius," *Saturday Review*, June 9, 1951; Malcolm Cowley, "Unshaken Friend," *The New Yorker*, April 1 and 8, 1944; and John Hall Wheelock's Introduction to *Editor to Author*, a selection of Perkins' letters. I am grateful to Mr. Cowley for lending me his research materials for the *New Yorker* profile.

I am grateful to the following for giving me access to their unpublished memoirs of Wolfe and/or Perkins: Madeleine Boyd, Eleanor Buckles Breese, Belinda Jelliffe, Helen K. Landon, Mrs. Edwin K. Large, Mrs. Maxwell Perkins, Garland Porter, David Randall, Max Whitson and William B. Wisdom. I am grateful to Miss Margaret Roberts for showing me her mother's unpublished notes on Wolfe, and to H. Seward Lewis for lending me his tape recordings of meetings of John Terry's Thomas Wolfe Biography Club.

I am grateful to Charles Scribner's Sons for allowing me to go through their complete authors' correspondence files—invaluable for what I learned not only about Wolfe and Perkins but about the literary history of the period. I am grateful to Perkins' wife Louise, to his daughter Bertha, and to his friend, Elizabeth Lemmon, for showing me his letters to them. I am grateful to Mrs. Peter Cusick for permitting me to quote the letters of her mother, Aline Bernstein.

Among numerous librarians who helped me, I am especially indebted to William Bond, Carolyn Jakeman and Joseph McCarthy of the Houghton Library at Harvard; to William Powell of the University of North Carolina Library whose fine Wolfe Collection is second only to Harvard's; and to Myra Champion of the Pack Memorial Library in Asheville. Wolfe is fortunate to have in his home town someone as dedicated as is Miss Champion to preserving his memory and widening the interest in his work.

For a critical reading of this book in manuscript—and I hasten to absolve them from its faults—I wish to thank Hilda Westall Bottomley, C. Hugh Holman, Belinda Jelliffe, Richard S. Kennedy, Felicia Lamport, Elizabeth Lemmon, Herbert J. Muller, Paschal Reeves, Mrs. Bradley Saunders, Henry Volkening, John Hall Wheelock and William B. Wisdom.

I am grateful to my editor, Burroughs Mitchell, for counsel and encouragement during a lengthy project, and to Gordon N. Ray and the John Simon Guggenheim Memorial Foundation for a fellowship which helped to underwrite it. I am grateful to Nina Holton and Dr. Guido Majno for technical advice.

Above all, I am grateful to the author's brother, Fred Wolfe, and to Paul Gitlin and Melville Cane, administrators of the Wolfe Estate, for granting me the privilege of undertaking the job in the first place.

A CHRONOLOGY OF THE MAIN
EVENTS IN WOLFE'S LIFE

1900	Oct.	Born in Asheville
1904	Nov.	Grover dies at St. Louis World's Fair
1905	Sept.	Enters Orange Street Public School
1906	Aug.	Julia Wolfe buys the Old Kentucky Home
1912	Sept.	Enters North State Fitting School. Meets Margaret Roberts
1916	Sept.	Enters University of North Carolina
1917	June	Romance with Clara Paul
1918	June	Goes to Norfolk for the summer
	Oct.	Ben dies
1919	March	Carolina Playmakers stage *The Return of Buck Gavin*
1920	Sept.	Enters Harvard Graduate School. Meets George Pierce Baker and Kenneth Raisbeck
1921	Oct.	Workshop stages *The Mountains*
1922	June	Father dies
1923	May	Workshop stages *Welcome to Our City*
	Dec.	Theatre Guild declines *Welcome to Our City*
1924	Feb.	Begins teaching at N.Y.U.
	Oct.	First trip to Europe
1925	Jan.	Quarrels with Raisbeck after month together in Paris
	Aug.	Meets Aline Bernstein on the *Olympic*
	Sept.	Resumes teaching at N.Y.U.
1926	June	Goes abroad with Aline
	July	Begins *Look Homeward, Angel* (original title, *O Lost*)
	Aug.	Stays in England to work on novel after Aline goes home
	Dec.	First visit to Germany
1927	Jan.	Returns to America and continues work on *Look Homeward, Angel* in Eighth Street loft
	July	Goes abroad with Aline

	Sept.	Resumes teaching at N.Y.U.
1928	March	Finishes manuscript of *Look Homeward, Angel*
	June	Leaves manuscript with agent and goes abroad by himself. Rift with Aline
	Sept.	Beaten up at *Oktoberfest*
	Nov.	Letter from Maxwell Perkins expressing interest in *Look Homeward, Angel*
	Dec.	Returns to America and makes up with Aline
1929	Jan.	Meets Perkins. Resumes teaching at N.Y.U. while revising manuscript of *Look Homeward, Angel*
	Aug.	"The Angel on the Porch" published in *Scribner's Magazine*
	Oct.	*Look Homeward, Angel* published
1930	Feb.	Stops teaching at N.Y.U. permanently
	March	Awarded Guggenheim Fellowship
	May	Goes abroad
	June	Meets Scott Fitzgerald in Paris
	July	Settles in Montreux
	Sept.	In the Black Forest during German national elections. Witnesses street fighting between Communists and Nazis
	Oct.	Settles in London
1931	Feb.	Meets Sinclair Lewis
	March	Goes home. Aline attempts suicide. Settles in Brooklyn
1932	Jan.	Definitive break with Aline
	April	*A Portrait of Bascom Hawke* in *Scribner's Magazine* —first publication since *Look Homeward, Angel*
	June	Wolfe submits his novel, *K-19*, to Perkins who persuades him to shelve it
	July	*A Portrait of Bascom Hawke* ties for first place in Scribner $5,000-prize short novel contest
1933	Jan.	Perkins persuades Wolfe to resume the story of Eugene where he dropped it in *Look Homeward, Angel*
	Dec.	Perkins tells Wolfe his novel is finished and their collaborative revision begins

1934	Sept.	Against Wolfe's wishes, Perkins sends the last half of the *Of Time and the River* manuscript to the printer while Wolfe is at the Chicago World's Fair
1935	March	Wolfe goes abroad. *Of Time and the River* published
	May	Fame in Berlin
	July	Returns to America. Attends University of Colorado Writers' Conference
	Aug.	First visit to West Coast
	Sept.	Settles in Manhattan, 865 First Avenue
	Nov.	*From Death to Morning* published
1936	March	Begins *The Vision of Spangler's Paul*
	April	*The Story of a Novel* published. Bernard De Voto's attack, "Genius Is Not Enough"
	Aug.	Visits Germany during the Olympics
	Oct.	Dorman law suit brings to a head Wolfe's dissatisfaction with Scribners
1937	Jan.	Trip to New Orleans and Chapel Hill
	March	"I Have a Thing to Tell You" serialized in *The New Republic*
	May	First visit to Asheville since publication of *Look Homeward, Angel*
	July	Rents cabin at Oteen
	Aug.	First attempts to find new publisher
	Oct.	Settles at Chelsea Hotel
	Dec.	Signs contract with Harpers
1938	May	Completes "George Webber" manuscript and gives speech at Purdue
	June	Tour of the national parks
	July	Taken ill with pneumonia. Hospitalized at Firlawns Sanitarium near Seattle
	Aug.	Transferred to Providence Hospital, Seattle
	Sept.	Operated on at Johns Hopkins. Dies

ILLUSTRATION ACKNOWLEDGMENTS

Grateful acknowledgment is made to the following sources for permission to reproduce the pictures listed below:

1–7, 9, 10, 18, 20–2, 24, 25, 27, 29. The Thomas Wolfe Collection, Pack Memorial Public Library; 8, 12. The Wolfe Collection at the University of North Carolina Library; 11. Mrs. F. G. Dawson, Alliance, N.C.; 13. The Harvard Theatre Collection; 14. The Carl Van Vechten Collection, Yale University Library; used by permission of Saul Mauriber, executor of the Carl Van Vechten photographic collection; 15. Doris Ulmann photograph from the Wolfe Collection at the University of North Carolina; 16. Private collection of Alexander Wainwright, the Princeton University Library, Princeton, N.J.; 17. Robert Disraeli Films, New York, N.Y.; 19. Photograph by Louise Dahl Wolfe from collection of Mrs. Peter Cusick, New York, N.Y.; 23. The Thomas Wolfe Collection of William B. Wisdom at Harvard; 26. Carl Mydans, *Life* Magazine © Time Inc.; 28. Mrs. E. C. Bigelow, New York, N.Y.

INDEX

J

11/09

mL